THE FUTURE
INFORMATION
SOCIETY

Social and Technological Problems

World Scientific Series in Information Studies
(ISSN: 1793-7876)

World Scientific Series in Information Studies — **Vol. 8**

THE FUTURE INFORMATION SOCIETY

Social and Technological Problems

Editors

Wolfgang Hofkirchner

Vienna University of Technology, Austria

Mark Burgin

University of California, Los Angeles, USA

 **World Scientific**

NEW JERSEY · LONDON · SINGAPORE · BEIJING · SHANGHAI · HONG KONG · TAIPEI · CHENNAI · TOKYO

Published by

World Scientific Publishing Co. Pte. Ltd.

5 Toh Tuck Link, Singapore 596224

USA office: 27 Warren Street, Suite 401-402, Hackensack, NJ 07601

UK office: 57 Shelton Street, Covent Garden, London WC2H 9HE

Library of Congress Cataloging-in-Publication Data

Names: Hofkirchner, Wolfgang, 1953– editor. | Burgin, M. S. (Mark Semenovich) editor. |
    International Society for Information Studies. Summit (2015 : Vienna, Austria)

Title: The future information society : social and technological problems /
    [edited by] Wolfgang Hofkirchner (Bertalanffy Center for the Study of
    Systems Science, Austria), Mark Burgin (UCLA).

Description: New Jersey : World Scientific, 2016. | Series: World scientific series in
    information studies ; volume 8 | Based on the Summit of the International Society for
    Information Studies on "The Information Society at the Crossroads : Response and
    Responsibility of the Sciences of Information" held in Vienna in June 2015.

Identifiers: LCCN 2016035657 | ISBN 9789813108967 (hc : alk. paper)

Subjects: LCSH: Information society. | Information technology--Social aspects. |
    Technological innovations--Social aspects.

Classification: LCC HM851 .F868 2016 | DDC 303.48/33--dc23

LC record available at https://lccn.loc.gov/2016035657

British Library Cataloguing-in-Publication Data

A catalogue record for this book is available from the British Library.

Desk Editors: V. Vishnu Mohan/Tan Rok Ting

Typeset by Stallion Press
Email: enquiries@stallionpress.com

Printed in Singapore

ABOUT THE EDITORS

Mark Burgin from UCLA has Ph.D. in Mathematics and is Doctor of Science in Logic and Philosophy. He is doing research, has publications, and taught courses in various areas of mathematics, artificial intelligence, information sciences, system theory, computer science, epistemology, logic, psychology, social sciences, and methodology of science publishing more than 500 papers and 21 books. He originated such theories as the general theory of information, theory of named sets, mathematical theory of schemas, theory of oracles, hyperprobability theory, system theory of time, theory of non-Diophantine arithmetics and neoclassical analysis (in mathematics) and made essential contributions to such fields as foundations of mathematics, theory of algorithms and computation, theory of knowledge, theory of intellectual activity, and complexity studies. Mark Burgin was the first to discover non-Diophantine arithmetics, the first to axiomatize and build mathematical foundations for negative probability used in physics, finance and economics, and the first to explicitly overcome the barrier posed by the Church-Turing thesis.

Wolfgang Hofkirchner is Professor for Technology Assessment at the Faculty of Informatics of the Vienna University of Technology. He works on ICTs and Society, Science of Information, and Complexity (see his book *Emergent Information — A Unified Theory of Information Framework*). He is member of the *International Academy of Systems and Cybernetic Sciences* (IASCYS), President of the *Bertalanffy Center for the Study of Systems Science*, Past President of the *International Society for Information Studies*.

ABOUT THE CONTRIBUTORS

Syed Mustafa Ali, Ph.D. in Computational Philosophy, Brunel University (1999), is a Lecturer in the School of Computing and Communications at The Open University, UK. His current research focuses on the development of a hermeneutic framework that can be used to inform critical investigations of computational, informational, cybernetic, systems theoretical and trans-/post-human phenomena. The framework is grounded in phenomenology, critical race theory and postcolonial/decolonial thought and is being used to engage with various areas in computing and ICT including artificial intelligence (the Turing test, situated robotics) and ubicomp (embodiment and social embedding).

Jörg Becker (born 1946) is Professor for Political Science at Marburg University in Germany. He was Guest Professor for Political Science and/or Communication Research at Universities in Roskilde in Denmark, Beirut in Lebanon, Hong Kong and Innsbruck in Austria.

Howard Bloom is the author of six books, including *The Lucifer Principle: A Scientific Expedition into the Forces of History* ("mesmerizing" — *The Washington Post*) and *The God Problem: How a Godless Cosmos Creates* ("Bloom's argument will rock your world" Barbara Ehrenreich). The office of the American Secretary of Defense hosted a workshop on Bloom's second book, *Global Brain: The Evolution of Mass Mind from the Big Bang to the 21st Century*, and brought in representatives from the *State Department*, the *Energy Department*, *DARPA*, *IBM*, and *MIT*. Bloom's scientific work has appeared in:

arxiv.org, the leading pre-print site in advanced theoretical physics and math; *PhysicaPlus*; *Across Species Comparisons and Psychopathology*; *New Ideas in Psychology*; *The Journal of Space Philosophy*; and in the books: *Research in Biopolitics* and *NASA's Cosmos and Culture*. His popular work has appeared in *The Washington Post*, *The Wall Street Journal*, *Wired*, *Knight-Ridder Financial News Service*, the *Village Voice*, *Cosmopolitan Magazine*, and the *Scientific American's* scientific american.com.

Gunilla Bradley is Professor Emerita in Informatics at Royal Institute of Technology (KTH) in Stockholm and has been a visiting professor at Stanford University. She has a broad background in the social/behavioral sciences and has authored 13 books in the field of Social Informatics. In 1997, she received the prestigious Namur Award from IFIP and lately created the IADIS international conference on "ICT, Society and Humans". Book in progress: *The Good ICT society — From Theory to Actions* (Routledge 2017). http://gunillabradley.se.

John Collier, Professor, now retired, has worked in six countries on five continents. His main work is foundational, assisting scientists in various fields involving information and complexity with conceptual issues in the foundations of their disciplines.

Mary Jo Deering is President of *Deering Health Associates*, which provides consulting services on health care transformation through consumer and patient empowerment and eHealth technologies. Dr. Deering served 26 years in the U.S. Department of Health and Human Services, where she developed policies for the nationwide health information network, with a special focus on the role of consumers and patients. She has published numerous book chapters and articles in these areas.

Yagmur Denizhan is Professor at the Electrical and Electronics Engineering Department and Head of the Graduate Program in Systems and Control Engineering of Bogazici University. Recent technical research areas are nonlinear dynamics, chaos control and modeling of biological systems, while wider fields of philosophical involvement include social impacts of technology, cognitive science, biosemiotics, systems theory and mythology.

José María Díaz Nafría, Ph.D. in Telecommunication Engineering by the Technical University of Madrid, M.Sc. in Philosophy by the National University for Distance Education (UNED), is currently Scholar at the University of León, Spain, National University of Santa Elena, Ecuador, and Munich University of Applied Science, Germany. Between 1997 and 2009, he was Associate Professor at the University Alfonso X el Sabio in Madrid. His research focuses on the interdisciplinary study of information and communication, perception, systems and complexity. He is board member of the *International Society for Information Studies* (Austria), the *Institute for Design Science* (Germany), and the *BITrum-Research Group* for the interdisciplinary study of information (Spain), and he is Fellow of the *Bertalanffy Center for the Study of Systems Science* (Austria).

Banu Durdağ is a Ph.D. candidate and research assistant in the Faculty of Communication at Ankara University in Turkey. Her research interests focus on the political economy of communication, the relationship between technology and social change, ICT policies and social inequalities, alternative media, and social movements. Her current research has appeared as a book chapter in *Social Inequalities, Media, and Communication: Theory and Roots* edited by Jan Servaes and Toks Oyedemi.

Thomas Fundneider is Founder and Managing Director of *theLivingCore* and has acquired extensive management knowledge by being responsible for numerous major projects. His introduction of innovative, entrepreneurial working and thinking to organizations has made a lasting impact on his clients. He is a board member of *PDMA Austria* as well as

Bertalanffy Center for the Study of Systems Science, and lectures at several European universities.

Armin Grunwald, Prof. Dr., studied physics, mathematics and philosophy at the universities of Münster and Cologne. After occupations in the industry and at *DLR* (German Aerospace Center) he became Vice Director of the *European Academy Bad Neuenahr-Ahrweiler* in 1996 and received the *venia legendi* for philosophy at Marburg University in 1998. Since 1999, Armin Grunwald has been head of the *Institute for Technology Assessment and Systems Analysis* (ITAS) at Karlsruhe Institute of Technology (KIT), since 2002 also director of the *Office of Technology Assessment at the German Bundestag* (TAB) and since 2007 also full professor of philosophy of technology at KIT.

Dirk Helbing is Professor of Computational Social Science at the Department of Humanities, Social and Political Sciences and affiliate of the Computer Science Department at ETH Zurich. He earned a Ph.D. in Physics at the University of Stuttgart and was Managing Director of the Institute of Transport & Economics at Dresden University of Technology in Germany. He is internationally known for his work on pedestrian crowds, vehicle traffic, and agent-based models of social systems. Furthermore, he coordinates the *FuturICT Initiative* (http://www. futurict.eu), which focuses on the understanding of techno-socio-economic systems, using smart data. Within the ERC Advanced Investigator Grant "Momentum" he works on social simulations based on cognitive agents. Helbing is an elected member of the prestigious *German Academy of Sciences "Leopoldina"* and received an honorary Ph.D. from Delft University of Technology.

Francis Heylighen is a Belgian Research Professor affiliated with the interdisciplinary Center Leo Apostel at the Vrije Universiteit Brussel (VUB), and Director of the *Global Brain Institute*. His research focuses on the self-organization of complex, cognitive systems from a cybernetic perspective, with an emphasis on their distributed intelligence. He has authored over 150 scientific publications in a wide variety of disciplines.

Marc Humbert is currently Professor of Political Economy at Rennes University and he has published more than 15 books and 100 of papers in Scientific Reviews. Until 2000, his main theme was the global economic competition among firms and nations. Since then, drawing upon a systemic approach, he started the project to build a political and ethical knowledge on economic activities and was the co-founder in 2010 of a new strand of thought in human sciences dealing with this project: "convivialism".

Stefan Hügel is the Chairperson of the *Forum Computer Professionals for Peace and Social Responsibility* (FIfF). In his professional life, he works as an IT consultant in the fields of IT governance, IT processes, project management, information security and risk management. He holds a Diploma in Computer Science from the University of Karlsruhe (now Karlsruhe Institute of Technology) and lives in Frankfurt/Main, Germany.

Nikhil Joshi is a Scientist, an Entrepreneur and the Founder of *Lifel*. *Lifel* is a non-profit initiative for collaborative scientific research to explore a multi-system "Big Picture" view of organization in living systems that spans biological, ecological, and socioeconomic domains. It further aims to leverage new insights from research to explore systemic solutions to sustainability in multi-system interactions between ecological, social and economic systems.

Asimina Koukou is a Ph.D. candidate at the Department of Communication, University of Vienna. She is researcher at the Media Governance and Industries Research Lab and the recipient of the "Ludwig von Bertalanffy PhD Scholarship", awarded by the *Bertalanffy Center for the Study of Systems Science* (BCSSS).

Hans-Jörg Kreowski is Retired Professor for Theoretical Computer Science at the University of Bremen (Germany) and member of board of the *Forum Computer Professionals for Peace and Social Responsibility* (FIfF). Moreover, he is member of the *Leibniz-Sozietät der Wissenschaften zu Berlin* vice-chairing the working group on Emergent Systems, Information and Society.

Uwe Krüger (born in 1978) is Assistant Professor in the Journalism Department at the University of Leipzig since 2012. He studied journalism and political science at the Universities of Leipzig and Rostov-on-Don (Russia) and worked as a journalist for daily newspapers and magazines, especially for the quarterly journalism magazine *Message*. He earned his Ph.D. in Communication Science with a work on leading German journalists and their networks among political and business elites.

Zoe Lefkofridi is Assistant Professor of Comparative Politics at the University of Salzburg. Her research interests lie in transnational democracy and representation in Europe, with a focus on inequality. Her work appears in *European Union Politics*, *West European Politics*, *European Political Science Review*, *Electoral Studies*, among others.

Robert K. Logan is an Emeritus Professor in Physics and a Fellow at St. Michael's College at the University of Toronto. He is also the Chief Scientist at the Strategic Innovation Lab at the Ontario College of Art and Design and a Fellow of the *Bertalanffy Center for the Study of Systems Science*.

Rüdiger Lohlker is Professor of Islamic Studies, University of Vienna, Austria, since 2003; teaching at the Universities of Göttingen, Kiel, Giessen, and working at the Bibliothèque générale et Archive, Rabat, Morocco, etc. His research focuses on history of Islamic ideas, Arab world and Islam online, contemporary Islamic movements.

Dietrich Meyer-Ebrecht, Prof (em) Dr-Ing, is Vice Chairman of *Computer Professionals for Peace and Social Responsibility* (FIfF). His present activities are on social impact and military abuse of information technology. Previously, he was in charge of the Institute of Image Processing and Computer Vision at RWTH Aachen University of Technology.

Markus F. Peschl is Professor for Cognitive Science and Philosophy of Science (University of Vienna). His focus of research is on the question of knowledge creation and innovation in various contexts: in natural and artificial cognitive systems, in science, in organizations, in educational settings, as well as in the context of knowledge technologies and their embedding in social systems. He follows a radically interdisciplinary approach integrating concepts from the natural sciences (cognitive science & neuroscience), philosophy (of science), from the humanities, organizational/innovation studies, as well as from (knowledge) technology. Currently, he is working in the field of radical innovation where he developed the concepts of Emergent Innovation and Enabling Spaces. M. Peschl has published six books and more than 130 papers in international journals and collections. For further information, see: www.univie.ac.at/knowledge/peschl/.

Tomáš Sigmund is Assistant Professor at the Department of System Analysis of the University of Economics in Prague, Czech Republic. His research interests encompass systems science, information ethics, media studies and phenomenological philosophy. He focuses on topics related to human identity, nontechnical aspects of IT and hermeneutics. He is a member of the *Bertalanffy Center for the Study of Systems Science*.

Sarah Spiekermann chairs the Institute for Management Information Systems at Vienna University of Economics and Business (WU Vienna). She has published a multitude of scientific articles on the social and ethical implications of computer systems and has given more than 100 presentations and talks about her work throughout the world. Her main expertise is electronic privacy, disclosure behavior and ethical computing.

Christian Stary received the Diploma in Computer Science, his Ph.D. in usability engineering, and Habilitation degree from the Vienna University of Technology, Austria. Since 1995, he is Full Professor of Business Information Systems with the University of Linz. His current research interests include the area of interactive distributed systems, focusing on method-driven learning and explication technologies for personal capacity building and organizational development.

Felix Tretter holds Dr.phil. in Psychology and Philosophy, Dr.rer.pol. in Social Science and Statistics, Dr.med. in Medicine. He was a researcher in Neuroscience, later Senior Physician in psychiatric hospital in addiction department (Munich). At present Fellow at the *Bertalanffy Center for the Study of Systems Science*, Vienna.

CONTENTS

Part III.   Meaningful Technology?   285

Chapter 1

Introduction:
Sociology of Information Processes
and the Development of Society

Mark Burgin[*,§] and Wolfgang Hofkirchner[†,‡,¶]

*University of California, Los Angeles
405 Hilgard Ave.
Los Angeles, CA 90095, USA
†Institute of Design and Technology Assessment
Vienna University of Technology
Argentinierstraße 6, 1040 Vienna, Austria
‡Bertalanffy Center for the Study of Systems Science
Paulanergasse 13, 1040 Vienna, Austria
§mburgin@math.ucla.edu
¶wolfgang.hofkirchner@bcsss.org

The information age is the age of the information societies, into which industrialized societies are gradually transforming under the influence of new information and communication technologies (ICTs), in the same way as the industrial age is the age of industrial societies, into which agricultural societies had been and are still transforming worldwide. However, a full-fledged development of science is still in need to catch up with the actual societal and technological development. The accelerated technological development of the modern society is not accompanied by an equally rapid growth in scientific insight, let alone foresight, into the impact of technology on the levels of society other than that of technological organization. Attempts to observe and understand the basic nature of these changes are still going on. The public use of the notion of "information society" has been reduced to denoting a society in which applications of modern ICTs are widely spread in order to facilitate the handling of the phenomenon commonly called "information". A scientific conceptualization of this transformation has not had time to develop. There is still no discipline that deserves the name "science of the information society" or "science of information".

That lag of science behind society and technology is particularly critical, since actual techno-social developments have been leading to aggravating ambiguities. On the one hand, the study and the engineering of information processes have been spreading and diversifying, while diffusing throughout the disciplines. As a result, there is a rich body of knowledge about diverse aspects of information; and in many cases valuable findings have been made. However, on the other hand, more often than not, information studies are not focused on contributing to the urgent needs of civilization in crisis, while research and development are undertaken to meet short-sighted economic concerns, one-sided military and political pursuits, and self-centered cultural interests being an obstacle to thinking big and hindering the social development of society. Thus, diversity still outbalances unity instead of providing the basis for information studies to become a science of information in its own right. It is vital to transform information studies into the science of information [Hofkirchner 2013]. A methodological and theoretical base for such a transformation is provided by the general theory of information, which suggests a way for a synthesized understanding of information phenomena and information processes unifying all diverse theoretical approaches and developing mathematical tools for investigation of information processes in all spheres of reality – in nature, society, human organisms and technical systems [Burgin 2010].

The goal of overcoming these obstacles was the main rationale for holding the Summit of the International Society for Information Studies on "The Information Society at the Crossroads – Response and Responsibility of the Sciences of Information" in Vienna in June 2015. This goal is reflected in the following statement (Call for Participation – bold style removed, M.B. and W.H.):

The information society has come with a promise – the promise, with the help of technology, to restore information as a commons: generated and utilised by everyone; for the benefit of every single person and all humanity; unfettered, empowering the people, truthful and reasonable, enabling constructive ways of living and a proper understanding of the environment.

The promise has not yet proven true. Instead, we face trends towards the commercialisation and commoditisation of all information; towards the totalization of surveillance and the extension of the battlefield to civil society through information warfare; towards disinformation overflow; towards a collapse of the technological civilisation itself as a consequence of the vulnerability of information networks and, in the most general terms, as a consequence of ignorance of the fundamental information processes at work not only in natural systems but also in social and artificial systems.

The social and technological innovations that are intended to boost cognition, communication and co-operation are ambiguous: their potential to advance information commons is exploited for purposes of self-aggrandisement rather than concern for the overarching communities in which every human self is embedded from the family to world society. Tools – computer and other – are made for profit, power or predominance; the goal of a flourishing and thriving of humanity as a whole takes a distant second place, if it runs at all.

Thus, the information society has reached a crossroads: without significant change, business as usual can even accelerate its breakdown. A breakthrough to a global, sustainable information society must establish an information commons as a cornerstone of a programme for coping with the challenges of the information age.

In order to set the course for the future development of the information society, the Summit provided beneficial conditions for the researchers involved in information studies to present and discuss the obtained results and created ideas developing the field of social and technological innovations based upon findings in information theory and methodology, in information society, and in information technology. Researchers working in the area of the fundamental research and exploring the nature of information processes in all realms of the real world also presented and discussed their results and ideas. Thus, we can elucidate three basic areas of information studies:

- *Sociological information studies* concentrate on the impact of the information sciences on society questioning how to "improve the design and implementation of social and technological applications for the advancement of a viable information society and individual autonomy."

- *Methodological information studies* focus on the foundations of the sciences of information questioning how to "improve the concepts we use for the study of information at all levels, from natural information processes to the information society and information technology, such that they open new vistas that allow for improved applications."
- *Theoretical information studies* develop information theories exploring the essence of information and regularities of information processes.

This book contains results and ideas of the selected Summit speakers and other leading experts in the first area dealing with problems of social issues of information processes, for the most part either from a critical perspective or in a pro-active design stance. Although the editors do not agree with some of these ideas and statements, they believe that it is necessary to provide a possibility for a free exchange of information and constructive discussion of different ideas and approaches in science. Violation of this ethical principle hinders the development of science.

Social information processes take place in any subdomain of society, that is, in the cultural, political, and economic sphere or subsystem as well as in that sector that provides the environmental basis of society and, last not least, in that sector that the provides the technological infrastructure of society. In any of these areas social information manifests itself in the cognitive capabilities of any social actor, in communicative capabilities of coupled cognitive social actors, and in the co-operative capability of entangled communicative social actors constituting a social entity on a higher level of organization.

Problems occur when social information processes are hampered due to social friction. The concept "social friction" was used at the beginning of the 20th century [Chapman 1912] and then was revitalized at the end of the 20th century [cf., for example, Nolen-Hoeksema *et al.* 1997; Mander 1998] becoming very popular in the 21st century [cf., for example, McGowan 2003; Heylighen 2007].

Being a fundamental aspect of everyday life, social friction is a negative process due to the state of co-operation where the pursuit of one actor's goals hinders the pursuit of other actors' goals and reduces the productivity and efficiency of the overall outcome. Such a state trickles down the ladder to communication and inhibits cognition. As a result, many problems of social information processes are caused by social friction, which decreases synergy of social organizations and thus, can be treated as negative synergy. While synergy is a feature of a multicomponent system to be able to achieve higher results than the simple combination of the results of its components, friction is the trait that hinders achievement of higher results. It is interesting that in business practice, synergy is represented by the expression "1 + 1 = 3", which describes that the "sum" of two systems or processes is greater than what they could achieve on their own [cf., for example, Tufte 1990; Angier 2015].

In spite of the hopes expressed by some researchers [cf., for example, Floridi 2007], ICTs alone do not have the potential of establishing a "frictionless" medium for functioning of social information. Even more, ICTs can even cause intensification of existing frictions or might instigate new frictions. The majority of social problems cannot be solved by the development of technical means alone. Without appropriate social organization and psychological growth of separate individuals and society as a whole, it is impossible to decrease social friction. Only interplay of social and technological changes can achieve this goal. First, it is necessary to accomplish the reconfiguration of relations between social actors in such a way that synergy grows up, while frictions are decreased. Second, it is necessary to base the development of ICTs on an efficient information theory, which takes into account social factors. Third, the redesigned and remodeled ICTs have to support unfettered information processes. Thus, it is vital not only to have and utilize diverse ICTs but also to know how to efficiently use them. Acquisition of this knowledge is the main goal of the sociological information studies presented in this book.

The first part of the book – *From Nature to the Organization of Society* – contains contributions to the study of information that aim at the creation of a grand social theory. They span the panorama from natural evolution to the specifics of social evolution and the role technology can play for reducing the frictions of information processes (chapters 2 to 7).

The second part – *Designing the Future* – continues with visions of how technology can be shaped to enable humanity to enter a new stage of its development by minimizing social frictions. Contributions start with a new framing for Technology Assessment, focus on co-operation of human collective intelligence that conceptualizes the Internet as Global Brain for a new community of the world citizens and touch innovations, learning and methods of how to take advantage of the rise in available information (chapters 8 to 15).

The last cluster of contributions – *Meaningful Technology?* – is devoted to concrete areas of frictions in particular social and technological fields. The contributions in the third part of the book analyze not only why those frictions hamper the development of society but demonstrate also approaches to overcoming those frictions. The range is from prejudices against cultural groups via the orientation of media coverage via the fallback of the European Union and its political implications via surveillance and military technology, robots and A.I., to health care technology (chapters 16 to 28).

References

Angier, M. (2015). One plus one equals three? http://www.smithfam.com/news2/synergy.html

Burgin, M. (2010). *Theory of Information: Fundamentality, Diversity and Unification*, World Scientific, New York/London/Singapore

Call for Participation, http://summit.is4is.org/calls/call-for-participation

Chapman, S. J. (1912). *Political Economy*, Williams and Norgate, London

Floridi, L. (2007). A look into the future impact of ICTs on our lives, *The Information Society*, 23/1, 59-64

Heylighen, F. (2007). Accelerating Socio-Technological Evolution, in: Modelski, G., Devezas, T., and Thompson, W. (eds.), *Globalization as an Evolutionary Process – Modeling Global Change*, Routledge, London, 286-335

Hofkirchner, W. (2001). *Emergent Information*, World Scientific, New York/London/Singapore

Mander, M. S. (Ed.) (1998). *Framing Friction: Media and Social Conflict*, University of Illinois Press, Urbana

McGowan, D. (2003). *From Social Friction to Social Meaning*: *What Expressive Uses of Code Tell Us About Free Speech*, Minnesota Public Law Research Paper No. 03-4

Nolen-Hoeksema, S., McBride, A., and Larson, J. (1997). Rumination and psychological distress among bereaved partners, *J. Pers. Soc. Psychol.*, 72(4), 855-862

Tufte, E. R. (1990). *Envisioning Information*, Graphics Press, Cheshire, CT

Part I

From Nature to the Organization of Society

Chapter 2

Information for a Global
Sustainable Information Society

Wolfgang Hofkirchner

Institute of Design and Technology Assessment
Vienna University of Technology
Argentinierstraße 6, 1040 Vienna, Austria
wolfgang.hofkirchner@bcsss.org

Starting point is the résumé of a systems theoretical analysis of the information age as an age of global challenges. Global challenges indicate a crisis in the evolution of humanity's social systems. They indicate a Great Bifurcation, one trajectory of which would signify another Great Transformation – a transformation into a Global Sustainable Information Society (GSIS). Such a social formation would be characterised by three properties that are concretisations of generic properties characteristic of any complex system. One of those properties refers to the information generation capacities of the agents of world society in *statu nascendi*. In order to promote the advent of such a social suprasystem, there are historical-concrete requirements to be met on each level of social information processes, which forms an imperative for human co-operative, communicative, and cognitive information in the information age. A new step in the evolution of social information is needed in order to avoid the extermination of civilised human life. Information technology – its development and implementation – is subject to that imperative.

1. The Information Society in the Course of Systems Evolution

Any science is characterised by praxiological, ontological and epistemological assumptions. So do systems sciences. Ludwig von

Bertalanffy's General System Theory provides us with a new world view concerning the aims of systems sciences, with a new world picture concerning the scope of systems sciences, and with a new way of thinking concerning the tools of systems sciences [Hofkirchner and Rousseau 2015].

Ervin Laszlo was among the early philosophers that took over Bertalanffy's ideas on the fate of civilisation [1972: 281-290] and he is known for having elaborated on them widely up till now. In line with that, what is termed information society can be understood in the course of the evolution of social systems as a transition phase from one social formation to another or as a distinct social formation in its own right, be it manifest or yet to come.

1.1. *The Multi-Stage Model of systems evolution*

The Multi-Stage Model of systems evolution was first put forward in Ellersdorfer and Hofkirchner [1994] and Fenzl *et al.* [1996] and was later on supplemented by assumptions concerning causality [Brunner and Klauninger 2003; Collier 2003].

The Multi-Stage Model combines evolutionary phases and systemic levels of whatever systems in evolution. The diachronic dimension accounts for metasystem transitions, that is, for leaps in quality by which ever new systems emerge that represent an increase in complexity while the synchronic dimension does justice to the hierarchy of the suprasystem (the nesting of systems) in which the new organisational relations exert dominance so as to compensate for the increased complexity. New systems emerge from the space of possibilities given with the existing systems by establishing a new order that incorporates the old systems as elements or subsystems of the new ones by imparting them a new dominant shape. In the diachronic dimension, there is a superposition of two Aristotelian causes, the efficient and the final cause such that the efficient one gets functionalised by the final one and becomes an end-directed efficient cause. In the synchronic dimension, there is another superposition, namely that of the other two Aristotelian causes, the material and the formal cause such that the material one gets structured by the formal one and becomes a formatted material cause. In the course of evolution, ever higher complex systems shift step by step towards increased end-directedness and increased formative power as well. This accounts for the differences between types of self-organisation as the dynamic of, and in, complex systems can be called [Hofkirchner 2013a: 89-94].

1.2. *The current stage of social systems evolution*

Social systems are but another type of self-organising systems. They are systems that are capable of teleologically producing themselves in that there is an explicit end and an artificial, invented form. Thus they go beyond the capability of controlling conditions to meet an in-built end given to them, which maintains their form, as with any living system, and they go beyond the capability of resulting in an end when conditions are met, by which they refer to their form, as with any prebiotic self-organising system [Hofkirchner 2013a: 110-115].

The agency of co-acting elemental actors (individuals or corporate actors) reproduces and/or transforms the system's structure (the social relations that work as organisational relations) that, in turn, enables, through constraints for the agency (by means of rules, regulations and resource dispositions), synergy effects that could not accrue otherwise for the actors [Hofkirchner 2014b: 120-121].

History moves social systems on trajectories in the course of which bifurcations occur. Bifurcations come up with a variety of possible future trajectories. The social system needs to choose one out of many. The more advanced history is, the greater the variety of future trajectories seems to be. However, with regard to the further development of the social system bifurcations offer opportunities and threaten with risks as well. In order to avert devolution (a path that leads to the breakdown of the system), a leap from the previous level-evolution on which the social system could enjoy a steady state onto a higher level which forms part of a successful mega-evolution (a breakthrough to a path that transforms the system into [Haefner 1992: 314; Oeser 1992: 103-104]) is mandatory. Amplified fluctuations of parameters indicate possible and necessary punctuations. Today, global challenges drive an accumulation of crises that mark a decisive bifurcation.

Since the second half of the last century the dominant way of using technological, environmental and human resources has turned out to be increasingly incompatible with a peaceful and harmonious future of societies. There are forceful impediments on the path to establishing sustainable international as well as intra-national relations (which exclude the use of military violence and other technological means that are detrimental to the good life); to establishing ecologically sustainable relations to nature (which excludes overuse of resources and their abuse as sinks for harmful waste); and to establishing sustainable relations amongst humans in the cultural, political and socio-economic context (which includes all producers and users in a fair production and usage of whatever is commonly produced). Enclosures of the commons have been aggravated to such a degree that all of them morphed into global challenges. As long as social systems could externalise the negative effects, their self-organisation was compatible with the enclosure of commons; now that they are interconnected as they are, the enclosure of the commons is not tenable any more.

It is an age of global challenges that human civilisation has entered. Global challenges are global because they affect humanity as a whole and because it is only humanity as a whole that can deal with them successfully. Global challenges have a 'dark' and a 'bright' side. The dark side is the imminent danger of the breakdown of differentiated interdependent social systems with the possibility of the falling apart of civilisation and exterminating civilised human life. The bright side marks a possible entrance to a new state of civilisation that brings about a peaceful, environmentally sound and socially and economically just and inclusive world society – the integration of differentiated interdependent social systems and the advent of a higher organisation. This is the Great Bifurcation that lies ahead of humanity. World society, humanity as one whole, as a unity through diversity, is in *statu nascendi*. The crises of today are the heralds of that change never seen before – of a possible and needful meta-system transition in which a supra-system is on the point of emerging. This supra-system would be a real world society that turns the current systems into its components. It would disclose the commons and make the social systems inclusive; it would warrant *eudaimonia* (good life in a good society); it would accomplish the adjustment of those structures that have become obsolete and doing justice to agency that cares for the whole. It would be a Global Sustainable Information Society (GSIS).

GSIS requires,

(1) for the first time in the history of our planet, on a higher social level – that is, globally –

(2) a reorganisation of the social relations within and in between the interdependent social systems such that sociogenic dysfunctions with respect to the social, the social-ecological and the socio-technological realms can be contained – that is, a transformation into sustainable development –

(3) through conscious and conscientious actors that are not only self- but also community-concerned – that is, under well determined informational conditions.

Hence the ingredients "globality", "sustainability", and "information-nality" of the GSIS concept [Hofkirchner 2014a; see also 2011, 2013b]. They form imperatives for three different features of complexity: the spatio-temporal dimension, the level of organisation, and the state of intelligence. One imperative necessitates the other. Being global implies being sustainable which, in turn, implies being informational. Informationality means there is information needed for sustainability; sustainability means there are sustainable relations needed for globality.

1.2.1. *The spatio-temporal dimension: the imperative of globality*

The first feature refers to an inherent tendency in every evolution of complex systems – that of wholeness and nestedness. When independent systems have become interdependent, level-evolution of these systems can be punctuated by the transition to a meta-system that forms a hierarchy: a suprasystem can emerge, nesting the formerly independent systems as its new elements. The suprasystem encapsulates them such that they become co-systems of each other.

This tendency is what can be found during globalisation. Formerly rather independent social systems in different parts of the globe have been becoming more and more dependent on each other. There has been going on a penetration of social systems in range and depth, there has been less and less left over, there is almost nothing "outside" any more. This is an objective rise of interdependence between social systems. And this paves the way for the development of forms of common governance for all those systems. Such a metasystem transition is possible. Moreover, it is imperative, for what can be conceived as constitutive partitions of humanity on earth cannot survive and thrive unless all and each of them become, in fact, integrative parts of a society of societies.

Evolution of globality can be conceptualised in the following way.

- After nomadicity with human foraging up to the neolithical revolution, after presumed self-sufficiency of the first agglomerations of human settlement with matrilineal societies [e.g. Eisler 1987; Bornemann 1975; but see also Eller 2000] and after connectivity that developed with ancient city-states along historical trade routes [Zimmermann 2014, 2015],
- which prevailing features of the social space were replaced by strict principles of territoriality manifest in the empires, nation states and regional unions that have followed,
- a third step seems possible that negates the exclusive feature of territoriality and resumes nomadicity [Lévy 1997], self-sufficiency and connectivity under the new circumstances. That new feature is a new cosmopolitanism, it is globality that – in the sense of R. Robertson's definition of the term glocalisation [1992] – embraces the bottom-up and top-down dynamics in a world system that – not in the sense in which Immanuel Wallerstein [1988] introduced the term – is a social system of nested social systems that run from the local level up to the global level. In that vein, nation states need not to be dissolved when it comes to the world system. They need only being reworked. Democracy needs to be strengthened from below as long as the global level is not hampered.

This points to the second feature.

- a possible third step would be the feature of a "wise society" as put forward by the High-Level Expert Group of the European Commission in 1997, namely an *unitas multiplex* [Morin 1992: 143-144], a universal without totality [Lévy 2001], integrating the differences in synergetic "Me"-"Us"-"Thee" triads – "Me"s and "Thee"s are "I"s and "You"s mediated by all of "Us" and "Us" is the "We" mediated by "Me" and "Thee", from the world system down to the most local system – that foster complementariness, a subsidiary composition made up of all differences.

Sustainability can come true only if and when informationality, the third feature, is achieved.

1.2.3. *The state of intelligence: the imperative of informationality*

The ability of a system to organise itself is co-extensive with the ability to generate information. "Information is generated if self-organising systems relate to some external perturbation by the spontaneous build-up of order they execute when exposed to this perturbation" [Hofkirchner 2013a: 172]. Information is that very process of relating or the result of that process which is the order itself. Intelligence is the capability of self-organising systems to generate that information that contributes in the best way to solving problems that occur to the systems when maintaining themselves or improving their performance. Collective intelligence is emergent from the single intelligences of the co-systems on the level of the suprasystem. Collective intelligence can do better than any single intelligence. In times of crises, systems are prompted to organise themselves onto a higher level to overcome the crises. The better their collective intelligence, that is, the better their problem solving capacity and the better their capability to generate information, the better their handling of the crisis and the order they can reach. This is a reformulation in informational terms of W. Ross Ashby's Law of Requisite Variety. That law states that a system is dynamically stable if the variety (the number of states) of its control mechanism is not less than the variety of that system that is to be controlled. Now, that system that is to be controlled can be the system itself or another system. That means, when increased complexity puts the performance or maintenance of a system at risk, it can catch up and solve the problem by activating the collective intelligence of the co-systems it is made up of and raise the complexity of its organisational relations or by activating the collective intelligence of its co-systems and raise the complexity of the system in which they are nested to match or surpass the complexity that is faced.

Applied to social systems, that law is the system theoretical expression of the law Karl Marx introduced into social science when postulating a dialectic between productive forces and relations of production and the substitution of relations of production and the whole societal superstructure when they do not meet any longer the requirements of the productive forces. Today, global challenges are complex and need complex solutions. Complex solutions would be possible, if humanity developed that information that is necessary to shift societal development onto a sustainable path. Moreover, such information is imperative. Otherwise the world system could not be governed, civilisation and the human race could go extinct.

A three-step logic would give the following sketch in the informational respect.

- First, when the transition from our ancestors to Homo sapiens started, this was done by the insertion of social factors in the biotic evolution and the reinforcement of their taking effect within the bounds of biotic evolution. An *animal sociale* formed. As illustrated by Alexei N. Leontyev's [1981: 210-212] hunter beater example in his activity theory and Michael Tomasello's [2014: 36-47] stag hunt example which stems from game theory and is used in his "shared intentionality" hypothesis to illuminate the co-operative turn in evolution, joint actions, joint goals, and joint attention coevolved together, joint intentionality dyads started off social selection by judgements about others and, eventually, when the new factor became so powerful that it took the lead over pre-human evolution and set human evolution going, collective intentionality could be carried out by group-minded individuals [Tomasello 2014: 80-81].

- Second, however, *homo economicus* appeared as a concrete example of generic *"homo idioticus"* who benefitted from "the creation of the private through the enclosure of public or commonly held resources", which "has historically been the primary means by which property has been secured for private use" [Curtis 2013: 12]. Instrumental rationality has prevailed since and has used even other persons for one's personal interests.

- Third, when collective intentionality would be set free from the current restrictions that instrumentalise co-operation for competition against other "Them"-groups, a true *"homo socialis"* [Gintis and Helbing 2015] could enter the stage. New cosmopolitans could enjoy a universalised, extended capability to act through a consciousness and conscience that takes care of the global commons.

2. Requisite Information in the Age of Global Challenges

Having discussed globality, sustainability and informationality, it becomes clear that all those features are currently emergent but far from being dominant to complement a third step in the evolution of social systems. They would need some further development to characterise information society as a social formation in its own right, which would be GSIS. Today, they characterise a transition time only, if anything.

As it turns out that informationality is the most basic foundation for the transformation into a GSIS, what the current social information requirements for the transformation into a higher-order social formation are is of utmost importance. The fine structure of the informational imperative deserves closer examination.

2.1. *The Triple-C Model of information structure*

Information processes serve different functions. An agent, while organising itself, generates at the same time information, that is, assumes a form by relating itself towards the environment. The process of relating is an information process and the form assumed is the result of that information process. Depending on the role the object plays to which the agent relates, three information functions can be distinguished [Hofkirchner 2013a: 184-196].

- The most general case is the object is some other system (or part of the system or a process performed by the system). Then the information function is a cognitive one.
- If that other system is a co-system (or part or process of a co-system), the information function is communicative. Communication is the coupling of cognitive co-systems.
- And if the other system is the suprasystem (or part or process of the suprasystem) the agent is part of, the information function is co-operative. Co-operation is the entangling of communicative co-systems such that the agent's relation to co-systems is mediated by the suprasystem's structure that is an emergent from, and dominates, the behaviour of all co-systems.

Cognition, communication and co-operation represent the three information functions. They form a hierarchy. That means the higher level shapes the lower one, although the higher depends on the lower. Therefore, cognition is a necessary condition for communication, and communication is a necessary condition for co-operation. Given a system of systems, co-operation of these very systems shapes their communication. This, in turn, shapes the cognition in each of them. In this way, cognition, communication and co-operation are mutually conditioning each another. That is the Triple-C Model.

2.2. *The current stage of social information (r)evolution*

Social information is information generated by social systems. Actors, whether individual or collective, can be conceived as social systems too. An actor behaves vis-à-vis the environment. When being perturbed they try to make sense of it. The actor responds by the creation of information that, from that point of time onwards, mediates the relation of the actor to the environment.

Social information refers to [Hofkirchner 2014: 132]

- the actualisation of the cognitive abilities of actors, which allows the reflexive discernment of wisdom to guide acting;
- the actualisation of their communicative abilities, which allows for empathetic understanding of other actors' appeals, thus being an extension and application, of cognition and feeding back to it; and

- the actualisation of their co-operative abilities, which allows them intentionally to share common goals, which is an extension and application of communication and, in turn, feeds back to their communication and – via it – to their cognition.

Let's discuss the anthropological features of the three social information functions that undergo in the age of global challenges a decisive change that gives the information age its meaning in reverse order, since the imperative comes from the top-most level. Let's start with co-operation.

2.2.1. *The co-operative function: the imperative of commonalism*

The rationale of every system is synergy. Because agents when producing a system produce synergetic effects, that is, effects they could not produce when in isolation, systems have a strong incentive to proliferate. In social systems synergism takes on the form of some social good. Actors contribute together to the good and are common beneficiaries of that good – the good is a common good, it is a commons. That good comes into being through the common effort of the actors' combined productive energies and is located on a social system's macro-level. It is a relational good that influences actors on the micro-level, since it enables or constrains the actors' participation in producing and consuming the good. All actors contribute to the emergence of that order that grants that their interactions become stable relations. The new structure relates the actors to each other.

The production of commons has been made possible through a new kind of co-operative information with humans. Tomasello contends that his "shared intentionality" hypothesis provides an evolutionary and structural explanation of the difference yielded by human co-operation, and presupposes different human communicative and, as a consequence, different human cognitive capabilities as well. The key idea is that it is conditions of co-operation that made the difference in evolution. Evolutionary pressure unfolded a ratchet effect that yielded ever higher complex co-operation. Early humans began to speciate only when they took advantage of going beyond "individual intentionality" and adopted "more complex forms of cooperative sociality" [2014: 31], which enabled them to achieve shared goals and brought about, in a first step, "joint intentionality" and, in a second one, "collective intentionality".

Co-operative information is anthropologically consensual. Collective intentionality refers to consensus about goals, about the here and now and about the way to reach those goals from the here and now in whole societies that go beyond the kinship groups. It is based on collective action that comes first. And it implies a dynamic at the end of which collective commitment appears, a dynamic that starts with discernment of the ultimate concern of individual actors at the cognitive level, goes on with deliberation and ends up with dedication that translates into collective commitment [Donati and Archer 2015: 127-142, 189].

That is how collective intelligence works with humans in a generic way. But what makes the difference now is that co-operative information is in need to transcend even whole societies. A global consciousness and conscience is requested. It is now the global commons that are at stake and need to be focused on. Through the growing interdependence any commons gets more and more integrated with the global commons. Thus co-operative information for a GSIS is requested to respect and collectively share the commitment to the conservation and flourishing of every part of the global commons. Now all commons need to be liberated to save our world. That is the imperative for co-operation today. That's what commonalism means – the orientation of co-operation towards caring for the commons.

2.2.2. *The communicative function: the imperative of all-inclusiveness*

In order to support the negotiation of joint goals and the coordination of collaboration, human communication originated with "a commitment to informing others of things honestly and accurately, that is, truthfully" [Tomasello 2014: 51]; "being committed to informing others of things honestly, for *their* not *our* benefit, is the starting point" [51-52]. Later on, discourse appeared in which "I must always honor the perspective of my recipient, and in cooperative argumentation I must be committed to accept the reasons and arguments of others if they are better than my own" [122].

Communicative information is anthropologically collaborative. Consilience is its task, the bringing together of several perspectives to bring about a common perspective on a higher level. This common perspective is convergent on objectivated knowledge. In anthropogenesis, so Tomasello [122], modern humans contrasted their own perspective "with some kind of generic perspective of anyone and everyone about things that were objectively real, true, and right from any perspective whatsoever – a perspectiveless view from nowhere." That means that the deliberation phase Margaret Archer is talking about is not only a discourse between individual actors who let a consensus emerge but, according to Tomasello [123], also a discourse that is done in "the perspective of the group as a whole, or any group member, Mead's 'generalized other.'" This is in full accordance with Bertalanffy's epistemological stance of perspectivism and objectivation of scientific knowledge through de-anthropomorphisation [2015: 247-248].

That is again the normal functioning of human collective intelligence. If civilisation today is in urgent need of efficient solutions for global problems, discourse and deliberation must take place as global conversation in order to mobilise any possible effort to create and implement the best ideas. That implies that no actor should be excluded or decapacitated to contribute to the common task of mitigating the challenges. As always with diversity in situations of crises, minority positions might offer potentials to build upon. All humanity needs to be embraced. That's the imperative for communication today.

2.2.3. *The cognitive function: the imperative of meta-reflexivity*

Cognitively, "when early humans began engaging in obligate collaborative foraging, they schematized a cognitive model of the dual-level collaborative structure comprising a joint goal with individual roles and joint attention with individual perspectives" [Tomasello 2014: 69]. Triangulation began. When communication started with modern humans to involve discourses about "objective" facts and needed compelling arguments, cognition turned into full-blown human reasoning. "In the context of cooperative argumentation, modern humans made explicit the reasons for their assertions, thus connecting them in an inferential web to their other knowledge, and then this social practice of reason-giving was internalized into fully reflective reason" [121-122].

Moreover, early humans "could also view the world at the same time from the perspective of the other" [78]. They even "self-regulated their behavioral decisions with others' evaluations in mind" [75]. With culture, says Tomasello, it is not "one individual evaluating another individual" any more but, rather, "modern group-minded humans" evaluating all others "in agent-neutral, transpersonal mode" [87]. That implies "an objective standard against which an individual's behaviour is evaluated and judged", i.e. the "group's agreed-upon evaluations", and a target that is in principle applicable to anyone belonging to the group [88-89]. Group members self-monitor and self-regulate their individual actions via group norms so as to co-ordinate with the expectations of the group.

And all that implies a new capability – the capability to reflect, to generalise, to think in concepts.

Archer calls "the regular exercise of the mental ability, shared by all normal people, to consider themselves in relation to their (social) contexts and vice versa" "reflexivity" [2007: 4]. Reflexivity is a human property only. Reflexivity thus enables humans to reflect upon themselves, and to reflect themselves as part of a bigger picture, that is, being reflexive about their immediate social situation, but also all the way up to society itself. The actions of members towards other members of society are mediated by this 'third': the structure of society. What is expected from the very fact of being a member of society? This reflection itself is a model for every mode of (complex) thinking. It is a model for grasping the general relationship between elements and system, parts and whole, of which individual and society are merely the model instantiation. It is a model for generalisations and subsuming of the specific under the general. Human cognition is thus concept-dominated rather than sensation-focused [Logan 2007]. It is conceptual. A concept is a generalisation of percepts, of sense data. It is not a complete induction, which would be a compelling deduction. It is a jump to another level that has a new quality and cannot be accomplished by deductive reasoning only. By being reflexive, able to generalise, conceptual, cognition is empowered to anticipate the co-ordination of tasks, the structure of action. Cognitive information is anthropologically co-ordinative. That is a common feature of human collective intelligence.

Now that the survival of mankind has been put at stake, that the hitherto existing modes of governance have failed, that battles over the global commons have broken out, new specifications for cognitive information are key.

The discernment phase that sorts out what matters most to an individual actor [Donati and Archer 2015: 127-142] is a phase in which the actor can refer to the general level of the social standard. The finding of an ultimate concern is the precondition for carrying out the deliberation and dedication phases that lead to the collective commitment. Margaret Archer and Pierpaolo Donati illustrate this in the example of the performance of an orchestra. Like musicians in an orchestra, individuals constitute "a collectivity that evaluates objectives (discernment), deliberates about realizing its common concerns (deliberation), and commits itself to achieving them (dedication)" [61-62]. The point is "about the *orientation of all the musicians to the collective performance*. A collective orientation to a collective 'output' is the core of collective reflexivity" [61]. That collective reflexivity emerges from what they call individual meta-reflexivity practised by each musician. An individual is meta-reflexive if "he reflects *on* the orchestra's performance and about how this performance could be improved were the musicians to relate to each other in a different way", that is, if he seeks "to alter the performance of the whole orchestra" and "to produce a different emergent effect" [61].

The orchestra example needs generalisation to the level of humanity. Cognition for a GSIS requires meta-reflexives that have the fate of humanity as their ultimate concern and orient towards the common good for all. That kind of reflexivity goes beyond confined varieties of reflexivity as well as a restrictive capability to act that does not take into consideration interests other than self-concerned [Holzkamp 1983]. It is imperative for cognition today.

3. Meaningful IT

What is currently called information society with respect to the penetration of society with information technology (IT) is not a full-fledged social formation. The fluctuations in social development in cultural, political, economic, ecological, and technological respects might be an indicator for preparing the grounds for another social formation that might be brought about by another Great Transformation that relies upon meta-reflexive social subjects, and IT might be part of it. But it is part of it, if and only if informatisation is subject to the informational imperatives, the commons-liberating, all-humanity-embracing, and meta-reflexive imperatives, and facilitates informationalisation.

Informatisation is the spread of IT that makes society more and more responsive to information. Informationalisation is the process of raising the problem-solving capacity of the nascent world society to a level that allows for successfully tackling the problems that arise from society's own development. Informationalisation can, and needs to be, based upon informatisation, but is not entailed by informatisation per se [see Hofkirchner 2015b: 287].

The penetration of society with IT is not a "mechanism" that leads to information society. "Mechanisms" are rooted in self-organisation. Far from being mechanical, they are contingent dynamisms. They are not based upon a one-to-one mapping of causes and effects. In spite of designing technological means serving particular social interests, supervenient features accrue in the shape of the designed technology and open the space for possible impacts on society different from those intended. This is an ineluctable property of the complexity of real-world systems. These impacts can add value to the system, can be neutral, or can be partly or overall detrimental to it. Detrimental impacts occur because social actors who are accountable behave as if they were autonomous systems, that is, restrict their focus to themselves and do not extend it to the social relations that assign to them the limits of positions they hold and of the roles they play.

The social system is characterised by a certain structure containing dysfunctionalities or not. IT has ambiguous impacts on the social system they support.

- On the one hand, it offers opportunities to improve the functioning of the produsage of any commons and can support the mitigation, and even elimination, of disparities;
- On the other hand, it can be functionalised for purposes detrimental to the reclaim of the commons and can reinforce existing disparities, quantitatively;
- Or spawn new disparities, qualitatively.

Thus, IT needs to be designed deliberately. Informatisation has to be tamed such that it can be harnessed for informationalisation.

The dialectic of informatisation and informationalisation is the generic dynamism in information society. As it is a manifestation of the dialectic of "socialization" and "individualization" characteristic of any social systems evolution, antagonisms hinder proper informationalisation and turn informatisation into a perverted form. Informatisation shows ambiguities between, in general, the potential of an informed world netizenship and the actualisation of a divide between the information rich and the information poor; between, in the cultural respect, the potential of enabling wisdom and the actualisation of an information blackout through information overflow and brainwash; between, in the political respect, the potential of empowering people and the actualisation of violations of the right to informational self-determination through surveillance and information warfare; between, in the economic respect, the potential of unfettering information and the actualisation of intellectual proprietarisation through commodification and commercialisation; between, in the ecological respect, the potential of optimising material and energy flows and the actualisation of IT-supported over-exploitation and degradation of nature; between, in the technological respect, the potential of lowering frictions in the functioning of technologies and the actualisation of an IT-induced vulnerability of the technological infrastructure of civilisation.

The term "meaningful technology" designates technology that is endowed with meaning by two conditions:

(1) The reflection, through integrated technology assessment and technology design, of its social usefulness, that is, its expected usage vs. its factual usage, and the consequences thereof; this includes a reflection of both
   (a) the aptness for the purpose (the utility) and
   (b) the purpose itself (the function the technology serves).
(2) Participatoriness, that is, the inclusion in the design process of those who are affected by its usage (transdisciplinarity in the broad sense).

In the age of global challenges, meaningful technology shall contribute to the capability of societies to safeguard their development and rule out a self-inflicted breakdown. By doing so, that technology fulfils the requirements for a GSIS.

Meaningful IT in the information age shall support the creation of wisdom, knowledge, data, that can guide action to transform the social systems with the objective to break up the enclosure of the global commons. By doing so, IT fulfils the requirements for a GSIS.

Concluding, it has been shown that, in line with Bertalanffy's General System Theory approach, criteria for practical recommendations on the issue of the information society and information technology can be derived. Evaluations can be achieved through analyses that are carried out with a methodology based upon an Evolutionary Systems Theory and a Unified Theory of Information [Hofkirchner 2013a]. A Science of Information, including a Philosophy of Information, is possible that grounds an understanding of problems of social information processes on an understanding of the fundamentals of generic information processes. And as soon as Computer Science and Informatics reflect the embeddedness of computer systems in social systems and consider specifications accordingly, they become part of such a Science of Information that can guide us on our way to a GSIS.

References

Archer, M. (2007). *Making our Way through the World: Human Reflexivity and Social Mobility*, Cambridge University Press, Cambridge
Bertalanffy, L. V. (2015). *General System Theory*, George Braziller, New York
Bornemann, E. (1975). *Das Patriarchat*, S. Fischer, Frankfurt am Main

Brunner, K., Klauninger, B. (2003). An Integrative Image of Causality and Emergence, in: Arshinov, V., Fuchs, C. (eds.), *Causality, Emergence, Self-Organisation*, NIA-Priroda, Moscow, 23-35

Collier, J. (2003). Fundamental Properties of Self-Organisation. in: Arshinov, V., Fuchs, C. (eds.), *Causality, Emergence, Self-Organisation*, NIA-Priroda, Moscow, 150-166

Curtis, N. (2013). *Idiotism: Capitalism and the Privatisation of Life*, Pluto Press, London

Donati, P., Archer, M. (2015). *The Relational Subject*, Cambridge University Press, Cambridge

Eisler, R. (1987). *The Chalice and the Blade: Our History, Our Future*, Harper and Row, San Francisco

Eller, C. (2000). *The Myth of Matriarchal Prehistory*, Beacon Press, Boston

Ellersdorfer, G., Hofkirchner, W. (1994). Informationsstrukturen auf zellulärer Ebene und Fragen des Reduktionismus/Antireduktionismus, in: Wessel, K.-F., Naumann, F. (eds.), *Kommunikation und Humanontogenese*, Kleine, Bielefeld, 105-115

European Commission, Directorate-General for Employment, Industrial Relations and Social Affairs (ed.) (1997). *Building the European information society for us all*, Final Policy Report of the high-level expert group, Office for Official Publications of the European Communities, Luxembourg

Fenzl, N., Fleissner, P., Hofkirchner, W., Jahn, R., Stockinger, G. (1996). On the Genesis of Information Structures: A View that is neither reductionistic nor Holistic, in: Kornwachs, K., Jacoby, K. (eds.), *Information: New Questions to a Multidisciplinary Concept*, Akademie Verlag, Berlin, 271-283

Gintis, H., Helbing, D. (2015). Homo Socialis: An Analytical Core for Sociological Theory, *Review of Behavioral Economics*, 2, 1-59

Haefner, K. (1992). Information Processing at the Sociotechnical Level, in: Haefner, K. (ed.), *Evolution of Information Processing Systems*, Springer, Berlin etc., 307-319

Hofkirchner, W. (2011). Information and Communication Technologies for a Good Society, in: D. M. Haftor, Mirijamdotter, A. (eds.), *Information and Communication Technologies, Society and Human Beings: Theory and Framework*, Information Science Reference, Hershey, Pennsylvania, 434-443

Hofkirchner, W. (2012). Sustainability and Self-Organisation: Sustainability in the Perspective of Complexity and Systems Science and Ethical Considerations, in: Nishigaki, T., Takenouchi, T. (eds.), *Information Ethics: The Future of the Humanities*, V2 Solution Publisher, Nagoya City

Hofkirchner, W. (2013a). *Emergent Information: A Unified Theory of Information Framework*, World Scientific, Singapore etc.

Hofkirchner, W. (2013b). Self-Organisation as the Mechanism of Development and Evolution in Social Systems, in: M. Archer (ed.), *Social Morphogenesis*, Springer, Cham etc., 125-143

Hofkirchner, W. (2014a). Potentials and Risks for Creating a Global Sustainable Information Society, in: Fuchs, C., Sandoval, M. (eds.), *Critique, Social Media and the Information Society*, Routledge, London etc., 66-75

Hofkirchner, W. (2014b). On the Validity of Describing 'Morphogenic Society' as a System and Justifiability of Thinking About it as a Social Formation, in: Archer, M. (ed.), *Late Modernity: Trajectories towards Morphogenic Society*, Springer, Cham etc., 119-141

Hofkirchner, W. (2015a). 'Mechanisms' at Work in Information Society. In: Archer, M. (ed.), *Generative Mechanisms Transforming the Social Order*, Springer, Cham etc., 95-112

Hofkirchner, W. (2015b). Ethics for a Global Sustainable Information Society, in: Doucek, P., Chroust, G., Oskrdal, V. (eds.), *IDIMT-2015: Information Technology and Society*, Trauner, Linz

Hofkirchner, W., Rousseau, D. (2015). Foreword, in: Bertalanffy, L. v., *General System Theory*, George Braziller, New York, 18th paperback printing, xi-xix

Holling, C. S. (1973). Resilience and Stability of Ecological Systems, *Annual review of Ecology and Systematics*, 4, 1-23

Holzkamp, K. (1983). *Grundlegung der Psychologie*, Campus, Frankfurt am Main

Jantsch, E. (1987). Erkenntnistheoretische Aspekte der Selbstorganisation natürlicher Systeme, in: Schmidt, S. J. (ed.), *Der Diskurs des Radikalen Konstruktivismus*, Suhrkamp, Frankfurt am Main, 159-191

Laszlo, E. (1972). *Introduction to Systems Philosophy: Toward a New Paradigm of Contemporary Thought*, With a Foreword by Ludwig von Bertalanffy, Gordon and Breach, New York etc.

Leontyev, A. N. (1981). *Problems of the development of the mind*, Progress, Moscow

Levy, P. (1997). *Collective Intelligence*, Plenium Trade, New York etc.

Lévy, P. (2001). *Cyberculture*, University of Minnesota Press, Minneapolis etc.

Logan, R. (2007). *The extended mind: the emergence of language, the human mind and culture*, University of Toronto Press, Toronto

Mouffe, C. (2013). *Agonistics: Thinking the world politically*, Verso, London

Morin, E. (1992). *Method, Towards a Study of Humankind, Vol. 1, The Nature of Nature*, Peter Lang, New York etc.

Oeser, E. (1992). Mega-Evolution of Information Processing Systems, in: Haefner, K. (ed.), *Evolution of Information Processing Systems*, Springer, Berlin etc., 103-111

Robertson, R. (1992). *Globalization*, Sage, London

Tomasello, M. (2014). *A Natural History of Human Thinking*, Harvard University Press, Cambridge

Wallerstein, I. (1988). *One World, Many Worlds*, Rienner, New York

Zimmermann, R. E. (2014). *H NEA ΠΟΛΥ: Neue Stadtbegriffe auf dem Weg in die Heimat*, LIT Verlag, Berlin

Zimmermann, R. E. (2015) Mesógios - Zur Struktur der Polis-Netzwerke, in: Faber, R., Lichtenberger, A. (eds.) Ein pluriverses Universum: Zivilisationen und Religionen im antiken Mittelmeerraum, Fink, Paderborn, 113-130

Chapter 3

Information Dynamics, Self-Organization
and the Implications for Management

John Collier

Philosophy, University of KwaZulu-Natal
Durban 4041, South Africa
collier@ncf.ca
http://web.ncf.ca/collier

I start with a brief summary of kinds of information used in science, showing how they are nested (or hierarchically arranged), with inner kinds inheriting properties of the outer kinds. I further argue that within each kind there is also hierarchical organization, and that the major kinds are distinguished by their dynamics, not just being ordered in a hierarchy, though similar principles apply at all levels. Next I argue that rules applying to non-equilibrium thermodynamics apply also to information systems, and I give some examples of resulting self-organization, or what we have called "rhythmic entrainment". I point out that entrainment that results from forces within a system are more efficient than ones that are entrained by outside forces. This gives a sort of resilience to such systems, and in higher kinds of information allows for self-adaptation via accommodating both external forces and internally generated forces. I then apply these lessons to management and argue that the most efficient and creative form of management comes not from severe control from the top, or from imposed "efficiency" but through self-organization allowed by a low degree of control and the encouragement of diversity. This form of management I call *facilitation*. There may be specific people assigned a facilitation role, but this is not required; any member of a group can act as a facilitator. What is required, however, is that members of the group are accustomed to being open-minded and flexible. This form of management is most compatible with anarchism as a political (and management) theory, but has benefits in pretty much any political system.

35

1. Introduction

Management is a process, so it is possible to look at it dynamically, like any other process. Although management is often represented as a structure, with control from the top down the presupposed process, it is more general to look at management in a free form, with information being the main currency within any management system. Typically management is of something. I will largely ignore anything external to the management process itself, treating incoming information as data and other externalities as outputs or products. It should be noted that management of some kinds of systems, especially complex ones, does not permit this sort of division between the managed and the management, and concessions need to be made to take this into account. For example ecological management must include the management system as part of the very ecology that is to be managed, thus effectively enlarging the management system by extending interactions from within the management system to the interior of the ecology itself. Viewed slightly differently, the ecology becomes a part of the overall management system. The general remarks I have to make about management can be extended to include such enlarged systems, so much the same principles apply as to management in particular. It is important, however, to move to an enlarged system whenever there are complex interactions between the management and the system to be managed; in these cases treating inputs as data, rather than processes of the system itself, is distinctly misleading. I will assume (hope!) that such situations can be taken recognized and taken into consideration.

Information plays two roles in management systems. One is as a process that connects the various nodes in the management. The other is as a constraint on such processes. In flexible management systems, and also depending on time scales, the two roles can be interchanged. However Shannon [1949] pointed out that logically the roles of information and constraint are interchangeable. When I introduce the idea of information flow later it will be evident that particulars carrying information are dual to classes that arrange information, which is similar in some ways to Shannon's equivalence. The duality allows us to see filters of information as informational in themselves, obeying the rules of information dynamics in general; likewise information can be seen as a classification and part of the structure of management. These dual roles emphasize the nature of management as a process rather than a structure. This more flexible approach has important consequences for what can constitute the most effective management systems.

The first part will deal with dynamical systems in general, noting some properties that I will use later, in particular the efficiency of use of resources. Then I will apply dynamics to information flow and draw some general principles that apply to all information systems. Lastly I will look at management in particular, and compare various forms of management in terms of the principles developed earlier, arguing for their advantages and disadvantages. I will conclude that the most effective form of management is what I call *facilitation*, which combines a certain degree of control, generated either externally or, preferably, internally within the constraints of what is to be managed, but encourages diversity and flexibility, which together encourage self-organization. I will argue that this form of management, despite appearances, is more efficient than either top-down or anarchistic alternatives. It can be compatible with anarchistic principles understood with Kropotkin's ideal of cooperation, but it can also benefit other forms of management, even when there are hostile parties.

2. Dynamical Systems: Energy versus Information Budgets

A dynamical system mathematically is any system with change, usually but not necessarily over time. I use a somewhat more restrictive notion of a system of interacting processes. Processes are causally connected sequences of states, with an early initial point and a later endpoint. I take it that processes are fundamental, and their states are useful fictions, but not a lot turns on this. Although qualitative processes can be described and included in theories (with many successes especially in movement studies, including speech) it is convenient if quantities can be applied. Most processes are at least restricted by energy inputs and outputs, and many are also best described in terms of information flows and changing constraints (which turns out to be another form of information flow). In many cases energy and information are more or less independent of (decoupled from) each other (assuming sufficient energy to support the information flows), but in other cases they interact with each other in ways that make them mathematically inseparable. For convenience I will deal mostly with cases in which the energy and information budgets can be separated. But later I will examine the consequences when this fails.

There are some general principles that apply to all dynamical systems with regard to their computability and predictability. In standard Hamiltonian mechanics of conservative or near conservative systems, boundaries are not time dependent (the systems are holonomic). This is the condition assumed in most of modern physics, and, by analogy to physics, much of modern science. Standard advanced texts on classical physics [such as Goldstein *et al*. 2000] make the assumption explicit when they introduce the Hamiltonian formulation. For this reason I have called such systems Hamiltonian [Collier 2008a, 2014], though the Hamiltonian formulation can in principle deal with non-holonomic systems. If the system is nearly holonomic, then it is possible to deal with deviations with perturbation theory, a standard method. At the other end we can deal with large changes as step functions between states. This is familiar to quantum physicists since at least the introduction of the Dirac delta function. In changes of state that can be modeled by step functions, both the boundary conditions and the local dynamics change abruptly to new conditions.

Hamiltonian systems are predictable in the following sense: the trajectory of a system is predictable if and only if there is a region η constraining the initial conditions at t_0 such that the equations of motion ensure that the trajectory of the system passes within some region ε at some time t_1, where the region η is chosen to satisfy ε. Indeterministic systems have probabilistic predictability (at best), but are otherwise much the same. It might be that there is no analytic universal solution to the equations governing the system (in three body gravitational systems, for example, and perhaps systems involving three collisions). Predictability for any finite time is still in principle possible, however, for any holonomic system, given enough computing power (though rounding due to computational limitations can give the appearance of nonpredictability when these systems are modeled on actual computers – this should not be confused with unpredictability in the system itself).

These methods fail in many types of systems in which the boundary conditions interact with system laws in a mathematically inseparable way. Such systems are radically nonholonomic. I have also called them radically non-Hamiltonian [Collier 2007, 2008a, 2014]. They badly fail both reducibility and predictability, and involve the formation of novel large scale properties, i.e., what has historically been called *emergence*. Conrad and Matsuno [1990: 67-68] made clear the consequences for dynamical systems:

> Differential equations provide the major means of describing the dynamics of physical systems in both quantum and classical mechanics. The indubitable success of this scheme suggests, on the surface, that in principle it could be extended to a universal program covering all of nature. The problem is that the essence of a differential equation description is a separation of itself from the boundary conditions, which are regarded as arbitrary.

Conrad and Matsuno go on to draw conclusions about the application of the method to the whole universe (they claim the system breaks down, but it is actually compatible with "no boundary conditions" constraints on cosmological theories). Of more significance here is the breakdown of the separation of differential equations and boundary conditions in nonintegrable systems, exactly the ones that are nonholonomic. In these systems, computation from partwise interactions fails, and the system is in a sense holistic. In any case, its dynamics cannot be reduced to the system dynamics and constraints arising from partwise relations.

How can a system fail to be holonomic? If we consider systems in which the energy budget dominates, basic physics tells us that energy is conserved, so that the Hamiltonian, which is the sum of the potential and kinetic energies, is constant. Non-Hamiltonian systems must gain or lose energy. The relevant energy here (to the system in question) is the available, or usable energy. To get this we must subtract the unavailable energy, which is entropic. We can compensate for this, though, through thermodynamics, taking the unavailable energy as heat, a form of disorder. Non-Hamiltonian systems must be such that we can't exclude heat energy. But this can happen within a system if it expels entropy to its surroundings, as noted often by Prigogine. In that case the system can do work on itself, altering its boundary conditions, and setting up a new dynamical regime that is more complex, the simplest case being Prigogine's dissipative structures. It might seem that we can redescribe the system more inclusively to include (or add in the dynamics of) the system into which the excess entropy is dumped, the larger system being holonomic. This is not always possible, though, at least not without including the whole universe into consideration [Collier 2011], since we may need to go ever outwards to get to an (effectively) isolated system. The problem is that the boundaries between attractors in complexly organized systems are fractal, with any two points in one attractor having a point between that is in another attractor. Complexly organized single attractor systems can be approximated by very carefully controlling boundary conditions and slowly changing the energy, as has been done in some exquisite experiments with Bénard like cells, using liquid Helium, but even in such cases there are at least two possible directions of rotation that are not determined by internal rules [Behringer and Ahlers 1982].

Many relatively simple energy budget dominated systems and the majority of complex ones are of this sort. At a minimum, three factors and external dissipation are required.[a] Reducibility and predictability both fail, reducibility because the equations governing the system have no complete analytical solution, and predictability because a stepwise approximation of the dynamics, no matter how big a computer we have, will never be enough, since the system reaches an endpoint (the new dynamical regime occupying the central region of the attractor) in finite time, solving equations for which would require a non-existent complete analysis rather than a piecewise approximation to an arbitrary degree of accuracy [Collier 2011a]. The dynamics of the system cannot be localized, and irreducible (novel) properties are manifested [Collier 2007, 2008a, 2014]. Despite this, the emergent properties and general system dynamics will have some highly regular general properties that I

[a]More mathematically, following Bertalanffy [1968], who follows Franks, noncomputable mathematical models occur in linear systems with partial differential equations using many parameters, and in nonlinear systems having more than one parameter, being partial differential, or in nonlinear algebraic systems with many parameters.

will return to below. These result from the fact that the system can do work on itself to modify its own boundary conditions, and this capacity to do work can be more or less efficient. The work done tends to be minimized, resulting in regular states (typically called attractors, though often they are also transitory, but with a much longer period than the regularities preceding them, perhaps *quasiattractor* would be better). This shift of system dynamics is a sort of phase change in which the system forms nonlocalizable regularities, with chaotic boundaries between, that get frozen into more local but still holistic regularities as noise dissipates. This can happen very quickly (as in the formation of Bénard cells) or rather slowly (as in planetary harmonic resonances, see [Collier 2011a]).

Interestingly, boundary conditions in such systems can no longer be described as specific values of physical parameters, since they are dynamic as well (being nonholonomic, after all). As usual, they are constraints on the system, but they are dynamical constraints. As Shannon famously argued [1949] the notion of constraint is an information theoretic notion: constraints are information. If we follow this, then the dynamics of constraints requires a dynamical theory of information. The notion of information in such a system can be aligned with physical properties using methods devised by Szillard in the 1920s to examine the thermodynamics of measurement, using Boltzmann's constant, and described by Brillouin [1962]. For details of the connections, see Collier [2007] for further developments, including information flow and complexity measures for information devised by Landauer [1961, 1987] and Charles Bennett [1982, 1985, 1987]. These ideas also allow connection to the physics of computation, opening up a way to discuss information flow in physical (and biological) systems. The notion of information flow was further developed by Barwise and Seligman [1997] (see below). These methods together allow connecting physical notions and information in constraints, as well as notions of information flow. For an account of causal process in information theoretic terms, see [Collier 1997]. I will not go into further detail here, but will merely assume that the strong analogy between energy and information budgets holds for systems in general. A summary of the basic connections justifying the analogy as a continuity of principles are to be found in [Collier 2007].

There are two ways that information can move (be dynamic) in a system. One is information flow, in which information at one point in the system is conveyed to another point in the system. The other is the constraints on the system itself can change. Often, changing the constraints will affect information flow as well. This is because information flows in channels, and the channels must be constrained to permit the flow, so changes in constraints on channels can change information flow. The information in constraints can change even if there is no information flow, because, as noted, in energy budget non-Hamiltonian systems the dynamics allow the system to work on itself to alter its boundary conditions. However, information flow depends on channel constraints. It is possible in principle for the channel constraints to change independently of the information flow, and also for the information flow to be dependent on changes in the channel constraints, but not vice versa. This is more or less like a Hamiltonian energy budget dominated system, if the constraints of the channel represent the system laws and the information flow represents the boundary conditions, and the two are independent of each other. Mathematically there is no difference. Most information systems, e.g., computers with their typical separation of program and data, and biological inheritance on the neo-Darwinian model assumes this separation. However, as has often been pointed out, there is no essential difference between program and data, so these models may be misleading if taken as generic of information systems. If the two interact, then it is possible for the information system to reorganize itself in much the same way as systems can do work on themselves to alter their boundary conditions.. This was proposed by Brooks and Wiley [1988] in biology (see also Collier [1986] for more detail about the conditions and processes required). They argued that biological information could self-organize on a strong analogy to energy dominated systems that are now fairly familiar, starting with dissipative structures and working towards more complicated systems, including evolutionary and developmental processes. This analogy can be strengthened further by noting that self-organization and the emergence of novel information requires the dissipation of information externally (e.g., through organism deaths and population extinctions). This sort of process can lead to speciation and increased diversity [Brooks and Wiley 1988, but see especially Collier 1986]. Basically, Brooks and Wiley assumed that the energy budget could pretty much take care of itself, maintaining an otherwise decoupled information budget with self-organizing properties. They gave many examples of cases in which this has appeared to occur in both development and evolution. Collier [2008b] argued that with a proper understanding of information channels (i.e., from Barwise and Seligman [1997]) we can recover a robust form of the expression of information in DNA that in its simplest version is just the neo-Darwinian view, but that also allows the Brooks and Wiley mechanism. On this account information is both substantive and has its own dynamics decoupled from the underlying but supportive energy dynamics. Information of this kind tends to form a natural hierarchy [described in some detail in Collier 2003].

The reader may doubt that information flowing and constraints are really comparable with each other, forming one pool of information. Aside from Shannon's [1949] observation that constraints are a form of information, Barwise and Seligman [1997] observed that the particulars carrying information and the classes that give it meaning in their channels are duals of each other. The exact details are rather complicated, but I think that the idea can be seen in the process of observation. Red light stimulates receptors in the retina, allowing them to stimulate nerves to carry information to the brain. The signals carry the information of a red impingement, as classified by the receptors, but the receptors are also individual units that carry the information that red light has struck them and a channel exists from the red receptors to the brain. So both the receptors and what they carry can be thought of as information about red. Basically, depending on what is useful for our analysis we can see the receptors as red classifiers or else as conductors of red information, as classified elsewhere in the perceptual system. This dual aspect of classification and content allows us to bring together the system constraints and what they carry as informational under the same heading, bringing together the informational nature of both the flow and what carries it. The two are separate, and have their own dynamical properties, but basically they deal with the same thing. When information flow is able to self-organize, this common basis allows a continuity between the processes, so that changes in the channel and what it carries change together.

We can generalize to information systems of all kinds: under the right conditions (external dissipation of information and system interactions such that the system can do work on its own dynamical conditions) then emergence of novel information can occur. If the novel information stabilizes, then it can provide a bed for further novelty to appear. The result will be a hierarchically arranged information system, with each level emerging from lower levels, but largely decoupled from them. From basic physics through to social systems increasingly complex kinds of information emerge from simpler systems by pretty much the same dynamic [Collier 2011b]. The basic dynamic is that of symmetry breaking [Collier 1996], leading to an intrinsic information grounded in system asymmetries [Muller 2007]. Although how the information is used might vary, it is the underlying processes that make it exist. Inasmuch as the causal processes in such systems are objective, so is the information. Information can have dynamical properties that do not depend on whether it is recognized or on how it is eventually used. This allows that there might be much going on beneath recognition of consciousness, or any purpose the information might eventually be put to, although these are certainly interesting issues worthy of scientific exploration. But to limit study of information dynamics just to perception and action would be to ignore much of what is going on.

3. General Properties of Complexly Organized Dynamical Systems

Since I have dealt with various aspects of these processes elsewhere [see Collier and Hooker 1999 for the basics], I will merely summarize the main points here:

- Although the simplest physical systems are Hamiltonian (or near Hamiltonian) many systems (or most, with Hamiltonian systems a vanishingly small proportion, see Robert Rosen [2000]) can show emergent properties.

- My main concern here is that boundary conditions deal with forms, and are best described by information methods.
- So the dynamics of information become important for systems with dynamical boundary conditions.
- The concept of information has been used in science from physics through economics, but the meanings and uses are somewhat different and should not be confused. One important difference is between information used as instrumentally, for convenient description and information used substantively. When used substantively information is assumed to really exist and plays a causal role [Collier 2008b].
- Some major classes of information used in science form a hierarchy [Collier 2011b]. Each level introduces new kinds of dynamics (novel properties), and can be said to be emergent from lower levels.
- Within each level of the hierarchy are further hierarchies of organization. These originate by self-organization (of two distinct types, reorganization through dissipation and self-organization through the promotion of perturbations). In some cases these levels are emergent but in others (reorganized information) they are not.
- The same basic systems principles apply across all levels, but new properties appear at higher levels due to new possibilities created at lower levels. The whole fits into the principles of General Systems Theory. There are some basic principles that apply at all levels (see next section).
- Each successive kind introduces further restrictions, which in turn create new immediate possibilities. This in turn feeds inwards, e.g.: the social requires communication between individuals, which creates new possibilities for the individuals in addition to social possibilities. This can be further iterated within the social kind.
- In general, negentropy (difference from equilibrium state, which is unique for each system) creates possibilities for self-organization, allowing the formation of new structural information (a form of negentropy itself). At the same time the new constraints permit variant complexions within the constraints, leading to an entropy of the structural information in addition to the energetic entropy. This can be iterated within through further levels once we have an information budget largely decoupled from the energy budget.

- These principles are grounded in growth and self-organization, but an important aspect is that there are natural system resonances and it is easier (requires less energy) to form and maintain these resonances than others. Spontaneous organization through rhythmic entrainment minimizes required work to maintain it [Collier and Burch 1998, 2000, Collier 2007]. These resonances are typical larger scale and often irreducible.
- In many higher level systems in the hierarchy the boundary conditions dominate, with the energy budget just maintaining a maintenance role. This is especially true in biology, but can also be true in purely physical systems, such as mineral formation, which can be surprisingly complex.
- The emergence of mind introduces a novel partially decoupled level that can work on its biological grounding, directing it and even working against its biological interests.
- Communication in social organisms introduces another partially decoupled level, which in turn creates new possibilities for more complex organization. This is most highly developed in human language. In turn, it allows for new forms of organization within the organisms themselves.
- The next level of information, made possible by communication, is social organization. This, in turn, creates the conditions required for management of social organization to be possible. In some social animals, like wolves, this management role is taken on by alpha males, whereas in others, like macaques, it is performed by mature females. In other animals it is distributed in more complex ways. Humans are special in being able to adopt a wide range of differing management styles at multiple levels from families to institutions.

I will end by arguing that certain management styles are much more efficient than others. These are the ones that work with the natural dynamics of the system to facilitate self-organization, rather than forcing a solution externally.

4. Naturally Resonant Systems through Self-Organization (Rhythmic Entrainment)

At the basic physical level we now understand fairly well how the levels of information kinds interact and form. They can be shown schematically as in the following diagram for some of the lowest levels (Fig. 1):

Common principles across levels (system theoretic)	**Minor levels hierarchical information** Molecules Atoms Basic particles
Self-organization creates new information within levels	**Minor levels negentropy** 'Clumped matter' Kinds of matter – kinds of radiation Matter – radiation
New forms of interaction produces new kinds of information	**Minor levels it from bit** Black hole horizons Event horizon, particle horizon Origin of universe (universe boundary)

Fig. 1. Basic physical phenomena

The Principles of General Systems Theory apply across all possible levels of organization. Some of the most important (referred to briefly above) are:

- Growth: Order and Entropy (disorder) can increase together. Order = S_{max} - S_{actual}, S being a statistical measure of entropy, the difference being commonly called *negentropy*, or information [Brillouin 1962].
- This "overhead", when growth exceeds the formation of order, permits self-organization:
- reorganization to lowest energy state by dissipation – noise dissipated, also natural selection;

- spontaneous self-organization (state change, bifurcation) through continuous dissipation of free energy → new information;
- creates new possibilities for interaction (reduced abstract possibility space constrains processes, making them more immediately likely).

These common principles allow the entropy concept to be generalized to substantive dynamical information, so that we can talk of an entropy of information and self-organization and emergence within information systems. The basic principles are as follows:

- The basic physical relation is given by Boltzmann's constant in a suitable form, leading to measures in entropy units or bits.
- Microstates, according to David Layzer, have microinformation. Part of this is the information of the macrostate in which they are contained, called macroinformation.
- Not all microinformation is accessible to a macroscopic entity (2nd Law of Thermodynamics)
- Macrostates, to be real, must be cohesive, binding over space and time.
- The same statistical principles apply to any system in which the microstates are not constrained by anything but the macrostate, so we can apply the related principles generally.
- In particular, we can talk of the macrostate of an information that has informational microstates. An example is the gene pool of a population or species. (Variation of the gene pool is taken to be random with respect to the properties of the species – in fact this is not always true and must be controlled for.)

These leads to the possibility for the spontaneous formation of levels through rhythmic entrainment [Collier and Burch 1998, 2000], though it can also be formed through external (or even internal) forcing:

- Rhythmic entrainment is a ubiquitous phenomenon that produces large scale coordination either through the elimination of interfering factors (re-organization) or through the emergence of higher level order (spontaneous self-organization).
- It produces new macrostates.
- In both cases the result is a sort of harmony at a larger scale while permitting variations at lower scales. Both produce new possibilities, as above.

- Entrainment can be produced either by forcing (constraining the system at a large scale), or spontaneously.
- The former requires more work (energy expenditure) to produce and maintain than the latter.
- It is worth noting that entrainment produces symmetries, and it is the symmetries that reduce the amount of work required. Externally forced systems are typically in more asymmetric states.

5. Some Simple Examples of Entrainment

The exemplary case with the fewest complications is the simple harmonic oscillator. It is noteworthy that it has a natural frequency at which the least work is required to get the largest response (Fig. 2).

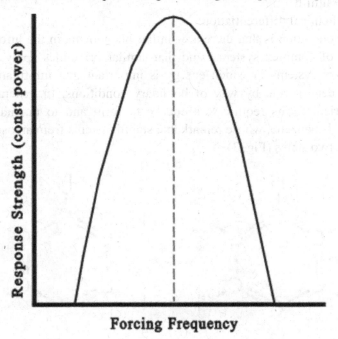

Fig. 2. Forced harmonic oscillator (*source*: author)

The harmonic oscillator is a paradigmatic case that can be modified by analogies to model a wide range of physical systems such as sound, light, seismic and other waves. However some of the basic principles also apply to a range of physical phenomena, once suitably modified to take into account the specifics of the particular systems. Resonances and phase changes are typical, however. Some examples are:

- Bénard cell convection and other vortices
- Planetary resonances (Earth-Moon, Mercury-Sun, Jupiter's major moons, Pluto and Neptune)
- Japanese satellite to the moon (energy required was minimized by moving the satellite near a chaotic region in its orbit in which Earth and Lunar orbits for the satellite were close to each other; it took longer than a more direct route, but the satellite had enough fuel to allow the relatively small shift)
- Various climate phenomena (el Niño, North Atlantic Oscillation, …)
- Old Faithful
- Geochemical differentiation

My contention is that there are similar phenomena in the information budgets of complex systems, and that similar principles apply. On the border are systems in which energy is important, but information also plays a central role by way of boundary conditions. In general, more symmetrical forms require less energy to form and to maintain. One example is benzene, whose remarkable stability stems from an oscillation between two states (Fig. 3).

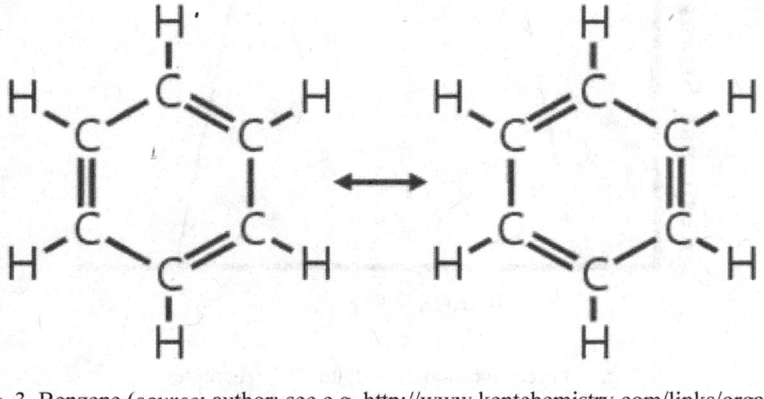

Fig. 3. Benzene (*source*: author; see e.g. http://www.kentchemistry.com/links/organic/Benzene.htm)

Another case involves the comparison between ethylene and butadiene [Harris and Bertolucci 1978: 288-297]. Ethylene is a double-bonded 2 carbon unit. Butadiene is a 4 carbon unit with 2 double bonds. To make all things equal, the energy of 2 molecules of ethylene is compared with one molecule of butadiene. The butadiene is more stable by 12 kJ. The usual explanation is that the bond energy is delocalized, but it is not clear why delocalizing something should lower its energy. The present explanation, that there is increased cohesion in the form of harmonic entrainment of the bonds explains why the energy of butadiene is lower (Fig. 4) [Collier and Burch 2000].

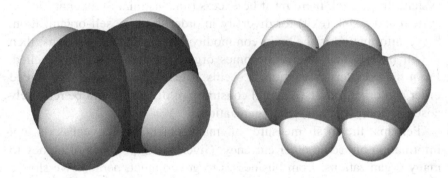

Fig. 4. Ethylene and Butadiene (*source*: http//:chemistry-reference.com)

Presumably more complex chemical systems as found in organisms increase stability through similar nonlocality (although not through double bounds, but networks of pathways, even though the individual molecules are not necessarily especially stable). The thing to note is that it is the whole network that inherits the stability.

These principles allow a remarkable range of mineral forms, for example, the conditions required appearing rarely, with some minerals being know at only one location on Earth. One example is Jeremejevite (Al6(BO3)5(F,OH)3), which requires special conditions to form and is found in only a few locations. You cannot get it merely by condensing the component chemicals.

6. Human Systems Management

I will jump over biological systems (on which there is now a vast
literature concerning self-organization and information) and move to
human systems in particular, especially as they pertain to management.
The general principles should apply to human systems, especially social
systems, but the problem is to find proper analogues of dissipation,
energy, information and other properties essential to self-organizing
systems. The domain of interest is communication of ideas and behaviors
and how these can self-organize. In line with other self-organizing
systems, there must be an excess of something that is expelled from the
system. In general, there must be excess (unconstrained) diversity in the
system and a sink (exit) for diversity in order to allow self-organization.
Since information is the main commodity of management systems, then
it will be information that becomes organized and which is expelled.
From the previous discussion, it seems at least highly likely that forced
order and organization (external constraint of diversity) will be relatively
costly in comparison to self-organization.

·Perhaps the best measure of management effectiveness is not
information but some other currency. Given the importance of money to
many organizations, from businesses to government, perhaps we should
use economic criteria to measure how well an organization functions.
Economics has the advantage of giving a clear and measurable currency.
Neoclassical economics assumes a sort of neo-Darwinian optimality
leading to equilibrium in the market. However incomplete information,
variations in trading times in the market, "animal passions", and most
importantly, unequal information, distort the market so that the
optimality assumption fails. This is verified by the regular failure of
neoclassical economics in both prediction and explanation. In general,
the market changes faster than it can equilibrate, and equilibrium
assumptions become questionable. Away from equilibrium, however,
dissipative but organizing processes become possible. So self-
organization should be expected in typical market conditions. It should
also be evident that divergent and diversely distributed information will
play a role in how the market changes.

But in general the currency of social systems is information, and it is passed more or less efficiently by communication. Money is just a special case. Open lines of communication, all other things being equal, will be advantageous to any organization. But that is not enough in itself, and more likely than not there will be plenty of communication that is or could be detrimental, let alone less than useful.

Productivity is a useful measure of efficiency if it is used wisely – the system should produce useful results relatively efficiently. These might be: sales (industry and commerce in general), societal benefit (governments, social agencies), or new ideas (think tanks, research units), but for society as a whole it should be overall flourishing and individual well-being. These last desiderata are harder to measure, but generally fall under the categories of happiness and satisfaction. These different ends will require different foci (on results) but it isn't clear that different management organization is required for each sort of end. However, different time scales for returns might justify different management methods. Generally, though, there should be minimization of unexpected (crises, disasters, externalities producing antagonism). Fortunately, these are also important general human desiderata, so there is at least some common ground for various management ends and general human ends.

There are various management systems that have been used or advocated over the years. A common one is a military style of organization with a central command that enforces the structure and function of the organization. Both experience and the theory proposed here suggests that this sort of organization will require a lot of excess effort to maintain. Authoritarian and totalitarian states put a premium on control. To some extent, they must rely on predispositions in their populations, but largely they rule by terrorist methods and fear. This requires a large concentration of political, economic and political power as well, since driving a system artificially requires a lot of power and waste of energy. This suggests that such states will be unstable. Unfortunately, whenever there are large concentrations of political, economic or physical power, there will be a tendency to use forced entrainment of ideology, however inefficient. A more efficient but less reliable method is propaganda and advertising, which attempt to drive or create resonances through subtle forcing. Herman and Chomsky [1988] describe a particularly insidious way in which consent is achieved, though it requires considerable investment by power seeking individuals in media. So this method still requires a concentration of power to exclude competitors. Such a social system is always fighting a gradient towards more efficient organizations. This is one of the primary social lessons we can derive from complexity theory: *forced control is unstable and expensive (wasteful)*.

Anarchists, and to a lesser extent libertarians, advocate a kind of flat social system. The idea is that everyone makes their own decisions, so there are no leaders or monarchs, the social relations are "flat". This yields a form of radical libertarian anarchism in its most extreme form but it is also compatible with some forms of democracy in which everyone gets to vote on everything without any mechanism for forming compromises and concessions. As Hobbes argued, this will likely lead to a vote for a central authority with no limits on its power and we are back at the previous case. Representative democracy comes someplace between, but in effect closer to the top-down model, just as direct democracy with votes required on all decisions comes closer to the flat model. But it is unclear how any of these involve room for the production of new social information, new ideas or visions. Besides, there is the problem of who gets to decide what is to be voted on.

An alternative is a consensus system, which has been used effectively in some communitarian organizations. Consensus governance requires full agreement on any group issue. It can work well with small groups with largely common beliefs, but the worry is always what to do about holdouts. Furthermore, common beliefs constrain possible solutions, perhaps overly (e.g., the Amish). So consensus seems to be either overly restrictive or else too difficult to achieve.

The management model that best fits the self-organized complexity model of social systems is to encourage diversity with minimal top-down control. I call this facilitation. Facilitators concern themselves with attaining group agreement, and focus on the whole. Their role is to suggest, not demand. Facilitators need not be a single person or the same people throughout. It is largely a voluntary role. When a facilitator finds themselves being treated as an authority, it is best they step back.

Facilitation is a variation on anarchism, but could be applied in varying degrees within many different management systems. Facilitators should encourage diversity while still helping to maintain focus, permitting self-organized solutions. Too much diversity "saturates" the system, whereas too little, or too little communication, makes it unstable. There has to be a certain amount of "overhead" in which ideas can be exchanged, compared, dissected and combined to produce novel solutions, otherwise the system will stagnate. This also requires that members remain actively involved in the management process. This is perhaps one of the hardest requirements to maintain. Often the introduction of a novel point will lead to re-organization of discussion around that point. This tends to be temporary unless resolution is reached. But it can help to keep people involved. A major disadvantage of facilitation style management is that its gentleness implies that it is slow (recall the Japanese satellite). On the other hand, this very fact makes it more likely that it will tend to satisfy human needs that go beyond the basics.

Some degree of control, or vision, is needed for this sort of management, however. It can't be implemented without the participants understanding its advantages and potential defects, not to mention the principles that underlie it. This will require considerable education before it is generally practical. Nonetheless, a stable social system is best founded on spontaneous entrainment. This is both more stable and more efficient than forced coordination and obedience, and it is more productive and ultimately more stable than a flat system of management. Its main problem is that it may lead to arbitrary and unproductive entrainments, basically pathological, so some control is mandatory except in the most advanced social systems, in which stability is already well entrained, and mechanisms for the dissipation of concentrations of power are already entrenched in the structure of the system. Great variety can be tolerated in such a system, with minimal control, and it allows both the greatest freedom and flexibility. Facilitators should also recognize that much of the organization in naturally self-organized systems occurs below the surface, neither fully recognized nor used systematically.

Otherwise, variety should be encouraged within limits, and organization should be facilitated by the wise manager rather than forced or otherwise controlled. This requires encouragement of variety and judicious application of force near critical points between emerging attractors. In contrast, a strong selection regime is counterproductive for finding natural solutions to problems, and requires more power to enforce and maintain. It is also more likely to get stuck on local maxima that are not more widely optimal, partly because it works through eliminating diversity.

References

Barwise, J., and Seligman, J. (1997). *Information Flow: The Logic of Distributed Systems*, University of Cambridge Press, Cambridge

Behringer, R. P., and Ahlers, G. (1982). Heat transport and temporal evolution of fluid flow near the Rayleigh-Bénard instability in cylindrical containers. *Journal of Fluid Mechanics*.125: 219- 258

Bennett, C. H. (1982). The thermodynamics of computation: A review. *International Review of Theoretical Physics* 21: 905-940 (reprinted in: Lef and Rex (eds.), Maxwell's Demon)

Bennett, C. H. (1985). Dissipation, information, computational complexity and the definition of organization, in: Pines, D. (ed.), *Emerging Syntheses In Science, Proceedings of the Founding Workshops of the Santa Fe Institute*: 297-313

Bennett, C. H. (1987). Demons, engines and the second law. *Scientific American* 257, no. 5: 108-116

Bertalanffy, L. von (1968). *General Systems Theory: Foundations, Development, Applications*, George Braziller, New York

Brooks, D. R., and Wiley, E. O. (1988). *Evolution as Entropy: Toward a Unified Theory of Biology, 2nd edition*, University of Chicago Press, Chicago

Collier, J. (1986). Entropy in evolution, *Biology and Philosophy*, 1, 5-24

Collier, J. (1996). Information originates in symmetry breaking. *Symmetry: Science and Culture*, 7, 247-256

Collier, J. (1999). Causation is the transfer of information, in: Sankey, H. (ed.), *Causation, Natural Laws and Explanation*, Kluwer, Dordrecht, 279-331

Collier, J. (2003). Hierarchical dynamical information systems with a focus on biology, *Entropy*, 5, 100-124

Collier, J. (2007). Rhythmic entrainment, symmetry and power, in: Richardson, K. A., and Cilliers, P. (eds.), *Explorations in Complexity Thinking: Pre-Proceedings of* the 3rd International Workshop on Complexity and Philosophy ICSE Publishing, Mansfield, MA, 78-91

Collier, J. (2008a). A dynamical account of emergence, *Cybernetics and Human Knowing*, 15, no 3-4, 2008, 75-100

Collier, J. (2008b). Information in biological systems, in: Adriaans, P., and Benthem, J. v. (eds.), *Handbook of Philosophy of Science, vol 8, Philosophy of Information*, NorthHolland, Dordrecht, Chapter 5f

Collier, J. (2011a). Holism and emergence: Dynamical complexity defeats Laplace's Demon. *South African Journal of Philosophy*, Vol. 30, no 2,229-243

Collier, J. (2011b). Kinds of Information in Scientific Use, *cognition, communication, co-operation*, Vol 9, No 2

Collier, J. (2014). Emergence in dynamical systems, *Analiza i Egzystencja (Analysis and Existence)*, 23, 17-40

Collier, J., and Burch, M. (1998). Order from rhythmic entrainment and the origin of levels through dissipation, *Symmetry: Culture and Science, Order/Disorder, Proceedings of the Haifa Congress, 1998*, Vol. 9, Nos. 2-4, 165-178

Collier, J., and Burch, M. (2000). Symmetry, levels and entrainment, ISSS 2000: Proceedings, International Systems Science Society, ACM

Collier, J., and Hooker, C. A. (1999). Complexly organized dynamical systems, *Open Systems and Information Dynamics*, 6, 241-302

Conrad, M., and Matsuno, K. (1990). The boundary condition paradox: a limit to the university of differential equations, *Applied Mathematics and Computation*, 37, 67-74

Harris, D. C., and Bertolucci, M. D. (1978). *Symmetry and Spectroscopy: An Introduction to Vibrational and Electronic Spectroscopy*, Oxford University Press, Oxford

Herman, E. S., and Chomsky, N. (1988). *Manufacturing Consent*, Pantheon Books, New York

Landauer, R. (1961). Irreversibility and Heat Generation in the Computing Process. IBM J. Res. Dev. 5: 183-191 (reprinted in Lef and Rex (eds.) Maxwell's Demon).

Landauer, R. (1987). Computation: A Fundamental Physical View. *Phys. Scr.* 35: 88-95. (reprinted in Lef and Rex (eds.) Maxwell's Demon)

Lef, H. S., and Rex, A. F. (1990). *Maxwell's Demon: Entropy, Information, Computing*, Princeton University Press, Princeton

Muller, S. J. (2007). *Asymmetry: The Foundation of Information*, Springer-Verlag, Berlin

Rosen, R. (2000). *Essays on Life Itself*, Columbia University Press, New York

Shannon, C.E., and Weaver, W. (1949). *The Mathematical Theory of Communication* University of Illinois Press, Urbana

Chapter 4

eSubsidiarity:
An Ethical Approach for Living in Complexity

José María Díaz Nafría

Universidad Estatal Península de Santa Elena/Senescyt, Ecuador
Universidad de León, Spain
jdian@unileon.es

It is needless to insist on the significant increase of the complexity we are living in. Whereas the social order arisen with modernity encompassed – at the level of the nation-states – a reduction of social complexity through cultural normalization, the new social and political order is nowadays, as a consequence of globalization, to be intercultural, multilingual and even multi-national. We may encounter a different way of diminishing the complexity at the level of the human agency, but we have to do it in a different way as modernity did it. The management of information and complexity in biology provides some clues to this endeavor. As we see, living beings through its management of complexity enact the subsidiarity principle that can equally be applied to the organization of decentralized political systems. It enables the decrease of complexity at the level of the heterarchical organized agents, while preserving the complexity at the global level. eSubsidiarity was essayed in Allende's Chile following Stafford Beer's Viable System Model and in many other human organizations. Could it become a new ethical paradigm at the information age?

1. The World We are Living in

Our current world is significantly determined by the geo-political, economic and social process of globalization which poses a number of complex challenges amounting to environmental and climatic issues, inequality and poverty, peace and security concerns, depletion of basic resources, financial instabilities, cultural conflicts, etc., as the author has elsewhere discussed [Díaz 2011, 2014; Díaz *et al.* 2014]. From a network perspective, the globalization process brings about an unprecedented increase of the complexity of the human network through the extension and multiplication of human interactions throughout the globe thanks to the development of ICT and transport technologies and facilities.

In a significant extent, the globalization is a consequence of the natural proclivity of capitalism to extend itself towards a "free, unobstructed, progressive and universal development" [Marx 1973: 540]. Nevertheless the globalization was actually deployed from the framework of liberal-democratic wealthy nation-states surrounded by significantly poorer countries with a narrow factual autonomy. In Marxian terms, it was the development of the productive forces within the framework of the existing productive relations – reflected and legitimized in the property relations – that led to the contradictions between the given productive forces and relations [Marx 1859], ending up in the obsolescence of the productive relations and the subsequent necessity to re-express them in the existing political framework [Elster 1983: 209-236]. This is what we see nowadays, for example, in all the continents through the endorsing of free-trade treaties, regional alliances and international institutions, legitimized by the nation-states. Thereby the productive forces, remarkably embodied in international corporations, get clearly expressed.

Still, if Marx was right, this cannot be the end of the history. As Hardt and Negri pointed out:

> Through processes of globalization, capital not only brings together all the earth under its command but also creates, invests, and exploits social life in its entirety, ordering life according to the hierarchies of economic value. In the newly dominant forms of production that involve information, codes, knowledge, images, and affects, for example, producers increasingly require a high degree of freedom as well as open access to the common, especially in its social forms, such as communications networks, information banks, and cultural circuits. [...] The content of what is produced – including ideas, images, and affects – is easily reproduced and thus tends toward being common, strongly resisting all legal and economic efforts to privatize it or bring it under public control. The transition is already in process: contemporary capitalist production by addressing its own needs is opening up the possibility of and creating the bases for a social and economic order grounded in the common [Hardt and Negri 2009: ix–x].

Is this 'commonist' horizon or Commonwealth – as Hardt and Negri like to speak of – evolving from a formless network really nearby? Or shall an effective autonomous agency (a sort of historical subject) emerge capable of taking these bulk tendencies of the 'Multitude' towards its effective expression?

What we can currently observe is, on one side, the individual overwhelmed by a carpet-bombing of information but at same time striving to use the digital tools and its mediated relations to get ahead through increasing problems. On the other side, corporations, governments and international institutions strive to take advantage of the ever-increasing realms of data provided by the peoples and the environment in order to make the adequate decision that keep or extend their concentrated power. Whereas the former side seem to have an ethical flavor – concerning how to carry a better life – the latter could be rather regarded as a political concern. But such a bifurcation is just an optical aberration stemming from the Christian separation – often opposition – between the realm of individual moral action and the realm of social, political agency: church vs. empire in Dante, ethics and politics in Locke, nature and society in Rousseau, etc. In the context of liberalism the separation is quite crude: while the political action should establish the space of trustworthiness and leeway for the individual, ethics can be expressed in such a space. But is this separation really meaningful in our contemporary world?

Whereas the social order arisen with modernity encompassed – at the level of the nation-states – a reduction of social complexity through cultural normalization, the new social and political order is nowadays as a consequence of globalization to be intercultural, multilingual and even multi-national. National life is more and more entangled with international relations, and cannot be conceived anymore with our backs turned to nature. All this makes that the traditional context of posing ethical questions is rather different. The universality paradigm that pervaded many classical approaches in ethics is not as convincing anymore. Anthropology, ethnography, intercultural ethics has shown the fragility of such pretentious positions. Its social and political correlate is bureaucracy, whose efficiency for the organization of the industrial enterprise and the state has been a decisive factor for the extension of its power. However when this organization accumulates unsolved problems, we must then encounter a different way of diminishing the complexity at the level of the human agency.

2. The Lessons Learnt from Biological Information and Complexity

Before dealing with the issue of how we should manage information in the benefit of a better life within the complexification of our current social and natural environments, let us look at how information is being used and managed in living beings.

We actually find a tremendous complexity in any organism and the question arises where all that comes from. The immediate answer provided by contemporary biology concerns genetic information as the heritable biological information coded in the nucleotide sequences of DNA and RNA. These nucleic acids – able to reproduce themselves through replication – contain the information which is used by a living cell to construct the proteins constituting the building blocks of the corresponding living being (be it just a cell or a multicellular organism). With these proteins, the organism builds and maintains the organic structures that enact the living form.

From the molecular perspective, the basic process consists in the translation by the cell machinery of the sequence of nucleobases – on the nucleic acid strand – into the specific sequence of amino acids that make up a particular protein, where a single amino acid corresponds to a codon or triplet composed by a set of three bases (belonging to the four nucleotide sorts).[a] This offers a set of $4^3 = 64$ different combinations that

---

[a]In eukaryotic cells according to the central dogma of molecular biology, the specific mechanism by which proteins are constructed consists in the transcription within the nucleus of the DNA information into the mRNA – intermediary molecule – which is being used by the ribosomes in the cytoplasm as a template to construct the protein strand. After a complex "regulation of the form, proteins are integrated as structural and/or functional units in the complex network of biological functions in the cell" [Lara, 2009: 376]. This complex regulation, not fully understood, concerns among other factors the set of nucleic acid sequences which do not code for proteins, but play a significant

code for 20 different amino acids needed for the protein synthesis together with 3 stop-codons that are also fundamental for protein construction. This represents a redundancy which is relevant to ensure the protein building processes but that states a relation to structural complexity of about: $\log_2 21$ bit/codon $\cong$ 1,5 bit/codon = 0,5 bit/base (assuming, for the sake of simplicity, a homogeneous distribution of amino acids and codons which is obviously not the case). Nevertheless not all the sequences code for proteins. If we take into account the difficulty to measure the regulatory value of the non-coding DNA together with the ongoing discussion about its actual functionality, the informational correspondence of the nucleic acids into the erection of the actual complexity of the organism is difficult to determine, but as an approximation we can hold the genome length in base-pairs (as shown in Fig. 1 for different species) as about the double of the potential information held by the genetic molecules, i.e., not what is being actually expressed by genomes but what can potentially be expressed in the evolutionary process.

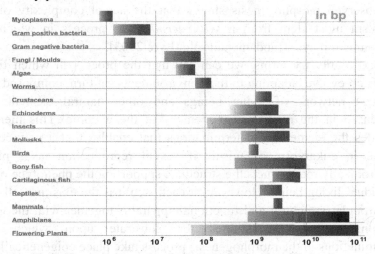

Fig. 1. Genome size ranges (in base pairs) of various life forms
Source: Abizar at English Wikipedia

role for instance as metadata for protein synthesis or evolution [Lyre 2003]. This uncertainty makes difficult to determine the information amount contained in the DNA [Farach *et al.* 1994].

As we can observe in Fig. 1, the genome's length is not always in direct correspondence with the observed complexity of the organism. Here the role of the non-coding genome seems to play a fundamental role concerning the complexity of the regulatory process that deploys the intricate network of biological structures and functions. Indeed as we can observe, there are flowering plants the genome of which contains much more information than the one of humans, whose organic complexity is much higher. Concerning the latter, it is worth comparing the amount of potential determinations that the human DNA can provide (of the order of 10^9 b) with the complexity of its organism. For instance, just the number of antibody molecules (from 10^8 to 10^{11}) that the human cells can synthetize seem to be over the determination ability of the DNA. Furthermore, the complexity of the nervous system comprises 10^{15} synapses among a network of 10^{12} neurons. Therefore considering neuronal plasticity (namely the leeway for synapse formation), the number of determinations needed to specify the actual structure of the nervous system is significantly far beyond the reach of the genome. Thus the observed morphogenesis shows that the actual complexity of the organism must stem from a *self-determination* process in which the environment plays a fundamental role [Lyre 2003].

In evolutionary terms, we can say that the process in which living beings co-evolve, adapting to their environments (in turn, composed by a complex network of living beings and other natural elements), is condensed in the nucleic acid memory of the genome. This memory provides the elementary determinations that enables that a new cell (a zygote in eukaryotic organisms if sexual reproduction takes place) diachronically reconstructs the structures supporting the phenotype of the individual living being. However, at each step it is the existing cell with its particular structural and functional apparatus together with the given environment what constitutes the substrate upon which new determinations in the morphogenesis process take place epigenetically.

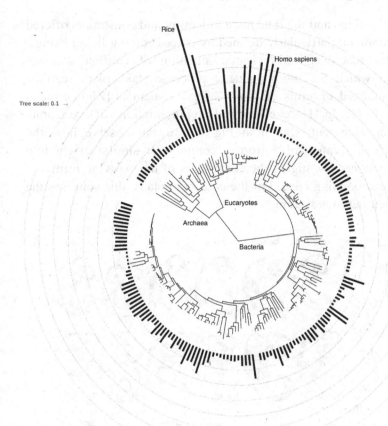

Fig. 2. A highly resolved tree of life on complete sequence genomes. From about 1 o'clock to about 10 o'clock: bacteria. From about 10 to about 11: archaea. From about 11 to about 1: eucaryotes. The surrounding bars correspond to the genome size for the corresponding branch. (adapted from: http://itol.embl.de/itol.cgi)

Figure 2 shows a highly resolved tree of life in which the evolutionary paths are shown from a common trunk, together with the genome sizes of the species. Again we can observe here that there is not a direct correspondence between the evolutionary determinations that are needed for the morphogenesis and the hereditary memory of the genome. In other words, life develops between the determinations provided by the genomic instructions and the fundamental leeway and constraints offered by the environment, particularly defined by other evolving living beings. As elsewhere discussed, this chaotic situation of conflict and co-evolution, in which the morphogenetic processes take place, can be fruitfully visualized in terms of Thom's logoi dynamics [Zimmermann and Díaz 2012]. In Haeckel's 1874 representation of vertebrate embryonic development, shown in Fig. 3, we can observe how the epigenetic process can evolve from a common or similar origin into different directions. The higher the complexity of the evolving form, the wider the corresponding cone. For the case of humans, this concerns the leeway of their nervous system.

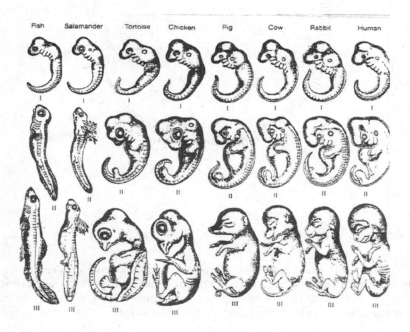

Fig. 3. Haeckel's 1874 version of vertebrate embryonic development. The top row shows an early stage common to all groups, the second row shows a middle stage of development, and the bottom row shows a late stage embryo. (Adapted from [Gilbert, 1997]).

From the physiological perspective, we can focus – following Beer [1981] – on the organization of the human organism as being mainly composed by three interacting parts: (i) the muscles and organs, (ii) the nervous system and (iii) the external environment. The first is being concerned with the primary activities, the basic work and interaction with the environment and is being regarded as the set of *operational units*; the second ensures that the operational units (muscles and organs) work in an integrated, harmonic manner and can therefore be regarded as a *metasystem* (with respect to the system of operation units); and finally the *environment* refers to the parts of the outside world directly relevant to the organism, namely in direct interaction with the organism – be it immediately or in the foreseen future (see Fig. 4).

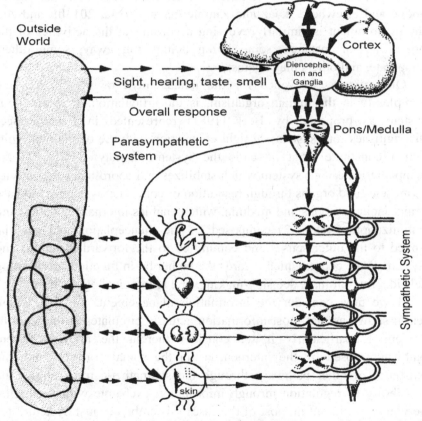

Fig. 4. The human organism is basically regarded as being composed by: operational units (muscles and organs) inscribed by circles; the nervous system (in turn composed by: the sympathetic system, the base brain, the diencephalon and ganglia, and the cortex); and finally the outside world, on the left (Illustration elaborated from: [Beer 1981: 131]).

Though the three parts are dynamic, there is a balance among them whenever the organism is in a sane situation. This means the three parts shall be constantly adapting upon each other: (i) according to the physical interactions and the metabolic activities, as well as the constant exchange with the nervous system: the muscles and organs will evolve in one way or another; (ii) according to the sensing interactions with the outer and inner environments, the neuromuscular coordination needed for the usual mobility, the mental activity performed to regulate the organism and its activities, the nutrients provided by the organs, etc., conforms the constant development of the nervous system (as argued above and elsewhere [Díaz and Zimmermann, 2013a, 2013b]; and (iii) the environment is similarly evolving according to the activities of the organism (for instance, some living beings run away, some others cooperate, and others play against).

Of particular relevance for the management of information and complexity in the human organism, is the articulation of the nervous system as proposed by Beer [1981] represented in Fig. 4. Beer distinguishes four systems in tight connection with the operational units which constitute what he calls the system, namely: System 1) the sympathetic nervous system which stabilizes and coordinates the activity of muscles and organs through resolution of conflicts; System 2) the base brain, including pons and medulla, which enables internal regulation and optimization; System 3) composed by the diencephalon and ganglia, linked to the outer senses and committed to the forward planning; and System 4) the cortex which regards the higher brain functions performing self-identity, ultimate decision-making, and axiological orientation.

If we now consider the information management, the first lesson learnt shows us that most information actually circulates at the level of System 1, particularly if we consider therein the afferent-efferent pathways closed by the interneurons in the spinal cord. Second, the existence of other pathways through the sympathetic trunk shows the possibility of regulation through information exchange with the higher nervous system, but in most of the cases this embraces just System 2 for the short-term coordination of organ activity, or System 3 if longer term coordination is required. Indeed a very small fraction of regulatory information reaches System 5 as proven by the fact that the bandwidth of conscious awareness is in the range of 100 b/s or less while, in contrast, the bandwidth of the information managed in the retina is of about 6×10^6 b/s [Anderson 2005; Norretranders 1998].

This reduction of information flow from the lower to the higher regulatory bodies corresponds to distributed and autonomous management of operational complexity and the concentration of the mostly relevant with respect to the dynamics of the whole. Thereby, if one is grabbing a flower most of the information flow to regulate the complex coordination of muscle fibers will be circulated at the lowest level, in which the corresponding network of synapses have 'learnt' how to do it, but if in the movement one is acutely pricked by a thorn, the information of the pain stimulus will circulate all the way up as to make – all the way down – the whole body to escape from the danger.

All in all, the biological management of information shows us that a proper hierarchical (or rather heterarchical as we have just seen) architecture of autonomous agency oriented to the resolution of issues at the lowest level and the coordination of actions among the parts enable a dramatic alleviation of information flow and the coping with a maximal complexity. Furthermore, the meaning of the information flow is fundamentally dependent of the environment

3. Reconciling Ethics, Politics and Nature: eSubsidiarity

Democracy since its Greek roots is conceived as linked to both equality and liberty [Aristotle 2004: VI, 2][b]. Equality with respect to the capacity to decide upon available common options; liberty with respect to the self-determination or autonomy of the community members, who should not depend on some authority in order to make really free choices. Equality thus concerns the right to participate equally (social value), but it also entails that a minimal satisfaction of needs is provided as to ensure real autonomy (material value). Therefore concerning material equity democracy admits a certain degree of inequality, but this is strictly

---

[b]In Aristotle these principles are aligned with the ethical virtues that in turn stem from the very human nature.

bounded by the need to guaranty autonomy [Post 2003]. As it has been proven, though democratization can be achieved under inequality conditions, in the long term, it undermines the consolidation of democracy [Houle 2009] and moreover, it is correlated to the decrease of democratic political engagement [Solt 2008]. This relation has even been stated by the OECD in the report concerning public engagement: "Decision-making is founded on broad participation and equality of citizens" [2009: 146].

From a historical perspective, it can be observed that despite the constantly growing global inequality since the 18th century (measured for instance through the Gini coefficient), the localized reduction of inequality has often been associated to democratic processes, as in Western Europe, where the strengthening of social security systems improved the autonomy of the citizens during the decades following World War II [Milanovic 2009]. But since the 1980s, we observe within these countries a heterogeneous increase of national inequality, as well as between EU countries. Again, this provides an additional clue to the EU democratic deficits.

To this respect, it is remarkable to recall that, it was in the context of the dramatically increasing inequality, observed in the industrialized areas of the 19th century Europe, that the principle of *subsidiarity* was developed and incorporated into the socio-political agenda [Nell-Breuning 1990]. Although the concept is historically rooted in the Calvinistic understanding of community, it was the contradiction between work and capital that made evident the undermined autonomy of the many and subsequently the inability to accomplish the principles of democratic liberalism. Hence, it progressively became a fundamental principle of democratic liberalism, a pillar of the Catholic Church social doctrine, and it is now one of the foundations of the EU who has coded the principle in the following terms: "Under the principle of subsidiarity, in areas which do not fall within its exclusive competence, the Union shall act only if and in so far as the objectives of the proposed action cannot be sufficiently achieved by the Member States, either at central level or at regional and local level, but can rather, by reason of the scale or effects of the proposed action, be better achieved at Union level." [EU 2008: art. 5]. Internationally, the principle has been coded as a foundation of decentralization and co-responsibility [UNDP 1997] and it has even been devised as a core concept for the organization of complex systems (for instance, in the field of neuropsychology and cybernetics), and this is in fact what underlays the aforementioned organization of organisms devised by Stafford Beer in his search of the principles of sustainable organizations.

Hitherto, this understanding of subsidiarity requires moving beyond the *negative* account of subsidiarity (as it has been extensively done in the EU in order to prevent action of public bodies) and developing instead a *positive* strive by public institutions to act where no other closer instrument is actually acting as to ensure fundamental rights, in particular those enabling the development of real democracy.

As we can see in Stafford Beer's *Designing Freedom* [1974] his positions clearly stands for a reconciliation of ethical and political action superseding the limitations of both the liberal ethics and the bureaucratic organization of economic and political life. As we saw, he learned the lesson of how to deal with complexity from biology, deriving the fundamental and necessary structure that any *viable system* – able to constantly adapt to its environment – should hold [Beer 1981]. The success of this architecture was shown in several organizations, but the most astonishing experiment is undoubtedly its implementation at the level of Chile's state by Allende's government of Popular Unity through the utilization of very simple but effective electronic means. Nevertheless, though this was the target of the Cybersyn project, the implementation just achieved the management of the nationalized economic companies between 1972 and 1973. Such economic control proved its strengths against the "soft" power supporting Allende's opposition and organizing two massive transport strikes, but it brutally collapsed under the bombs of the hard power in the other black 9/11 of 1973 [Church 1975; Atina 2008; Rivière 2010].

The case is of significant interest because it addresses at a time the question of individual life (ethics) and the question of social life (politics) and it has been extensively documented, in particular since the last book of Medina [2008, 2012; Beer 1975, 1981]. Nevertheless, despite Allende's strong concern of furthering radical democracy in an efficient way, it must be borne in mind its direct connection to nation-state political-economy and how the leeway of the latter has significantly changed since, but the scalability of the organizational core model of subsidiarity is capable to address the additional complexification that should be addressed in order to handle eSubsidiarity at a global scale [Díaz, 2011; Díaz *et al.* 2015].

4. Study Case: Cybersyn Project, Democratically Seizing the State

The project CyberSyn was initiated in 1971 by the invitation by the National Company Corfo to Stafford Beer, who enthusiastically accepted. The objective of the project – directed by Fernando Flores, Beer and Raúl Espejo – was the implementation, at the national level, of the scientific approaches derived by Beer towards organization and management to cope in real time with economic crisis by means of a coordination of actions under the monitoring of the information from all the related national companies. To dissipate any Orwellian interpretation, it is worth highlighting Allende's insistent claim to ensure that the system behave in a "decentralising, worker-participative, and antibureaucratic manner" [Medina 2008].

The CyberSyn team integrated scientists of different disciplines and deployed a well-organized information network – though based upon very limited technological resources – as a backbone of the economic system at national scale. Figure 5 shows the "Viable System Model" (VSM) the project aimed at implementing. The VSM allegedly structures the organization of any viable system, i.e., any organized system that combines the survival demands in a changing environment. As observed above for the human physiology, it consists of 3 different parts that incubate the management and dynamics of the processes at: (a) the environment of the organism; (b) the operations area, (c) the metasystem. As illustrated, the system is integrated by the following subsystems: activity, information, internal management, environmental monitoring and global management; and there are five control and information levels.

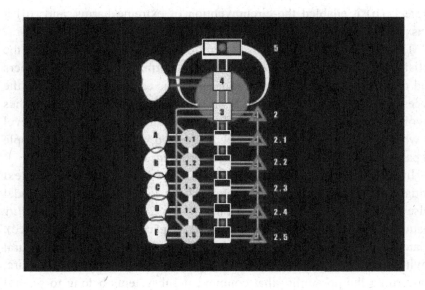

Fig. 5. Schema of CyberSyn's Viable System Model. The clouds on the left represent environments (A-E operational, global at the top); 1: operational units; 2: coordination; 3: current internal management; 4: environmental and future monitoring; 5: political decisions of the organization aimed at balancing global necessities (OR-AM 2006).

Although the systems could not be fully implemented, in October 1972, the CyberSyn team faced the truck strike – supported by the CIA and the US 40 Committee [Church 1975]. CyberSyn endeavored organizing the 200 loyal truckers (against 40.000 in strike) to warrant the most essential transports. The survival to this crisis made the project respectful. Furthermore, Flores was appointed as Economic Minister. Pitifully, as said above and before the project could be fully developed, the bombs and guns of the hard power finished the experiment in the 9/11 of 1973, and Flores spent three years in the concentration camps of Pinochet's Chile [Rivière 2010].

The probe that, from the viewpoint of procurement of freedom and appropriate individual and social life – in the sense of being able to cope with its issues –, the CyberSyn project was a clear example of it, is based upon the following facts: (i) the political, social and economic stability was dramatically threatened during the period of development of the project, (ii) it enabled the circumvention of extreme harms, and (iii) it was posed as a provision of freedom [Medina 2008].

The Cybersyn approach was committed, on one side, to guarantee the satisfaction of basic needs to enable self-determination of the members and the equality among parts (in our case, this can be translated into the necessary autonomy of the university community members and bodies involved); on the other, to bring off that relevant issues reaches the level in which they can be most efficiently addressed, thus enabling the people to participate in the decision-making at different levels.

In order to address the problems linked to the globalization context initially posed, four additional features have to be added to the model (elsewhere discussed by the author [Díaz 2011]): a) *sustainability* feature, as principle for determining the space of freedom (choice), related to the carrying capacity of the socio-economic and natural environment in which it is immersed; b) *heterarchical* feature, concerning the possibility that component subsystems belong to several systems; c) *fuzzy* boundary feature, for enabling the emergence of new relations or entities; d) *horizontal networking* capabilities have to be ensured to avoid the security threats of a too hierarchical structure. An architecture to deploy the model at a global scale for sustainability issues has recently been posed by Schwaninger [2005]. Are we not before a sound ethical/political approach for living in global complexity?

References

Anderson, C.H. *et al.* (2005). Directed visual attention and the dynamic control of information flow, in: Itti, L. *et al.* (eds.), *Neurobiology of Attention*, Elsevier, Netherlands, 11-17

Aristotle (2004). *Politics: A Treatise on Government*, Trad. W. Ellis. Gutenberg Project, http://www.gutenberg.org/ebooks/6762 [1 March 2014]

Atina Chile (Team) (2008). La historia del Proyecto "Cybersyn". *La opinión, August 2008*, http://www.laopinon.cl/admin/render/noticia/10505 [26 January 2011]

Beer, S. (1975). *Designing Freedom*, John Wiley, New York, USA

Beer, S. (1981). *Brain of the Firm*, 2nd ed., Wiley, UK

Church, F. (Chairman) (1975). Church Report: Covert Action in Chile 1963-1973. Select Committee To Study Governmental Operations With Respect to Intelligence

Activities, Washington: U.S. Government Printing office, 63-372, http://foia.state.gov/Reports/ChurchReport.asp [26 January 2011]

Díaz Nafría, J.-M. (2011). The Need for an Information System Approach to Security. *TripleC*, 9(1), 93-121

Díaz Nafría, J.-M. (2014). Ethics at the age of information, *Systema*, 2, 43-52

Díaz Nafría, J.-M., Alfonso Cendón, J., Panizo L. (2015). Building up eParticipatory decision-making from the local to the global scale. Study case at the European Higher Education Area, *Computers in Human Behavior*, 47, 26-41

Díaz Nafría, J.-M., and Zimmermann, R. (2013a). Emergence and Evolution of Meaning: The General Definition of Information Revisiting Programme—Part II: The Regressive Perspective: Bottom-up, *Information*, 2013, 4, 240-261

Díaz Nafría, J.-M., and Zimmermann, R. (2013b). Emergence and Evolution of Meaning, *TripleC*, 11, 1, 13-35

Elster, J. (1983). *Explaining Technical Change*, Cambridge University Press, UK

EU (European Union) (2008). Treaty on European Union and the Treaty on the Functioning of the European Union. *Official Journal C*, 115, 1-388, http://eur-lex.europa.eu/LexUriServ/LexUriServ.do?uri=OJ:C:2008:115:0001:01:en:HTML [5 March 2014]

Farach, M., Noordewier, M., Savari S., Shepp, L., Wyner, A., and Ziv, J. (1994). On the Entropy of DNA: Algorithms and Measurements based on Memory and Rapid Convergence. *Proc. of the Sixth Annual ACM-SIAM Symposium on Discrete Algorithms*, 48-57

Gilbert, S. F. (1997). *Developmental Biology*, Sinauer Associates, Sunderland, MA, USA.

Hardt, M., and Negri, A. (2009). *Commonwealth*, Cambridge University Press, Massachusetts

Houle, (2009). Inequality and Democracy: Why Inequality Harms Consolidation but Does Not Affect Democratization, *World Politics*, 61(04), 589-622

Lyre, H. (2002). *Informationstheorie. Eine philosophisch-naturwissenschftliche Einführung*, W Fink Verlag, Germany

Marx, K. (1859 –orig.). Prologue. A Contribution to the Critique of Political Economy. Moscow: Progress Publishers, 1977. Also available in the Marxists Internet Archive. http://www.marxists.org/archive/marx/works/1859/critique-pol-economy/preface.htm [20 January 2011]

Marx, K. (1973). *Grundrisse*. Nicolaus (trans.). London: Penguin. Available at the Marxists Internet Archive. http://www.marxists.org/archive/ marx/works/1857/grundrisse/index.htm [22 January 2011]

Medina, E. (2008). Designing Freedom, Regulating a Nation: Socialist Cybernetics in Allende's Chile, *J. Lat. Amer. Stud.* 38, 571-606

Milanovic, B. (2009). Global Inequality and the Global Inequality Extraction Ratio. The Story of the Past Two Centuries, *Policy Research Working Paper 5044*. World Bank - Development Research Group

Medina, E. (2012). *Cybernetic Revolutionaries: Technology and Politics in Allende's Chile*, MIT Press, USA

Nell-Breuning, O. v. (1990). *Baugesetze der Gesellschaft. Solidarität und Subsidiarität*, Freiburg, Germany

Norretranders, T. (1998). *The User Illusion*, Viking, New York, USA

OECD (2009). *Focus on Citizens: Public engagement for better policy and services*, OCDE Publishing, Paris

OR-AM (2006). *CyberSyn. Cybernetic Synergy*. Chile: Art/Scicen Research Studio OR-AM, http://www.cybersyn.cl/ingles/cybersyn/index.html [10 January 2015]

Post, R. (2003). Democracy and Equality, *Annals of the American Academy of Political and Social Science*, 603, 24-36

Rivière, P. (2010). Allende, l'informatique et la révolution, *Le Monde Diplomatique*, 57(676), 27

Solt, F. (2008) Economic inequality and democratic political engagement, *American Journal of Political Science*, 52(1), 48-60

Schwaninger, M. (2005). Organizing for sustainability: a cybernetic concept for sustainable renewal, *Kybernetes*, 44(67), 935-954

UNDP (1997). *Decentralized Governance Programme: Strengthening Capacity for People-Centered Development*, New York: UNDP-Management Development and Governance Division, Bureau for Development Policy, http://www.undp.org/content/dam/aplaws/publication/en/publications/democratic-governance/dg-publications-for-website/decentralised-governance-for-development-a-combined-practicen ote-on-decentralisation-local-governance-and-urban-rural-development/DLGUD_P N_English.pdf

Zimmermann, R., and Díaz Nafría, JM. (2012). Emergence and Evolution of Meaning: The General Definition of Information Revisiting Programme—Part I: The Progressive Perspective: Top-Down, *Information*, 2012, 3, 472-503

Chapter 5

Multilevel Research:
Exploring Natural Roots of Socio-Economic Organizations

Nikhil Joshi

Lifel.Org
201 TV Industrial Estate, S.K. Ahire Marg, Worli, Mumbai, 400030, India
Nikhil.Joshi@lifel.org

This article is a part of a collaborative, interdisciplinary research effort to develop multilevel models of organization in living systems, with a broader aim to develop new scalable solutions to enable multilevel sustainability between economics and ecosystems. To facilitate further interdisciplinary collaboration and research, an initial scaffolding of multilevel ideas and observations has been put out. It presents a multilevel view of organization in living systems that spans across molecular, cellular, ecological, and social systems. In developing the scaffolding, some definitions of key organizational characteristics have been put forth. An examination of multilevel living systems through the lens of these definitions reveals two common multilevel level organizational patterns (CMOP). These CMOPs provide new insights into the possible natural roots of our socio-economic human society. The research also points to possible organizational and role similarities between subsoil Mycorrhiza networks, gut bacterial networks, and our financial investment networks. New insights from the CMOPs have been discussed, important implications outlined, a possible new direction for multilevel sustainability between economic and ecosystems has been presented, questions and areas for further research have been put out.

1. Introduction

Some of the most pressing ecological and social problems facing us today are known to arise through interactions between self-organizing processes across two or more different levels in organization [Joshi 2015]. For instance, ecological changes and ecosystem degradation [World Wildlife Fund 2014] that accompany socioeconomic development are often attributed to interactions between our socioeconomic organizations and underlying ecosystem organizations [Daly 2007]. A deeper understanding of such multilevel phenomena requires efforts to develop organizational models and insights that span multiple levels.

This article is a part of a collaborative, interdisciplinary research effort to develop multilevel models of organization in living systems, with a broader aim to develop new scalable solutions to enable multilevel sustainability between economics and ecosystems. To facilitate further interdisciplinary collaboration and research, an initial scaffolding of multilevel ideas and observations has been put out in the form of common multilevel organizational patterns (CMOP).

This paper presents two important common multilevel organizational patterns (CMOP) in organization of living systems that point to the possibility that some key organizational aspects of human socio-economic organizations could be an extension of a larger multilevel pattern in organization in living systems. These CMOPs provide new insights into the possible natural roots of our socio-economic human society. They also serve as multilevel "scaffolding" of ideas and observations for new research aimed at exploring similarities in organization and underlying processes across multiple levels in living systems. Such research could eventually help us better understand how our socio-economic organizations fit into the larger scheme of organization and evolution in living systems.

Prior research across different levels in natural organization has revealed that organization in living systems at one organizational level leads to the emergence of new entities that enable organization at the next higher level. For instance, organization in molecular systems in the course of prebiotic evolution leads to the emergence of living cells [Morowitz and Smith 2007; Pratt 2011; Luisi 2014]. Organization in living cells then gives rise to their multicellular forms [Bonner 1998; Furusawa and Kaneko 2002] and ecosystem networks comprised of autotrophic and heterotrophic species [Ulanowicz 2009; Solé and

Bascompte 2006]. Organization in heterotrophic species populations (including humans) then leads to social organization comprised of families, communities [Hamilton *et al.* 2007] and eventually leading to the emergence of formal businesses, and a socio-economic system of exchanges and organization that is described in economic, social and organizational theories [Padgett and Powell 2012; Hordijk 2013; Scott 2011; Searle 2010].

It has also been previously observed that certain multilevel organizational patterns arise in living systems. For instance cooperation [Stewart 2014; Axelrod and Hamilton 1981] has been observed as a multilevel organizational pattern in living systems. Autocatalysis is another multilevel organizational pattern in living systems [Ulanowicz 2009; Hordijk 2013]. In order to look for common multilevel organizational patterns in the organization of living systems, one needs to first develop useful definitions of general organizational characteristics of systems that could be applicable across multiple levels. A multilevel view using such defined organizational characteristics can then be used to look for multilevel patterns in the organization of living systems.

For instance, in the widely studied common multilevel organizational pattern involving "cooperation" [Axelrod and Hamilton 1981; Stewart 2014], systems belong to the class of unitary systems (like atoms, unicellular organisms or species individuals) "cooperate" or share their dynamic to give rise to the class of composite systems (like molecules, multicellular organisms, or species social groups). In multilevel systems, it is only when one looks at such systems using an organizational characteristic of "unitary systems" across multiple levels giving rise to systems with an organizational characteristic of "composite systems with a shared dynamic" across multiple levels, that cooperation as a multilevel organizational pattern becomes evident.

In this article, new definitions of classes of coupled-composite systems, decoupled-composite systems, alphabetic catalysts, and the concept of modulatory systems have been used to capture important characteristics of internal organization in living systems across multiple levels. Such a definition allows one to look for organizational similarities across multiple levels; hence allowing for a multilevel comparison of organization across three different levels molecular level, cellular level and social level.

An examination of multilevel living systems through the lens of these definitions and concept reveals a common pattern in organization of living systems across multiple levels. The CMOP extends across levels from molecular organization in cells, to cellular organization of species in ecosystems, and the organization of people in human society.

2. Definitions

First the idea of a "composite system" in the context of multilevel organization in living systems is presented and then used to define two classes of systems called "coupled-composite systems" and "decoupled-composite systems". These definitions are then used to reveal a common multilevel organizational pattern in organization of living systems.

From a systems theory perspective in its broadest conception, a "system" may be described as a complex of interacting components together with the relationships among them that permit the identification of a boundary-maintaining entity or process [Laszlo 1998]. A composite system in living organization then is a combined system that is comprised of two or more systems at the same level in organization (i.e. each system is now a sub-system of the composite system), such that the organization of the entire composite system fulfils the boundary maintaining condition.

At different levels in living systems internal organization that constitutes a composite system is based on relationships (or bonds) between elements based on sharing or exchange. For instance, composite systems in the form of molecules arise through relationships (bonds) between atoms through sharing of electrons. Cellular composite systems in the form of multicellular species arise through relationships or bonds between cells through sharing of biomolecules and biochemical pathways. Social composite systems in the form of families, communities, and businesses arise through relationships or bonds between species individuals through sharing of species resources for work in the course of collective adaptation. A summary of composite systems at different levels in organization of living systems referenced in this study is presented in Table 1.

In such exchange-based relationships that give rise to composite systems, the dynamic of exchange is sometimes asymmetrical, in that one sub-system acts as a *donor* and other acts as an *acceptor* of the medium of exchange (i.e. shared resource) at that level. For instance, in molecules that are formed through the exchange of electrons, differential electron affinities [Sanderson 1988] between atoms can make some atoms (or atomic groups) act as electron donors and some act as electron acceptors within the same molecule. In such a case of asymmetrical exchange two classes of composite systems can be defined: (1) The class of coupled-composite systems, and (2) The class of decoupled-composite systems.

2.1. *The class of coupled-composite systems*

Composite systems that are comprised of both donor and acceptor sub-systems (at a given level in organization), within the same composite system organization are said to belong to the class of *"coupled-composite systems"*.

For instance, a water molecule (H_2O) that is comprised of an electron donor atom (H) and an electron acceptor atom (O) in the same molecule belongs to the class of "coupled-composite systems" at the molecular level. Carbon dioxide (CO_2) molecule that is comprised of an electron donor (C) and an electron acceptor (O) in the same molecule is also said to belong to the class of coupled-composite systems at the molecular level. Similarly, multicellular autotrophic or multicellular chemoautotrophic species are coupled-composite systems at the cellular level, because the biomass producing donor cells (photosynthetic cells or chemosynthetic cells) and biomass acceptor cells (non-photosynthetic cells or non-chemosynthetic cells) are present within the same multicellular system. Likewise, kinship based social groups are coupled-composite systems at the species level because species producing groups (i.e. reproducing members or families) and functionally specialized species deploying working groups are present within the same family or kinship-based community composite system comprised of many different related families.

2.2. *The class of decoupled-composite systems*

When donor and acceptor sub-systems exist in separate composite systems, such composite systems are said to belong to the class of *"decoupled-composite systems"*.

For instance, carbohydrate (CH_2O) molecules are produced in the course of photosynthesis from oxidized molecules like CO_2 and H_2O by separating electron donor Hydrogen atoms from electron acceptor Oxygen atoms through the photolysis of water and the release of electron acceptor Oxygen. Carbohydrates are reduced molecules and have a deficiency in the electron acceptors (compared to CO_2 and H_2O) hence such reduced molecules belong to the class of decoupled-composite systems at a molecular level.

Similarly, unicellular and multicellular heterotrophic species are decoupled-composite cellular systems at a cellular level, because unlike multicellular autotrophic species that have both net biomass producing photosynthetic (donor) cells and net biomass consuming non-photosynthetic (acceptor) cells, heterotrophic multicellular species do not have net biomass producing photosynthetic cells within their cellular organization. Hence they have an internal deficiency in biomass production (in the context of a production-consumption dynamics) [Yodzis and Innes 1992] and belong to the class of decoupled composite systems.

Likewise, non-kinship based social groups are decoupled-composite systems at the species level, because unlike kinship based social groups that internally produce their own human resources (or species resources), non-kinship based social groups like formal businesses do not have species producing groups (i.e. reproducing families) within their internal organization. Hence, non-kinship based social groups, like modern day formal businesses must depend on kinship based social groups for their human resources (or species resource) needs, hence they are classified as decoupled-composite systems at the level of social organization.

2.3. A comparative definition

It is important to clarify that the classes of coupled-composite systems, and decoupled-composite systems are not absolute definitions of composite systems, but they are distinct classes of systems that arise through a comparison between organizations of two sets of species. Hence both H_2O and CO_2 as molecules do not belong to the class of coupled-composite systems in any absolute sense. Both H_2O and CO_2 molecules have a very different internal balance between electron donors and acceptors. However, it is only through a comparison of molecular organization of related coupled-composite molecular systems – H_2O and CO_2, and decoupled-composite molecular systems – carbohydrates, that the organizational distinction between coupled-composite systems and decoupled-composite systems becomes evident.

2.4. Alphabetic catalysts

Another common multilevel pattern in organization in living systems is the emergence of catalysts and networks of such catalysts that operate at different levels in organization. At the molecular level, enzyme proteins are known to catalyze transformations between molecules [Alberts *et al.* 2002] in living cells. At the cellular level, DNA catalyzes cellular and multicellular organization in species. Finally, at the level of organization of species populations, human language allows collective social "rule making" that creates preferred behavioral paths in society and "catalyzes" social organization [Knight 2005; Searle 2010; Logan 2007; Padgett and Powell 2012].

In defining catalysts here we have used an extended definition of catalysts and catalysis. It is proposed that a catalyst is a system that enhances the rate of transformation of a set of input objects into a set of output objects, without itself undergoing any permanent change. In this way a catalyst creates preferred paths in the transformation of input objects into output objects. Such an extended definition of a catalyst and catalysis to include all sets of objects not just molecules and their reactions, allows for the extension of the concept of catalyst and catalysis beyond chemical reactions, and to any process that involves the mediated transformation of input entities into output entities. Similar extended definition of catalysts and catalysis have also been attempted elsewhere [Cabell 2011; Padgett and Powell 2012].

Further, in all these cases such catalysts are known to evolve to have a certain alphabetic character [Ji 1999]. Protein catalysts are made up of alphabets of 20 amino acids, DNA is made up of alphabets of 4 nucleotide base pairs, and human languages have their own phonetic and alphabetic character. For the sake of drawing organizational similarity across multiple levels in this study such catalysts have been termed "alphabetic catalysts".

The coupled and decoupled-composite systems across multiple levels and alphabetic catalysts (that are referenced in this study) are tabulated in Table 1.

Table 1. A summary of composite species that arise through sharing of resources at different levels in organization in living systems is presented. Further, coupled-composite systems and decoupled-composite systems and alphabetic catalysts (that are referenced in this study) at different levels in organization of living systems are presented.

Org. level	Systems	Shared resource	Composite Systems	Coupled-composite systems	Decoupled composite systems	Alphabetic catalysts
I	Atoms	Electrons	Molecules	Oxidized molecules	Reduced molecules	Proteins
II	Living Cells	Bio-molecules	Multi-cellular species	Multicellular autotrophic species	Heterotrophic species	DNA
III	Species individuals	Species resources	Families, extended families, business entities	Kinship based social groups (like families)	Non-kinship social groups (like formal businesses)	Human language based collective social rules

2.5. *Characterizing modulator systems*

Modulation is a term that has been often used in the context of communication technologies. Frequency Modulation (FM) and Amplitude Modulation (AM) are two popular technologies in radio communication (RF) [Hudson and Luecke 1999]. In each case there is a "carrier wave", a radio wave that defines the base level dynamics of system, which is altered or "modulated" by a modulator wave to encode new information like music or news in the carrier wave. Such systems are essentially comprised of two independent dynamics: (1) the dynamics of the carrier wave (base dynamics) and (2) the dynamics of the modulator system. The resultant dynamic after modulation represents the combined effect of the two dynamics. In such a system, a "modulator" is a device whose input is used to "modulate" the dynamics of the carrier wave [Hudson and Luecke 1999]. Similarly, modulation is also possible where a light beam acts as a carrier. Using a similar conceptual framework in optical systems, an optical modulator is defined as a device that is used to modulate a beam of light [Ramaswami and Sivarajan 2002].

In the brain as well, a number of "neuromodulators" like dopamine, and serotonin, are known to change (i.e. modulate) the patterns of flow of stimulus through neural networks [Arias-Carrión *et al.* 2010; Weiger 1997; Doya 2000]. A neuromodulator is defined as something (as a polypeptide) that potentiates or inhibits the transmission of a nerve impulse but is not the actual means of transmission itself. The dopamine system in the basal ganglia in the brain is one of the most widely studied neuromodulator networks. Every dopaminergic neuron is extensively branched and a single dopaminergic neuron can synapse with a very large number of target neurons [Arias-Carrión *et al.* 2010]. Here again the neuronal network system can be represented through two different dynamics. The first is the base level dynamic of stimulus flow in the neuronal network that is enabled through the release of neurotransmitters, and the modulation of this dynamics by the modulator system is based on dynamics of the release of neuromodulators like dopamine. The combined effect of the two determines the overall dynamics of stimulus flow in the neuronal network. In the case of the dopamine system this helps an organism choose between different behavioral choices and learn to choose those that predict a reward [Arias-Carrión *et al.* 2010].

For the sake of the discussion in this article, we define a modulator system, as a system whose input modulates the dynamics of the base system. The base system is assumed to have its own dynamics independent of the modulator system. The combined dynamics of the entire system is then a combination of the two.

3. Common Multilevel Organizational Patterns (CMOP)

A multilevel view of organization in living systems, using the definitions in the previous section reveals two common multilevel organizational patterns. The first CMOP appears in the form of a triad comprised of interacting systems. The second CMOP is seen in exchange networks at three different levels in organization.

3.1. *CMOP in molecular, cellular and social organization*

The first CMOP in the form of a triad is seen at three different levels of organization in living systems. At each organizational level this triad is comprised of interactions between three classes of systems- coupled-composite systems (1), decoupled-composite systems (2) and a network of alphabetic catalysts (3), as presented in Fig. 1 (numbers in parenthesis refer to those in Fig. 1).

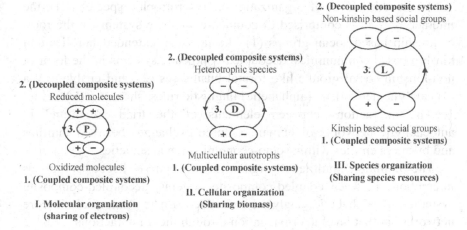

Fig. 1. Common multilevel organizational pattern of a triad of interactions between coupled-composite systems (1), decoupled-composite systems (2) and alphabetic catalysts (3), across three levels of organization in living systems, as described below

At the first level of molecular organization into autotrophic or chemoautotrophic living cells (I), the interacting triad is comprised of coupled-composite systems in the form of oxidized molecules (1), decoupled-composite systems in the form of reduced molecules (2), and enabled by (3) networks of alphabetic protein catalysts, shown in center of the figures as (P) in Fig. 1. The interactions between elements of this triad are found in the autocatalytic molecular "metabolic core" [Morowitz and Smith 2007; Smith and Morowitz 2004; Luisi 2014] within living cells. The metabolic core is one of the earliest autocatalytic molecular systems in the evolution of chemoautotrophic living cells, and is now universally found in living cells. The metabolic autocatalytic core is further coupled with other cellular metabolic pathways that expand metabolic range and sustain living cells [Smith and Morowitz 2004].

At the second level of cellular organization (II), the interacting triad is comprised of coupled-composite systems in the form of multicellular autotrophic species (1), decoupled-composite systems in the form of heterotrophic species (2), and is enabled by a (3) network of alphabetic DNA catalysts, shown as (D) in Fig. 1. The interactions between elements of the triad are found in autocatalytic networks of autotroph-heterotroph interactions within species ecosystems [Ulanowicz 2009].

At the third level of organization of heterotrophic species (III), the interacting triad is comprised of coupled-composite systems in the form of kinship based social groups (1) like families, extended families and kinship based communities, decoupled-composite systems in the form of non-kinship social groups like formal businesses (2), and enabled by a (3) catalytic network of (alphabetic) linguistic rules, shown as (L) in Fig. 1. The interactions between elements of the triad are found in autocatalytic networks of human resource exchanges between families and business entities within socio-economic human societies.

The common multilevel organizational pattern hence comprises interactions between coupled-composite systems, decoupled-composite systems and alphabetic catalysts, and gives rise to "autocatalytic core networks" at that level in organization through these interactions.

3.2. *CMOP in exchange networks*

The second CMOP observed is based on new research findings from soil microbiology, and gut bacteriology. These research findings reveal interesting organizational similarities between sub-soil Mycorrhiza networks, gut bacterial networks in heterotrophic species, and financial investment networks in socioeconomic communities. When examined together with the multilevel organization of living systems outlined in Fig. 2, this research reveals a common pattern where at each of the three levels of exchange networks (Levels II and III in Fig. 2) Mycorrhiza networks, gut bacterial networks and financial investment networks modulate the flows of exchange materials across exchange networks comprised of competing species. At three different levels these networks are known to modulate the growth rates of species, and hence increase or decrease the salience of different network paths that comprise the total flow of resources through the entire network. These modulator networks have been marked as "M" (Mycorrhiza), "G" (gut bacteria), and "B" (Banks and financial networks) in Fig. 2. Current research that presents organizational and role similarities between modulator networks that operate at three different levels in organization in living systems has been compiled below.

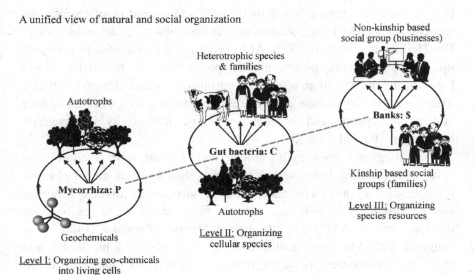

A unified view of natural and social organization

Non-kinship based
social group (businesses)

Heterotrophic species
& families

Autotrophs

Banks: $

Gut bacteria: C

Kinship based social
groups (families)

Mycorrhiza: P

Autotrophs

Level III: Organizing
species resources

Geochemicals

Level II: Organizing
cellular species

Level I: Organizing geo-chemicals
into living cells

Fig. 2. Three levels of exchange networks seen in living systems. The organization at the third, social level is based on the previously proposed CMOP (section 3.1). The first level (Level I) involves organization of geochemical molecules into autotrophic species and gives rise to networks of exchange between autotrophic species and bio-geochemical cycles, the second level involves ecological networks of exchange between autotrophs and heterotrophs. The next level involves species organization into socio-economic society and gives rise to networks of exchange between kinship based and non-kinship based social groups. Research points to the existence of three levels of modulator systems: the Mycorrhiza networks (M) in roots of terrestrial autotrophs, gut bacterial networks (G) in guts of heterotrophic species, and banks and financial networks (B), as discussed in sections 3.2 and 3.3. The dotted line illustrates the possibility of synergizing across the three levels of organization as discussed in section 4.7

3.3. *Important research findings supporting Mycorrhiza, gut bacterial, and financial investment networks as modulator systems*

3.3.1. *Arbuscular mycorrhizae (AM)*

Arbuscular mycorrhizae (AM) are ancient fungal habitants going back more than 400 million years [Parniske 2008]. They are mainly involved in the transfer of water and mineral nutrients, in particular phosphate

(Pi), to their host plants. Roots of over 90% terrestrial plant species can associate with AM fungi, establishing endosymbiotic relationships [Van Der Heijden and Horton 2009]. AM exchanges are estimated to consume up to 20% of the photosynthetic production of terrestrial plants (approximately 5 billion tonnes of carbon per year) [Parniske 2008]. Therefore, AM symbiosis contributes significantly to global phosphate and carbon cycling and influences primary productivity in terrestrial ecosystems [Parniske 2008].

AM fungi are coenocytic, that is their hyphae have a continuous cytoplasm (without cross walls) in which thousands of nuclei coexist, forming a syncytium. The nuclei encode surprisingly diverse genomes and several lines of evidence indicate that the nuclei themselves are diverse, that is AM fungi are heterokaryotic [Parniske 2008]. This suggests that AM fungi could have a wide range of metabolic and symbiotic capabilities. Its long evolutionary history, its highly conserved primitive cellular form, combined with its ubiquitous symbiosis with terrestrial autotrophs leads us to believe that AM probably occupy an important ecological niche in the subsoil ecosystem comprising plants, bacteria and geochemical cycles [Johnson *et al.* 2005].

Subsoil networks of AM fungi are known to interconnect multiple species of autotrophic plants [Van Der Heijden and Horton 2009; Heijden *et al.* 2015]. They modulate [Van der Heijden *et al.* 1998] and influence plant community structure [Montesinos-Navarro *et al.* 2012] and alter plant-plant interactions by supplying and recycling nutrients [Van Der Heijden and Horton 2009].

AM fungi symbiotically provide phosphorous (and Nitrogen) from the soil in exchange for carbohydrates from plants. The extent of symbiosis in the plant root system is dependent on the plants Phosphorous and Nitrogen status and its photosynthetic capacity (carbohydrate production) [Van Der Heijden and Horton 2009]. Since AM exchange subsoil Phosphorous for Carbohydrates from plants, they are able to simultaneously sense the status of subsoil geochemical cycles, and the photosynthetic productivity of the associated plant species. Through their modulator effects AM fungi are known to have both positive and negative effects on plant growth [Van Der Heijden and Horton 2009], hence modulate flows in interspecies networks comprised of autotrophs, bacteria, and biogeochemical cycles [Bonfante and Anca 2009].

While Phosphorous is predicted to be the major limiting element in terrestrial ecosystems high-energy Carbon is the limiting element for decomposers [Cherif and Loreau 2009]. Hence by exchanging Phosphorous for high-energy Carbon (carbohydrate) from plants, AM could be able to allocate growth limiting Phosphorous to modulate overall production of carbohydrate across networks of competing species of autotrophs and their subsoil bacterial ecosystems [Walder *et al.* 2012].

3.3.2. *Gut bacterial networks*

The bacterial-host mutualism is ubiquitous and is seen even in the simplest of heterotrophic species [Thomas *et al.* 2010]. The pervasive and extensive mutualism between gut bacteria and their heterotrophic hosts points to the possibility that gut bacteria could play an essential role in enhancing environmental adaptation of their hosts [Norris *et al.* 2013].

From the point of view of their role in the host-food dynamic, gut bacteria occupy a strategic position in the autotroph to heterotroph flow of biomass. The flow of biomass in the exchange between autotrophs and heterotrophs occurs through the guts of the heterotrophic species. From this unique vantage point gut bacteria can sense the changing nature of food supply from autotrophs (i.e., changing diets of heterotrophs) as well as the internal states of the heterotrophic species [Norris *et al.* 2013]. This could enable them to modulate the absorption and utilization of resources in the gut of the host based on changing composition of food supply and internal states of the host. Hence, gut bacteria can determine how much of the consumed food-energy the host can assimilate and how much passes out back to the ecosystem.

Gut bacteria are known to modulate host appetite as well as their internal state of satiety [Norris *et al.* 2013]. Research provides evidence that gut bacteria can even determine metabolic phenotypes in humans [Li *et al.* 2008]. Gut bacteria have also been shown to modulate growth rates and reproduction rates in some species [Storelli *et al.* 2011]. The species composition of gut bacteria biome can influence the level of absorption of nutrients. For instance, in human populations certain species of bacteria are associated with higher fat absorption and lead to obesity in their hosts [Turnbaugh *et al.* 2006; Ley *et al.* 2006].

One of the most prominent food classes whose absorption is influenced by gut bacteria is carbohydrates [Hooper *et al.* 2002; Flint *et al.* 2012]. Most mammals cannot digest and absorb complex polysaccharides from plants. Gut bacteria digest these sugars in the gut and break them down into short chain fatty acids that are readily absorbed by the host. By modulating carbohydrate metabolism gut bacterial biomes can significantly influence the calories available to a species [Flint *et al.* 2012].

The species composition of gut bacterial biome is known to be dependent on the diet of the host [Jumpertz *et al.* 2011]. Further, changes in diets produce changes in species composition [David *et al.* 2014]. Such changes in species compositions of gut bacteria could be associated with changes in growth rates in host species [Storelli *et al.* 2011]. Hence it is possible that the bacterial colonies in the gut can sense changing patterns in food production (from changes in dietary intake of its hosts) and change its species composition and growth rates of species. Gut bacteria can also affect the nutritional state, motivational state [Norris *et al.* 2013] and activity levels in host species.

Certain species of gut bacteria also produce plant hormone like substances when faced with nutritional stress and such signaling could influence metabolic states in plants [Goffin *et al.* 2010]. Recent findings suggest that gut bacterial compositions play a vital role in the evolutionary emergence of new species [Brucker and Bordenstein 2013], hence defining metabolic niches for species in an ecosystem. Interestingly, gut bacterial biomes show geographical variation even within the same species [Suzuki and Worobey 2014]. This evidence broadly suggests that ecological factors could influence composition of gut bacterial biomes and such biomes could play a role in defining metabolic niches for species.

Evidence presented above suggests that changes in the composition of colonies of gut bacteria can significantly modulate the energy and nutrients available, activity levels, and reproduction rates in heterotrophic species. In doing so, could gut bacteria serve to modulate species compositions in autotrophic-heterotrophic exchange networks in ecosystems? Further, could this also modulate the distribution of plant production between competing heterotrophic species, so as to maximize the overall benefit to the entire autotroph-heterotroph ecosystem? While definitive answers require further research, preliminary findings point to an important role of gut bacteria in modulation of flows of biomass between competing ecosystem exchange networks.

3.3.3. *Banks and financial investment networks*

Banks and investment institutions provide money to such businesses that not only require investment for growth, but also present the best promise for profit, and hence provide good returns for the investment. Businesses in turn use this money to generate profits by providing ever-changing repertoire of products and services to fulfill changing needs of its customers [Werker 2003; Schumpeter 1934]. In economic models it is hence believed that banks and equity markets, dynamically modulate the flows of human, material, and other resources across networks of competing business entities in an economy by changing the levels of investments across businesses entities and economic sectors based on their growth rates and predicted returns. Hence, in doing so banks and financial investment networks serve as community level modulators by investing across a mix of competing business entities and sectors of the economy to derive optimum overall growth for the economy as a whole. Growth in banking and financial markets is hence often correlated with growth and development in an economy [Boot and Thakor 1997; Schumpeter 1934; Levine 1997].

3.4. *Common characteristics of modulator systems – Mycorrhiza, gut bacterial and financial investment networks*

There are a few common features of network modulator systems across multiple levels:
(1) They differentially modulate growth rates across dependent species in an ecosystem or economy.

Hence at the first level in organization sub-soil Mycorrhiza networks are known to modulate growth rates of different autotrophic species across groups of competing autotrophic species in ecosystem networks [Van Der Heijden and Horton 2009; Walder *et al*. 2012]. At the next higher level, gut bacterial networks are known to modulate growth rates and activity levels in across different heterotrophic species [Turnbaugh *et al*. 2006; Storelli *et al*. 2011]. At the next higher level, banks and financial investment networks are known to invest across competing business entities and hence modulate growth rates across competing business entities [Boot and Thakor 1997].

(2) They modulate growth rates by "differentially altering" the flow of rate-limiting scarce resource (s) across different dependent species in exchange networks.

Mycorrhiza networks are known to differentially allocate phosphorous across different competing autotrophic species [Van Der Heijden and Horton 2009], hence modulating growth rates across competing species of autotrophs. Since phosphorous is an important constituent in the energy metabolism of autotrophs, and a rate limiting resource in ecosystems [Cherif and Loreau 2009], changing the availability of phosphorous, alters growth rates of autotrophs. Gut bacterial networks are known to modulate the growth rates in heterotrophic species by modulating the availability of carbohydrates and small chain fatty acids that provide energy for species growth and activity [Hooper *et al*. 2002; Flint *et al*. 2012]. By modulating these flows, they can alter growth and size in heterotrophic species [Storelli *et al*. 2011; Ley *et al*. 2006]. Finally, banks and financial investment networks modulate growth in businesses by altering the availability of money and financial resources across competing business entities [Schumpeter 1934; Boot and Thakor 1997]. Altering the availability of money changes growth and activity levels in business entities.

(3) They appear to "invest" the rate-limiting scarce resource across species networks giving rise to community effects and enabling group level adaptation and group learning.

Mycorrhiza networks appear to allocate (or invest) phosphorous to such species of plants that in the given environment, provide the highest growth and hence highest return of carbohydrate to the Mycorrhiza network across a community of plants [Walder *et al.* 2012]. The differential allocation of phosphorous across competing autotrophs gives rise to community effects, and could enable group adaptation [Van der Heijden *et al.* 1998; Montesinos-Navarro *et al.* 2012; Van Der Heijden and Horton 2009]. Similarly, banks and financial investment networks allocate money (or invest) across such businesses and sectors that in a given environment provide optimum financial risk/reward proposition for the bank or investor. At the level of the entire economy the differential allocation of financial capital across business entities and economic sectors gives rise to community effects by dynamically allocating financial resources to produce optimal overall economic growth and financial returns for the investor. While, gut bacterial networks are known to modulate the availability of carbohydrates in heterotrophic species [Hooper *et al.* 2002; Flint *et al.* 2012] whether they give rise to community effects, and facilitate group adaptation across species in ecosystems is still unknown and merits further research.

(4) They occupy a strategic position in the flow of nutrients into the dependent species organization hence being able to effectively modulate resource flows.

Mycorrhiza networks occupy a strategic vantage in the "roots" of plants, where they alter the absorption of geochemical molecules by modulating the availability of phosphorous [Walder *et al.* 2012]. Gut bacteria occupy a strategic vantage in the guts of heterotrophic species, where they can sense the availability of nutrients in the food, and also alter their absorption [Storelli *et al.* 2011; David *et al.* 2014]. Finally, banks and financial networks are said to be the "roots" or the "stomach" of business organizations [Duisenberg n.d.] and modulate the availability of finance to the business [Levine 2004; Boot and Thakor 1997]. In doing so they can modulate the availability of human resources and other human controlled resources to business entities. It is interesting to note that within the social context, people do not require to be paid money to work within kinship based social groups (like in one's own family), however money is required to work in non-kinship based social groups like businesses. Hence money can be said to play an important role in sustaining non-kinship based social groups (like businesses), and banks and financial investment networks play an essential role in enabling modern day socio-economic organizations.

(5) They create highly branched networks that connect to a large number of dependent species in the base system network.

Mycorrhizae are known to interconnect to a large number of terrestrial plants through their sub-soil network [Van der Heijden *et al.* 1998]. This forms a subterranean network for the flow of nutrients across terrestrial plants. Banks and financial investment networks are also known to connect to a large number of business entities, and give rise to highly branched networks where banks form key nodes in such networks [Vitali *et al.* 2011]. Gut bacteria are ubiquitously present in guts of heterotrophic species from the simplest heterotrophs [Taylor *et al.* 2007] to human beings, and there is a rapid exchange of genetic and environmental information between communities of gut bacteria [Jacob *et al.* 2004]. While it is possible that such exchanges between gut bacterial communities across heterotrophic species can give rise to community effects, a definitive answer to the question 'do gut bacteria enable inter-species community effects between heterotrophic species?' requires further research.

4. Discussion

4.1. *Common multilevel organizational pattern in organization of living systems*

The common multilevel organizational pattern presents kinship based social groups like families, non-kinship based social groups like formal businesses, and human language in social organization as an extension of a larger multilevel pattern the organization of living systems. The notion that businesses, families, communities and exchanges that constitute our modern society could be a part of a larger pattern in living systems serves to initiate new thinking towards a unified view of organization in social and natural systems.

The two classes of composite systems defined in this study reveal an important pattern in the form of "core networks" comprised of a triad of interactions at each level in organization of living systems. Across ascending levels of organization in living systems, the triad involves interactions between coupled-composite systems, decoupled-composite systems, and alphabetic catalysts that give rise to autocatalytic organization with increasing spatial and temporal scales. The sub-microscopic scale molecular triad of interactions comprises the autocatalytic core metabolic molecular network [Smith and Morowitz 2004; Morowitz and Smith 2007] in living cells. The triad of interactions at the cellular level gives rise to an autocatalytic species ecosystem organization [Ho and Ulanowicz 2005; Ulanowicz 2009] that has a greater spatial and temporal scale, and finally the triad of interactions at the species level gives rise to our autocatalytic socio-economic society [Padgett and Powell 2012; Hordijk 2013] that is organized at even greater spatial and temporal scale.

4.2. *Stability and ecological scope of coupled and decoupled composite systems*

It is important to point out that for self-organizing living systems that are dependent on a constant flow of materials and energy for their sustenance [Prigogine 1997], producing decoupled-composite systems that must depend on other systems for their source of energy and exchange resources is a major evolutionary feat. From an energetic perspective, the evolution of living cellular species from chemoautotrophic or autotrophic unicellular systems to multicellular (chemo-)autotrophic systems extends the flow of energy and materials from producing photosynthetic cells to consuming (non-photosynthetic) cells within the same composite system organization (coupled-composite system). However, the evolutionary emergence of cellular heterotrophic species that must depend on their relationships with (chemo-)autotrophic species for their sustenance extends this flow of energy and materials across different species to create a new level of ecosystem dependence between producing and consuming species.

Yodzis and Innes [1992] have shown that autotrophs, and multicellular autotrophs, where producing and consuming sub-systems exist within the same composite systems organization (coupled-composite systems) have a larger ecological scope (i.e., they are ecologically more stable). Heterotrophic cellular species (decoupled-composite systems) that do not produce their own high-energy biomass have a smaller ecological scope (i.e., they are ecologically less stable). Further, within heterotrophic species the ecological scope decreases with growing deficit between production and consumption of high-energy biomass. Hence, cold-blooded heterotrophic species that are less deficient in high-energy biomass are ecologically more stable than warm-blooded heterotrophic species that require a higher rate of flow of high-energy biomass per unit species mass.

Yodzis and Innes provide an important conceptual framework to understand stability differences between coupled- and decoupled-composite systems in ecosystems. This raises the question can these ideas be generalized to examine the scope for coupled and decoupled-composite systems across multiple levels in the organization of living systems?

According to the species-class definitions in this paper, non-kinship based social groups and heterotrophic species both belong to the class of decoupled-composite systems, and kinship based social groups and multicellular autotrophic species both belong to the class of coupled-composite systems. If ideas presented by Yodzis and Innes on the differences in ecological scope between autotrophic and heterotrophic species are extended to social ecosystems, then kinship based social networks like families, extended families and kinship based communities that produce and deploy human resources within the same composite system should be ecologically more stable than non-kinship based social networks that must depend on external sources of species resources to fulfill their organizational needs.

Evidence suggests that this might indeed be the case. It is interesting to observe that Dunbar and others in their study of social networks in human society have found that bonds between individuals in kinship based social networks are stronger than those between individuals in non-kinship based social networks [Roberts and Dunbar 2011; Curry *et al.* 2013]. Generally speaking, stronger bonds between elements are usually associated with more stable organizations. Could this mean that kinship based social networks are more stable than non-kinship based social networks? The higher ecological stability of Kinship based social networks like families, and communities is supported by the observation that kinship based social networks for species reproduction are found across many species of heterotrophs, and have existed much before the emergence of non-kinship based formal social groups in human society. Behavioral evidence also points to important differences in affinity between individuals in kinship and non-kinship based social groups. For instance, one does not require an external reward like money to take care of ones own family (i.e., a kinship based social group), whereas people require external rewards like money to work within non-kinship based social groups (like businesses). This lends support to the idea of higher relative stability of kinship based social groups. Could this mean that, like in ecological organization, in social organization also the decoupled-composite systems also have a lesser ecological scope (or are less stable) than the coupled-composite systems? This is a question that requires further research.

4.3. *Autocatalysis in exchange networks*

In living systems the emergence of new levels of dependence, is also accompanied by the emergence of autocatalytic networks between coupled and decoupled-composite systems at each new level in organization. Hence, the emergence of dependence between oxidized molecules and reduced molecules in an autotrophic or chemoautotrophic living cell is accompanied by the emergence of an autocatalytic metabolic core that is highly conserved and seen across living species [Smith and Morowitz 2004]. The emergence of dependence between autotrophic species and heterotrophic species is also accompanied by the emergence of an autocatalytic species networks in ecosystems [Ulanowicz 2009]. The emergence of dependence between kinship based social groups (like families) and non-kinship based social groups (like businesses) is also accompanied by the emergence of autocatalytic networks of exchange between businesses and families [Padgett and Powell 2012]. The question is why and how does the emergence of dependence give rise to autocatalytic networks? This is a question that requires further research.

4.4. *The role of alphabetic catalysts*

Alphabetic rule-making catalysts are known to enable interactions between decoupled and coupled-composite systems at two different levels in organization of living systems. Alphabetic protein catalysts are known to catalyze transformations of coupled molecular systems like Carbon dioxide, and water into decoupled molecular systems (like carbohydrates, and other cellular biomolecules) within living cells [Alberts *et al.* 2002]. Similarly, another alphabetic catalyst, human language, is thought to enable social rule making that enables the emergence of rules-based non-kinship based social organizations in human society [Bingham 2009; Knight 2005]. Is it possible that alphabetic catalysts also play a role in the emergence of dependence between autotrophic and heterotrophic species in ecosystems? Extrapolating the common multilevel level pattern prompts a speculation that DNA could have an important role to play in enabling the emergence of cellular heterotrophy and in enabling ecological relationships between autotrophic and heterotrophic species. Could the emergence of DNA have allowed cellular systems to decouple producing and consuming metabolic pathways to give rise to heterotrophic cells that do not produce their own biomass? Recent research reveals that extensive areas of external DNA are dynamically inserted into species DNA through viruses [Witzany 2012], and points to significant DNA exchanges across species through viruses. Could this be an outcome of the role of DNA as an ecosystem level rule-making catalytic system that is similar to the role of human language in social organization, as suggested by inter-level similarity considerations? This is a question that requires further research.

While catalysts enable dependence between coupled-composite systems and decoupled-composite systems, autocatalysis in exchange networks are also thought to shape networks of catalysts. Recent research suggests that autocatalysis in prebiotic cellular metabolism, could have a role in the selection of only one enantiomer in amino acids in proteins [Kafri *et al.* 2010]. Autocatalysis has been suggested to play a role in the emergence of human language as well [Logan 2007]. Could autocatalysis have a role in the emergence of the alphabetic character in alphabetic catalysts in living systems? This is a question that requires further research.

4.5. *Common multilevel organizational pattern in exchange networks*

Observations suggest a common multilevel organizational pattern in organization of living species across levels- ecological and social. They point to the possibility that financial investment networks and banks could belong to a larger class of modulator systems that arise in the course of organization of exchange networks within both ecosystems and socio-economic systems. Further research could provide new insights into the roots of financial and investment networks in the larger scheme of organization in living systems.

4.6. *Modulator systems in multilevel alignment*

Aligning and synergizing self-organizing exchange networks across multiple levels, like aligning economic exchange networks with ecosystem exchange networks, is one of the most difficult challenges we face today. Here we look at how connections between modulator systems at two different levels in ecosystems could play a role in aligning and synergizing exchange networks across two different levels in ecosystems.

Within ecosystems there are two levels of energetically and materially coupled exchange networks. At the first level of exchange networks geochemical molecules are organized into different autotrophic species (Level I). Different autotrophic species then become food for the different heterotrophic species hence giving rise to the next higher level of exchange networks in ecosystems (Level II), see Fig. 2.

At Level I, Mycorrhiza networks are known to modulate growth rates across different autotrophic species by providing phosphorous to different autotrophic species in quantitative exchange for carbohydrates [Van Der Heijden and Horton 2009; Heijden *et al*. 2015]. Autotrophic species (or groups of autotrophic species) that provide more carbohydrate hence get more phosphorous. Hence carbohydrate production influences phosphorous allocation across different autotrophic species connected to a Mycorrhiza network. At the next higher level in the exchange networks between different autotrophic species and different heterotrophic species gut bacteria use carbohydrates to modulate energy availability to heterotrophic species [Hooper *et al*. 2002; Flint *et al*. 2012].

Hence carbohydrates seem to play a role both in influencing dynamics in exchange networks at Level I, as well as in influencing dynamics in exchange networks at Level II. Could such an organization where carbohydrates are a common influencing factor in exchange at both levels serve to align both levels towards increasing overall carbohydrate production in ecosystems (hence increasing the overall primary production in ecosystems) by synergizing dynamics across both levels? Could this two-level role of carbohydrates provide new insights on aligning the third level of exchange networks (economics) with underlying ecosystem exchange networks at Levels I and II?

4.7. *New avenues for aligning ecosystems and economic systems*

It is interesting to note that at each of the three levels modulator systems use a scarce resource to modulate species growth rates across competing networks of exchanges. Mycorrhizae use Phosphorous which is an ecologically scarce resource [Cherif and Loreau 2009] that limits the growth in autotrophs, gut bacteria use carbohydrate which is a growth limiting resource both for soil bacteria [Cherif and Loreau 2009], and heterotrophic species, and banks and financial investment networks use money, which is a growth limiting scarce resource for business entities [Lietaer 2001]. This multilevel view points to the possibility that using a scarce, rate-limiting resource to modulate network dynamics could be a larger pattern in modulatory systems of using different scarce resource as "currencies" for "investment" across competing exchange networks at different levels.

In such a scenario, can it be possible to envision a system for currency exchanges that could allow for the equitable exchanges and reciprocity between human economics and natural economics? For instance, can human currencies be made exchangeable for the mycorrhizal "currency" of phosphorous?

A simple way to imagine how such a currency exchange could work is by using an analogy from global trade. For instance, when people from country A that use pounds (£) as their currency, exchange goods or services with people from country B that use dollars ($) as their currency, a global system of currency exchanges enables a cross-border transaction between people in two different economies. Similarly, can one imagine two different exchange networks or "economies" (for a lack of a better word): (1) A "natural economy" that operates on an embedded phosphorous currency and mediated through "bankers" in the form of Mycorrhizae, and (2) a human economy that operates on human currencies (like a dollar, pound, and others) mediated through banks and financial investment networks?

In such a case, can one think of a system for currency exchanges that can allow for "cross-border" trade and investments between natural economy and our human economy? Could digital currencies that mirror phosphorous flows through mycorrhizal networks capture the dynamics in subsoil ecosystems? Can human exchanges with ecosystems be "valued" in terms of such a digital ecosystem currency? Can people and human organizations be incentivized to grow the subsoil economy through an exchange between the two currencies? Can such a strategy create new employment in ecological regeneration? These questions capture both the problems and possibilities brought forth by new insights from multilevel research.

Undoubtedly there are many unanswered questions, however ideas like an economic-ecosystem exchange are unique new perspectives that arise through a multilevel worldview. A multilevel worldview could provide new insights that lead to solutions that cannot be envisioned in the current two-system worldview that completely separates economics and ecosystem dynamics. It is important to note that what is presented above are only possible directions for further exploration and are presented only to illustrate possibilities for further discussion and collaborative exploration.

5. Conclusion

The chapter presents two important common multilevel organizational patterns (CMOP) seen in organization of living systems. The first pattern is revealed when one looks at systems and their interactions through the lens of the definitions of the two types of composite systems presented here. The second CMOP is seen in exchange networks at different levels in organization.

The first CMOP presented here, reveals important similarities in organization between natural and social systems and paves the way towards the development of multilevel organizational models that can provide a unified view of both natural and social systems.

The idea that our socio-economic organization, comprised of formal businesses, families and their shared communities, and enabled through language based rule-making, could be a part of a larger pattern in the evolution of living systems provides new insights into the natural roots of our socio-economic systems.

The CMOP also serves as a conceptual scaffolding to facilitate multilevel and cross-disciplinary scientific research to explore if there could be common processes underlying the CMOPs. The CMOP leads to important new questions that provide opportunity for further research [Joshi 2015] to explore the organization of multilevel living systems, and sustainability in such multilevel systems.

The second CMOP presented here points to high-level organizational similarities between exchange networks at three levels. A comparison is drawn between modulator systems operating at three different levels. New insights on how ecosystem exchange networks at two different levels could be aligned using a common scarce commodity in exchange across two levels have been presented. Important questions that present opportunities for further research have been put out.

This chapter presents early ideas that are intended to seed new multilevel research aimed at exploring the roots of our financial and socio-economic systems in the organization of living systems. It is believed that multilevel research and a multilevel view could not only enhance our understanding of natural systems, but could also provide new insights in how our economic systems could be synergized with life supporting ecosystems. It hoped that ideas presented here motivate domain level researchers to look beyond their research domains to collaboratively explore cross-disciplinary and multilevel research leading to a deeper understanding of living systems.

References

Alberts, B., Johnson, A., Lewis, J., Raff, M., Roberts, K., and Walter, P. (2002). *Molecular Biology of the Cell,* 4th Ed., Garland Science, New York

Arias-Carrión, O., Stamelou, M., Murillo-Rodríguez, E., Menéndez-González, M., and Pöppel, E. (2010). Dopaminergic reward system: a short integrative review, *International archives of medicine,* 3, 24

Axelrod, R., and Hamilton, W. D. (1981). The evolution of cooperation, *Science,* 211(4489), 1390-1396

Bingham, P. (2009). On the evolution of language: Implications of a new and general theory of human origins, properties and history, in: Larson, R., Deprez, V., and Yamakido. H. (eds.), *The Evolution of Language,* Cambridge

Bonfante, P., and Anca, I.-A. (2009). Plants, mycorrhizal fungi, and bacteria: a network of interactions, *Annual review of microbiology,* 63, 363-383

Bonner, J. T. (1998). The origins of multicellularity, *Integrative Biology,* 1, 27-36

Boot, A. W. A., and Thakor, A. V. (1997). Financial system architecture, *Review of Financial Studies,* 10(3), 693-733

Brucker, R. M., and Bordenstein, S. R. (2013). The hologenomic basis of speciation: gut bacteria cause hybrid lethality in the genus Nasonia, *Science,* 341, 667-669

Cabell, K. R. (2011). Catalysis: cultural constructions and the conditions for change, *Journal of Integrated Social Sciences,* 2(1), 1-12

Cherif, M., and Loreau, M. (2009). When microbes and consumers determine the limiting nutrient of autotrophs: a theoretical analysis, *Proceedings. Biological sciences / The Royal Society,* 276, 487-497

Curry, O., Roberts, S. G. B., and Dunbar, R. I. M. (2013). Altruism in social networks: evidence for a "kinship premium", *British Journal of Psychology (London, England: 1953,* 104(2), 283-295

Daly, H. E. (2007). *Ecological Economics and Sustainable Development: Selected Essays of Herman Daly*, Edward Elgar, Cheltenham, UK

David, L. A., Maurice, C. F., Carmody, R. N., Gootenberg, D. B., Button, J. E., Wolfe, B. E., Ling, A. V, Devlin, A S., Varma, Y., Fischbach, M. A, Biddinger, S. B., Dutton, R. J., and Turnbaugh, P. J (2014). Diet rapidly and reproducibly alters the human gut microbiome, *Nature*, 505, 559-563

Doya, K. (2000). Complementary roles of basal ganglia and cerebellum in learning and motor control Summary: Specialization by Learning Paradigms, *Current Opinion in Neurobiology*, 10(6), 732-739

Duisenberg, D. W. F. (2001). Speech delivered by Dr. Willem F. Duisenberg, President of the European Central Bank, at the Economics Conference "The Single Financial Market: Two Years into EMU" organised by the Oesterreichische Nationalbank in Vienna on 31 May 2001, https://www.ecb.europa.eu/press/key/date/2001/html/sp010531_content.en.html

Flint, H. J., Scott, K. P., Duncan, S. H., Louis, P., and Forano, E. (2012). Microbial degradation of complex carbohydrates in the gut, *Gut microbes*, 3(August), 289-306

Furusawa, C., and Kaneko, K. (2002). Origin of multicellular organisms as an inevitable consequence of dynamical systems, *The Anatomical record*, 268(3), 327-342

Goffin, P., Bunt, B. van de, Giovane, M., Leveau, J. H. J., Höppener-Ogawa, S., Teusink, B., and Hugenholtz, J. (2010). Understanding the physiology of Lactobacillus plantarum at zero growth, *Molecular Systems Biology*, 6(413), 413

Hamilton, M. J., Milne, B. T., Walker, R. S., Burger, O., and Brown, J. H. (2007). The complex structure of hunter-gatherer social networks, *Proceedings Biological Sciences / The Royal Society*, 274(July), 2195-2202

Ho, M.-W., and Ulanowicz, R. (2005). Sustainable systems as organisms? *Bio Systems*, 82(1), 39-51

Hooper, L. V., Midtvedt, T., and Gordon, J. I. (2002). How host-microbial interactions shape the nutrient environment of the mammalian intestine, *Annual review of nutrition*, 22, 283-307

Hordijk, W. (2013). Autocatalytic Sets: From the Origin of Life to the Economy, *BioScience*, 63(11), 877-881

Hudson, J., and Luecke, J. (1999). *Basic Communications Electronics*, Master Publishing. Lincolnwood, Illinois

Jacob, E., Ben, Becker, I., Shapira, Y., and Levine, H. (2004). Bacterial linguistic communication and social intelligence, *Trends in Microbiology*, 12(8), 366-372

Ji, S. (1999). The Linguistics of DNA: Words, Sentences, Grammar, Phonetics, and Semantics, *Annals of the New York Academy of Sciences*, 870, 411-417

Johnson, D., Ijdo, M., Genney, D. R., Anderson, I. C., and Alexander, I. J.. (2005). How do plants regulate the function, community structure, and diversity of mycorrhizal fungi? *Journal of Experimental Botany*, 56(417), 1751-1760

Joshi, N. (2015). Science, Organization and Sustainability: A Multilevel Approach, in: *Proceedings of ISIS Summit Vienna 2015—The Information Society at the Crossroads*, I003, http://sciforum.net/conference/isis-summit-vienna-2015/paper/ 2923

Jumpertz, R., Le, D. S., Turnbaugh, P. J., Trinidad, C., Bogardus, C., Gordon, J. I., and Krakoff, J. (2011). Energy-balance studies reveal associations between gut microbes, caloric load, and nutrient absorption in humans, *American Journal of Clinical Nutrition*, 94(1), 58-65

Kafri, R., Markovitch, O., and Lancet, D. (2010). Spontaneous chiral symmetry breaking in early molecular networks, *Biology direct*, 5(1), 38

Knight, C. (2005). The Human Revolution. In *Alice V., and David H. Morris Symposium on Evolution of Language*, Stony Brook University, October 14-16, 2005: Stony Brook University, New York

Laszlo, A. (1998). Systems Theories: Their Origins, Foundations, and Development BT - Systems Theories and A Priori Aspects of Perception, *Systems Theories and A Priori Aspects of Perception.*, 47-74

Levine, R. (2004). Finance and Growth: Theory and Evidence. *NBER WORKING PAPER SERIES; Handbook of Economic Growth*, (September), 0-117

Levine, R. (1997). Financial development and economic growth: Views and agenda, *Journal of Economic Literature*, 35(2), 688-726

Ley, R., Turnbaugh, P., Klein, S. and Gordon, J. (2006). Microbial ecology: human gut microbes associated with obesity, *Nature*, 444(7122), 1022-1023

Li, M., Wang, B., Zhang, M., Rantalainen, M., Wang, S., Zhou, H., Zhang, Y., Shen, J., Pang, X., Zhang, M., Wei, H., Chen, Y., Lu, H., Zuo, J., Su, M., Qiu, Y., Jia, W., Xiao, C., Smith, L. M., Yang, S., Holmes, E., Tang, H., Zhao, G., Nicholson, J. K., Li, L., and Zhao, L. (2008). Symbiotic gut microbes modulate human metabolic phenotypes, *Proceedings of the National Academy of Sciences of the United States of America*, 105(6), 2117-2122

Lietaer, B. (2001). *The Future of Money: Beyond Greed and Scarcity*, Random House

Logan, R. K. (2007). *The Extended Mind: The Emergence of Language, the Human Mind, and Culture*, University of Toronto Press

Luisi, P. L. (2014). Prebiotic metabolic networks? *Molecular Systems Biology*, 10, 729

Montesinos-Navarro, A., Segarra-Moragues, J. G., Valiente-Banuet, A., and Verdú, M. (2012). Plant facilitation occurs between species differing in their associated arbuscular mycorrhizal fungi, *New Phytologist*, 196, 835-844

Morowitz, H., and Smith, E. (2007). Energy flow and the organization of life, *Complexity*, 13(1), 51-59

Norris, V., Molina, F., and Gewirtze, A. T. (2013). Hypothesis: Bacteria control host appetites, *Journal of Bacteriology*, 195(3), 411-416

Padgett, J. F., and Powell, W. W. (2012). The Problem of Emergence, in: Padgett, J. F., and Powell, W. W. (eds.), *The Emergence of Organizations and Markets*, Princeton University Press, 1-30

Parniske, M. (2008). Arbuscular mycorrhiza: the mother of plant root endosymbioses. *Nature Reviews, Microbiology*, 6, 763-775

Pratt, A. J. (2011). Prebiological evolution and the metabolic origins of life, *Artificial life*, 17, 203-217

Prigogine, I. (1997). *The End of Certainty*, Simon and Schuster, New York

Ramaswami, R., and Sivarajan, K. N. (2002). *Optical Networks: A Practical Perspective*, Morgan Kaufmann, San Francisco, California

Roberts, S. G. B., and Dunbar, R. I. M. (2011). Communication in social networks: Effects of kinship, network size, and emotional closeness, *Personal Relationships*, 18, 439-452

Sanderson, R. T. (1988). Principles of electronegativity. Part I. General nature, *Journal of Chemical Education*, 65(2), 112-118

Schumpeter, J. (1934). The Theory of Economic Development, *Joseph Alois Schumpeter*, 61-116

Scott, B. R. (2011). *Capitalism – Its Origins and Evolution as a System of Governance*, Springer-Verlag, New York

Searle, J. (2010). *Making the Social World: The Structure of Human Civilization*, Oxford University Press

Smith, E., and Morowitz, H. J. (2004). Universality in intermediary metabolism, *Proceedings of the National Academy of Sciences of the United States of America*, 101(36), 13168-13173

Solé, R. V, and Bascompte, J. (2006). *Self-Organization of Complex Ecosystems*, Princeton University Press

Stewart, J. E. (2014). The direction of evolution: The rise of cooperative organization, *Bio Systems*, doi:10.1016/j.biosystems.2014.05.006

Storelli, G., Defaye, A., Erkosar, B., Hols, P., Royet, J. and Leulier, F. (2011). Lactobacillus plantarum promotes drosophila systemic growth by modulating hormonal signals through TOR-dependent nutrient sensing, *Cell Metabolism*, 14, 403-414

Suzuki, T. A., and Worobey, M. (2014). Geographical variation of human gut microbial composition, *Biology Letters*, 10, 20131037

Taylor, M. W., Radax, R., Steger, D., and Wagner, M. (2007). Sponge-associated microorganisms: evolution, ecology, and biotechnological potential, *Microbiology and Molecular Biology Reviews: MMBR*, 71(2), 295-347

Thomas, T., Rusch, D., DeMaere, M. Z., Yung, P. Y., Lewis, M., Halpern, A., Heidelberg, K. B., Egan, S., Steinberg, P. D., and Kjelleberg, S. (2010). Functional genomic signatures of sponge bacteria reveal unique and shared features of symbiosis, *The ISME Journal*, 4(12), 1557-1567

Turnbaugh, P. J., Ley, R. E., Mahowald, M. A., Magrini, V., Mardis, E. R., and Gordon, J. I. (2006). An obesity-associated gut microbiome with increased capacity for energy harvest, *Nature*, 444, 1027-1031

Ulanowicz, R. E. (2009). *A third window: natural life beyond Newton and Darwin*, Templeton Foundation Press

Van Der Heijden, M. G., Martin, F. M., Selosse, M.-A., and Sanders, I. R. (2015). Mycorrhizal ecology and evolution: the past, the present, and the future, *New Phytologist*, 205, 1406-1423

Van Der Heijden, M. G., and Horton, T. R. (2009). Socialism in soil? The importance of mycorrhizal fungal networks for facilitation in natural ecosystems, *Journal of Ecology*, 97, 1139-1150

Van der Heijden, M. G., Boller, T., Wiemken, A., and Sanders, I. R. (1998). Different Arbuscular Mycorrhizal Fungal Species Are Potential Determinants of Plant Community Structure, *Ecology*, 79(6), 2082-2091

Vitali, S., Glattfelder, J. B. J., and Battiston, S. (2011). The network of global corporate control. *PloS one*, 6, p.e25995

Walder, F., Niemann, H., Natarajan, M., Lehmann, M. F., Boller, T., and Wiemken, A. (2012). Mycorrhizal Networks: Common Goods of Plants Shared under Unequal Terms of Trade, *Plant Physiology*, 159(June), 789-797

Weiger, W. (1997). Serotonergic modulation of behaviour: a phylogenetic overview. *Biological reviews of the Cambridge Philosophical Society*, 72(1), 61-95

Werker, C. (2003). Innovation, market performance, and competition: lessons from a product life cycle model, *Technovation*, 23, 281-290

Witzany, G. (ed.) (2012). *Viruses: Essential Agents of Life*, Springer Science and Business Media, Dordrecht

World Wildlife Fund (2014). *WWF Living Planet Report 2014*

Yodzis, P., and Innes, S. (1992). Body Size and Consumer-Resource Dynamics, *The American Naturalist*, 139, 1151

Chapter 6

Conviviality:
A Choice of Civilisation

Marc Humbert

Faculty of Economics, University of Rennes, France

My presentation is relevant to all people who are searching for an alternative to the present way in which our world is managed. It draws upon the diagnosis posed by Ivan Illich in 1973. According to him a radical move is necessary. People must choose convivial tools if they want to avoid being crushed by machines and to save their freedom and their dignity. I will try to present the characteristics of these convivial tools as they are described in the convivialist Manifesto. This Manifesto presents four basic ethical and political principles, on which we must organize our societies in line with Illich's argument. These principles are not new, they are drawn from doctrines, religions and philosophies in so far as their recommendations made possible, and helped to improve, a sustainable life altogether (*cum-vivere*). It is necessary to go on with a strong intellectual promotion of these ideas to have a chance to escape from the looming threats on humanity.

1. Introduction

This chapter presents an analysis that has been elaborated collectively to bring an alternative way of thinking, to break with the mainstream strand of thought. The reason is that we share, with so many people on earth, a discontentment regarding the way the leaders are trying to deal with the challenges that are in front of us. Their sole idea is to restore old ways of doing things. Thus they push relentlessly to come back to "business as usual". We are a growing number of people who want a more relevant answer to these challenges that are actually facing us with a fundamental question: how do we want to live and how can we set up a new way of living?

I want to convey three basic messages about that[a]. First, I would like to make explicit why we have to address this question "how do we want to live?". Clearly, a lot of people are fed up with the way they have been living (or surviving) for long. In a nutshell, human civilization, that is *the total culture and way of life*[b] of human beings, is at stake because it has been almost exclusively focussed on a rationalistic search for economic and technical excellence, whereas this axis of evolution has reached a dead end.

My second message delivers what the core of the convivialist manifesto is: a set of general principles allowing a bearable life for all of us and for the future generations. Doing this, the Manifesto brings some first ideas about rules of organisation that a society should adopt to set up a mode of working complying with these principles. The target is to define the rules on which a society must work so that conviviality prevails. In other words, the Manifesto proposes a set of principles that are a basis to make a choice for a different civilization to build.

Finally, I will try to convince the reader that we have to take stock of the radicalism of the necessary move. It means that a series of small incremental changes will not switch us from this world to a better one. Even if the myriadization of such tiny changes could make us close to a radical move, a real upheaval is necessary to escape from the looming catastrophes. This is a choice of civilisation.

2. The Human Civilization at Stake

For a few decades the forces of life have had to confront a steamroller of technical and economic efficiency. The operators of the machine ignore billions of people who are hungry and excluded and whose livelihoods hang by a thread. They ignore a long warning by established intellectual authorities about the state of the environmental degradation and

---

[a]My contribution to this debate follows in the line of the ideas introduced by Ivan Illich [1973].
[b]According to the definition given by the *Collins Concise English Dictionary*.

exhaustion [e.g. Meadows *et al.* 1972] and recent ones about the endogenous end of growth [e.g. Gordon 2012 and Krugman 2013]. They do not mind about these announced catastrophes that could have a detrimental effect on the majority as they believe that an exit from actual crises will be found by a hyper-cyborg-humanity that might be formed by an oligarchy of the best performers.

The leaders of nations and operators of the mega-machine [Mumford 1964] want to go on along this technical axis that made our species the champion of all species, able to act on the whole world around us, on other species and on itself. Those who promote it are from the same lineage of our distant ancestors who managed to control fire, long before the birth of humanity, that is, before *homo sapiens* appeared. They are the heirs of those who improved our language skills and who invented and miniaturised cut stone tools over hundreds of thousands of years. *Homo sapiens* went on to domesticate the natural environment, develop the cultivation of plants and animal husbandry. The result was a proliferation of our species, the urbanisation of groups, the appearance of writing and the formation of vast empires. These new changes to the planet forged a deep gulf with other species.

Gradually *homo sapiens* colonised the whole Earth. And step by step – longer steps followed by less longer ones – came the Industrial Revolution and an ever growing gap between us and crude nature: artificiality, specific to mankind, has spread out. Steam power and no natural energies, speciality steels and no raw material, information technology and not instinctive moves. The techno-scientist can insert chips underneath our skin that enable us to be recognised, localised, and protected, or rather monitored and controlled, maybe. And why not generate genetically modified humans living away from illnesses and escaping from mortality? The reality of excess – a crazy dream.

A crazed confidence emerged in the mind of the elite, that even in the worst situations, thanks to the progress of science and technology, it is possible to find solutions to get by. Not only in physical matters but also in organizing society thanks to society's technicians, that is to say, thanks to cute politicians and shrewd financiers. For this foolish elite, it is no doubt possible to emerge from the crisis along the technological axis that our leaders call: exiting the crisis from the top.

The technical axis is supported by the efficiency of competition between individuals, competition that is stimulated by the pursuit of individual enrichment and the promise of boundless economic growth. This promise is the carrot for all at the global level. The trickle-down effects expected ensure that everyone stick to the collective project to go on further on the same track. Tomorrow everyone will be wealthier: this false hope is nurturing the collective fantasy, the desire ever more to consume which is boosted by a deluge of advertising.

However, between 95% and 99% of people of all nations are fed up with the way they have been living (or surviving) for long, under this technical axis, and they all have a feelings of considerable discontent. Ivan Illich posed the same diagnosis in 1973: "The crisis I have described confronts people with a choice between convivial tools and being crushed by machines" [1973: 107]. If the decision is not made for conviviality, "Freedom and dignity will continue to dissolve into an unprecedented enslavement of man to his tools" [12]. The move supposes "the shared insight of people that they would be happier if they could *work* together and *care* for each other" [50].

3.   A Set of General Principles as a Basis to Build a Convivial Society

The *Convivialist Manifesto* [2014] brings a few basic ethical and political principles, on which we must organize our societies as convivial societies, in order to achieve what is in line with Illich's argument: "the only response to this crisis is a full recognition of its depth and an acceptance of inevitable self-limitations" [1973: 107], or, said differently, to accept a universal interdependence. Let us examine these four principles proposed by the Manifesto as a necessary common doctrinal basis on which it is possible to build convivial societies and a convivial world.

3.1. *The principle of common destiny*

The principle of common destiny acknowledges the inescapable fact of observation that anyone is a member of a single common humanity that is living within a common universe[c]. To us, the universe is the observed totality from which everything is part, as we are, as a species and as an individual as well. We cannot escape that, it is our common destiny, we are an ephemeral[d] part of that. We are used to word it LIFE. "There is no wealth but life[e]." There is no other value but life. There is no point measuring this value, there is no equivalent. Life is the air we breathe, the source of sunshine and the earth. It is a swarming interacting mass that has existed from the Big Bang right out to the unknown extremities of the universe. Locally, LIFE is nature and the human beings are one of nature's species, who came late to this Earth and which is only one among 9 million species living on the planet. Humanity is born within our natural environment. We owe it our lives that are part of it and we must pay attention to it and respect it. All human beings are made up of cells, DNA, molecules and physicochemical matter. The gift of a tiny part of life is there to be received by any human person. The sun, air, water, sky and stars, her or his parents, her or his family, and their groups interact with any of them from their birth and even before.

Whatever the initial differentiations, and whatever subsequent differentiations become, because of their personal life-stories and different living environments, all human beings share the necessary humility to recognise that life has been given to them and that they share the destiny of a universe. Consequently, "beyond differences in skin-colour, nationality, language, culture, religion and wealth, gender and

---

[c]I must say that the Manifesto reads only "the principle of common humanity" but I believe it is in order to express the largest recognition of what we all have in common, that is our common humanity which, to its turn, is sharing the lot of all that is around us in the universe: living creatures, the biosphere and the cosmos.

[d]It is worth remembering that the stars themselves, on a different time-scale to that of humans, are ephemeral. One day they too will disappear, as will our sun, and blend into life as it continues…

[e][Ruskin 1860] inspired Gandhi who translated this book into Gujarati in 1908.

sexual orientation, there is only one humanity, and that humanity must be respected in the person of each of its members" [2014: 30].

3.2. *The principle of common sociality*

Human beings are social beings and their greatest wealth lies in their social relationships [Convivialist Manifesto 2014: 31].

Received life cannot flourish in individual solitude. Mankind's offspring cannot survive from birth. It cannot move or feed itself independently and it takes several years to acquire the aptitudes necessary for survival. Human beings are beings whose lives can only be led together, in interaction between them and with the natural environment. As Maurice Godelier writes [2012], because of humanity's group existence, it takes more than a man and a woman to make a child. In order for human life to flourish, humans have to become a part of the group. They must not only develop physiological and physical aptitudes, but also aptitudes for life, i.e. for interaction with others and with their environment: they have to learn the gestures, language, words, and attitudes that are suitable at the right moment, in the right place. An individual's construction begins physically and culturally by training, an education received by the human being. Our life together gives us characteristics unique to our species – above and beyond the planet's vast diversity – and which make our humanity unique. Today, there is only one single human species.

3.3. *The principle of individuation: individuals blossom by interdependence*

Always bearing in mind these two first principles, a legitimate politics is one that allows each of us to assert our distinctive evolving individuality as fully as possible by developing our *capabilities*, our potential to be and to act without harming others' potential to do the same, with a view to achieving *equal freedom for all*. [Convivialist Manifesto 2014: 31].

Every human being is welcomed into and educated by a group that is part of a concrete natural environment where she/he gradually creates and constructs her/his own unique individuality by developing her/his power to be and to act (Spinoza). The ideal of paying attention to others implies to give recognition to everyone [Honneth 1992] and to give to everyone the autonomy necessary for the affirmation and evolution of her/his own individual life, which responds to everyone's universal need.

This freedom to exercise one's power to be and to act offers individuals an autonomy that does not extend to autarkic independence that would enable her/him to make an abstraction of others and the natural environment. Autonomy and solitude can only be relative, as is their role in the construction of everybody's individuality. Interactions with the environment and with others are permanent and essential. In parallel, we must refuse the idea that individuality is only a product of environmental conditioning and of one's social group, on a given physicochemical basis. But as long as any subsequent outside influence on the thinking, acting individual does not lead to dependency, outside influence is essential. Combined with autonomy it enables us to consider that individuality is formed and is living in a state of interdependency[f]. Interdependency between human beings and with an environment constitutes a fundamental reality that humanity in search of conviviality has to recognise. Recognising this overall interdependency is the corollary of recognising the gift of life.

3.4. *The principle of managed conflict or creative interdependence*

> Given that each of us has the power to express our distinctive individuality, it is natural that human beings should sometimes oppose one another. But it is only legitimate for them to do so as long as this does not jeopardize the framework of common sociality that ensures this rivalry is productive and non-destructive. *Good politics* is therefore politics that allows human beings to be individual by accepting and managing conflict [Convivialist Manifesto 2014: 31].

---

[f] Interdependence is opposed to both dependence and independence, and simultaneously it is a combination of both dependence and independence; this reasoning that goes beyond the definitive opposition of two terms is contrary to the law of the excluded middle (*tertium non datur*), it is consistent with the logics of the tetralemma.

All human beings have to recognise the gift of life and to build their lives together, in interdependence with each other and with the natural environment, within constituted groups. Every human being is a locus for one of an infinity of life forces, the interactions of which have been modulated to constitute, without endangering, their common sociality within a group. Each member of a group is relatively dependent on this and benefits from relative autonomy.

The word "collective" could apply to the informal personalisation of the common sociality of individual human beings living in a group, within an environment, a group that is then forming an "us". This group will follow a same direction, sharing a common destiny, provided that certain conditions exist. It supposes that a general will can form to clearly express the framework accepted and respected by all. This is the Common Law, under which all human beings can interact with the feeling of living altogether, a good, worthy, just life.

The harmony between individuals and the natural environment cannot be established spontaneously. Rivalry and conflict create futures and often lead to destruction in the present. Earthquakes, volcanic eruptions, and the fangs and venom of other species remind humans that the forces of nature are powerful. A crushed shell liberates its seed that in turn dies so that the plant can bear fruit. As long as the natural equilibrium is respected, ploughed soils and drained swamps improve human environments without deteriorating them.

Struggle engages the body and makes it stronger. Ideas collide so that minds may expand and so that discussion and negotiation might take place between conflicting positions. Conviviality has to transform enemies into adversaries so that conflict can take place without massacre, and so that collectives may flourish in order for everyone to live to the full. The common social bond must be preserved. Peace must reign. Enemies must disappear, as well as the desire to kill, or at least the enactment of this desire.

The illusion of liberal democracy rests on the hypothesis that trade on free markets will radically change the landscape of conflicts. The confrontation of people would be displaced in the pacific economic scene, turning enemies into competitors. This is a fallacy that has been quite hidden as long as unlimited growth seemed possible. As long as an expected better future seemed plausible in a tamed capitalism[g], it played the role of a hypnotic drug for the victims of the economic massacre.

But the sheer reality is that humanity still suffers from both kind of wars, that of physical terror and that of economical terror. To preserve the common social bond, everyone must limit both his desire to kill and his desire to get more than what is collectively considered as his fair part. This was pointed out by Illich under the wording "an acceptance of inevitable self-limitations" [1973: 107]. This means to stop the desire for always more, which is greed. Plato linked the interdiction of greed, conceptualised as pleonexia ($\pi\lambda\varepsilon o\nu\varepsilon\xi\acute{\iota}\alpha$), with justice. As incest is still a taboo to preserve the social bond, pleonexia should be taken again as a taboo [Dufour 2015], in order to preserve the sustainability of our societies by keeping hubris at bay.

4. As a Conclusion

To be sure, it is a herculean task to try to have our societies, to have the whole humanity, working on the basis of these principles.

To a certain extent, a large proportion of humanity is convinced of our common destiny: the international community approved the universal declaration of human rights that is the simplest version of the manifesto's first principle. However, its enforcement is still a work in progress.

As far as the second principle is concerned, the idea that the social bond is preeminent is widespread in the population. But this is not the position of the dominant school of economists, followed by a significant group of social scientists and essayists. Recently, an ever-larger proportion of governments, listening to these "experts", have reduced their social policies even if the politicians who head them are not known as adepts of neo-liberal ideas. The dominant thinking among politicians is that of Friedrich Hayek [1988] who wrote that "society" is a term deployed when people "do not quite know what they are talking about." In order to have a society working under the second principle of the

---

[g] Tamed thanks to the revolts of the oppressed and by the introduction of countervailing powers [Galbraith 1952] into the working of societies mainly after the Great Crisis (1929).

Manifesto, democracy should be strong enough to impose the people's will to the present oligarchy.

On the other hand, to get a majority of people understanding and accepting the contents of the last two principles seems to be a very big challenge. As a matter of fact, the search for independence by any individuals is the basis of the deification of freedom, a victory of enlightenment and liberalism against thousands of years of dependence, exploitation, enslavement. To forbid greed, and to make it as a taboo in order to stop the economic massacre of humanity and nature is a terrific move. It is to break into pieces the collective dream of unlimited growth and to replace it by fair sharing of the results of the work of all, which is upsetting the common way to think and to act. Such a move supposes "the shared insight of people that they would be happier if they could *work* together and *care* for each other" [Illich 1973: 50].

To be sure here and there, millions of localised changes are already implemented by perhaps 100 million people – this means around 1.5% of the world population – who do share this insight. They organise at least a small part of their individual and collective life, at a micro-level, according to these principles: this is what is done, e.g. by activities which are known as solidarity economy. At the level of societies, of nation-states, there are no such significant moves, in spite of attempts by activists to get some laws limiting the detrimental effects of the mega-machine. For instance, unconditional basic income or limitation to the extent of the income scale are still targeted in vain by various political and activist movements in different nation states.

Nevertheless, who may believe that such a series of small incremental changes, already present at the micro level or that could emerge at a macro-level in some nation state, would be able to switch us from this world to one which could be based on these four principles? The move we need is radical and a real upheaval is necessary to build such a better and sustainable world and, doing so, to escape from the looming catastrophes. What could it be? How will it be operated?

Personally, even if I think that along with the intellectual battle of ideas it will be necessary to have a political fight, I share the optimism showed by Illich [1973: 103]: "Some fortuitous coincidence will render publicly obvious the structural contradictions between stated purposes and effective results in our major institutions. People will suddenly find obvious what is now evident to only a few: that the organization of the entire economy toward the 'better' life has become the major enemy of the *good* life. Like other widely shared insights, this one will have the potential of turning public imagination inside out. Large institutions can quite suddenly lose their respectability, their legitimacy, and their reputation for serving the public good. It happened to the Roman Church in the Reformation, to Royalty in the Revolution. The unthinkable became obvious overnight: that people could and would behead their rulers".

References

Convivialist Manifesto – A declaration of interdependence (2014). With an introduction by Adloff, F., [translated from Manifeste convivialiste – Déclaration d'interdépendance (2103), Editions le Bord de l'eau, Paris, by Clarke, M.], Center for Global Cooperation Research, Global Dialogues 3, Duisburg

Dufour, D-R. (2015). *Pléonexie,* Le Bord de l'eau, Lormont

Galbraith, J. K. (1952). *American Capitalism – The Concept of Countervailing Power,* Houghton Mifflin, Boston

Godelier, M. (2012). *The Metamorphoses of Kinship,* Verso, London [translated from: Godelier, M. (2007). *Au fondement des sociétés humaines. Ce que nous apprend l'anthropologie,* Albin Michel, Paris]

Gordon, R. (2012). *Is U.S. Economic Growth Over? Faltering Innovation Confronts the Six Headwinds,* Working Paper n° 18315, National Bureau of Economic Research.

Hayek, F. (1988). *The Fatal Conceit: The Errors of Socialism,* Routledge, London

Honneth, A. (1992). *Kampf um Anerkennung. Zur moralischen Grammatik sozialer Konflikte,* Frankfurt/M. [translated as The Struggle for Recognition – The Moral Grammar of Social Conflicts, Polity Press, Cambridge (UK) in 1995]

Illich, I. (1973). *Tools for Conviviality,* Harper & Row, New York

Krugman, P. (2013). Secular Stagnation, Coalmines, Bubbles, and Larry Summers, http://krugman.blogs.nytimes.com/2013/11/16/secular-stagnation-coalmines-bubbles-and-larry-summers/?_php=true&_type=blogs&_r=0

Meadows, D. H., Meadows, D. L., Randers, J., and Behrens III, W. W. (1972). *The Limits to Growth,* Universe Books, New York

Mumford, L. (1964). *The Myth of the Machine, The Pentagon of Power,* Harcourt Brace Jovanovich, New York

Ruskin, J. (1860). *Unto this Last,* Cornhill Magazine, London

Chapter 7

In Search of Wisdom in the ICT Society

Gunilla Bradley

Royal Institute of Technology (KTH), Sweden

The convergence model illustrates ongoing changes in the Net Society. The theoretical model synthesises the theoretical framework in the author's research on the psychosocial environment and computerisation. Interdisciplinary research programmes were initiated by the author in the 1970s, leading to an analysis of societal changes related to various periods in 'the history' of ICT. The description of the convergence model is structured with reference to the core concepts of Globalisation, ICT, Life Environment, Life Role, and Effects on Humans. Convergence and Interactions are important features of the model that organises analysis at individual, organisational, community, and societal levels. This chapter then focuses on the Effects on Human Beings and which aspects are most sensitive to the use of ICT, followed by a section entitled "From Theory, Visions to Actions" where the author reflects on actions for achieving a good and sustainable society.

1. Introduction

Let me begin with some history of how the Convergence Model and its conceptual components were developed. To do this, we need to return to the 1970s, when countries like Sweden were attempting to build political, economic, and social structures to shape a sustainable democratic society but also provide a balance between the main political systems of capitalism and socialism. This was a great challenge for a small country geographically located between the super powers that represented these political systems. In 1977, the Act on Employee Participation in Decision-Making (MBL) was signed. The concept of a *psychosocial work environment* was integrated in Swedish law and in agreements between the labour market parties. Over the next 20 years, Sweden was well on its way to introducing economic democracy through distributed citizen ownership of production. By the early 1990s, however, public anxiety increased, subsequently leading to the election of a liberal government and many of the structures shaped during the former governments were dissolved. The evolution of societal structures and their representation in political action at the time were later described for international readers in *Computers and the Psychosocial Work Environment* [Bradley 1989].

During these two decades, the 1970s and 1980s, advanced studies examined the corresponding structures in work life that were facilitated by available superstructures at the societal level. The focus of information and communication technology (ICT)-related research was on participation in the development of computerised information systems. Some research programmes also addressed the broader work life structures [Bradley 1977].

For many years, theories, methods, and results from my research were published in the Swedish language alone. *Computers and the Psychosocial Work Environment* was my first international book. The research programmes I initiated and led dealt with the *four principal historical periods of computerisation and ICT:* from the mainframe period with the use of batch processing systems; to the online period and use of display terminals; later to micro-computerization following the emergence of microchip technology; and to the net period where communication technologies have played a dominant role in the convergence of computer, tele-technology, and media technologies.

2. The Convergence Theory on ICT, Society and Human Beings

2.1. *Structures in interaction with human beings*

The model is primarily a graphical representation of ongoing changes in the Net Society whose important features are Convergence and Interactions. *Convergence* here is used to mean a move towards a common content. *Interaction* means that technology interacts in the social world with values and beliefs. The *psychosocial environment* refers to the process involving the interaction between the objective structural and subjective perceived environments.

The important key processes in the model are Convergence, Interaction, Participation, Psychosocial processes, Globalisation, and Democratic processes. These processes are characterised by complexity. There are four levels of analysis: individual, organisational, communal, and societal, and their ongoing processes are graphically reflected by converging circles. There is ongoing interaction between the 'clusters of circles'. Structures impact on human beings but human beings also impact structures.

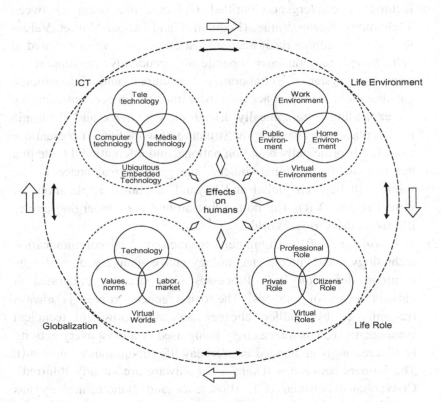

Fig. 1. Convergence Model depicting ICT and the Psychosocial Life Environment [Bradley 2000, 2001, 2005, 2006, 2011]

Essential concepts in the psychosocial work environment include factors such as contact patterns and communication, organisational structure and design, work content and workload, participation in decision-making, promotional and development patterns, salary conditions and working hours. The process of interaction is not the same in authoritarian and democratic regimes.

The principal constituents of convergence theory are presented in Fig. 1. The description of its components is organised with reference to concepts in the outer circle: Globalization, ICT, Life Environment, Life Role, and Effects on Humans (in the middle).

(1) *Globalisation* (lower left in the circle in Figure 1): This component represents what many theorists define as the societal structural factors. A convergence entitled *Globalisation* occurs between Technology, Norms/Values (Economy), and Labour Market. Values related to the economic system are a strong driver. Values related to culture and religion may operate independently or support an economic system. Collaborative structures and international collaboration, including access to new markets (in economic terms), are expanding geographically. Electronic commerce and electronic market places are changing the structure of work life. At present our work life is principally based on national and international trade that has become more global. Indeed, the geographical space of the future will be both global and beyond, including applications of virtual reality (VR). The dotted line around the converging circles illustrates the Virtual Worlds.

(2) *ICT* (upper left): Computer technology, telecommunication technology, and media technology have converged with the common definition ICT. Processes have become integrated at various levels of analysis. The convergence process is always (re-)enforced by smaller, cheaper and more powerful technical components. ICT is increasingly being used in almost every activity and increasingly embedded in everyday life (ubiquitous computing). The borders between software and hardware are already 'blurred'. Convergence between ICT, Bioscience and Nanotechnology has contributed to invisible convergences. Knowledge companies and

knowledge workers are increasing in number and knowledge is being managed in new ways. In the twenty-first century multiple communication channels are available. Meta-level channels, e.g. meta-media of virtual reality (VR) and controlled reality environments (environments that we manipulate and manage in VR) are increasingly available. ICT capabilities of influencing are used for governance structures and processes. The dotted line around the three circles illustrates embedded (pervasive, ubiquitous) technology.

The interaction between the 'ICT' and 'Globalisation' clusters gives a powerful push to the main direction of the speed of the 'wheel'.

(3) *Life Environment* (upper right): The Work Environment, Home Environment, and Public Environment converge into a Life Environment where work and public environments move into our homes. It is important to place new emphasis on certain dimensions in the current psychosocial environment and identify new dimensions in the psychosocial environment. We have to be open for unanticipated implications. The dotted line around the three circles illustrates the Virtual Environments. In Media research the term 'environment' is often replaced by 'spheres' and the discourse is about the work sphere, the public sphere, and the private spheres. The concept of 'landscape' is also coming into use.

(4) *Life Role* (lower right): The Professional Role, the Private Role, and the Citizen's Role converge into a Life Role. A Role is the position, task, or function a person has in a particular context and the norms and expectations associated with this position or task. Every person has a set of roles played in various contexts; role conflict takes place when integration of various roles is difficult. Role appears where psychology and sociology meet; social psychology emphasises the corresponding interaction between the levels of analysis of social structures and the individual. In democracies people can create and influence their roles; they are not solely a 'victim' of societal structures.

Changes are taking place in the home and home environment where professional, private, civic, and educational roles converge. The home can be regarded as a communication sphere that encompasses an extended family centre, a care centre, a multimedia centre, a centre for democratic dialogue, a market place, a learning centre, and an entertainment centre. The home is moving towards encompassing both virtual and physical space. Technologies such as ICT have become embedded and have already altered behavioural patterns in the home and home environments on several continents [Bradley and Bradley 2000, 2001; Bradley Linda 2005; Danielsson 2007; Jansson and Bradley 2005].

(5) *Effects on Humans* (in the centre): The Effects on Humans are represented by the circle in the centre with arrows pointing in two directions similar to a flower or a compass, illustrating interactions. The individual is affected by ICT, by the Life Environment with its three sub-environments, by the Life Role with its three sub-roles, and by Globalisation with its three components of values, technology, and labour market. Individuals influence and are influenced by technology, the environment, their own roles, by phenomena at organisational and societal level and by the new virtual reality with its subparts. The individual can influence and is influenced by the clusters of circles or single circles as illustrated by the double direct arrows between the inner circle 'Effects on Humans' and the clusters of circles around it. Effects on the individual have become more multi-faceted and complex. The way in which humans react to their situations can be roughly categorized as either active or passive, which is represented in the middle of Fig. 1. Examples of active reactions are involvement, creative behaviour, and protest. Examples of passive reactions are alienation and certain psycho-physiological symptoms.

(6) *Virtual Reality* (VR) as a summarizing concept is illustrated by the four circles marked with dotted lines that surround the four clusters of converging circles and represents our participation in cyberspace at various levels. In the lower left section we can talk about *Virtual Worlds* at the global level. Within the concept of ICT the phrase *Embedded (Pervasive, Ubiquitous)* makes the technology less obvious to the individual and to society as a whole; the tempo of the embedded processes is accelerating. *Virtual Environments* in the upper right part of the figure has been a common concept for some

time; other names are online communities and virtual communities. *Virtual Human Roles* (lower right section) are emerging. The main tools are the Internet and web technologies, mobile phones, and new software applications known as social media (Facebook, Twitter, etc.) that are transforming work, private, and citizen roles. More time is spent on the net. The professional role has real and virtual components. The private role is increasingly dominated by one's presence in cyberspace. In a more extreme form, VR can be expressed by another persona/personality that people assume, for example, an avatar in online games. VR is also a significant factor in reshaping the power balance between authority and the grassroots and strengthening civil society.

2.2. *Convergence theory and the effects on humans*

The human aspects that we have identified as *sensitive to the use of* ICT are:
- Identity and self-perception (web community identity)
- Social competence
- Integrity
- Trust (security, privacy - the terms vary)
- Dependency (Addictiveness)
- Empowerment
- Empathy
- Stress

Regarding Effects on Humans in the centre of Fig. 1, we can conclude that the use of ICT has thus far changed the human qualities of identity and self-perception, social competence, creativity, integrity, trust, dependency, and vulnerability. For example, the identity of humans has acquired new and additional bases through participation in various virtual and online communities. Each of those qualities can be either strengthened or weakened. In stress-theoretical terms we often talk about the importance of balance. ICT contributes to a balance or imbalance between, for example, the emotional and rational components of life, between female and male aspects, and between involvement and alienation.

Research indicates an accelerated tempo in the (post-)industrialised world. Certain types of 'ICT stress' are related to increased dependency on computers and networks and to an increased expectation that these technologies are functioning well. Stress phenomena in the Internet world are information overload, contact overload, demands for availability, lack of organisational filters, and difficulty in separating 'noise' from essentials. Changing levels of expectations by others and ourselves and altered perceptions of time and space are basic factors that contribute to ICT-related stress.

Tasks, roles, and environments that expose people to one of the two poles of over-stimulation and under-stimulation should be avoided due to the risk of stress (the individual level); the risk of a fragmented labour force (group/organisation levels); the risk of a digital divide in nation-states; and the risk of marginalisation and exclusion from the mainstream of society (individual, group, and societal levels) [Bradley 1989].

More attention needs to be given at the individual level with respect to interaction between ICT–Society–Individual. There are both positive and negative impacts on the individual. In the current flexible network organisation too much responsibility is placed on the individual who loses permanent employment. In the current highly competitive market place, knowledge workers have become members of a 'peripheral work force', wholly responsible for their competency development and for marketing themselves. Although this may be seen as freedom from paid work in a traditional sense and freedom to choose your life, nonetheless, we all need basic security as employees and citizens. There needs to be a balance between a strong society and strong individuals. Most people are not 'strong' throughout life. We need to think in terms of sustainability in both the physical and social environment and to develop ways to create sustainable human beings. The increasing number of courses in mindfulness, preventive stress, cognitive behaviour therapy, provide sources for reflection.

2.3. *Dynamics of the model: speed and complexity*

The *thin double-directed arrows* in the outer part of the large circle represent interaction between *the clusters* of circles and *the broad arrows* represent the *main direction* for the movement in the circle model. The main direction is emphasised by an increasing change in society due to globalisation and to the *accelerated speed* within R&D in ICT. *The interaction between the clusters entitled "ICT" and "Globalisation" gives a powerful push to the speed of the "wheel". Accelerated speed of economic transactions by robotisation increases the risk that the world economy will collapse.*

Transferring this reasoning to *actions, we* can in our professional role, private role and/or citizen's role influence our life environment on various levels of analyses, but *an awareness of the speed of change, its causes and the complexity* is required. To *"simplify the complexity"* I would like to refer to the phenomenon of *"Societal Self-Production"*. "Human Beings" contribute to the production and reproduction of themselves, including the emergence of "Social" but also "Nature" and the artifact "ICT" is increasingly reproducing itself. Everything appears to be interacting with everything else. In this ambivalent move towards *the dialectic reproduction of "physical" and "cultural spheres"* we need an *ethical compass.* This takes us over to reflect on the question of: what is the Good ICT Society?

3. What is the Good ICT Society?

Internationally *the first official statements* of goals for the ICT society were formulated at the first World Information Technology Forum (WITFOR) in Lithuania in 2003 [Bradley 2004]. The so-called *Vilnius Declaration* identified the following goals:
- Information access for all
- Wellbeing and *quality of life* for all
- Deepening and broadening of *democracy*
- *Integration* and respect for *diversity*
- *Enrichment* in the social contact between people
- Greater *autonomy* for the individual
- Prevention of various kinds of overload and stress
- E-cooperation and *peace*
- Sustainability

This was the first time that researchers met with and had a dialogue with politicians at ministry level both from developed and developing countries. I conclude that the dialogue there served to plant the seed representing the insight that ICT could be used to broaden and deepen democracy.

WITFOR was followed up by the World Summit of the Information Society (WSIS) largely held in the developing countries and involving NGO's and civic society, after which there emerged an *awareness process around the world* of the *potential of ICT*. Examples of this are the Arabic Spring, the Occupy Wall Street movement etc. Thoughts about the good society are not new – there are many examples in politics, religion, and cultural spheres.

Visions are shared about well-being, democracy, and the quality of life for all as well as social, economic, and ecological sustainability, as illustrated by the convergence of circles in Fig. 1. We can all be actors in this process, whether it be in nongovernmental organisations or as researchers, teachers, IT professionals, and individuals.

In 2006, the United Nations began a review of the issue of Human Rights; global use of ICT has made the need for this review clear. Sustainability has increasingly become the principal criterion for a Good Information and Communication Society [Bichler *et al.* 2010; Jansson and Bradley 2005]. Sustainability and the use of ICT are closely connected. Important theoretical approaches are system dynamics, holism, human aspects, bottom-up, common good, equality and equity. Many of the concepts overlap and may be analysed from various perspectives. Action-oriented and value-oriented research is moving to the fore.

4. From Theory, Visions to Actions

At the time of the Millennium shift in 2000 considerable enthusiasm could be noted for ICT in Sweden and in most other western countries. New applications popped up all the time – now, in the 2010s, we call them "apps". At that time – 15 years ago and in the following years – I firmly believed that *market forces* would regulate the journey, that *consumer power* would be so strong that we were facing a wonderful future with all this marvellous technology, increased self-determination and influence, reduced poverty, freedom of speech etc. In my work at the Telecommunication department at KTH *"Interactivity"* was the leading word, the Internet centre was next door. A new IT-university was being created, to be subsequently transformed into the School of ICT. Further a centre for wireless computing appeared.

However the Net has since been occupied by terrorist organisations; giving rise to misuse and adverse effects. There is *bullying, hate, sexual abuse, dishonesty and mutual distrust* due to competing sources of information etc. *Anonymity and speed* are drivers. In addition *cyber-attacks* are taking place and we face the risk of a *global cyber war, the end of humankind.* Whole societies and civilisations are very *vulnerable* and their *infrastructures* can suddenly be wiped out.

ICTs have grown *out of control* for human beings – advanced applications require *wisdom.* Technology Development is widely discussed, but nothing is said about *Humane Development. Humane Development* must occur in parallel with Technology Development – it involves not only IQ but also emotional (EQ) and social competences (SQ) – applied wisdom [Bradley 2015].

ICT is all about *"Power"* on various levels or *"Politics"* if you like. In theory we are all "empowered". Each one of us can make an impact. Technology has taken a *leap into our hands and pockets.* The question is: Have we become more powerful or not? There is an increasing risk in enforcing *centralization, surveillance and power misuse.* The visions and goals for the Good ICT society for Human Beings require *stronger recognition and actions at all levels of society – including the global level.*

In a forthcoming book *"In Search of Wisdom in the ICT Society"* [Bradley and Whitehouse 2016] those issues will be further developed and related to the clusters/levels and the dynamics of the convergence theory.

5. Final Words

ICT can and should be used to narrow the gap between subcultures; it could show similarities, emphasize the synergy of the various cultural blocks, and bring us all into a thrilling, fruitful dialogue. We need quite a different approach. The goal must be "unity and diversity". In practice it is important to discuss and develop perspectives on the role of the citizen. What competences do we need, how should responsible citizens act in the ICT society, what life styles are important? We are all on the way to becoming global citizens. "The Golden Rule" could serve as a simplified guiding principle; perhaps we need an app with the Golden Rule. The ancient creed says, "Treat other People as you would want them to treat You".

The Distribution issue (distribution of power and resources) is still a key question and could easily be solved through ICT (distribution of resources both human and material). Accumulation of capital and other resources is speeded up by ICT. Distribution of resources could also be facilitated by ICT. Structures, Human development, dialogue are all golden keys for action. Each one of us can and should reflect on the actions we would prioritise in our country, community, work place, and home environment, and consider which actions we wish to convey to national and international bodies.

For many years I have declared and written that "ICT should be used for Deepening of Humane and Societal Qualities". There is an inherent opportunity for creating the Good and Sustainable Society. What is it all about? It is our responsibility for the Next Generation and the Planet.

References

Bichler, R. M., Bradley, G., and Hofkirchner, W. (2010). Editorial Comment. Sustainable Development and ICTs. *Information, Communication & Society*, 13(1), Routledge, London, UK

Bradley, G. (1977). *Datateknik, arbetsliv och kommunikation. (Computer technology, work life, and communication)*. The Swedish delegation for long term research. FRN. Liber (in Swedish), Stockholm, SE

Bradley, G. (1989). *Computers and the Psychosocial Work Environment*. Taylor & Francis (in Swedish 1986), London

Bradley, G. (2000). The Information and Communication Society: How people will live and work in the new millennium. *Special issue of "Ergonomics", Vol. 43, No. 6 and included in the congress CD-ROM proceedings at the IEA/HFES 2000 Congress*, San Diego, USA, Taylor & Francis, London

Bradley, G. (ed.) (2001). *Humans on the Net. Information and Communication Technology (ICT) Work Organization and Human Beings*, Prevent, Stockholm, SE, ISBN 91-7522-701-0

Bradley, G. (2004). ICT for Deepening Human and Societal Qualities, in: Khakhar, Dipak, (ed.), *WITFOR 2003 (WORLD IT FORUM) White Book. Key note contributions and panel discussions from the 8 commissions*, IFIP Press, Luxemburg

Bradley, G. (2005). The Convergence Theory on Information and Communication Technology (ICT) and the Psychosocial Life Environment - The Connected Home, in: Smith, M., and Salvendy, G. (eds.), *Proceedings of the HCI International 2005 conference*, Lawrence Erlbaum Associates, Inc, Mahwah, NJ

Bradley, G. (2006). *Social and Community Informatics-Humans on the Net*, Routledge, London/NY

Bradley, G. (2011). The convergence theory on ICT, society and human beings. Towards the good ICT society, in: Haftor, D., and Mirijamdotter, A. (eds.), *Information and Communication Technologies, Society and Human Beings. Festschrift in Honor of Gunilla Bradley*, IGI Global, New York, 30-46

Bradley, G. (2015). TED-talk on YouTube *Understanding the Change of Habits in the ICT Society*, http://tedxtalks.ted.com/video/Understanding-the-Change-of-Hab

Bradley, G., and Whitehouse, D. (2016). *In Search of Wisdom in the ICT Society*. Forthcoming

Bradley, L. (2005). *Home of the future Japan. Information and communication technology (ICT) and changes in society and human patterns of behavior in the network era.* KTH Research report ISBN 91-7178-052-1, Royal Institute of Technology (KTH), Stockholm

Bradley, L., and Bradley, G. (2000). Home of the Future and ICT - Integration of professional and private roles. *Special issue of "Ergonomics", Vol. 43, No. 6 and included in the congress CD-ROM proceedings at the IEA/HFES 2000 Congress*, San Diego, USA, Taylor & Francis, London

Bradley, L., and Bradley, G. (2001). The Home as a Virtual and Physical Space - Experiences from USA and South-East Asia, in: Smith, M. J., and Salvendy, G. (eds.), *Systems, Social and Internationalization Design Aspects of Human - Computer Interaction*, Lawrence Erlbaum Ass. Inc., Mahwah, NJ, 81-85

Danielsson, U. (2007). *Relationships between information communication technology and psychosocial life environment : Students and young urban knowledge workers in the ICT-era.* Doctoral dissertation at Department of Informatics, Mid Sweden University

Jansson, E., and Bradley, G. (2005). Sustainability in Collaborative Network Structures - with focus on the Psychosocial Work Environment in Distributed Teams. *Proceedings of the CIRN Conference on Sustainability and Community Technology: What does this mean for Community Informatics?* Monash Centre, Prato, Italy

Part II

Designing the Future

Chapter 8

Responsible Research and Innovation (RRI): Limits to Consequentialism and the Need for Hermeneutic Assessment

Armin Grunwald

Institute for Technology Assessment and Systems Analysis (ITAS)
Karlstr. 11, 76133 Karlsruhe, Germany
armin.grunwald@kit.edu

For decades, social scientists and philosophers, citizens and politicians have been engaged with scientific and technological progress, its intended and unintended consequences and cultural implications but also with opportunities for shaping new technologies according to social desires and ethical values. These activities are currently considered under the heading of "Responsible Research and Innovation". The ideal behind is to anticipate the implications of scientific and technological advances in order to provide societal and political orientation, e.g. for decision-making. However, this consequentialist approach comes up against limits because many future developments can be anticipated neither in a predictive way nor by identifying a set of plausible scenarios. Therefore it is the purpose of this paper to systematically examine an aspect of reflections of technology and technology assessment that has hitherto been considered only sporadically: its *hermeneutic side*. While the consequentialist idiom deals with assessing statements about possible futures in terms of their plausibility, the hermeneutics of discourse on technological futures focuses on the *meaning* of these debates for contemporary attitudes towards new technologies.

1. Introduction

For decades, social scientists and philosophers, citizens and politicians have been engaged with scientific and technological progress, its intended and unintended consequences and cultural implications. Fields of research and reflection have emerged including technology assessment, risk research, the ethics of science and technology, the whole area of STS (science, technology & society) studies, ELSI (ethical, legal and social implications) analyses, and EHS (environment, health & safety) research. Many of these areas of concern are currently considered under the heading of "Responsible Research and Innovation" (RRI). The ideal behind these endeavors is to *anticipate* the implications of scientific and technological advances and to *assess* the results of the anticipations with respect to social desires, political goals and ethical values in order to provide societal and political *orientation*, e.g. for decision-making in regard to the promotion or regulation of research. Thus, these approaches such as technology assessment follow a consequentialist approach.

The RRI debate [e.g. von Schomberg 2012; Owen *et al.* 2013] emerged out of the reflections on new and emerging technologies (NEST) such as nanotechnology [e.g. Fiedeler *et al.* 2010; Grunwald 2014a], nanobiotechnology [e.g. Grunwald 2012], human enhancement [e.g. Jotterand 2008], robotics [Böhle and Bopp 2014] or ubiquitous computing. The clue with respect to the issue of this paper now is that exactly in these fields there is only little if any reliable knowledge about future consequences available [e.g. Nordmann 2007; Coenen and Simakova 2013]. Because of the early stage of development in those fields there is no valid knowledge about specific innovation paths and products or about consequences and impacts of production, use, non-intended side-effects and disposal of future products. That means that the consequentialist approach comes up against limits as to the extent to which future developments may be anticipated [Nordmann 2014].

The rationale of this paper is to explore what this constellation means with respect to responsibility, in particular taking seriously that the traditional consequentialist approach does not work in this situation [Grunwald 2013]. Beyond the consequentialist paradigm the intention is to systematically examine an aspect of reflections of technology and technology assessment that has hitherto been considered only sporadically: Namely its *hermeneutic side*, which is concerned with a comprehensive *understanding* of the *meaning* of new developments in science and technology, particularly as regards ethical, cultural and social implications. While the consequentialist idiom deals with assessing statements about possible futures in terms of their plausibility in order to evaluate their consequences, the hermeneutics of discourse on technological futures focuses on the *meaning* of these debates for contemporary attitudes. The 'hermeneutic turn' views the lively and controversial debates about new fields of science or technology not as anticipatory, prophetic or quasi-predictive presumptions of the future, but as expressions of our present day.

The chapter is structured as follows. After this introduction the first task is to clarify the relation between the notion of responsibility and its epistemological prerequisites (section 2). This allows deepening the analysis of epistemological constraints to the classical consequentialist paradigm of responsibility ethics in the NEST fields (section 3) and to distinguish three modes of orientation of which the third one, the hermeneutic orientation, is novel in the RRI field. This type of orientation is then described in some detail (section 5), followed by drawing conclusions for responsibility debates in NEST areas.

2. The EEE Concept of Responsibility[a]

The very idea of responsibility and responsibility ethics is, following Max Weber's distinction between *Verantwortungsethik* and *Gesinnungsethik*, related with a consequentialist approach. Taking over responsibility or assigning responsibility to other persons, groups, or institutions indispensably requires, in this paradigm, the availability of valid and reliable knowledge, or at least of a plausible picture of the consequences and impact of decisions to be made or of actions to be performed. The familiar approach of discussing responsibilities is to consider future consequences of an action (e.g. the development and use of new technologies) and then to reflect these consequences from an ethical point of view (e.g. with respect to the acceptability of technology-induced risk). Thus, without a rather clear picture of those future consequences any ethics of responsibility falls under the suspicion either

---

[a] This concept has been developed through several stations [cp. Grunwald 2012, 2014a].

to fail, or to lead to mere arbitrary conclusions [Hansson 2006], or to end up in mere political rhetoric.

Having responsibility or not having it is the result of social processes, namely of *assignment acts*, either if actors assign responsibility to themselves or if the assignment of responsibility is made by others. There are three dimensions which have to be considered: (1) The process of assigning responsibility takes place according to social rules based on ethical, cultural and legal considerations and customs [Jonas 1979: 173). Thus, the socio-political dimension of responsibility has to be considered. (2) The rules and criteria of assigning responsibility must be reflected on which opens up the bridge to philosophical ethics. And (3) the question for the knowledge available about possible consequences of the decision under consideration and the quality and reliability of this knowledge is decisive in the consequentialist paradigm. My thesis is that *all* three dimensions must be considered in prospective debates in the NEST field [following Grunwald 2014b]:

- The *empirical dimension* of responsibility takes serious that the assignment of responsibility is an act done by specific actors and affecting others. It refers to the basic social constellation of assignment processes. Attributing responsibilities must, on the one hand, take into account the possibilities of actors to influence actions and decisions in the respective field. Issues of accountability and power must be involved. On the other, attributing responsibilities has an impact on the *governance* of that field. Shaping that governance is the ultimate goal of debating issues of assigning and distributing responsibility *ex ante*. Relevant questions are: How are capabilities, influence and power to act and decide distributed in the field considered? Which social groups are affected and could or should help decide about the distribution of responsibility? Do the questions under consideration concern issues to be debated at the "polis" or can they be delegated to groups or subsystems? What consequences would a particular distribution of responsibility have for the governance of the respective field and would it be in favor of desired developments?

- The *ethical dimension* of responsibility is reached when the question is posed for *criteria and rules* for judging actions and decisions under consideration as responsible or irresponsible, or for helping to find out how actions and decisions could be designed to be (more) responsible. Insofar as normative uncertainties arise, e.g. because of ambiguity or moral conflicts, ethical reflection on these rules and their justifiability is needed. Relevant questions are: What criteria allow distinguishing between responsible and irresponsible actions and decisions? Is there consensus or controversy on these criteria among the relevant actors? Can the actions and decisions in question (e.g. about the scientific agenda or about containment measures to prevent risks) regarded responsible with respect to the rules and criteria?

- The *epistemic* dimension asks for the knowledge about the subject of responsibility and its epistemological status and quality. This is a relevant issue in particular in debates on scientific responsibility because frequently statements about impacts and consequences of science and new technology show a high degree of uncertainty. The comment that nothing else comes from "mere possibility arguments" [Hansson 2006] is an indication that in debates over responsibility it is essential that the status of the available knowledge about the futures to be accounted for is determined and is critically reflected from an epistemological point of view [Nordmann 2007; Grunwald 2014c]. Relevant questions are: What is really known about prospective subjects of responsibility? What could be known in case of more research, and which uncertainties are pertinent? How can different uncertainties be qualified and compared to each other? And what is at stake if worse comes to worst?

Debates over responsibility in technology and science often suffer from narrowing their focus on the *ethical dimension* only while considering issues of assignment processes and epistemic constraints secondary issues. However, the ethical dimension is important but only part of the game. Meeting familiar criticisms towards responsibility reflections of being simply appellative, of showing epistemological blindness, and of being politically naïve is claimed to be possible by considering all the three EEE dimensions of responsibility together.

3. Epistemological Constraints to Consequentialism

In early stages of development of any R&D (e.g. in the above-mentioned NEST fields) the epistemic dimension of responsibility becomes decisive. Ethical debates in this situation mostly consider narratives about possible future developments involving visions, expectations, fears, concerns and hopes that can hardly be assessed with respect to their epistemological validity (this was the main line of criticism against the 'speculative nano-ethics', see [Nordmann 2007]). Questions arise such as: What could be subject to responsibility debates in the absence of valid knowledge about consequences of NEST developments? Is it possible to identify sources of providing orientation for responsibility debates and assignments beyond consequentialism?

In the past decade, there has been a considerable increase in visionary communication on future technologies and their impacts on society. In particular, this has been and still is the case in the fields of nanotechnology [Fiedeler *et al.* 2010; Ferrari *et al.* 2014], human enhancement [Jotterand 2008; Coenen 2010] and synthetic biology [Giese *et al.* 2014] but also in ICT-related fields such as robotics [Böhle and Bopp 2014] or ubiquitous computing. Visionary scientists and science managers have put forward far-ranging visions in these fields. Futuristic visions are more or less speculative narratives about possible scenarios for techno-visionary sciences and their impacts on society. As a rule, little if any knowledge is available about how the respective technology is likely to develop, about the products which such development may spawn and about the potential impact of using such products.

Recently it has been discussed whether anticipatory stories about futures in this field might narrow our thinking in a techno-morph [Nordmann 2014] or reifying [Boenink 2014] way. This debate is obviously relevant also for the issue of responsibility. One crucial aspect would be, following the critics of anticipation, to ask not only for the responsibility for anticipated specific developments based on technological advance but also to ask for a broader view on future developments not narrowed by looking through the "lens" of projected technologies and their anticipated consequences.

A misleading conclusion facing this diagnosis could be: it might still be too early to seriously think about chances and risks of synthetic biology or any other NEST development. Let the researchers do their work and come back with questions for responsibility as soon as better knowledge will be available - and then discuss in the familiar consequentialist manner. But there are good arguments not to wait [Grunwald 2014c]. While futuristic narratives often appear somewhat fictitious in content, it is a fact that such narratives can and will have real impact on scientific and public discussions [Brown *et al.* 2000]. Even a narrative without any scientific plausibility at all can influence debates, opinion-forming, acceptance and even decision-making. For example visions of new science and technology can have a major impact on the way in which political and public debates about future technologies are currently conducted. The factual power of futuristic narratives in public debate and for decision-making on funding is a strong argument in favor of carefully and critically analyzing and assessing them already in early stages of development.

4. Modes of Orientation

The situation characterized above was the reason to distinguish the possibilities to extract orientation from techno-futures according to their different kind and different epistemic quality. Recently it was proposed [Grunwald 2013] to distinguish between three methods of providing orientation:

- *Mode 1 (i.e. prognostic) orientation:* The prognostic imagination of future technologies and their consequences is supposed to produce a reliable basis for decision-making. Knowledge about future developments may be taken in this mode as information on boundary conditions within the Rational Choice paradigm in order to inform and optimize decision-making. Experience and theoretical analyses have shown, however, that as a rule this mode does not work in considering the consequences of technology [e.g. Grunwald 2009].
- *Mode 2 (i.e. scenario-based) orientation:* Scenarios have become the established means in many areas of prospective analyses. In this mode

we reflect systematically on a future that is in principle open. The necessary precondition for mode 2 orientation to be applicable is the existence of well-founded corridors of the envisaged future development, or at least an imagination of such corridors agreed upon by relevant persons or groups. Frequently, the space of plausible futures is imagined between a 'worst case' and a 'best case' scenario.

- *Mode 3 (i.e. hermeneutic) orientation*: This mode comes into the play in case of overwhelming uncertainty, that means if the knowledge of the future is so uncertain or if the images of the future diverge so strongly that there are no longer any valid arguments for employing scenarios to provide orientation. For this situation rendering any form of consequentialism non-applicable a *hermeneutic turn* is proposed [Grunwald 2014c]. The change of perspective consists of raising the question what could be learned by analyzing the visionary narratives *about the contemporary situation.* Beyond the consequentialist paradigm the expectation is that we could benefit from a hermeneutic analysis and assessment of those narratives for a better understanding of our present situation.

Because the epistemological quality of knowledge comprises a continuum between full and certain knowledge at the one end (mode 1) and the full ignorance at the other (mode 3), the distinguished modes of orientation overlap with gradual transitions between them. Thus, the distinction is not a logical one but rather shall orientate different approaches of providing orientation and provide an umbrella view. In the NEST debates, neither the mode 1 nor the mode 2 approach is applicable (see above). Therefore we have to focus on the hermeneutic mode (3). This focus leads to the necessity for us to concern ourselves with the hermeneutic constellation and to look for an adequate methodology.

5. Hermeneutic Analysis of Techno-Futures

Techno-futures (e.g. in the NEST field but also beyond) are images of the future development of society in which technology and scientific-technical progress play a perceptible role. They can include elements from specific areas of technology such as future mobility, energy supply, water management, or the regulation of complex technical, social, or virtual systems, such as with regard to the transformation of the energy system. They can also extend to more general issues such as the future of the nature of humans, the impact of technology's becoming increasingly autonomous, or developments in the relations between humanity, technology, and nature. Techno-futures which cannot be classified with respect to epistemic quality – that means which are more or less speculative – only can be made subject to hermeneutical analysis. This type of analysis asks for the *meaning* that is given to new technology by relating them with techno-futures [Grunwald 2014c]. Compared to the consequentialist paradigm with its central focus on questions as to the possible impacts of new technologies, how we assess these, and whether and under what circumstances we welcome or reject these implications, this perspective places the focus on entirely different questions [following Grunwald 2014c]:

- What are the implications of the new developments in science and technology for the present and future of man and society, which fundamental constellations (man/technology, man/nature, etc.) do they change, and "what is at stake?" e.g. in ethical, cultural, and social terms?
- How is a philosophical, ethical, social, cultural, etc. *meaning* attributed to scientific-technological developments, which after all are nothing initially but scientific-technological developments? What role do e.g. (visionary) techno futures play in this context?
- How is meaning being created, communicated, and discussed? What roles do they play in the major technological debates of our time? What forms of communication and linguistic resources are being used and why? What extra-linguistic resources (e.g. movies, works of art) play a role in this context and what does their use reveal?
- Why do we discuss scientific-technological developments in the way we do and with the respective attributions of meaning rather than in some other way?
- How does man as an historical being see himself in discourses about techno-futures? What future concepts are being applied if the future is presented either as though it were possible to shape it technically or politically, or as what will contingently come about and will never be

quite adequate in terms of a historical responsibility to bring about a better world?

Futures in general and techno-futures in particular do not exist per se but rather are 'made' and constructed – they are social constructs. Techno-futures, whether they are forecasts, scenarios, plans, programs, or speculative fears or expectations, are produced using a whole range of ingredients such as the available knowledge, value judgments, and suppositions. They are made by specific authors who always pursue specific purposes and intentions, for example, supporting political decisions, sensitizing the public for problematic developments, mobilizing support for research, creating a vision for regional development, warning at an early stage about potential problems, etc. Thus, inseparably linked with the hermeneutical analysis of techno-futures as such is, on the one hand, an understanding of their *origin and construction* and, on the other, an understanding of their *diffusion* in communicative processes and the *consequences* of these processes.

The hermeneutic analysis of pictures of the future hardly tells us anything about the future in the sense of a present in the time to come, but rather *about us today*. If projections of the future are interpreted in a way that makes it clear why we aggregate certain current ingredients to specific futures and argue dedicatedly about them, then we have learned something *explicitly* about ourselves, our societal practices, subliminal concerns, implicit hopes and fears, and their cultural roots. By investigating alternative approaches to the future of humans and society with or without different techno-visionary developments, such reflection may ultimately promote democratic debate on scientific-technical progress and help preventing the narrowing of alternative options for the future by anticipatory thinking [Nordmann 2014] (see also below).

6. Conclusions

The hermeneutical approach will make it possible to add meta-information to the RRI debates and should thus be able to enrich those debates. The added value should consist of information about *the respective current world* in which the techno-futures and the related meaning of NEST developments are created and communicated. This meta-information should heighten a debate's reflection and transparency and thus help make the debate open and unbiased in the sense of a deliberative democracy. This is what a hermeneutic orientation can achieve [Grunwald 2014c] – a modest contribution. What this could mean at the occasion of a specific RRI debate, perhaps in a specific NEST field, depends on the context. However, it seems possible to propose at least three more general lines of thinking that could enrich and orientate ongoing RRI debates:

(a) *Focus on present developments instead of trying to anticipate the future:* If the epistemological dimension of responsibility does not allow for applying consequentialist patterns of deriving orientation the first conclusion is: responsibility considerations should focus on what's going on in the present already and on its ethically relevant aspects. Considering synthetic biology, for example, the subject of responsibility should be seen more in the processes of current research rather than in speculative future products. Taking over responsibility therefore means being responsible for current processes of research, defining the research agenda, determining objectives and goals and supporting current societal debates on synthetic biology instead of talking about responsible or irresponsible future outcomes of synthetic biology. In spite of the fact that it often will be impossible to completely renounce on thinking about possible future outcomes and developments the major awareness is then given to more to-date questions of e.g. risk of today's research, of elements of the research process (e.g. whether animal experiments really would be helpful or even necessary) or of the allocation of resources and budgets in current research. This idea is in line with Nordmann's criticisms against a too speculative 'nano-ethics' [2007] and his warning against a possible misleading allocation of the resources of ethics.

(b) *Avoidance of narrowing future development through a technocratic lens:* Recently Nordmann [2014] warned against a specific aspect of approaches to anticipate the future. His concern is that anticipations could set up a kind of self-fulfilling process in approaching the future. Insofar anticipations usually are done based on today's models, today's knowledge and today's assessments – and indeed, there no alternative to make anticipations according to the current state of the art – and on current anticipation techniques Nordmann is afraid that the anticipated futures merely will be a prolongation of present time. If we would narrow our minds by looking at anticipations of this type we are, according to Nordmann, in danger to lose critical potential and new ideas for improving futures. Thus his lea is not to anticipate but more to think about wishful futures [Nordmann 2010]. Nordmann thus makes us aware of a specific risk associated with anticipatory thinking. Taking his concern seriously meets the case of the hermeneutic mode of orientation (see subsection 4.3). In this case anticipation is not possible on any sound epistemic ground – and the thesis of this paper is that we should accept this and look for a type of orientation beyond consequentialism. Doing this leads to the hermeneutical turn, which avoids considering techno-futures as anticipations. Their analysis should provide us with insight into their premises and biases and, thus, helps avoiding a too narrow focus on future possibilities but should contribute to opening up the field in order not only to take anticipations of the current world into the focus but also other possible 'worlds' [Nordmann 2014]. By this the subjects to be reflected in an RRI debate also should be widened in order to cover a broader picture of possible developments.

(c) *Contributing to more transparent democratic debate:* The hermeneutic analysis of techno-futures can contribute to societal orientation, public debate and decision-making in a modest manner, which, however, should not be underestimated. Beyond consequentialism, the remaining way of providing orientation is uncovering the "ingredients", the premises and presuppositions, the knowledge but also the hopes, assumptions, cultural biases, Zeitgeist issues and concerns included in the respective techno-futures. This "meta-knowledge" about those futures then could inform and enlighten democratic debate and deliberation and thus contribute to more transparency and a more rational debate.

References

Böhle, K., and Bopp, K. (2014). What a vision: The artificial companion. A piece of vision assessment including an expert survey, *Science, Technology & Innovation Studies* (STI Studies) 10(2014)1, 155-186

Boenink, M. (2014). Anticipating the future of technology and society by way of (plausible) scenarios: fruitful, futile or fraught with danger? *Int. J. Foresight and Innovation*

Brown, J., Rappert, B., and Webster, A. (eds.) (2000). *Contested Futures. A Sociology of Prospective Techno-Science*, Ashgate Publishing, Burlington

Coenen, C. (2010). Deliberating visions: The case of human enhancement in the discourse on nanotechnology and convergence, in: Kaiser, M., Kurath, M., Maasen, S., and Rehmann-Sutter, Chr. (eds.), *Governing future technologies. Nanotechnology and the rise of an assessment regime*. Dordrecht *et al.*: Springer, 73-87 (Sociology of the Sciences Yearbook 27)

Coenen, C., and Simakova, E. (2013). STS Policy Interactions, Technology Assessment and the Governance of Technovisionary Sciences, *Science, Technology & Innovation Studies* 9 (2), 3-20

Ferrari, A., Coenen, C., and Grunwald, A. (2012). Visions and Ethics in Current Discourse on Human Enhancement, *Nanoethics* 6 (3), 215-229. doi: 10.1007/s11569-012-0155-1.

Fiedeler, U., Coenen, C., Davies, S. R., and Ferrari, A. (eds.) (2010). *Understanding Nanotechnology: Philosophy, Policy and Publics*, Akademische Verlagsgesellschaft, Heidelberg

Giese, B., Pade, C., Wigger, H., and von Gleich, A. (eds.) (2014). *Synthetic Biology. Character and Impact*, Springer, Heidelberg

Grunwald, A. (2009). Technology Assessment, in: Meijers, A. (ed.) *Philosophy of Technology and Engineering Sciences*, Vol. 9 of the *Handbook of the Philosophy of Science*. Amsterdam, North-Holland, 1103-1146

Grunwald, A. (2012). *Responsible Nanobiotechnology. Philosophy and Ethics*. Singapore

Grunwald, A. (2013). Modes of Orientation Provided by Futures Studies: Making Sense of Diversity and Divergence, *European Journal of Futures Studies*, 15, 30

Grunwald, A. (2014a). Synthetic Biology as Technoscience and the EEE Concept of Responsibility, in: Giese, B., Pade, C., Wigger, H., and von Gleich, A. (eds.), *Synthetic Biology. Character and Impact*, Springer, Heidelberg, 249-266

Grunwald, A. (2014b). Responsible research and innovations: an emerging issue in research policy rooted in the debate on nanotechnology, in: Arnaldi, S., Ferrari, A., Magaudda, P., and Marin, F. (eds.), *Responsibility in nanotechnology development*, Dordrecht, Springer, Niederlande, 191-205

Grunwald, A. (2014c). The hermeneutic side of Responsible Research and Innovation. *Journal of Responsible Innovation* 1(2014)3, 274-291

Hansson, S. O. (2006). Great Uncertainty about small Things, in: Schummer, J., and Baird, D. (eds.), *Nanotechnology Challenges – Implications for Philosophy*, Ethics and Society, Singapore, 315-325

Jonas, H. (1979). Das Prinzip Verantwortung. Versuch einer Ethik für die technologische Zivilisation. Frankfurt

Jotterand, F. (2008). Beyond Therapy and Enhancement: The Alteration of Human Nature, *Nanoethics*, 2, 15-23

Lenk, H. (1992). Zwischen Wissenschaft und Ethik. Frankfurt

Nordmann, A. (2007). If and Then: A Critique of Speculative NanoEthics, *Nanoethics*, 1, 31-46

Nordmann, A. (2014). Responsible Innovation, the Art and Craft of Future Anticipation, *Journal of Responsible Innovation* 1 (1), 87-98

Owen, R., Bessant, J., and Heintz, M. (eds.) (2013). *Responsible Innovation: Managing the Responsible Emergence of Science and Innovation in Society*. Wiley

van der Burg, S. (2014). On the Hermeneutic Need for Future Anticipation, *Journal of Responsible Innovation*, 1 (1), 99-102

von Schomberg, R. (2012). Prospects for Technology Assessment in a Framework of Responsible Research and Innovation, in: Dusseldorp, M., and R. Beecroft, R. (eds.), *Technikfolgen abschätzen lehren: Bildungspotenziale transdisziplinärer Methoden*, Springer, Wiesbaden, 39-62

Chapter 9

The Biological Tricks that Knit a Global Brain

Howard Bloom

705 President Street, Brooklyn, NY 11215, USA
howlbloom@aol.com

The accepted view in evolutionary biology is that we humans and our animal cousins are built with a survival instinct, an instinct that watches out for our personal survival ahead of everything else. Yet when we encounter a saber tooth tiger on a pathway, we have three modes of response: not just fight or flight, but fight, flight, or freeze. And freeze can be suicide. When you are fired or your wife tells you she is leaving you, your survival instinct should put your mind into overdrive, hunting with energy and creativity for your next step. But that high-power cognitive processing is not what your biology serves up. Instead, it bogs you in depression, a state in which it's hard to think of even tying your shoes. How could natural selection possibly favor such obvious self-destruct mechanisms? The answer is in the algorithms that power collective intelligences and massively parallel processing learning machines like neural nets, supercomputers, and the immune system.

1. Introduction

We are told that when we run into a saber tooth tiger on our path, we have two responses: fight or flight. And we are told that fight and flight are proof of something smashingly basic in our nature. Basic in every plant and animal. Something profoundly selfish. We are told that fight and flight are proof of our survival instinct. Fight, flight, and the survival instinct have been gospel since the fight or flight mechanism was first hinted at by William McDougall in 1908 and popularized by Walter Bradford Cannon in his 1915 book *Bodily changes in pain, hunger, fear, and rage*. But the fight and flight concept is incomplete. When we encounter a saber tooth tiger on our path, we respond with more than just fight or flight. We have three modes of response: fight, flight, or freeze. And freeze can be the very opposite of selfish. Freeze can be suicide.

David Livingstone, of "Dr. Livingstone I presume" fame, describes how he met the sensation of freeze up close and personal during his travels in the uncharted wilds of Africa:

> I saw the lion just in the act of springing upon me.... He caught my shoulder as he sprang, and we both came to the ground below together. Growling horribly close to my ear, he shook me as a terrier does a rat. The shock produced a stupor similar to that which seems to be felt by a mouse after the first shake of the cat. It caused a sort of dreaminess in which there was no sense of pain, nor feeling of terror, though [I was] quite conscious of all that was happening. It was like what patients partially under the influence of chloroform describe, who see the operation but feel not the knife [Livingstone, 1860].

Livingstone's freeze, his "sort of dreaminess", may have been a nice anesthetic. But it was the very opposite of a survival instinct. If anything, it helped the lion more than it helped the good Christian doctor between the lion's teeth.

Freeze is not the only suicidal mechanism locked into our biology. When you're about to take that all-important math test and you've studied for weeks, then you finally open the test booklet, your mind locks up. It refuses to remember a thing. That anxiety blackout is not a product of a patriarchal civilization, industrialism, or capitalism. It is a product of your biology.

When you are fired or your wife tells you she is leaving you, your survival instinct should put your mind into overdrive. It should give you the juice to hunt with energy and creativity for your next step. But high-power cognitive processing is not what your biology serves up. Instead, it bogs you in depression, a state in which it's hard to think of even tying your shoes.

How do mental paralysis and depression up your odds of survival? How do freeze and "dreaminess" guarantee that your selfish genes will make it into the next generation? They don't.

So what gives? How could natural selection possibly favor such obvious self-destruct mechanisms? The answer is in the algorithms that power collective intelligences, massively parallel processing systems, mass learning machines like neural nets, supercomputers, beehives, and your immune system. Rules that turn down the flow of resources and influence to the nodes that fail to cope with the problems of the moment and turn up the resource-flow and the influence of the nodes that have a handle on things. Rules that turn you and me into components of a larger intelligence. Rules that turn a group into a collective brain. And rules that turn a planet of competing and cooperating groups, from groups of seven trillion bacteria in a single colony to seven billion human beings, into a global brain.

This secret of self-destruct mechanisms, this secret of massively parallel processing intelligences, if it's true, implies a revolution for evolutionary biology. Not to mention a revolution for economics and the social sciences. Why? The common wisdom – the dogmatically enforced view – in evolutionary biology is that we humans and our animal cousins are built with a survival instinct. An instinct that watches out for our personal survival, and for our personal survival ahead of everything else. Richard Dawkins sums up the catechism of personal survival best in his concept of the selfish gene. A selfish gene watches out for its own interests and for the interests of its exact duplicates. It watches out for the interests of its identical twins. And a selfish gene watches out for nothing else. What's more, in Dawkins' view, all genes are selfish. They are greedy little bastards. And their combined greed powers evolutionary creativity. Yes, the greed of genes, says Dawkins, determines every breakthrough of biology and every decision you make.

Which means that when it comes to your deepest, darkest nature, there's a whole lot of assuming going on. The fight or flight folks tell you that your biology has forced you into an overwhelmingly narcissistic instinct for survival. The selfish gene folks tell you that you are driven by greedy genes. And there's yet another pack of scientists accusing you of egotism out the kazoo. They're the rational-choice modelers and their followers, rational-choice-obsessed specialists like economists and evolutionary psychologists. The rational-choicers claim that you are pre-programmed for more than just survival at all costs. You are wired, they say, to maximize your personal gains.

These accusations about your most intimate nature are concealed in the very foundations of many of the social and evolutionary sciences, from the afore-mentioned evolutionary biology and evolutionary psychology to political science, sociology, philosophy, and economics. They are buried deep below the surface in the form of assumptions – often hidden assumptions. But these assumptions about your innermost self are only half-right. More important, they are half-wrong. And the half that's wrong throws evolutionary and social sciences way off base. Which may explain why one of the most lauded and mathematically savvy economists of his day, Irving Fisher, told the *New York Times* in mid-October, 1929, that stocks were about to go "a good deal higher within a few months." Then on October 29th came Black Tuesday and the great crash of 1929. Fisher was dead wrong. Why? Could the problem have been his assumptions?

There's a bottom line. If self-destruct mechanisms are built into your biology, then the notions of the survival instinct, the selfish gene, and the rational choice model may have to be abandoned. Trashed. Negated. Or, at the very least, modified. Modified profoundly. And integrated into a new big picture. A new paradigm.

So the first question is this: do self-destruct devices really exist? And the answer is a resounding yes. The grandfather of all self-destruct mechanisms is found in every cell. It's called an apoptotic mechanism. Technically known as a pre-programmed cell death mechanism. A suicide device. A poison pill. Built into every cell. Apoptosis is a firecracker string of molecules very much like the traps you probably built for birds when you were a kid. You propped up a box with a stick, put a piece of food on the ground below the box, and waited for a bird to come along. If a feathered flier took your bait, you yanked a string and the box fell down, trapping the poor bird. Apoptotic mechanisms are spring-like molecules held apart by a molecular prop. If the prop is pulled, the cells come together and, poof, you are on your way to death. A self-destruct routine of this sort is pre-programmed into every living cell. Its prop is pulled when the cell receives signals that it is no longer useful to the larger community [Ruoslahti 1997]. Apoptosis was one of the most studied phenomenon in the biology of the late 20th century. A search for apoptosis on Google Scholar brings up over 1,98 million hits. And, surprisingly, apoptosis is the default state of the cell. Just as resting firmly on the ground is the default state of that box you propped up with a stick. Yes, death, not life, is the cell's default state. Self-inflicted death. And that built-in suicide mechanism makes mincemeat out of the theory that we are driven solely by a survival instinct.

You can see apoptosis at work in the development of your fingers. Once upon a time, when you were an embryo, your hand was a clump of tissue like an M&M candy. It had no fingers. So how were fingers carved from this blob of meat, this clumsy ball? Some cells went apoptotic. They killed themselves off, thus making spaces in the blob. The spaces between your fingers. Without those spaces, you'd have a softball-like knob on the end of your arm today. And brushing your teeth or buttoning your shirt would be impossible. So every time you twiddle your thumbs or point to emphasize what you're saying, thank death in life. Thank your pre-programmed cell death mechanisms. Thank apoptosis.

Then there are the ways in which apoptosis carved your brain and shaped what you know as your mind today. When you were born, you had twice as many brain cells – neurons – as you needed. Why? You were equipped for a wide range of possibilities. For example, for the first six months of your life, you were capable of understanding and repeating every sound ever used in every language on earth. But in reality, you only heard one or two languages from your parents and from the others who cared for you. From the people who cradled you, and made a fuss over you. You had cell assemblies ready to understand the click sounds of the Kalahari Kung San and the sing song of the Chinese. But you probably never heard these strange tongues. So the cell assemblies you didn't need did you a favor. They said good-bye and committed suicide. They went apoptotic.

The same sort of thing happened with the facial recognition mechanisms in your fusiform gyrus. Early in life, if you'd been shown pictures of the faces of sheep and chimpanzees, the distinction between the face of one sheep and the face of another would have been as clear to you as the difference between the face of your father and the face of your best friend. The same would have held true for chimps. In your mind, each face would have stood out with a unique individuality. But when you grew up, if you never saw the faces of sheep and chimpanzees, the cell assemblies that could have been superb at facial recognition of other species would have committed suicide so that your brain could focus its energies on differentiating the faces of the sorts of animals and people you actually did grow up with.

Cell assemblies work on a simple rule. If they reach out to other cell assemblies and they receive the chemical equivalent of a hearty welcome, they thrive. If they reach out to other cell assemblies and those others do the chemical equivalent of turning their backs, the rejected cell assemblies die. The identity you call yourself today is made from the cell assemblies that survived. But you owe your uniqueness to cell assemblies that committed suicide.

There is a clan of evolutionary biologists who try to explain away the existence of self-destruct mechanisms. They're called the individual selectionists. These august and talented folks try to give you the impression that their work is part of the Central Dogma of Biology. Basing their arguments on the mathematical work of W. D. Hamilton and Robert Trivers, individual selectionists say that cells kill themselves to enhance the survival of others who carry identical genes. In your body, the genes in all of your cells are the same. Evolution, say the individual selectionists, is driven by the selfish. It's driven by a cousin of the survival mechanism. It's driven by selfish genes.

Explain the individual selectionists, a gene can enhance its survival by killing off the cell in which it lives. Sounds impossible, right? How can a gene possibly advance its selfish interests by doing something altruistic, by doing something self-sacrificial, by doing something that goes against its survival instinct? Here's the answer. With its death, a cell can increase the success rate of identical selfish genes in the cells that are its twins. If cells in your embryonic fist are selfish and refuse to die, you will be born with a hand that looks like a softball. You will never be able to use a tool, much less invent one. But selfless suicide, say the individual selectionists, is really greed in disguise. The cells that kill themselves off to carve out your fingers are upping the odds of survival of the cells that remain. Identical twins. Sister cells. Sisters that carry the same set of genes as the cell that died. And the more those sisters are fruitful and multiply, the more copies of the suicidal cell's genes will march into generations yet to come.

Has the suicide of the cells between fingers worked out? Has it advanced the genetic interests of the cells that died? Has it allowed identical genes to be fruitful and multiply? Today some folks think that human genes dominate the planet. They think human dominance has gone so far that we *homo sapiens* are killing all that's good, green, and natural. So the ploy of the genes that killed themselves between your fingers in order to make more copies of themselves has worked. Human genes are all over the place. In part thanks to fingers. In part, thanks to the apoptotic suicide of cells.

That's kin selection – making moves that increase the number of your genes in generations yet to come. Favoring your identical twins. But does the apoptotic mechanism come into play when the genes of your friends, your work mates, or your platoon mates are not at all identical to yours? Or, to put it differently, do apoptotic self-destruct mechanisms show up on more complex levels of life? You bet.

In 1945 the Japanese had been fighting American soldiers for six years. They had known they could not lose. Their gods [Reischauer 1981] had made them a superior people. They had swept through China and the Pacific Islands in the 1930s like an avenging wind, taking vast territories, conquering hordes of "inferior" peoples, showing the heaven-given supremacy of their race. The enemy who faced them was a contemptible lot – unblessed by the divinity that buoyed Japan, and crippled by racial impurity.

Yet the mongrels from the West were accomplishing the unthinkable. They were beating the warriors of Japan. By the time the Americans reached Okinawa, the Japanese could see that heaven had deserted them. The shame was unendurable. Four thousand Japanese killed themselves in Okinawa's underground naval headquarters. Another 30,000 military men and civilians threw themselves from a nearby cliff [Toland 1970].

On the Japanese homeland, pilots volunteered to keep the American marines in Okinawa from getting supplies. Those flyers were promised honor ... and death. Their mission was to guide their planes to the enemy and stay at the controls as the explosive-laden aircraft slammed into the enemy's ships. "I will be doing my duty by dying", they wrote in final letters to their families. Fifteen thousand of them fulfilled that fatal obligation. One network television commentator, describing the kamikaze experience forty years after the fact, explained that, "Japan is a society of groups, not individuals".

Here's the point. According to the standards used by the individual selectionists, by the selfish gene clique, and by the rational choice crew in economics and the social sciences, the genes of these Japanese were radically different. They did not show the degree of relatedness demanded by Hamilton's and Trivers' mathematics. Or, as the founder of sociobiology, E. O. Wilson says, the concept of kin selection has been appealing. So appealing that Wilson himself was once a believer. But in the end, the math never worked out. It proved itself wrong. So wrong that Wilson abjured it in an article in *Nature* in August of 2010 [Nowak *et al.* 2010] Then Wilson abjured it again at length two years later in his 2012 book *The Social Conquest of Earth* [Wilson 2012].

If our actions are geared to increasing the odds that our personal genes or those of our near relatives will make it into the next generation, what is the reason for suicide's existence?

And what about the other bits of death-in-life built into the human psyche? Why do you and I sometimes feel like crawling off into a corner and dying? There is an answer but it doesn't quite square with the notion of genes fighting for themselves no matter what. We are part of a larger organism and occasionally we find ourselves expendable in its interests.

But we are not just part of any organism. We are part of a collective brain. We are parts of a massively parallel processing intelligence. We are part of a complex adaptive system. We are modules, components in a mass-learning machine. We follow a rule that makes learning machines, from bacterial colonies and beehives to the immune system and brains, work. What's that rule?

It's a rule that you can see at work in two radically different kinds of learning machines: neural networks [Parikh and Pratap 1984] and immune systems [Farmer *et al.* 1987]. Both apply an algorithm – a working rule – best expressed by Jesus of Nazareth: "To he who hath it shall be given; from he who hath not even what he hath shall be taken away" [Mark 4:25]. In other words, turn up the flow of resources to the modules that are succeeding in confronting the problems of the moment. Turn down the flow of resources to those that are failing. And turn down something just as important – influence. Turn down the ability of failures to reach out to others and have an impact on their behavior. To he who hath it shall be given. From he who hath not, even what he hath shall be taken away. And, strange as it sounds, that rule is built into you and me. When we feel we are failing, when we feel that no one wants us, we don't fight or flee. We freeze. We go apoptotic. We are seized by something built into our biology. We are seized by self-destruct mechanisms.

Neural nets are hordes of individual electronic switch points wired in a complex mesh. They are used today for character recognition, image compression, stock market prediction, medicine, security, loan applications, football predictions, self-driving cars, and to read the minds of rats, chimps, and humans so that a paraplegic can someday have prosthetics that understand her thoughts and move when she wants them to [Roberts 2000]. Or so that your smart phone can someday read your mind and do what you want it to without forcing you to clumsily root through your pocket and peck away at icons and keys. The network linking the switches of a neural net together has an unusual property. It can beef up or turn down the number of connections and the amount of energy channeled to any switch points in the grid. It can turn some nodes into isolated paupers and some into big time winners. It can sideline the nodes that don't contribute to solving the problem of the moment and it can make the nodes that have a handle on things the equivalent of rich and famous. A neural net applies a rough equivalent of a self-destruct mechanism to some of its citizens. Why? In order to solve problems. In order to do a machine equivalent of thinking.

An immune system is a team of free agents on a far, far grander scale. It contains between ten million and ten billion different antibody types. Both the immune system and the neural net follow the Biblical rule, the self-destruct rule. Agents that seem able to contribute successfully to the solution of a problem are snowed with resources and influence. But woe be unto those unable to assist the group. You can see the principles of self-destruct and self-denial at work in a flood of entities known as "individual virus-specific T cells". In your immune system, T cells on patrol encounter the molecular signs of an invader [Chmielowski *et al.* 1998]. Each T cell is armed with a different arrangement of receptors – molecular grappling hooks. A few of your T cells discover that their weaponry allows them to snag and disable the attackers. These champions are allowed to reproduce with explosive speed, and are given the raw material they need to increase their clones dramatically [Welte *et al.* 1999; Matzinger 1998]. But T-cells whose receptors can't get a grip on the invaders go through the opposite experience. They are robbed of food, of the ability to multiply, and often of life itself. Each is subject to destruction from within via apoptosis' pre-programmed-cellular suicide [Vespa *et al.* 1999]. Most are merely left to languish in an impoverished state. After all, their grappling hooks might be needed to cope with a virus on some other day. But each runs the risk of being deemed unnecessary and having the plug pulled by its self-destruct mechanisms.

Then there's influence. In the computerized neural net, nodes whose guesswork contributes to the solution of a problem are rewarded with more electrical energy and with connections to a far-flung skein of switch points they can recruit to their cause [McClelland and Rumelhart 1986]. The nodes whose efforts prove useless are fed less electrical juice, and their ability to recruit connections from others is dramatically reduced. In fact, their failure drives connections away. Successful nodes put out the equivalent of attraction cues. But nodes that aren't needed put out the equivalent of repulsion cues. Just like you and I do when we're depressed. That's the self-destruct mechanism at work in electronic gadgetry.

Both T cells and neural network nodes compete for the right to commandeer the resources of the system in which they abide. And both show a seeming "willingness" to live by the rules that dictate self-denial. This combination of competition and selflessness turns an agglomeration of electronic or biological components into a learning machine with a puzzle-solving power vastly beyond that of any individual module. It makes a society smart. It powers a collective intelligence, a group IQ.

The same *modus operandi* is built into the biological fabric of most social beings. Which means it is built into you and me. But for clues to the self-destruct mechanisms in your psyche and mine, let's go to the world of our not-so-distant relatives – rats. And let's dive into evidence from the phenomenon that its discoverers call "learned helplessness" [Seligman 1985]. In 1968, Rockefeller University's Jay Weiss [Weiss 1968] hooked the tails of 192 rats to a live electric wire. He gave some of the rodents a control switch, but left the others to simply grin and bear the pain. When a jolt of electricity struck, the unsuspecting rodents would at first scurry and jump to find a quick way out. The luckier of the beasts would soon discover their control buttons. When the current sizzled their sterns, they would lunge for the switch and turn it off, rescuing both themselves and their switchless fellow sufferers. Remember, both the rats with control and those without it were hooked to the same live wire. Both were jolted with shocks at the very same time. And both were saved when the rat with the switch cut the juice. Yet some of the rats whose frantic searches resulted in no discovery of a means of control would eventually give up their struggle, lie down on the cage floor, and accept their shocks with an air of resignation. Even worse, the rats without the control levers would end up physical wrecks – scrawny, unkempt, and ulcerated – while those who could slam the current off stayed reasonably plump and fit. All this despite the fact that each and every rat received exactly the same surge of current for exactly the same amount of time and at exactly the same instant. Rats with control stayed relatively active. Rats with no control over their fate became as passive as Livingstone in the jaws of the lion. And their ulcers and sores were signs of something deeply biological that hits those with no control – self-destruct mechanisms.

As "learned helplessness" experiments continued, it was discovered that more than mere laziness crippled the beasts who couldn't find a way to abort their punishment. Their immune systems no longer protected them from disease. If given a way to escape their situation, their perceptions were too bleary to notice something as simple as an open door, a clear way out. If you put dogs in a shock cage, a cage with an electrified floor, at first the dogs jumped and scurried when the electricity was turned on. Then 20% of them became lethargic, lay on the electrified floor, and simply took the punishment. And here's the strangest part. When the cage door was opened and the escape route was staring them in the face, the dogs afflicted with learned helplessness did not take the hint and bolt or amble out the door. They continued to lie there and suffer every shock. Their self-destruct mechanisms had taken control. Among other things, their immune systems nosedived. The result was just what it had been in rats: sores, ulcers, and other physical afflictions. Afflictions produced by the dogs' own bodies.

All indications are that the self-maiming reflexes of learned helplessness are physiologically pre-programmed. They are the very opposite of survival mechanisms. They are self-destruct mechanisms.

At the base of learned helplessness is an endogenous chemical, a chemical the body cranks out automatically – Substance P. Substance P is a self-disabling chemical. It is the very opposite of a survival hormone.

Again, the experimental animals that were given a control button had a handle on the situation. Literally. They were NOT hit with learned helplessness. They retained a vigorous immune system, a relatively keen perception of the world around them, and remained energetic – despite the periodic spurts of abuse.

The rats and dogs without control switches were sabotaged by their own bodies, poisoned by their own stress hormones. How could this internally-inflicted damage aid the victims in projecting their precious genes into the next generation? Apparently no one asked. The answer is simple. Individuals only survive so long as the group they are a part of thrives. And individuals are equipped with self-destruct mechanisms to contribute to a group IQ.

Give health, food, and influence to the group members who have a grip on things, and they can lead you out of the wilderness. Give your attention to those who haven't got a clue, and your society will be clueless too.

In other words, your body is set up to enact the primary learning machine rule – to he who hath it shall be given; to he who hath not even what he hath shall be taken away. Your body, like the bodies of rats and dogs, is programmed to weaken your health and dim your insights. Your body is set up to take things away from itself. It is set up to become puritanical – to deny itself. It is programmed to measure your circumstances, and to sometimes shun the use of "material things". Your body and mine have self-destruct mechanisms. Apoptotic mechanisms. Learned helplessness mechanisms. And those mechanisms make us a part of a collective intelligence.

2. Massively Parallel Processed Intelligence – A Bit More Biological Evidence

A collective intelligence? You've got to be kidding me. How could apoptosis make a society of animals or a gaggle of humans smart? How could it produce a group IQ? How could it allow one society to outsmart others in the constant competition between groups?

Part of the answer is in our very first foremothers, creatures who appeared on this planet a mere billion years after the planet's formation, the bacteria of 3.5 billion years ago. From the very beginning, we living things have been yanked together by the tug of sociality. Three-and-a-half billion years ago, our cellular ancestors, bacteria, did not evolve as selfish loners. They evolved as groups, as mobs, as communities. They evolved in colonies.

For generations bacteria have been thought of as lone cells, each making its own way through the treacherous world of microbeasts. This is a misimpression, to say the very least. The work of The University of Chicago's James A. Shapiro and the University of Tel Aviv's Eshel Ben-Jacob has shown that bacteria are social to the nth degree [Shapiro 1998; Ben-Jacob 1998]. A bacterium 3,5 billion years ago or today can't live without the comfort of rubbing against its neighbors. For example, two myxobacteria must be in body contact before either is "motivated" to go about its business. In fact, if you are a bacterium, making body contact with as many other bacteria as possible is more important to you than sidling up to a food source. More important, if you are separated from your companions, you will rapidly divide to create a new society filled with fresh companions you can chummily rub against [Chang and Dworkin 1994]. You will divide to produce a highly populous society.

A bacterial colony the size of your palm contains seven trillion individuals. Yes, seven trillion. That is true of bacteria today. And it was true 3,5 billion years ago. The result? 3,5 billion years ago when our bacterial foremothers first arose, each colony of a trillion-plus faced warfare, disaster, the hunt for food, and windfalls of plenty. But bacteria did not face these traps and opportunities as a scatter of individuals. They mined the material around them and avoided catastrophes as a collective intelligence, a group IQ, a massively parallel processing network, a social brain.

What's the evidence for this collective intelligence? Roughly 3,5 billion years ago [Marshall 1997] the first bacterial colonies began to make indelible marks upon the face of the early seas. And those marks bore the clues to collective problem solving. The bacterial monuments I'm talking about are called stromatolites. They are mineral deposits in the shallows of tropical lakes and of the ocean's intertidal pools, deposits with their roots in the bottom of the shallows and their heads extending above the surface of the water, deposits ranging from a mere centimeter across to the size of a mattress [Golubic *et al.* 2000]. Stromatolites were manufactured by societies of cyanobacteria, [Xiao *et al.* 1998] organisms so internally crude that they had not yet gathered their DNA into a nucleus. But in their first eons of existence, these primitive cells had already mastered one of the primary tricks of society: the division of labor [Shapiro 1998]. Some colony members specialized in photosynthesis, [de Duve 1996] storing the energy of sunlight in ornately complex molecules of ATP. The sun-powered assemblers took in nutrients from their surroundings and deposited the unusable residue in potentially poisonous wastes. Their vastly different bacterial sisters, on the other hand, feasted on the toxic garbage [Shapiro 2000] that could have turned their photosynthetic siblings into paste.

The mass of these interdependent beings were housed in an overarching shelter of their own construction. As cyanobacterial [Legroux and Magrou 1920] founders multiplied, they formed a circular settlement. The waters within which the homestead was established washed a layer of clay and soil over the encampment. Some of the bacteria sent out filaments to bind these carbonate sediments in place. Tier by tier, the colony created its infrastructure, a six-or-seven-foot-long, sausage-shaped edifice as large compared to the workers who had crafted it as Australia would be to a solitary child with a pail and a sand shovel.

Another capacity of the colony outshone even its architecture. Evidence indicates that each bacterial megalopolis possessed a staggeringly high collective IQ. The clue is in a pattern extremely familiar to those few scientists who study the intelligence of microbial societies. The fossil remains of stromatolites spread like ripples from a common center – the key to a game plan of exploration and feeding that would persist for the next 3,5 billion years, even among higher species. Technically it's called a fission fusion strategy. But for convenience, let's call it the strategy of spread out and explore, then settle down and feast. A strategy still alive today in human patterns of boom and bust. But boom and bust is a story for another time.

A bacterial spore lands on an area rich in food. Using the nutrients into which it has fallen, it reproduces at a dizzying pace [Sturdza 1975]. But eventually the initial food patch which gave it its start runs dry. Stricken by famine, the individual bacteria, which by now may number in the millions, do not, like the citizens of Athens during the plague of 430 B.C. [Thucydides 1996], merely lay down and die. Instead these prokaryotes embark on a joint effort aimed at keeping their colony alive.

The first progeny of a colony's spores were shaped as digesters – creatures built to feed on the chow around them and steadfastly stay in place. They were homesteaders. Being rooted to the spot made sense when your microbit of turf was overflowing with treats. But when food ran low, sitting still and swallowing fast was no longer a winning strategy. Out of hunger or sheer restlessness [Esipov and Shapiro 1998], the bacterial cells now faced with scarcity switched gears [Driks *et al.* 1990]. Rather than reproducing homesteaders like themselves, they marshaled their remaining resources to generate daughters of a different kind [Allison and Hughes 1991] – rambunctious rovers [Harshey 1994] built to spread out in a search for new frontiers [Rauprich *et al.* 1996]. Members of this restless generation sported an array of external whips [Moens *et al.* 1995] with which they could snake their way across a hard surface or twirl through water and slime. These adventurous daughters gathered in cohorts of ten thousand, then left [Allison and Hughes 1991] in mass migrations to seek their fortune, expanding outward [Budrene and Berg 1995] from the base established by their ancestors. When their travels brought them to new lands of milk and honey, they issued the signal to change ways and put down solid roots again. The successful explorers produced whipless daughters equipped to hunker down and mine the riches of just one spot just as their grandparents had done [Smit and Agabian 1982]. These stolid homesteaders dug into the banquet discovered by their parental kin. But when the homestead's food ran low, wanderlust again set in. The rooted homesteaders sent forth new daughters whose whips propelled them on another expedition into the great unknown.

Each generation of explorers left few traces in the wilderness that it raced across to get to the next bonanza [Brenner *et al.* 1998]. Only when it found a land of plenty did it stay in place, forming a visible ring, a dark circle made by crowd-power, made by the mobs that put down roots to suck the riches from a new virgin home. Modern bacteria still shift from explorers to homesteaders and back to explorers again. In the process, they leave ripples of concentric circles clear as a dartboard's rings.

Ripples of exactly this type appear in the ancient stromatolites – an indication that bacteria three and a half billion years ago used the intricate social system of alternating explore and feast. Evidence that ancient bacteria used the fission fusion search strategy. Clues that a collective discovery mechanism was at work. A collective information processing strategy. A group IQ.

Where does apoptosis fit into the picture? How did self-destruct mechanisms make the bacterial mega-communities of 3,5 billion years ago smart? How did pre-programmed cell death turn a colony of over a trillion bacteria into a mass mind, a parallel processing intelligence, a collective brain? There was no "each woman for herself" in those deep, dark, early days a mere billion years after the birth of our planet. To the contrary. Modern research hints that primordial communities of bacteria were elaborately interwoven by communication links [Allison *et al.* 1993]. Their signaling devices were

- chemical [Salmond *et al.* 1995] outpourings with which one individual transmitted its findings to all in its vicinity [Muñoz-Dorado and Arias 1995],
- fragments of genetic material drifting from one end to the other of the community,
- and a variety of other devices for long-distance data broadcasting, including "collective vibrational modes" that one pair of researchers called singing [Norris and Hyland 1997].

These turned a colony into a collective processor [Gray 1997] for sensing danger, for feeling out the environment [Gray 1997], and for inventing radical adaptations to survive and prosper. The resulting learning machine was so ingenious that Eshel Ben Jacob has called its modern bacterial counterpart a "creative web" [Ben-Jacob 1998].

Evolutionary ethologist Valerius Geist says that all signals in animals and humans boil down to two things – attraction cues and repulsion cues. And attraction and repulsion cues were one key to bacterial brainpower. The other was the self-destruct mechanism of apoptosis – programmed cell death. When famine struck, some of the troops of ten thousand found food. And some did not. Instead, their trail led to territory as barren as that from which they'd fled. But the failed expeditions did not suffer their fate in silence. They neatly folded up their DNA in a package that said "do not go here, do not follow where I have gone." A package that the folks back home and fellow teams of wanderers read as a clear repulsion cue. Then the failed bacterial explorers killed themselves. They committed mass suicide, just like the 30,000 Japanese on Okinawa who walked off a cliff when American troops reached their island. The bacteria underwent apoptosis. And here's the trick. These bacterias' self-destruct mechanisms turned ten thousand failed explorers into a sensory tentacle with which the larger group felt out its *terra incognita* [Ben-Jacob *et al.* 1994]. Self-destruct mechanisms did not act as survival mechanisms for the individual. But they DID contribute to the survival of something larger: the colony.

The death of the unsuccessful served its purpose – adding survey reports to an expanding knowledge-base. Adding to a group IQ.

Other bacterial cells encountered turbulent conditions whose menace destroyed them utterly. But they, too, managed to ship back information about their fate. The chaotic fragments of their shredded genomes sent a message of danger to the colony back home. Then there were the voyagers whose trek took them to a new promised land. These sent out a chemical bulletin of an entirely different kind. Loosely translated, it meant, "Eureka, we've found it. Join us quickly and let's thrive. Ain't it grand to be alive."

If the colony's strategy of spread out and seek, of discover and feast, proved useless, and none of the groups of ten thousand explorers found anything to eat, if all they found was barren emptiness, the messages sent back to the center did not unleash new waves of emigrants. It triggered something very different. The incoming communiqués provided raw data for genetic research and development. Informationally-linked microorganisms [Holland 1995] possessed a skill exceeding the capacities of any massively parallel processing supercomputer from Cray Research or Fujitsu [Silicon Graphics 1999; Aoki 2013]. In a crisis, bacteria did not rely on deliverance via a random process like mutation [Kiely 1990], but instead unleashed their genius as genetic engineers [Shapiro 1997]. For bacteria were the first to use the tools that now empower biotechnology's genetic tinkerers: plasmids, vectors, phages, and transposons – nature's gene snippers, duplicators, long-distance movers, welders, and reshufflers. Overcoming disaster sometimes involved plugging in prefabricated twists of DNA and reverting to ancestral strategies. When tricks like this didn't work and the stakes were life or death, the millions – and often trillions – of bacteria in a colony used their individual genomes, says Eshel Ben-Jacob, as individual computational devices, meshing them together, combining their data, and forming a group intelligence capable of literally reprogramming their species' shared genetic legacy in ways previously untried and previously unknown [Ben-Jacob 1998].

The microbial global brain – gifted with long-range transport, data trading, genetic variants from which to pluck fresh secrets, and the ability to reinvent genomes – began its operations some 91 trillion bacterial generations before the birth of the Internet. Ancient bacteria, if they functioned like those today, mastered the art of worldwide information exchange [Sonea and Panisset 1983; Margulis and Sagan 1986]. They swapped snippets of genetic material like humans trading computer programs [Mazel *et al.* 1998]. And those snippets could be carried thousands of miles by the currents of the sea and by the whufflings of the wind. This system of molecular gossip allowed microorganisms to telegraph an improvement from the seas of today's Australia to the shallow waters covering the midwest of today's North America. The nature and speed of communication was probably intense. At least eleven different bacterial species [Schopf 1993] apparently exchanged trade secrets by three billion B.C.

And self-destruct mechanisms, the mechanisms that make a bacterium or you and me broadcast repulsion cues – played a vital role in this social intelligence. So did the ultimate self-destruct mechanism, cell suicide, apoptosis.

One more little detail on how your self-destruct mechanisms can threaten your personal survival but boost the IQ of the group. Bacterial colonies do not merely contend with the slings and arrows of an outrageous environment to survive. They contend with armies of others. Yes, our bacterial foremothers invented war. Industrialism, patriarchy, and capitalism had nothing to do with it. When there's a rich food source in the ocean, as many as seven bacterial colonies will compete for it. And that competition can turn nasty. If the struggle becomes violent, bacterial colonies will blast each other with weapons of mass destruction.

Chemical weapons. The weapons we borrowed from microorganisms between 1928 and the mid-1940s. The bacterial weapons we call antibiotics.

In war, the smartest armies tend to win. And the least smart can be exterminated utterly. So it pays to live in a smart colony. Even if the price of smarts is depression, paralyzing anxiety attacks, and the occasional thought of suicide.

The conclusions? Rational choice models don't work. Just look at Irving Fisher's failure to predict the Great Depression. And individual selection, kin selection and the theory of the selfish gene don't work either. Despite their considerable brilliance. We need a new paradigm. One that explains depression, brain freeze, and suicide. And we've got it. A society is a learning machine. So is an economy. That's why we have self-destruct mechanisms.

In other words, a social group is a collective brain. A group IQ. And an entire planet of social groups – from groups of bacteria to battling civilizations – is a cerebral cortex. A planet of competing and cooperating social groups is a global brain.

One last conclusion: nature may have built us to self-destruct when we're not useful to others. But nature has also built us to defy and reinvent her. And one of our biggest jobs as individuals is to defy our self-destruct mechanisms, to find new ways to help our fellow humans, and to push our minds and emotions to clarity no matter how much we may suffer. Our task is to turn every defeat into a victory. Our job is to mine the riches even in distress. Our job is to overcome our biological mechanisms of death-in-life, our apoptotic mechanisms. And to learn from them.

References

Allison, C., and Hughes, C. (1991). Bacterial swarming: an example of prokaryotic differentiation and multicellular behavior, *Science Progress*, 75: 298 Pt. 3-4, 403-422.C

Allison, C., Lai, H.C., Gygi, D., and Hughes, C. (1993). Cell differentiation of Proteus mirabilis is initiated by glutamine, a specific chemoattractant for swarming cells, *Molecular Microbiology*, 53-60

Allman, W. F. (1986). Mindworks. *Science, 86*, 23-31

Aoki, T. (2013). Getting the Best Performance From Massively Parallel Computer, Fujitsu

Ball, P. (1999). The Self-Made Tapestry: Pattern formation in nature. Oxford University Press, USA

Beasley, W.G. (1972). *The Meiji Restoration*, Stanford University Press, California, USA

Ben-Jacob, E. (1993). From Snowflake Formation to the Growth of Bacterial Colonies. Part I. Diffusive Patterning in Azoic Systems, *Contemporary Physics*, 34, 247ff.

Ben-Jacob, E., Tenenbaum, A., Shochet, O., Cohen, I., Czirók, A., and Vicsek, T. (1994). Communication, Regulation and Control During Complex Patterning of Bacterial Colonies, *Fractals*, Vol. 2:1, 14-44

Ben-Jacob, E., Tenenbaum, A., Shochet, O., Cohen, I., Czirók, A., and Vicsek, T. (1994). Generic Modeling of Cooperative Growth Patterns in Bacterial Colonies, *Nature*, 368, 46-49

Ben-Jacob, E., Tenenbaum, A., Shochet, O., Cohen, I., Czirók, A., and Vicsek, T. (1995). Cooperative Formation of Chiral Patterns During Growth of Bacterial Colonies, *Physical Review Letters*, 75, 1226-1229

Ben-Jacob, E. (1996a). Personal communication, April 23, 1996

Ben-Jacob, E. (1996b). Personal Communication. May 9, 1996

Ben-Jacob, E. (1997). From Snowflake Formation to the Growth of Bacterial Colonies. Part II. Cooperative formation of complex colonial patterns, *Contemporary Physics*, 38, 205-241

Ben-Jacob, E. (1998). Bacterial wisdom, Godel's theorem and creative genomic webs, *Physica A*, 248, 57-76

Bernstein, C., and Bernstein, H. (1997). Sexual communication, *Journal of Theoretical Biology*, September, 69-78

Bible, Mark 4:25.B.Y.

Brenner, M. P., Levitov, L. S., and Budrene, E. O. (1998). Physical mechanisms for chemotactic pattern formation by bacteria, *Biophysical Journal*, 1677-1693

Budrene, E. O., and Berg, H. C. (1995). Dynamics of formation of symmetrical patterns by chemotactic bacteria, *Nature*, July 1995, 49-53

Chang, B. Y., and Dworkin, M. (1994). Isolated fibrils rescue cohesion and development in the Dsp mutant of Myxococcus xanthus, *Journal of Bacteriology*, December 1994, 7190-7196

Chmielowski, B., Muranski, P., and Ignatowicz, L. (1998). In the Normal Repertoire of CD4+ T Cells, a Single Class II MHC/Peptide Complex Positively Selects TCRs with Various Antigen Specificities, *The Journal of Immunology*, 162, 95-105

Clark, N. D. L. (1999). Stromatolite, Hunterian Museum, Glasgow: University of Glasgow.   http://www.gla.ac.uk/Museum/HuntMus/earth/strom.html   [accessed January 1999]

de Duve, C. (1996). The Birth of Complex Cells, *Scientific American*, April 1996, 52

DeLong, E. (1998). Archaeal Means and Extremes, *Science*, April 24, 542-543

Douglas, C. W., and Bisset, K. A. (1976). Development of concentric zones in the Proteus swarm colony, *Journal of Medical Microbiology*, November, 497-500

Driks, A., Schoenlein, P. V., DeRosier, D. J., Shapiro, L., and Ely, B. (1990). A *Caulobacter* gene involved in polar morphogenesis, *Journal of Bacteriology*, April, 2113-2123

"Early Life on Earth: Stromatolites." Afton, MN: Worldwide Museum of Natural History. http://www.wmnh.com/wmel0000.htm, downloaded from the World Wide Web January 1999

Esipov, S., and Shapiro, J. A. (1998). Kinetic model of Proteus mirabilis swarm colony development, *Journal of Mathematical Biology*, 36, 249-263

Farmer, D., Lapedes, A., Packard N., and Wendroff, B. eds. (1985). *Evolution, Games and Learning: Models for Adaptation in Machines and Nature.* Proceedings of the Fifth Annual International Conference of the Center for Nonlinear Studies, Los Alamos, NM 87545, USA, North Holland Physics Publishing, Amsterdam

Farmer, J. D., Kauffman, S. A., Packard, N. H., and Perelson, A. S. (1987). Adaptive Dynamic Networks as Models for the Immune System and Autocatalytic Sets, In Koslow, S. H., Mandell, A. J., and Shlesinger, M. F. (eds.) *Perspectives in Biological Dynamics and Theoretical Medicine*, New York Academy of Sciences, New York, 118-131

Fujitsu. The Fujitsu Limited Home Page, http://www.fujitsu.co.jp/index-e.html [accessed February 1999]

Goleman, D. (1985). Vital Lies, Simple Truths: The Psychology of Self-Deception. Simon and Schuster, New York

Golubic, S., Seong-Joo, L., and Browne, K. M. (2000). Cyanobacteria: architects of sedimentary structures. In Riding, R., and Awramik, S. M. (eds.) *Microbial Sediments*, Springer, Berlin, 57-67

Gray., K. M. (1997). Intercellular communication and group behavior in bacteria, *Trends in Microbiology*, May 1997, 184-188

Grotzinger, J. P., and Rothman, D. H. (1996). An abiotic model for stromatolite morphogenesis, *Nature*, October 3, 423-425

Harshey, R. M. (1994). Bees aren't the only ones: swarming in gram-negative bacteria, *Molecular Microbiology*, May 1994, 389-394

Holland, J. H. (1995). *Hidden Order: How Adaptation Builds Complexity.* New York: Addison-Wesley, 31

Hopfield, J. J. (1982). Neural networks and physical systems with emergent collective computational abilities, *Proceedings of the National Academy of Sciences of the United States of America*, April 1982, 2554-2558

Hopfield, J. (1988). personal communication, November, 1988

Hussain, N. H., Goodson, M., and Rowbury, R. J. (1998). Recent advances in biology: intercellular communication and quorum sensing in micro-organisms, *Science Progress*, 81, 1998 (Pt 1), 69-80

Kiely, T. (1990). Rethinking Darwin, *Technology Review*, May/June 1990, 19-20

Koch, A. L. (1988). Speculations on the growth strategy of prosthecate bacteria. *Canadian Journal of Microbiology*, April 1988, 390-394

Legroux, R., and Magrou, J. (1920). État organisé des colonies bactériennes. *Annales de l'Institut Pasteur*, 34, 417-432

Lipkin, R. (1995a). Bacterial Chatter: How patterns reveal clues about bacteria's chemical communication, *Science News*, March 4, 1995, 137

Lipkin, R. (1995b). Stressed bacteria spawn elegant colonies, *Science News*, September 9, 1995, 167

Livingstone, D. (1860). *Missionary Travels And Researches In South Africa*. Harper & Brothers, New York, 12

Margulis, L., and Sagan, D. (1986). *Microcosmos: Four Billion Years of Microbial Evolution*, Summit Books, New York

Marshall, C.R., and Schopf, J.W. (1996). *Evolution and Molecular Revolution*, Sudbury, MA: Jones & Bartlett

Marshall, C. R. (1997). The Center for the Study of Evolution and the Origin of Life at UCLA, personal communication January 31, 1997

Matzinger, P. "The Real Function of the Immune System or Tolerance and the Four D's (danger, death, destruction and distress)." http://kcampbell.bio.umb.edu/MamTox/Presentations/Session11/polly.html [accessed 22 November 2015]

Mazel, D., Dychinco, B., Webb, V. A., and Davies, J. (1998). A Distinctive Class of Integron in the Vibrio cholerae Genome, *Science*, 605–608

McClelland, J. L., Rumelhart, D. E., and the PDP Research Group (1986). Parallel Distributed Processing: Explorations in the Microstructure of Cognition Volume 2: Psychological and Biological Models. The MIT Press, Cambridge, MA

Miller, W. R., and Seligman, M. E. (1975). Depression and learned helplessness in man. *Journal of Abnormal Psychology*, June, 228-238

Mitchell, D., and Smit, J. J. (1990). Identification of genes affecting production of the adhesion organelle of Caulobacter crescentus CB2, *Bacteriology*, 5425-5431

Miller, W. R., Rosellini, R. A., and Seligman, M. E. P. (1985). Learned Helplessness and Depression, In J.C. Coyne (ed.) *Essential Papers on Depression*, New York University Press, New York

Moens, S., Michiels, K., Keijers, V., Van Leuven, F., and Vanderleyden, J. (1995). Cloning, sequencing, and phenotypic analysis of laf1, encoding the flagellin of the lateral flagella of Azospirillum brasilense Sp7, *Journal of Bacteriology*, October 1995, 5419-5426

Muñoz-Dorado, J., and Arias, J. M. (1995). The social behavior of myxobacteria, *Microbiologia*, 429-438

Norris, V., and Hyland, G. J. (1997). Do bacteria sing? Sonic intercellular communication between bacteria may reflect electromagnetic intracellular communication involving coherent collective vibrational modes that could integrate enzyme activities and gene expression, *Molecular Microbiology*, 879-880

Nowak, M. A., Tarnita, C. E., and Wilson, E. O. (2010). The Evolution of Eusociality, *Nature*, 466(26)

Ong, C. J., Wong, M. L., and Smit, J. (1990). Attachment of the adhesive holdfast organelle to the cellular stalk of Caulobacter crescentus, *Journal of Bacteriology*, 1448-1456

Parikh, J. C., and Pratap, B. (1984). An evolutionary model of a neural network, *Journal of Theoretical Biology*, 31–38

Pennisi, E. (1988). Of Great God Cybernetics And His Fair Haired Child, *The Scientist*, 5, 23

Pennisi, E. (1996). Teetering on the Brink of Danger, *Science*, 1665-1667

Pennisi, E. (1998). Versatile Gene Uptake System Found in Cholera Bacterium, *Science*, April 24, 521-522

Rauprich, O., Matsushita, M., Weijer, C. J., Siegert, F., Esipov, S. E., and Shapiro, J. A. (1996). Periodic phenomena in Proteus mirabilis swarm colony development, *Journal of Bacteriology*, November 1996, 6525-6538

Reischauer, E. O. (1981). *The Japanese*, The Belknap Press of Harvard University Press, Cambridge, Massachusetts, 217-219

Ridge, J. P., Fuchs, E. J., and Polly Matzinger (1996). Neonatal Tolerance Revisited: Turning on Newborn T Cells with Dendritic Cells, *Science*, 1723–1726

Roberts, E. (2000). *Neural Networks, Other applications of neural networks*, http://cs.stanford.edu/people/eroberts/courses/soco/projects/2000-01/neural-networks/Applications/ miscellaneous.html [accessed 22 November 2015]

Rudner, R., Martsinkevich, O., Leung, W., and E. D. Jarvis (1998). Classification and genetic characterization of pattern-forming Bacilli, *Molecular Microbiology*, 687-703

Ruoslahti, E. (1997). Stretching Is Good For A Cell, *Science*, 1345-1346

Salmond, G. P., Bycroft, B. W., Stewart, G. S., and Williams, P. (1995). The bacterial 'enigma': cracking the code of cell-cell communication, *Molecular Microbiology*, 615-624

Seligman, M. E. (1972). Learned Helplessness, *Annual Review of Medicine*, Vol. 23, 407-412

Schneegurt, M. A. (1999). Cyanosite: A Webserver for Cyanobacterial Research, http://www.cyanosite.bio.purdue.edu/images/images.html [accessed September 1999]

Schopf, J. W. (1976). Are the oldest 'fossils', fossils? *Origins of Life and Evolution of the Biosphere*, 19-36

Schopf, J. W., and Klein, C. (eds.) (1992). *Proterozoic Biosphere: A Multidisciplinary Study*. Cambridge University Press, New York

Schopf, J. W. (1993). Microfossils of the Early Archean Apex Chert: New Evidence of the Antiquity of Life, *Science*, April 30, 640-646

Schopf, J. W. (1999a). director of the Center for the Study of Evolution and the Origin of Life at UCLA, home page http://www.igpp.ucla.edu/cseol/schopf.html [accessed 1999]

Schopf, J. W. (1999b). *Cradle of Life: The Discovery of Earth's Earliest Fossils.* University of California Press, Berkeley

Shapiro, J. A. (1992). Natural genetic engineering in evolution, *Genetica*, 86:1-3, 99-111

Shapiro, J. A. (1993). Natural genetic engineering of the bacterial genome, *Current Opinion in Genetics and Development*, December 1993, 845-848

Shapiro, J. A. (1995). The significances of bacterial colony patterns, *Bioessays*, Vol 17 Issue 7

Shapiro, J. A. (1997). Genome organization, natural genetic engineering and adaptive mutation, *Trends in Genetics*, March 1997, 98-104

Shapiro, J. A. (1998). Thinking About Bacterial Populations as Multicellular Organisms, *Annual Reviews in Microbiology*, 52, 81-104

Shapiro, J. A. (1999a). Personal Communication, February 9, 1999

Shapiro, J. A. (1999b). Personal Communication, September 24, 1999

Shimkets, L. J. (1990). Social and developmental biology of the myxobacteria, *Microbiology Reviews*, December 1990, 473-501

Sicard, R. E. (1986). Hormones, neurosecretions, and growth factors as signal molecules for intercellular communication, *Developmental and Comparative Immunology*, Spring 1986, 269-72

Silicon Graphics. The Silicon Graphics Cray supercomputers Web site. http://www.cray.com/ [accessed 1999]

Smit, J., and Agabian, N. (1982). Cell surface patterning and morphogenesis: biogenesis of a periodic surface array during Caulobacter development, *Journal of Cell Biology*, 41-49

Sommer, J. M., and Newton, A. (1989). Turning off flagellum rotation requires the pleiotropic gene pleD: pleA, pleC, and pleD define two morphogenic pathways in *Caulobacter crescentus*, *Journal of Bacteriology*, 392-401

Sonea, S., and Panisset, M. (1986). *A New Bacteriology.* Boston: James and Bartlett.

Sonea, S. (1988). The Global Organism: A New View of Bacteria, *The Sciences*, July/August, 38–45

Sturdza, S. A. (1975). Expansion phenomena of Proteus cultures. I. The swarming expansion, *Zentralblatt fur Bakteriologie* [Orig A], 505-530.

Terrana, B., and Newton, A. (1976). Requirement of a cell division step for stalk formation in Caulobacter crescentus, *Journal of Bacteriology*. 456–462

Thucydides. History of the Peloponnesian War. Translated by Richard Crawley. In Library of the Future, 4th Edition, Ver. 5.0. Irvine, CA: World Library, Inc., 1996. CD-ROM

Toland, J. (1970). The Rising Sun: The Decline and Fall of the Japanese Empire, Random House, New York

Vespa, G. N. R., Lewis, L. A., Kozak, K. R., Moran, M., Nguyen, J. T., Baum, L. G., and Miceli, M. C. (1999). Galectin 1 Specifically Modulates TCR Signals to Enhance TCR Apoptosis but Inhibit IL 2 Production and Proliferation, *Journal of Immunology*, January 15, 1999, 799-806

Weiss, J. M. (1967). Effects of coping behavior on development of gastrointestinal lesions in rats, *Proceedings of the Annual Convention of the American Psychological Association*, 2 1967, 135-136

Weiss, J. M. (1968). Effects of coping responses on stress, *Journal of Comparative and Physiological Psychology*, 65, 251-260

Weiss, J. M. (1968). Effects of predictable and unpredictable shock on development of gastrointestinal lesions in rats, *Proceedings of the Annual Convention of the American Psychological Association*, 3 1968, 263-264

Weiss, J. M. (1971). Effects of coping behavior in different warning signal conditions on stress pathology in rats, *Journal of Comparative & Physiological Psychology*, October 1971, 1-13

Weiss, J. M. (1972). Influence of psychological variables on stress-induced pathology, *Ciba Foundation Symposium*, 8 1972, 253-65

Weiss, J. M. (1972). Psychological factors in stress and disease, *Scientific American*, June 1972, 104-13

Welte, T., Leitenberg, D., Dittel, B. N., al-Ramadi, B. K., Xie, B., Chin, Y. E., Janeway Jr., C. A., Bothwell, A., Bottomly, K., and Fu., X.-Y. (1999). STAT5 Interaction with the T Cell Receptor Complex and Stimulation of T Cell Proliferation, *Science*, 8 Jan 1999, 222-225

Wolfe, A. J., and Berg, H. C. (1989). Migration of bacteria in semisolid agar. *Proceedings of the National Academy of Sciences of the United States of America*, September 1989, 6973-6977

Xiao, S., Zhang, Y., and Knoll, H. (1998). Three-dimensional preservation of algae and animal embryos in a Neoproterozoic phosphorite, *Nature*, 4 February, 553-558

Chapter 10

Distributed Intelligence Technologies:
Present and Future Applications

Francis Heylighen

Global Brain Institute, Vrije Universiteit Brussel,
Brussel, Belgium

This chapter surveys a wide variety of potential applications of *distributed intelligence technologies*. These are systems that tackle complex challenges in a distributed manner, by collecting, processing and routing information and actions that are spread across a global network of human and technological agents. The eventual integration of all these systems is expected to produce a distributed intelligence at the planetary scale, the *Global Brain*. Supporting technologies for such distributed problem solving include Wikipedia, the Semantic Web, the Internet of Things and the Smart Grid. These and future extensions will facilitate the propagation and coordination of information, knowledge, energy, physical objects, actions and personal identity. By extrapolating from existing applications such as social media, data mining, online shopping and MOOCs, it is argued that these technologies can in principle satisfy all our material, health, safety, social, achievement, cognitive, and even self-actualization needs.

1. Introduction

Over the past two decades, the Internet has taken over ever more social, economic and technological functions from other communication systems, and this at an absolutely staggering speed. At the same time, it has been opening up a seemingly infinite variety of new applications. People use the Internet for applications as diverse as ordering groceries, organizing political rallies, watching movies, financing new inventions, selling second-hand goods, discussing global problems, keeping in touch with family, monitoring buildings remotely, guiding self-driving cars, publishing photos, articles and books, keeping stock in warehouses, distributing intricate calculations across thousands of independent computers, tracking public transport, exchanging scientific information, "crowdsourcing" tasks to anonymous workers, and remotely following courses at prestigious universities. Yet, for every successful new service or application, plenty of equally promising new ventures seem to fail.

This explosion in the number of actual and potential applications of the Internet is overwhelming. The resulting confusion makes it very difficult to discern stable trends – except for a general growth in Internet use. Long-term prediction of these multifarious developments seems especially daunting. Yet, there exists a paradigm that promises to bring some order to this tangle of seemingly chaotic, yet interdependent developments: the *Global Brain* [Bernstein *et al.* 2012; Goertzel 2002; Heylighen 2011; Mayer-Kress and Barczys 1995; Russell 1995].

The Global Brain paradigm conceives the Internet as the nervous system of a *global superorganism*, a planetary system consisting of all humans, their artifacts, and the social, economic and technological links that tie them together [De Rosnay 2000; Heylighen 2007a; Stock 1993]. The idea is that global exchanges have made the people on this planet interdependent to such a degree that together they form a single "living system" [J. G. Miller 1965, 1995]. The function of the nervous system is to coordinate the different activities taking place in the organism. More in particular, a brain needs to gather information about what is going on in and around the system, process the information in order to decide what this means and what should be done about it, and finally initiate appropriate actions to deal with the perceived challenges.

Contemporary science sees societies, organisms and brains as *complex adaptive systems* [Ball 2012; Holland 1992; J. H. Miller and Page 2007]. This means that they consist of a vast number of relatively autonomous agents (such as cells, neurons or individuals) that interact locally via a variety of channels. Together these channels form a complex, dynamic network. Out of these non-linear interactions, some form of coherent, coordinated activity emerges – a phenomenon known as *self-organization* [Camazine *et al.* 2003; Heylighen 2013]. The resulting organization is truly *distributed* over the components of the system: it is not localized, centralized or directed by one or a few agents, but arises out of the interconnections between all the agents.

In the case of the Global Brain (GB), the self-organization of this distributed capacity for information processing is still in the early stages: the global system is far from having settled into a stable, coordinated regime. However, the breakneck speed that characterizes the spread of the Internet clearly exemplifies the accelerating pace of such a process of global coordination [Heylighen 2008, 2016], which is driven by the positive feedback of new applications enabling and inspiring further applications. While such a non-linear process cannot be predicted in any detail, the Global Brain paradigm provides us with a long-term, qualitative view of the most likely outcome: an integrated, intelligent system for processing all the information relevant for the survival and development of the planetary superorganism [Heylighen 2015a].

The present paper will start from this broad view in order to derive a more concrete list of present and future applications of the Internet. The emphasis will be on the distributed character of global information processing, because this is what most fundamentally distinguishes the new paradigm from the older paradigm, which sees political, economic or cognitive organizations as centralized, hierarchical systems. Therefore, we will first investigate what it means for an information-processing system to be distributed. Then, we will examine in more detail some of the specific technologies that will be needed to support a distributed intelligence at the global level. Finally, we will survey how such distributed intelligence can satisfy the basic needs of human individuals. This will give us a more concrete view of some major applications that can be foreseen.

2. Distributed Intelligence

2.1. *From individual to distributed intelligence*

To better understand which kind of applications would be part of a global brain, we need to define *distributed intelligence* [Fischer 2006; Heylighen 2014a]. This will allow us to distinguish technologies that are effectively founded on some form of distributed intelligence from those that merely support traditional functions. For example, a centralized database to which people can get individual access via the Internet to check records is not essentially different from the card catalogs that were used in libraries before the advent of computers. Similarly, using your smartphone to send a photo to a friend is not essentially different from sending a postcard via the mail. These Internet applications are merely more efficient versions of traditional communication media, and will simply continue to become quicker, cheaper and easier to use.

We will define intelligence as "the ability to gather and process information so as to efficiently solve problems and exploit opportunities". What are considered problems, opportunities – or more generally *challenges* [Heylighen 2014a] – will depend on the goals and values of the decision-maker, who can be an individual organism, an organization, or the global superorganism. Efficiently dealing with a challenge means selecting and performing the right actions that solve the problem or exploit the opportunity. It is the process of adequate selection that is the essence of intelligence [Ashby 1956].

Traditional models of intelligence in cognitive science and artificial intelligence see the process of problem solving as a sequential search through a space of potential solutions. The attempts to simulate the neural networks used by our brain, however, led to the notion of parallel, *distributed* processing of information [Bechtel and Abrahamsen 1991; McLeod *et al.* 1998; Rumelhart and McClelland 1986]. The idea is that different units or "neurons" deal simultaneously with different aspects of the problem or question. In other words, the problem is split up into parts or aspects that are processed by several autonomous agents (active units) working in parallel, without central supervision or direction. Their contributions are then reassembled or aggregated into a collective solution.

A fundamental advantage of this approach is flexibility and robustness. The many contributions ensure redundancy of function: individual units may be unavailable, produce erroneous results, or lack relevant data, but the resulting errors tend to be compensated by the signals coming from the other units, so that the aggregate result normally is informative – even in the most confused situations. In a centralized, sequential process, on the other hand, a single malfunction along the line can be sufficient to throw everything off-course, so that no useful result is produced. Another advantage is that the different agents can represent a wide variety of skills, perspectives, or experiences, thus allowing a balanced, integrated approach of the most complex problems.

The same mechanism of compensating for individual ignorance or bias by aggregating a large variety of contributions characterizes successful applications of *collective intelligence* [Heylighen 1999, 2013; Malone *et al.* 2010; Surowiecki 2005]. But in typical social systems, distributed intelligence is more than collective intelligence: contributions do not only come from the people in a collective, but from a variety of artifacts, tools and technologies that sense, register, store, process or transfer information. This is the perspective of *distributed cognition*, originally proposed by the ethnographer Hutchins [Clark 1998; Heylighen *et al.* 2004; Hutchins 2000]. In real-world problem solving, we routinely rely on tools such as pen and paper, maps, cameras, telephones and calculators to gather and process information. We also rely on other people to provide us with their unique observations, skills or ideas. For a complex system – such as a Navy ship [Hutchins and Lintern 1995] – to function well, all the people and artifacts involved need to work together in a *coordinated* manner, by sending the right messages at the right moments to the right destinations.

2.2. *Emergence of distributed intelligence*

In truly complex systems, such distributed coordination is typically the result of *self-organization* [Heylighen 2013], not of central planning. However, self-organization is usually a slow and difficult process that needs to overcome a variety of obstacles, given that it needs to produce global coordination out of local interactions between agents that have only a very limited perspective on the whole. This is where Internet technologies can play a crucial role. They make it in principle possible for any agent (human or artificial) to interact in real-time with any other agent, while keeping a detailed trace of such interactions and their outcomes. This makes it easier to find, select and reinforce the interactions that are most effective in tackling problems, while eliminating the less useful ones [Heylighen 2008; Heylighen *et al.* 2012]. As a result, coordination and distributed intelligence can evolve much more widely, quickly and effectively.

Internet technology not only facilitates globally distributed intelligence, it makes it virtually inevitable. Suppose that there exist two systems that perform at first sight separate functions, independently of each other. Imagine, for example, a medical database keeping track of individuals' disease records, and a cellular phone network, routing calls from one person to another. The Internet makes it possible to connect them together, but why would anybody want to do that? A fundamental reason for interconnection is that the people who use these technologies are themselves interconnected, and so are their problems – simply because they are all members of the same planet-wide society. There is not a single aspect of one person's life that is not potentially relevant for another aspect of another person's life. For example, my medical record may be relevant to your cellular phone record, because I carry a highly contagious disease and your cellular phone use shows that you were in the same place as I was at the same time. Or perhaps the record of our communications shows that we have both closely interacted with the same friend, who may well be the source of the infection.

Imagine that a system is developed to interconnect the two first systems – say, the medical database and the cellular network. Initially, this interconnection may exhibit some shortcomings, like poor protection of privacy, or vulnerability to computer viruses or to hacking. Through trial-and-error (which is the same as variation and natural selection), flawed versions will eventually we replaced by better versions. At that moment, we have an integrated system that is potentially much more powerful than the two initially disconnected systems. In the present example, the interconnection makes it possible to track the spread of infectious agents, and to warn potential carriers of their risk of infection.

The same reasoning extends to all systems that are not interconnected yet: sooner or later an interface will be developed between them, which allows the one system to benefit from the information produced by the other, and vice versa. The principle is simple: because all individuals and systems are part of a coherent global superorganism, every piece of information produced in one part of that superorganism is potentially useful when decisions need to be made in some other part. Without interconnection, this information would remain inaccessible to the other components of the global system. As a result, these other parts would lack some relevant data, and therefore produce suboptimal decisions.

This principle explains why links between systems and components are more likely to be added and reinforced than to be removed. Eventually, all systems will become interconnected, and their pattern of interconnection will become increasingly efficient, maximizing synergies while minimizing conflicts or frictions [Heylighen 2008, 2013, 2016], so that information can take the most direct route from those that produce it to those that need it. That is why there is a continuing trend for all information technologies to merge into one giant distributed intelligence.

2.3. *Aspects of distributed intelligence*

Let us analyze more concretely what is needed for a technology to support distributed intelligence. Intelligent information processing can be decomposed into the following stages:

(1) *input*: collecting a variety of data about phenomena that are potentially relevant for the system (this is the sense of "intelligence" as information gathering).

(2) *processing*: aggregating, filtering and recombining the input information so as to recognize the challenges most important to the system, and developing strategies to deal with those challenges (this is the sense of "intelligence" as interpretation and problem solving).

(3) *output*: sending the derived decisions to the components of the system that are in contact with the outside world, so that they can address the observed challenges.

(4) *feedback*: monitoring the effect of the performed actions, and using this information as new input for a next iteration of the process, so as to correct for mistakes and unforeseen disturbances.

Each of these functions can be performed in principle either in a distributed or in a centralized manner. We will call a technology "distributed" if it performs at least one function in a distributed manner. Let us consider the underlying mechanisms in more detail.

Distributed input means that the information is gathered in parallel by a variety of human and/or artificial agents. For example, the spread of a global epidemic can be tracked by having doctors worldwide enter new cases into a shared database the moment they observe them. Their observations may be complemented by automatic monitors that track e.g. the temperature, heart rate and blood pressure of the hospitalized patients. A simple computer program can analyze these data to show the present dispersal of the disease on a world map, and to establish typical patterns in the disease progression, so that doctors can get an idea in which stages they may have to cope with fever or a possibility of cardiac arrest.

This first processing of the input information, which might happen in a centralized system, can now be combined with a very different type of information, such as the records of phone conversations, flights, or public transport journeys. This requires not only a very different source of input, but also a very different method of processing that will typically be performed on a different system. While the first system computes the static distribution of cases, the second one computes the pattern of movement of people. Their integration in a third system then makes it possible to extrapolate where the next cases of infection are most likely to appear. The final interpretation will moreover rely on a variety of human experts who complement the results of computer algorithms with their intuitions and experience. This illustrates *distributed processing*: different human and/or artificial agents simultaneously work on (different aspects of) a common problem, while pooling their results into an overall solution.

The next stage in our example is distributed output: the prediction of the most likely future outbreaks and what to do about them now needs to be communicated to the agents involved. These will typically be medical personnel in a variety of locations. The distributed system can provide each of them with guidelines, which may be adapted to the individual (e.g. different for doctors and for nurses) and to the local circumstances (e.g. different for countryside and for city locations). These guidelines may include the most likely subjects to carry the germ (e.g. elderly people arriving from Bangkok), the symptoms to look out for, the most likely progression of the disease, and the recommended treatment for each stage of the illness, as based on the experiences up to now of various doctors worldwide. The human guidelines can be complemented by automatic programs downloaded to monitoring equipments that spot typical configurations of symptoms that tend to announce a crisis.

More generally, *distributed output* means that the system sends recommendations on how to act to a variety of human and/or artificial agents in different parts of the world, who then perform the action appropriate for their local situation. Instead of a single centralized decision, various local decisions are made and executed, albeit in a coordinated manner.

The final stage of *distributed feedback* consists of two mechanisms:

(1) correcting for unforeseen (external) disturbances. This requires additional actions to compensate for the deviations created by the disturbances.

(2) correcting for (internal) mistakes in selecting the right actions. This is the process of *learning* in which the information processing system becomes better by adapting its organization according to its experience.

The first mechanism can be implemented simply by feeding the new situation, as affected by the output, back to the input and processing stages. Assuming that all these stages are distributed, feedback will be distributed as well: a variety of input sensors will register the aggregated results of a variety of output effectors as affected by external events. The second mechanism is more subtle, as it requires some degree of "rewiring" of the connections between the distributed components: some links need to become stronger, others weaker. Distribution in this case means that a variety of links are affected by the aggregate effects of a variety of actions. A "neural" mechanism for this is proposed in our mathematical model of the Global Brain [Heylighen *et al.* 2012]: links that produce benefit are reinforced, the others weakened.

Let us illustrate such distributed feedback with the example of the global disease monitoring system. A disturbance could be an outbreak of infections in a location as yet unknown by the system. The counteraction is simply to analyze the data and send the appropriate recommendations for treatment and containment to the agents in that location. Learning in this case means updating the map of disease spread and establishing a direct link between the medical personnel in these locations and the rest of the medical community and system involved in tackling the epidemic.

3. Enabling Technologies

To implement such distributed intelligence systems, we need supporting technologies. These may not be intelligent in themselves, but they provide the infrastructure necessary for an effective distribution and coordination of intelligent activity. Let us survey some basic enabling technologies that either already exist or are being developed.

3.1. *Distribution of information*

The world-wide distribution of information was the original function of the *Internet*: by hooking up to this "network of networks", any computer in any place could in principle send information to any other connected computer in a quick and reliable manner. This was made possible by the TCP/IP protocol for transmitting information between computers [Leiner *et al.* 2009]. This protocol breaks up the message into small packets that each find a route from the sender to the receiver via a number of intermediate computers. If some packets get lost on the way, the sender is warned and immediately resends them, possibly via a different route. Thus, travelling information is distributed across different nodes and routes of the TCP/IP network.

This makes the communication particularly robust, since it will continue to function even if several of the intermediate nodes are unavailable, because of malfunction, overload or any other disturbance. The protocol was designed so that it could survive a nuclear war that would take out the major centers of communication. This decentralized, adaptive design is part of what makes the Internet such a flexible medium for information distribution, allowing programmers to build a variety of more complex systems on top of it, without having to worry about the underlying communication flows.

This infrastructure has been widely available in most developed countries since about the year 2000, but is still spreading into some of the more remote regions. This further spread is facilitated by the explosive development of *wireless* communication protocols, which make it easy to bridge many physical gaps without needing to install cables. More importantly, wireless technologies provide ubiquitous access to information, even while moving around. This enables more interactive applications, such as location-aware navigation or recommendation.

The *World-Wide Web* is a layer of protocols (HTML, HTTP, and URL) built on top of the Internet [Berners-Lee and Fischetti 1999; Heylighen 1994]. It allows a transparent distribution of information storage: webpages on one computer contain hyperlinks to other webpages that can be situated on any computer anywhere in the world. By clicking on the link, the user is "transported" from the one computer to the other, without needing to be aware of the location of the information. Thus, complex networks of linked data can be built that are distributed over a variety of servers. This approach is developed further in *cloud storage* technology, where the distribution is so flexible and efficient that the user cannot even find out anymore exactly where the data are stored. The advantage is transparency and robustness: if a particular server is not available for whatever reason, a copy of the data will be retrieved from another server, without the user having to worry about what is stored where.

3.2. *Distribution of knowledge*

Information is not yet knowledge: available data first need to be processed in order to extract more general and reliable concepts and rules. This is typically done collaboratively by a variety of human experts, supported by ICT. This is the domain in which the worldwide web seems to have made the largest contributions to date, by making accepted knowledge, observations, new ideas, and plausible hypotheses freely available for discussion, analysis and reorganization.

Perhaps the best existing example of a "Global Brain"-like system emerging from such worldwide discussion is *Wikipedia*, the Internet encyclopedia that is being read and written by millions of people [Jemielniak 2014; Kittur and Kraut 2008]. The input is clearly distributed as thousands of people are simultaneously, but independently, editing different Wikipedia articles, in order to extend, update or correct the facts that they contain. This is a very efficient way of harvesting, organizing and publicizing the collective knowledge of humanity. It can be seen as a contemporary implementation of the óld ideal that H. G. Wells called the "World Brain" [Wells 1937; Rayward 1999]. Input not only comes from people, but from a variety of software agents called "bots", which perform various housekeeping tasks, such as correcting formatting errors, adding links and references, and gathering related articles together.

In this case, input and processing cannot really be separated as much of the input consists of reformulation or reformatting of existing material. The output too is distributed as all people with an Internet connection can (and most likely will) consult the material, while being influenced in their actions by what they find there. For example, a person suffering from a disease such as gout will find in Wikipedia a detailed exposition of the most important things known about the causes, outlook, and possible treatments for that disease, while getting suggestions about the kinds of foods or circumstances to avoid (e.g. alcohol, red meat, and cold), but also about the ones that may help mitigate the disease (e.g. coffee, water, and heat). Output also goes to software agents, who e.g. produce statistical analyses, maps and taxonomies starting from the material in Wikipedia.

The *Semantic Web* is an emerging set of protocols to code such knowledge in an explicit format that is understandable and dependable not just for people, but for computer programs [Berners-Lee and Fischetti 1999]. These programs can make non-trivial inferences, thus allowing them to answer questions for which the answer is not written down as such, but derivable via logical inference. For example, while an article about penguins may note that penguins are birds, it is unlikely to also state that they are warm-blooded. A standard "inference engine", on the other hand, should be able to correctly answer the question "Are penguins warm-blooded?" by combining the knowledge that penguins are birds with the knowledge that birds are warm-blooded.

3.3. *Distribution of material objects*

Distributed intelligence not only steers the development of knowledge, but the development of artifacts. Several existing or planned technologies support this function. The success of Wikipedia is due in part to its "open access" or "open source" philosophy, according to which individual or collaborative information products can be freely used and modified by anyone [Heylighen 2007b; Weber 2004]. The advent of *3D printers* makes it possible to extend that philosophy to physical products: a design for a material object (e.g. a bottle opener, a machine component, or a decorative vase) can be published on the Internet, downloaded and if necessary adapted by a person interested to use it, and then "printed" straight into the correct three-dimensional shape so that it is ready to use [Lipson and Kurman 2013]. Even when no 3D printer is available, many designs are made especially so that they are easy to realize with commonly available materials and components. This inspires people across the world to again start making things themselves, instead of buying industrially assembled artifacts, a trend that has been called the "*maker movement*" [Stangler and Maxwell 2012].

The advantage is that objects can be literally made to measure, satisfying the highly specific preferences of each user, while still being much less expensive than purchased goods. Moreover, specialized parts and tools become available in places (like villages in developing countries) where market supply rarely reaches, or is prohibitively expensive. Again, input (all the designs created by people, individually or collaboratively, supported by software), processing (the many variations, improvements and extensions of available designs), and output (the many artifacts built from these designs) are all distributed. The servers that store, list and organize the available designs function here as the medium of coordination between the agents involved.

3.4. *Distribution of energy*

Not just the production of informational and material goods, but the production of energy can be distributed in an intelligent manner. This is the idea behind various projects to build an adaptive electricity network, sometimes called *Enernet*, or *smart grid* [Li *et al.* 2010; Massoud and Wollenberg 2005]. In the traditional approach, electricity is produced in a centralized manner, by a few large power plants running on oil, coal, or nuclear power, and then distributed via a network of electrical cables to millions of consumers. In the new approach, there are potentially millions of producers, since any company or household that owns solar panels, a windmill, watermill, or some other small-scale energy-supplying installation can add the generated electricity to the network.

Physically, this is not a problem, since the same cables can be used to both extract and inject electrical current. The problem is one of coordination: these independent producers will produce variable amounts of energy at variable times (e.g. solar panels only during the day, windmills only when there is wind), independently of the demand from the consumers (e.g. more demand in the evening because of electrical lighting). Therefore, supply will not in general match demand. This means that there is a risk of shortages or overloads at crucial moments, and a general waste of capacity whenever demand is low.

Part of the solution is in providing reservoirs able to store unused energy. But the most important part will be in implementing distributed intelligence. This may gather information from a variety of sensors (e.g. for wind speed, solar strength, temperature…) and sources (e.g. weather forecasts and statistics on energy use) in order to estimate present and future supply and demand. On that basis, the system can decide to power up or power down local energy-producing or energy-consuming installations, or adjust the price of energy according to local demand, so as to most efficiently allocate the load across the grid. The benefits of such a smart grid are obvious: less waste, less need for non-renewable, polluting resources, less risk for blackouts because a particular power plant or high-voltage line is overloaded, and more incentives for ordinary citizens to invest in clean, efficient energy.

3.5. *Distribution of action*

Regulating the movement of energy can be extended to the movement of physical objects. This is the idea behind the *Internet of Things*, an emerging network infrastructure for monitoring and controlling the position and state of objects such as machines, devices, goods, and building materials [Atzori *et al.* 2010; Welbourne *et al.* 2009]. It suffices to equip each object with an RFID tag or other small device that can be wirelessly consulted in order to quickly get an overview of what is located where. This is particularly useful for controlling inventory, logistics and factory assembly lines, an application domain called the *industrial Internet* [Bruner 2013], which is expected to significantly reduce the costs of production and distribution of goods. The implication is that not just people and computers but even simple material things will keep in touch via the network, thus effectively becoming part of the global brain.

Some objects will not only be able to send information about their state or location, but to receive and execute commands that tell them what to do. For example, your home thermostat may receive a message that you are on your way, and start heating so that the temperature would be pleasant by the time you arrive. Similarly, your coffee machine may already prepare an espresso, while the blinds can open in order to let in the sunlight. The different tools in a complex, automated factory may similarly receive continuously updated commands about which items to produce in which quantities, and how best to assemble them, so as to optimally take into account the varying demands of the clients. The produced goods may leave the factory via remotely controlled transport systems, making sure the right goods reach the right clients.

Tools that affect the outside world function as "actuators" or "effectors" for the global superorganism: they convert information (commands received) into physical action. The most sophisticated effectors, which can autonomously move and manipulate objects while using sensory feedback, are commonly called "robotic". Examples are industrial robots, self-driving cars that can be controlled remotely, autonomous submarines that explore oceanic depths, robotic arms that perform operations while being directed by a surgeon, and the drones used by the military for monitoring and attacking enemy forces. Of these technologies, drones in particular appear very promising given that they are relatively easy to build and operate, while having the great advantage that they can move in three dimensions, and thus reach vantage points inaccessible to humans [Krajník *et al.* 2011]. For example, a swarm of -

small flying drones can quickly survey a remote region, e.g. to locate a lost person, detect forest fires, or map the effects of flooding. Such tools make it easy to distribute sensing (input) and acting (output) capabilities across large and complex spaces.

Processing and feedback too can be distributed in this way, by letting the "robots" communicate locally with each other via wireless connections, in order to coordinate their perceptions and actions by means of self-organization [Baldassarre *et al.* 2006]. An additional benefit of such self-organizing swarms of sensors and effectors is that they can produce "ad hoc" communication networks, locally propagating information from agent to agent until it reaches the fixed Internet, from where it can communicate with the rest of the world [Dressler 2008; Elmenreich *et al.* 2009]. Such wireless "mesh" networks [Akyildiz *et al.* 2005] provide improvised, yet robust communication in complex situations, such as war zones, jungles, or crowds of people with mobile phones.

3.6. *Distribution of identity*

Ideally, the global brain should be able to tailor its messages to each individual. For example, in the spreading epidemic scenario, different recommendations should be sent depending on whether the recipient is a doctor-specialist, a nurse, an immigration official, or a (potential) patient. In the case of a patient, the recommendations should ideally take into account the full medical record and health state of that person, so that e.g. the patient would not be suggested to take drugs that interfere with other drugs the person is already taking.

To ensure that such messages do not get to the wrong person, the distributed intelligence system should be certain about the identity of the recipient. At present, this is normally achieved by letting the user login to the system with a user name and password. This is highly inefficient, as users need to type in their data each time again in different systems, while trying to remember dozens of different passwords. Moreover, it is insecure, as people tend to use easily memorable passwords or write them down in lists, so that hackers have little difficulty in guessing or harvesting other people's passwords. This enables the novel crime of *identity theft,* in which person A pretends to be person B, thus being able to exploit person B's property or privileges (e.g. by buying goods with B's credit card details, or by posting offensive messages in B's name).

A key enabling technology for the future global brain will be a universal, secure standard for unambiguously establishing a person's identity. Several, albeit uncoordinated steps have already been made in order to create such a standard, including web-enabled electronic ID-cards in several European countries, the OpenID standard [Recordon and Reed 2006], and ORCID [Evrard *et al.* 2015], an attempt to ensure that publications are attributed to the right author. The reasons why standardization is slow to emerge tend to be social, economic and political rather than technological, as different corporations, governments and organizations are not inclined to exchange the valuable information they hold. An additional obstacle is people's legitimate fear for invasion of privacy and abuse. However, without universal regulation, abuse of private information by hackers, corporations or governments is more rather than less likely, as no one knows who has access to which personal information, and as hardly any laws exist that specify what organizations can and cannot do with the information they possess.

Technologically, it is perfectly possible (albeit non-trivial) to develop secure schemes that anonymize data so that only the ones that really need information about an individual can get access to the specific data they require, and to nothing else. For example, a doctor who finds you collapsed in the street should be able to consult your medical record, and to send a message to your next of kin, but should not have access to your financial record. Your bank, on the other hand, should know the transactions made from your account, but not your state of health.

Next to the technological challenge, the larger challenge will be to institute a system of rules and laws that specify exactly who can use which information about a person. This system should be perfectly transparent to the individual, so that you can find out exactly what happens with your data, and have the right to withhold information that is not crucial to the functioning of an organization. The general principle is that you should be able to act anonymously for any non-crucial transaction, but that the distributed intelligence system should be able to maximally extract the collective (anonymous or non-anonymous) information that will help it to make better decisions, while being able to securely and transparently address a specific individual with personalized recommendations. Once such a computational and legal technology is in place, interactions across the Internet are likely to become much safer and more efficient.

4. Satisfying Needs with DIT

Now that we have a general idea of what distributed intelligence technologies (DIT) are capable of, we need to understand what they are most likely to be used for. Normally, an artifact is adopted because it fulfills some need, i.e. its users can achieve something valuable with the tool that would have been more difficult (or impossible) to achieve without it. For example, a refrigerator makes it easy to store food safely and thus to ensure that fresh food is available whenever needed. Note that we here use "need" in the psychological sense, as something desirable that makes us feel and function better, not in the strictest sense as something without which we would not be able to survive. For example, it is possible to live without sex, without a home, or without friends, but life would be pretty miserable in those circumstances. Therefore, whenever some innovation appears that makes it easier to satisfy a need, people will systematically (though not necessarily universally) tend to adopt that invention.

In the case of distributed technologies, there are in a sense two types of users: the local individuals, and the global system or "super-organism". Given the size and complexity of human society, the super-organism as a whole needs to survive and thrive in order for the individual humans to survive and thrive. Without the sophisticated agricultural, industrial, economic and social infrastructure of modern civilization, our planet might at most sustain a few million human individuals, rather than the billions that it harbors now. Global problems, such as famines, wars, pollution and poverty, can be seen as remaining malfunctions or shortcomings of the superorganism. Their solution will require a better technological and institutional infrastructure and organization, something that the emerging global brain effectively facilitates [Heylighen 2015a, 2016].

Tackling global problems in particular requires *coordination* between all the stakeholders involved in these problems. Coordination [Crowston *et al.* 2006; Heylighen 2013] mediates between humans, artifacts, and the collective systems that they form. It ensures that the different local needs do not come into conflict at higher levels, e.g. like when one person's need for entertainment clashes with his neighbor's need for peace and quiet. It also ensures that individual needs do not oppose global needs, as when local demand for fish undermines the sustainability of global fish stocks. Distributed intelligence can greatly facilitate coordination, via mechanisms such as stigmergy [Heylighen 2007b, 2008, 2015b], challenge propagation [Heylighen 2014a] and offer networks [Goertzel 2015; Heylighen 2016].

As a complement to these existing studies on how DIT can satisfy global and coordination needs, the present paper will focus on the needs of individual people. For this, we can rely on classic psychological theories of motivation, such as Maslow's need hierarchy [Maslow 1970], and on empirical research about the conditions of happiness [Heylighen and Bernheim 2000; Veenhoven 1997]. After a brief definition of each need, we will try to imagine how present or future DIT may satisfy that need in the most efficient manner. This will provide us with a systematic list of likely future applications.

4.1. *Material needs*

Individuals first of all need material resources to survive. These include food, water, and oxygen, but also various raw materials, as well as the tools, clothes, shelters etc. manufactured with them. Extraction of raw materials from the environment is a function that is better addressed at the global level, since virtually no people still gather their own food, wood or wool, while sustainability requires highly coordinated action. However, individuals still need to acquire the right resources at the right time and place. In our present consumption society, this is typically done by visiting a shop, collecting the desired goods, and bringing them back home. The associated journey wastes time, space, energy, and attention, as illustrated by the ever-present curse of traffic jams.

A by now well established DIT application is Internet shopping: selecting goods from a web catalog with the help of a personalized recommender system and having them delivered wherever they are needed. This still requires travel for the delivery truck, but if distributed orders are combined in an intelligent manner, the route of the truck can be optimized for minimal cost in time and energy. The DIT application centered on 3D printing eliminates even this cost, as it removes the need for material goods to travel [Lipson and Kurman 2013]. However, even the most sophisticated future printers will still need raw materials, and are unlikely to produce certain goods such as food. A conceivable solution is to develop an automated physical distribution network, which e.g. uses self-driving vehicles, drones or underground tubes to shuttle basic goods and materials from producer to consumer [Heylighen 2007a].

Such DIT applications will not only change transport and production of goods, but also their economics. Generally speaking, as their production is further automated, material goods become ever less expensive. This trend will only accelerate with technologies such as 3D printing, and eventually nanotechnology [Drexler 2013]. Moreover, the "open access" model [Heylighen 2007b] of sharing designs will completely change the price structure, making a wide range of goods practically free. Future renewable energy technologies supported by a smart grid are likely to have a similar effect on energy prices. Eventually, the resulting intelligent network may do away with money altogether, satisfying needs by directly matching offers with demands – a vision that has been called the peer-to-peer economy, sharing economy, gift economy, collaborative commons, or offer network [Goertzel 2015; Heylighen 2016; Rifkin 2014]. This lets us envisage an age of true abundance, where poverty or scarcity no longer exist [Diamandis and Kotler 2012; Heylighen 2015a].

4.2. *Health needs*

Our need for health, in the sense of absence of disease, is obvious enough. But health can be defined more positively as physical fitness, strength, and quality of life, i.e. an optimal state for our body characterized by a sense of well-being, long life and the capability to take on a variety of challenges [Heylighen 2014b].

At present, health care requires an extremely expensive infrastructure that includes medical personnel, hospitals, and pharmaceutical firms. An important part of that cost is because the medical research to elucidate the causes of diseases and to develop new treatments is very slow and inefficient, requiring the collaboration of thousands of researchers, doctors and patients. A DIT approach likely to accelerate the process is *data mining*: finding patterns in massive databases that contain billions of medical observations [Yoo *et al.* 2011]. Eventually, all medical files maintained by doctors, hospitals and nurses will become available on the Internet, in a format suitably protecting privacy. As people start to use more and more Internet-connected sensors, these files will not just contain doctor-prescribed diagnoses and treatments, but a variety of health indicators, such as heart rate, blood pressure and temperature, as well as lifestyle elements, such as diet, exercise, exposure to sunlight, etc. There already exist a variety of smartphone apps that keep track of heart rate, running speed, temperature, altitude and other variables during their user's training sessions [Mandl *et al.* 2015].

Data mining algorithms will be able to explore these "big data" collections to find correlations between various symptoms, lifestyle elements, and diseases. This will help researchers to discover new syndromes, or to establish causal connections, e.g. between a particular diet and the risk of developing a particular disease. Moreover, the distributed database will allow researchers to quickly test the effectiveness of a particular treatment by immediately determining which portion of patients actually improved with that treatment, and in what ways.

Another source of health costs is medical consultation with a highly trained expert. As expert knowledge, complemented by patterns derived from data mining, is gradually converted into computer programs, diagnosis can become largely automated. Such an expert system (e.g. The Analyst™ (www.diagnose-me.com) or IBM's Watson [Ferrucci *et al.* 2013]) would start by asking the patient a variety of initially general, then increasingly focused questions while combining the answers with publicly available data about that patient. On that basis, it would then infer and suggest the most likely diagnoses and treatments. Only in the most difficult cases would this diagnosis need to be confirmed by one or more people, thus saving many human-hours of highly qualified work. Moreover, the computer diagnostician can take into account many more factors than any individual person could, thus making it more likely that all potentially relevant tracks are covered.

Finally, DIT systems can monitor and support the treatment regime, by ensuring that the necessary medicines are taken and expected recovery stays on course. In case of emergency, the system can locate and warn the nearest doctor or ambulance, while immediately transmitting all the vital data as monitored. In more ordinary circumstances, such systems can mobilize the patient to improve his lifestyle, e.g. by stimulating the person to do the right kind of exercises and to eat the right kinds of food [Heylighen *et al.* 2013; Intille 2004]. Here too a variety of smartphone apps are being developed and quickly adopted [Kratzke and Cox 2012]. This last application will be most important for disease prevention, and most generally for maximizing overall fitness. It may well have the largest impact on medical costs, simply by preventing the most common and costly chronic diseases, such as type II diabetes, that presently plague civilization [Carrera-Bastos *et al.* 2011].

4.3. *Safety needs*

Another basic need is feeling safe from danger. Apart from the health problems discussed before, the most common dangers in our present society are accidents and crime. Accidents are most frequently caused by traffic, followed by working with machinery. The spread of sensors and self-regulation in vehicles, buildings and machines will make it increasingly easy for DIT applications to prevent potential accidents. For example, sensors that keep track of the positions and speeds of the cars in a lane can send a braking signal to the motor as soon as the preceding car slows down too much, thus avoiding a collision. Google has built driverless cars that combine sensors such as these with a wireless connection that allows the vehicle to plan its journey taking into account road maps and traffic conditions [Hars 2015; Luettel *et al.* 2012]. These self-driving vehicles are reputedly already safer than human-driven ones.

Sophisticated sensors and control programs can similarly reduce the risk of crime, e.g. by using biometric data such as iris scans, fingerprints, and voice recognition to identify an individual, and thus make sure that only the rightful owner of a car, smartphone or house gets access to it. If access cannot be fully secured, sensors aided by smart algorithms can warn the police whenever a suspicious activity (such as the breaking of a window or an intrusion) takes place. Distributed intelligence relies on more than such devices, though: it makes full use of human eyes, ears and brains. Smartphone technology already makes it easy for people to immediately warn the police whenever they witness a crime, or any apparent preparation for it, including detailed data such as place, time, and video recordings. Distributed databases, such as Ushahidi, moreover make it easy to share, organize and visualize such data, so as to produce an overview of what is happening where. This makes it easier to plan and coordinate interventions in confuse situations such as fires, riots, or natural disasters [Gao *et al.* 2011]. Self-organizing sensor networks may even provide ad hoc guidance in situations where all traditional communications have broken down, such as an explosion in a tunnel [Dressler 2008]. After the events, data mining on the collected information should allow uncovering the most common causes of accidents, violence and crime, and thus help to formulate guidelines and precautions for preventing them.

4.4. *Social needs*

Being able to rely on others is another fundamental human need. To be truly happy, everybody needs friends, lovers or family, and the feeling of belonging to a community. Such relationships are easily supported by DITs.

At present, such social applications are perhaps the most popular ones of all, as illustrated by the explosive development of "*social media*" or "social networks", such as Facebook, Twitter and LinkedIn, together with a seemingly endless list of Internet communities, forums and discussion groups. Critics have a point in observing that social interactions sustained in this way are often superficial compared to the more traditional ones. But this is most likely due to the novelty of the medium, and the fact that people like to play and explore the many new functions, without as yet having learned to distinguish services that satisfy true needs from gadgets that produce cheap thrills. On the other hand, since its early days the Internet has been used to create and sustain deep personal and professional relationships across distances too large to allow for face-to-face contacts [Baker 2005].

The most obvious DIT application is to use the variety of data available about people worldwide to suggest good "matches", i.e. others that you might like to get to know, as professional partners, friends, or potential lovers. Relevant data include existing social connections, interests, personality traits, age, location, and professional, educational, social and cultural background. Matchmaking sites are one of the great success stories of the web [Whitty *et al.* 2007]. According to surveys, in one third of recent American marriages the couple met online. Such relationships started online even appear slightly more successful than the traditional ones [Toma 2015]. With more data becoming available and smarter recommendation algorithms, the effectiveness of online dating can only continue to increase.

Moreover, with the spread of high-bandwidth video communication and future, more sophisticated sensing methods (e.g. virtual reality, emotion recognition, telepresence), remote interaction becomes increasingly more similar to face-to-face interaction. This will help people to communicate subtle feelings across the net, and thus experience a true emotional connection with their communication partners.

Finally, the Internet has an impressive track record in establishing new *communities*, i.e. groups of people with a shared interest exchanging information and doing things together. People with unusual interests (e.g. those suffering from a rare disease, having an uncommon hobby, or non-standard sexual preferences) in the past would have felt lonely and alienated in their local environment. Now these people can easily find like-minded people who will not only accept them for what they are, but provide them with encouragement, feedback and support. The effect on personal well-being can be profound, as people no longer feel excluded, but rather appreciated for their contributions to the community, while always having someone available to give advice or help.

4.5. *Achievement needs*

To be truly happy, people need to develop a sense of achievement or mastery, of feeling that their actions are effective and that they have some degree of power or control over their situation. Moreover, people like to be recognized by others for such achievements, so that they can enjoy a sense of esteem, respect or status.

One of the reasons for the popularity of Internet communities and social media is precisely that they make it easy for people to get recognition for their contributions from peers, thus allowing them to build up a good reputation. The popularity of games, on the other hand, is due for an important part to the fact that they provide immediate feedback about the actions performed by the player, in the form or points, scores, and awards [Heylighen *et al.* 2013]. This creates a sense of achievement, as players can graduate into increasingly advanced "levels" of expertise in the game. While these gaming applications may seem rather frivolous, the underlying psychological mechanism of *flow* makes a real contribution to people's level of happiness [Chen 2007; Cowley *et al.* 2008; Nakamura and Csikszentmihalyi 2002]. Moreover, this mechanism can be extended by techniques such as "gamification" to tasks that are very serious indeed, such as studying mathematics, or increasing fitness [Deterding *et al.* 2011].

The concept of *mobilization system* [Heylighen *et al.* 2013] refers to a new type of DIT that encourages and helps people to work towards a worthwhile objective, thus boosting their sense of achievement. In addition, a number of Internet community forums (e.g. Stack Overflow [Mamykina *et al.* 2011]) are developing tools for measuring individuals' overall contribution, thus automating the development of reputation [De Alfaro *et al.* 2011], and rewarding helpful people for their good work.

4.6. *Cognitive needs*

People have an innate desire to know, to learn and to understand the world around them. Providing such knowledge is another one of the best-established uses of DIT. Search engines, such as the one of Google, have learned to anticipate and understand the most common questions that people have, and to find the documents most likely to provide a high-quality answer. Wikipedia harnesses the collective intelligence of all people to produce standard accounts of all knowledge domains about which some degree of consensus exists [Jemielniak, 2014], while the Semantic Web makes such knowledge available to machines as well as to people.

Both Wikipedia and the Semantic Web will continue to grow in the size and the quality of the knowledge they cover, until they contain all the knowledge discovered by humanity. At that moment, any question someone may ask for which an answer is possible given the present state of knowledge will receive that answer immediately. This is the practical equivalent of *omniscience*, a property that was hitherto considered an attribute of God [Heylighen 2015a; Otlet 1935].

The most commonly used knowledge should not just be available via the network, but as much as possible inside people's own brains, so that they immediately can apply it to the situation at hand. This can be achieved by *learning*. DIT are starting to revolutionize the process of education, thus making learning much easier, more efficient and more enjoyable [Heylighen *et al.* 2013]. One of the advantages is that learning can be perfectly tailored to the individual, by providing the right kind of challenges at the right moment, depending on the interests and capabilities of the learner, and not on the time or place where that learner resides. This is already achieved to some degree by "Massively Online Open Courses" [Rodriguez 2012], such as the Khan Academy, Coursera, and edX, and by an endless variety of apps that use gaming techniques to make learning fun [Michael and Chen 2005; Thompson 2011].

A straightforward extrapolation of these developments tells us that in the near future, people anywhere in the world will be able to study and obtain degrees on any subject, from basic literacy and numeracy to PhD level science, by freely following inspiring course materials remotely, while getting feedback from automatic evaluation programs, peers studying the same material, and – if need be – teachers. This will boost the education level of humanity to such a degree that it is as yet difficult to ascertain the consequences: imagine a world where every minimally gifted adult has at least a Masters degree in an advanced domain, while having a broad and deep general education covering a variety of common and uncommon topic.

4.7. *Self-actualization or growth needs*

At the highest level of Maslow's hierarchy of needs is the desire to maximally develop one's own capabilities, i.e. to realize one's potential, or to grow psychologically [Heylighen 1992; Maslow 1970]. This need is the final one in the sense that it has no endpoint, as one can always grow wiser or more capable. It ensures that no one will ever get bored because of having achieved all her desires.

The Internet can be seen as a space for unlimited exploration, allowing individuals to discover new opportunities, to take on new challenges, to develop new insights, to learn new skills, and to meet new people [Last 2016]. Indeed, new resources join the Internet at a much faster pace than any individual could explore them, thus ensuring that there is always much more to discover than what people already know. In that sense, the Internet allows an unlimited growth in knowledge, social connections, resources and wisdom, even for people who are too old or too frail to leave their homes.

Moreover, distributed intelligence algorithms will recommend activities or domains to explore that are tailored to an individual's personal interests and competences, while challenging them to go ever further in their endeavors. The path of learning can even be optimized by taking into account the experiences of others that followed a similar path before [Gutiérrez *et al.* 2007]. This ensures that people are constantly stimulated to develop themselves further and to take on more difficult challenges, so that personal development never needs to come to an end.

5. Conclusion

This chapter has tried to survey the major present and future applications of what we have called "distributed intelligence technologies". These are systems that tackle complex challenges in a distributed manner, by collecting input from many different sources, storing and processing that information simultaneously in different places, and sending their outputs to different human or technological agents working in parallel.

To achieve this, such systems need a global communication network, such as the Internet, to interconnect all people, computers and machines that are involved in solving the problem. Moreover, they need to make sure that the inputs and actions of all these agents are efficiently coordinated, so that they produce a coherent result. Supporting technologies for such distributed problem solving, such as the Semantic Web, the Internet of Things and the Smart Grid, are being developed at a rapid pace. They at least need to enable the efficient distribution of information, knowledge, physical objects, energy, actions and personal identity. The integration of all these technologies is expected to produce a distributed intelligence at the planetary scale, the *Global Brain*.

The capabilities of a Global Brain in tackling the problems of our planetary society have been surveyed elsewhere [Heylighen 2007a, 2015a, 2016]. The present paper has therefore focused on its applications at the level of individuals: how can distributed intelligence technologies satisfy our basic human needs? By extrapolating from existing applications, such as social media, data mining, online shopping and computer-supported education, we have shown that these technologies can in principle fulfil our material, health, safety, social, achievement, cognitive, and even growth needs. Once we have learned to deal more effectively with these technologies – and in particular some of their stress-producing side effects, such as information overload, distraction, and unpredictability [Heylighen 2015a; Heylighen *et al.* 2013] – this should greatly facilitate personal fulfilment and well-being.

References

Akyildiz, I. F., Wang, X., and Wang, W. (2005). Wireless mesh networks: a survey, *Computer Networks, 47*(4), 445-487, http://doi.org/10.1016/j.comnet.2004.12.001

Ashby, W. R. (1956). Design for an intelligence-amplifier. *Automata Studies*, 215-234

Atzori, L., Iera, A., and Morabito, G. (2010). The internet of things: A survey. *Computer Networks, 54*(15), 2787-2805

Baker, A. J. (2005). *Double click: Romance and Commitment Among Couples Online.* Hampton Press.

Baldassarre, G., Parisi, D., and Nolfi, S. (2006). Distributed coordination of simulated robots based on self-organization. *Artificial Life, 12*(3), 289-311

Ball, P. (2012). *Why Society is a Complex Matter: Meeting Twenty-first Century Challenges with a New Kind of Science* (2012th ed.). New York: Springer

Bechtel, W., and Abrahamsen, A. (1991). *Connectionism and the mind: An introduction to parallel processing in networks.* Basil Blackwell

Berners-Lee, T., and Fischetti, M. (1999). *Weaving the Web: The Original Design and Ultimate Destiny of the World Wide Web by Its Inventor.* Harper San Francisco, http://portal.acm.org/citation.cfm?id=554813

Bernstein, A., Klein, M., and Malone, T. W. (2012). Programming the Global Brain. *Communications of the ACM, 55*(5), 1

Bruner, J. (2013). *Industrial Internet.* O'Reilly Media, Inc.

Camazine, S., Deneubourg, J. L., Franks, N. R., Sneyd, J., Theraula, G., and Bonabeau, E. (2003). *Self-organization in biological systems.* Princeton University Press

Carrera-Bastos, P., Fontes-Villalba, M., O'Keefe, J. H., Lindeberg, S., and Cordain, L. (2011). The western diet and lifestyle and diseases of civilization. *Research Reports in Clinical Cardiology*, 15, http://doi.org/10.2147/RRCC.S16919

Chen, J. (2007). Flow in games (and everything else). *Communications of the ACM, 50*(4), 31-34

Clark, A. (1998). Embodied, situated, and distributed cognition. *A Companion to Cognitive Science*, 506-517

Cowley, B., Charles, D., Black, M., and Hickey, R. (2008). Toward an understanding of flow in video games. *Computers in Entertainment (CIE), 6*(2), 20

Crowston, K., Rubleske, J., and Howison, J. (2006). Coordination theory. *Human-Computer Interaction and Management Information Systems: Foundations*, 120

De Alfaro, L., Kulshreshtha, A., Pye, I., and Adler, B. T. (2011). Reputation systems for open collaboration. *Communications of the ACM, 54*(8), 81-87

De Rosnay, J. (2000). *The Symbiotic Man: A new understanding of the organization of life and a vision of the future.* Mcgraw-Hill, http://pespmc1.vub.ac.be/books/DeRosnay.TheSymbioticMan.pdf

Deterding, S., Sicart, M., Nacke, L., O'Hara, K., and Dixon, D. (2011). Gamification. using game-design elements in non-gaming contexts. In *Proceedings of the 2011 Annual Conference Extended Abstracts on Human Factors in Computing Systems*, 2425-2428

Diamandis, P. H., and Kotler, S. (2012). *Abundance: The Future Is Better Than You Think*. Free Press

Dressler, F. (2008). A study of self-organization mechanisms in ad hoc and sensor networks. *Computer Communications, 31*(13), 3018-3029

Drexler, E. K. (2013). *Radical Abundance: How a Revolution in Nanotechnology Will Change Civilization*. PublicAffairs

Elmenreich, W., D'Souza, R., Bettstetter, C., and de Meer, H. (2009). A Survey of Models and Design Methods for Self-Organizing Networked Systems. *Self-Organizing Systems*, 37-49

Evrard, A. E., Erdmann, C., Holmquist, J., Damon, J., and Dietrich, D. (2015). Persistent, Global Identity for Scientists via ORCID. *arXiv:1502.06274 [astro-Ph, Physics:physics]*, http://arxiv.org/abs/1502.06274

Ferrucci, D., Levas, A., Bagchi, S., Gondek, D., and Mueller, E. T. (2013). Watson: Beyond Jeopardy! *Artificial Intelligence, 199-200*, 93-105 http://doi.org/10.1016/j.artint.2012.06.009

Fischer, G. (2006). Distributed intelligence: extending the power of the unaided, individual human mind, in: *Proceedings of the Working Conference on Advanced Visual Interfaces*, ACM, New York, NY, USA, 7-14, http://doi.org/10.1145/1133265.1133268

Gao, H., Barbier, G., and Goolsby, R. (2011). Harnessing the crowdsourcing power of social media for disaster relief. *Intelligent Systems, IEEE, 26*(3), 10-14

Goertzel, B. (2002). Creating internet intelligence: Wild computing, distributed digital consciousness, and the emerging global brain. Kluwer Academic/Plenum Publishers

Goertzel, B. (2015). Beyond Money: Offer networks, a potential infrastructure for a post-money economy, in: Goertzel, B., and Goertzel, T. (eds.), *The End of the Beginning: Life, Society and Economy on the Brink of the Singularity*, Humanity+ Press, 522-549

Gutiérrez, S., Valigiani, G., Jamont, Y., Collet, P., and Delgado Kloos, C. (2007). A swarm approach for automatic auditing of pedagogical planning, in: *Advanced Learning Technologies, 2007. ICALT 2007. Seventh IEEE International Conference on*, 136-138, http://ieeexplore.ieee.org/xpls/abs_all.jsp?arnumber=4280973

Hars, A. (2015). Self-Driving Cars: The Digital Transformation of Mobility, in: Linnhoff-Popien, C., Zaddach, M., and Grahl, A. (eds.), *Marktplätze im Umbruch* Springer Berlin, Heidelberg, 539-549, http://link.springer.com/chapter/10.1007/978-3-662-43782-7_57

Heylighen, F. (1992). A cognitive-systemic reconstruction of Maslow's theory of self-actualization. *Behavioral Science*, *37*(1), 39-58, http://doi.org/10.1002/bs.383037 0105

Heylighen, F. (1994). World-Wide Web: a distributed hypermedia paradigm for global networking, in: *SHARE EUROPE SPRING MEETING*, 355-368

Heylighen, F. (1999). Collective Intelligence and its Implementation on the Web: algorithms to develop a collective mental map. *Computational & Mathematical Organization Theory*, *5*(3), 253-280. http://doi.org/10.1023/A:1009690407292

Heylighen, F. (2007a). The Global Superorganism: an evolutionary-cybernetic model of the emerging network society. *Social Evolution & History*, *6*(1), 58-119

Heylighen, F. (2007b). Why is Open Access Development so Successful? Stigmergic organization and the economics of information, in: Lutterbeck, B., Baerwolff, M., and Gehring, R. A. (eds.), *Open Source Jahrbuch 2007*, Lehmanns Media, 165-180, http://pespmc1.vub.ac.be/Papers/OpenSourceStigmergy.pdf

Heylighen, F. (2008). Accelerating socio-technological evolution: from ephemeralization and stigmergy to the global brain, in: *Globalization as evolutionary process: modeling global change*, Routledge, 284, http://pcp.vub.ac.be/papers/AcceleratingEvolution.pdf

Heylighen, F. (2011). Conceptions of a Global Brain: an historical review, in: Grinin, L. E., Carneiro, R. L., Korotayev A. V., and Spier, F. (eds.), *Evolution: Cosmic, Biological, and Social,* Uchitel Publishing, 274-289, http://pcp.vub.ac.be/papers/GB-conceptions-Rodrigue.pdf

Heylighen, F. (2013). Self-organization in Communicating Groups: the emergence of coordination, shared references and collective intelligence, in: À. Massip-Bonet and A. Bastardas-Boada (eds.), *Complexity Perspectives on Language, Communication and Society*, Springer, Berlin, Germany, 117-149 http://pcp.vub.ac.be/Papers/Barcelona-LanguageSO.pdf

Heylighen, F. (2014a). Challenge Propagation: Towards a theory of distributed intelligence and the global brain, *Spanda Journal*, *V*(2), 51-63

Heylighen, F. (2014b). Cybernetic Principles of Aging and Rejuvenation: the buffering-challenging strategy for life extension, *Current Aging Science*, *7*(1), 60-75, http://doi.org/10.2174/1874609807666140521095925

Heylighen, F. (2015a). Return to Eden? Promises and Perils on the Road to a Global Superintelligence, in: Goertzel, B., and Goertzel, T. (eds.), *The End of the Beginning: Life, Society and Economy on the Brink of the Singularity*. Humanity+ Press, http://pespmc1.vub.ac.be/Papers/BrinkofSingularity.pdf

Heylighen, F. (2015b). Stigmergy as a Universal Coordination Mechanism I: definition and components. *Cognitive Systems Research* (submitted)

Heylighen, F. (2016). Towards an Intelligent Network for Matching Offer and Demand: from the sharing economy to the Global Brain. *Technological Forecasting & Social Change* (in press)

Heylighen, F., and Bernheim, J. (2000). Global Progress I: Empirical Evidence for ongoing Increase in Quality-of-life. *Journal of Happiness Studies, 1*(3), 323-349, http://doi.org/10.1023/A:1010099928894

Heylighen, F., Busseniers, E., Veitas, V., Vidal, C., and Weinbaum, D. R. (2012). *Foundations for a Mathematical Model of the Global Brain: architecture, components, and specifications* (GBI Working Papers No. 2012-05). http://pespmc1.vub.ac.be/papers/TowardsGB-model.pdf

Heylighen, F., Heath, M., and Van Overwalle, F. J. (2004). The Emergence of Distributed Cognition: a conceptual framework. In *Proceedings of collective intentionality IV*.

Heylighen, F., Kostov, I., and Kiemen, M. (2013). Mobilization Systems: technologies for motivating and coordinating human action. In Peters M. A., Besley T. and Araya D. (Ed.), *The New Development Paradigm: Education, Knowledge Economy and Digital Futures*. Routledge.

http://pcp.vub.ac.be/Papers/MobilizationSystems.pdf

Holland, J. H. (1992). Complex adaptive systems. *Daedalus*, 17-30

Hutchins, E. (2000). Distributed cognition, in: Smelser, N. J., and Baltes, P. B. (eds.), *International Encyclopedia of the Social and Behavioral Sciences*. Elsevier Science

Hutchins, E., and Lintern, G. (1995). *Cognition in the Wild* (Vol. 262082314). MIT press Cambridge, MA, http://books.google.be/books?id=AfupQgAACAAJ&dq= Cognition+in+the+Wild&hl=en&sa=X&ei=YjLWT6PGLaOn0QWwyqiBBA&red ir_esc=y

Intille, S. S. (2004). A new research challenge: persuasive technology to motivate healthy aging. *Information Technology in Biomedicine, IEEE Transactions on, 8*(3), 235-237

Jemielniak, D. (2014). *Common Knowledge?: An Ethnography of Wikipedia*. Stanford University Press

Kittur, A., and Kraut, R. E. (2008). Harnessing the wisdom of crowds in wikipedia: quality through coordination, in: *Proceedings of the 2008 ACM Conference on Computer Supported Cooperative Work*, 37-46, ACM, New York, NY, USA, http://doi.org/10.1145/1460563.1460572

Krajník, T., Vonásek, V., Fišer, D., and Faigl, J. (2011). AR-Drone as a Platform for Robotic Research and Education, in: Obdržálek, D., and Gottscheber, A. (eds.), *Research and Education in Robotics - EUROBOT 2011*, Springer Berlin Heidelberg, 172-186, http://link.springer.com/chapter/10.1007/978-3-642-21975-7_16

Kratzke, C., and Cox, C. (2012). Smartphone Technology and Apps: Rapidly Changing Health Promotion. *International Electronic Journal of Health Education, 15*, 72

Last, C. (2016). Self-actualization in the Commons. *Technological Forecasting and Social Change* (submitted)

Leiner, B. M., Cerf, V. G., Clark, D. D., Kahn, R. E., Kleinrock, L., Lynch, D. C., and Wolff, S. (2009). A Brief History of the Internet. *SIGCOMM Comput. Commun. Rev., 39*(5), 22-31, http://doi.org/10.1145/1629607.1629613

Li, F., Qiao, W., Sun, H., Wan, H., Wang, J., Xia, Y., and Zhang, P. (2010). Smart Transmission Grid: Vision and Framework. *IEEE Transactions on Smart Grid*, *1*(2), 168-177. http://doi.org/10.1109/TSG.2010.2053726

Lipson, H., and Kurman, M. (2013). *Fabricated: The New World of 3D Printing*. John Wiley & Sons

Luettel, T., Himmelsbach, M., and Wuensche, H. J. (2012). Autonomous Ground Vehicles—Concepts and a Path to the Future. *Proceedings of the IEEE, 100*(13), 1831-1839

Malone, T. W., Laubacher, R., and Dellarocas, C. (2010). The collective intelligence genome. *IEEE Engineering Management Review, 38*(3), 38

Mamykina, L., Manoim, B., Mittal, M., Hripcsak, G., and Hartmann, B. (2011). Design lessons from the fastest q&a site in the west. In *Proceedings of the 2011 annual conference on Human factors in computing systems* (pp. 2857-2866). New York, NY, USA: ACM. http://doi.org/10.1145/1978942.1979366

Mandl, K. D., Mandel, J. C., and Kohane, I. S. (2015). Driving Innovation in Health Systems through an Apps-Based Information Economy. *Cell Systems, 1*(1), 8-13 http://doi.org/10.1016/j.cels.2015.05.001

Maslow, A. H. (1970). *Motivation and personality* (2nd ed.). New York: Harper & Row.

Massoud Amin, S., and Wollenberg, B. F. (2005). Toward a smart grid: power delivery for the 21st century. *Power and Energy Magazine, IEEE, 3*(5), 34-41

Mayer-Kress, G., and Barczys, C. (1995). The global brain as an emergent structure from the Worldwide Computing Network, and its implications for modeling. *The Information Society, 11*(1), 1-27

McLeod, P., Plunkett, K., and Rolls, E. T. (1998). *Introduction to connectionist modelling of cognitive processes*. Oxford University Press Oxford

Michael, D. R., and Chen, S. L. (2005). *Serious games: Games that educate, train, and inform*. Muska & Lipman/Premier-Trade

Miller, J. G. (1965). Living systems: Basic concepts. *Behavioral Science, 10*(3), 193-237.

Miller, J. G. (1995). *Living systems*. University Press of Colorado

Miller, J. H., and Page, S. E. (2007). *Complex Adaptive Systems: An Introduction to Computational Models of Social Life*. Princeton, N.J: Princeton University Press

Nakamura, J., and Csikszentmihalyi, M. (2002). The concept of flow. In C. R. Snyder (Ed.), *Handbook of positive psychology* (pp. 89-105). New York, NY: Oxford University Press

Otlet, P. (1935). *Monde: Essai d'Universalisme*. Brussels: Mundaneum

Rayward, W. B. (1999). H. G. Wells' s idea of a World Brain: A critical reassessment. *Journal of the American Society for Information Science, 50*(7), 557-573

Recordon, D., and Reed, D. (2006). OpenID 2.0: A Platform for User-centric Identity Management. In *Proceedings of the Second ACM Workshop on Digital Identity Management*, 11-16. New York, NY, USA: ACM. http://doi.org/10.1145/1179529.1179532

Rifkin, J. (2014). *The Zero Marginal Cost Society: The Internet of Things, the Collaborative Commons, and the Eclipse of Capitalism,* Palgrave Macmillan, http://www.bookdepository.com/Zero-Marginal-Cost-Society-Jeremy-Rifkin/9781137278463

Rodriguez, O. (2012). MOOCs and the AI-Stanford like Courses: two successful and distinct course formats for massive open online courses. *European Journal of Open, Distance, and E-Learning.* http://www.eurodl.org/materials/contrib/2012/Rodriguez.htm

Rumelhart, D. E., and McClelland, J. L. (1986). *Parallel distributed processing.* San Diego: University of California Press

Russell, P. (1995). *The global brain awakens: Our next evolutionary leap.* Global Brain, Inc.

Stangler, D., and Maxwell, K. (2012). DIY Producer Society. *Innovations: Technology, Governance, Globalization, 7*(3), 3-10. http://doi.org/10.1162/INOV_a_00134

Stock, G. (1993). *Metaman: The Merging of Humans and Machines Into a Global Superorganism.* Simon & Schuster

Surowiecki, J. (2005). *The Wisdom of Crowds.* Anchor

Thompson, C. (2011). How Khan Academy is changing the rules of education. *Wired Magazine,* (August), 126

Toma, C. L. (2015). Online Dating. In *The International Encyclopedia of Interpersonal Communication.* John Wiley & Sons, Inc., http://onlinelibrary.wiley.com/doi/10.1002/9781118540190.wbeic118/abstract

Veenhoven, R. (1997). Advances in Understanding Happiness. *Revue Québécoise de Psychologie, 18*(2), 29-74

Weber, S. (2004). *The success of open source.* Cambridge University Press.

Welbourne, E., Battle, L., Cole, G., Gould, K., Rector, K., Raymer, S., and Borriello, G. (2009). Building the internet of things using RFID: the RFID ecosystem experience. *Internet Computing, IEEE, 13*(3), 48-55

Wells, H. (1937). *World Brain.* Ayer Co Pub.

Whitty, M. T., Baker, A. J., and Inman, J. A. (2007). *Online matchmaking.* Palgrave Macmillan.
http://www.palgrave.com/rights/pdfs/Cultural%20and%20Media%20Studies.pdf

Yoo, I., Alafaireet, P., Marinov, M., Pena-Hernandez, K., Gopidi, R., Chang, J.-F., and Hua, L. (2011). Data Mining in Healthcare and Biomedicine: A Survey of the Literature. *Journal of Medical Systems, 36*(4), 2431-2448. http://doi.org/10.1007/s10916- 011-9710-5

Chapter 11

Smart Data:
Running the Internet of Things as a Citizen Web

Dirk Helbing

ETH Zurich, Clausiusstrasse 50, 8092 Zürich, Switzerland
dirk.helbing@gess.ethz.ch

The Internet of Things is an emerging Information and Communication Technology with revolutionary potentials. Its areas of application include (1) the real-time measurement of the state of our techno-socio-economic-environmental systems, (2) the development of a Global Systems Science to manage our world more successfully, (3) greater awareness of chances and risks to support everyone's decision-making, (4) possibilities to enable self-organizing systems, and (5) opportunities to create collective intelligence. I will, in particular, reveal plans to build a "Planetary Nervous System" as a Citizen Web, which is envisioned to be an open and participatory information system to unleash the power of the Internet of Things for everyone in the world.

The Planetary Nervous System is a large-scale distributed research platform that will provide real-time social mining services as a public good. It is an open, privacy-preserving and participatory platform designed to be collectively built by citizens and for citizens. The Planetary Nervous System aims at seamlessly interconnecting a large number of different pervasive devices, e.g. mobile phones, smart sensors, etc. A novel social mining paradigm shift is enabled: Users are provided with freedom and incentives to share, collect and, at the same time, protect data of their digital environment in real-time. In this way, social mining turns into a knowledge extraction service for public good. The social mining services of the Planetary Nervous System can be publicly used to build novel innovative applications. Whether you would like to detect an earthquake, perform a secure evacuation or discover the hot spots of a highly frequented city, the Planetary Nervous system makes this possible by collectively mining social activities of participatory citizens.

Moore's law, describing the exponential explosion of processing power and data production, is currently driving a fundamental transformation of our economy and society. While processing power doubles every 18 months, data volumes double every 12 months, which means that we literally produce as much data in one year as in the entire history of humankind (i.e. all previous years). However, this is not the end of the digital revolution. More and more "things" are now equipped with communicating sensors – fridges, coffee machines, tooth brushes, smartphones and smart devices. In ten years, this will connect 150 billion "things" with each other – and with 10 billion people. This creates the "Internet of Everything" and data volumes that double every 12 hours rather than every 12 months. How will this impact our society?

First of all, we will have an abundance of data about our world. Data will be cheap, and Big Data analytics can reach entirely new levels [Helbing 2015]. Can we soon know everything? Can we build a Crystal Ball depicting and perhaps even predicting the course of events [Helbing 2014]? Can we build superintelligent systems to run the world in a better way, based on cybernetic control principles [Wiener 1954; Medina 2011]? Would humans be steered by information [Kramer *et al.* 2014]? It seems that such technologies may now be built. For example, Baidu has started to work on a China brain project, which will learn to predict peoples' behaviors based on their Internet searches.[a] China has further initiated a project that rates the behavior of its citizens.[b] This will make loans and jobs dependent on personal scores, which also depend on the links clicked in the Web – and on political opinions. Is Orwell's Big Brother coming? Or is this the technology we need? Can the state act like

---

[a]http://www.wantchinatimes.com/news-subclass-cnt.aspx?id=20150307000015&cid=1101

[b]http://www.zeit.de/politik/ausland/2015-07/china-plangesellschaft-xi-jinping
http://www.volkskrant.nl/buitenland/china-rates-its-own-citizens-including-online-behaviour~a3979668/;

a "wise king"? Or is a state that determines, how its citizens should be happy, a despot, as Immanuel Kant concluded?[c]

In fact, there is no scientific method to determine the 'goal function of society' that ought to be maximized: should it be GDP per capita, sustainability, average life span, peace, or happiness? This is not clear and, furthermore, people are not like ants. The concept of omni-benevolence can't work, because people pursue different goals, have different conceptions of good life. On the one hand, their pluralism results from social specialization, economic differentiation and cultural development. On the other hand, such pluralism hedges the risks to society and increases its ability to master unexpected disruptions. Consequently, as the complexity of a society increases, pluralism needs to increase as well.

The concepts of top-down optimization and control are limited by a number of factors: (1) Data volume grows faster than the processing power. A growing share of data will never be processed. This creates a "flashlight effect": we may see anything we want, but we need to know what to pay attention to. However, some systems are irreducibly complex, so every little detail can matter [Kondor *et al.* 2014]. (2) Due to limited communication bandwidth, an even smaller fraction of data can be processed centrally, such that a lot of local information, which is needed to produce good solutions, is ignored by a centralized optimization attempt. (3) Systemic complexity can prevent real-time optimization, such that decentralized control approaches may perform better. This has been shown for self-organized traffic lights, which are flexibly and efficiently controlled by local traffic flows, while traffic control centers often fail to control traffic flows well [Lämmer and Helbing 2018; Helbing 2013]. (4) Further problems may be caused by overfitting, spurious correlations, meaningless patterns, noise and related classification errors – problems that are quite common in Big Data analytics. Another concern is that powerful information systems are

---

[c]http://oll.libertyfund.org/titles/kant-kants-principles-of-politics-including-his-essay-on-perpetual-peace/simple [Online Library of Liberty] and
http://plato.stanford.edu/entries/kant-social-political/ [Rauscher 2012].

attractive to organized criminals, terrorists and extremists, so they would sooner or later be corrupted or hacked.

To unleash the value of Big Data, it often takes theoretical models to look at the data in a useful way, as it is done in experiments at CERN's elementary particle accelerator (which just keeps the 0,1% of all measurement data – the data that are actually needed to test a particular theoretical prediction). A similar finding is made when trying to predict epidemic spread: a model-based analysis with little data is more powerful than brute force Big Data analytics such as Flu Trends [Lazer *et al.* 2014]. Therefore, Michael Macy recently concluded: "Big Data is the beginning of theory, not the end", and most experts agree. This is in sharp contrast to Chris Anderson's earlier claim that "The data deluge makes the scientific method obsolete."[d]

Some might say that Singapore, which considers itself a "social laboratory"[e], is a good example for a country that has greatly benefited from data-driven decision-making. Western democracies envy the country for its quick development and economic growth rate, but we must also consider that Singapore has been a tax heaven, and it largely profits from imported innovations originating predominantly in Western democracies. Moreover, the political party in power has steadily lost votes over the past years, despite all its successes. This is irritating, and we should therefore listen to Geoffrey West, the former president of the Santa Fe Institute, who studied cities extensively. He points out that the country of Singapore is run like a company. However, 40-50% of the Top 500 companies disappear in a time period of just 10 years, while cities persist for hundreds of years due to their usually more inclusive governance approach. The reason for this is that even powerful decision-makers make mistakes, but when this happens, the mistakes tend to be big.

Where do we stand today? Big Data analytics is far from being able to understand the complexity of human behavior, but it is advanced enough to manipulate our decisions by individualized information such as personalized ads or nudging. Such approaches use a few thousand

---

[d]http://archive.wired.com/science/discoveries/magazine/16-07/pb_theory

[e]http://foreignpolicy.com/2014/07/29/the-social-laboratory/

metadata that have been collected about every one of us. However, manipulating our decision doesn't seem to be a good idea, because it undermines the "wisdom of crowds" – an effect on which the functionality of democracies and financial markets is based [Lorenz *et al.* 2011]. Moreover, manipulating our decisions is likely to narrow down the variance of our choices, i.e. socio-economic diversity. On the one hand, this can foster political and societal polarization (or fragmentation) [Andris *et al.* 2015]. On the other hand, diversity is key for innovation, economic development, societal resilience, and collective intelligence [Page 2008]. Losing socio-economic diversity is equally bad as losing bio-diversity. It can cause systemic malfunction or collapse [Tainter 1990; May *et al.* 2008; Diamond 2011].

Moreover, given that about 50% of today's jobs in the industrial and service sectors will be lost in the next 10-20 years, our societies are under pressure to come up with many new jobs in the emerging digital sector (or at least with sufficient income and meaningful activities to give our lives a meaning).[f]

All of this calls for a fundamentally different strategy and an entirely new approach, particularly as we are faced with an increasing number of existential problems: an economic and public spending crisis, financial and political instability, increasing dangers of large-scale international conflicts or cyber wars, climate change with a mass extinction of species, and growing antibiotic resistance, to mention just a few of our global threats. We need to have more innovation capacity, and this means we need to unleash the creativity of people. Diversity can help trigger innovation, while information platforms and digital assistants can support coordination in a diverse and culturally rich world. A participatory approach, which allows everyone to contribute with his/her skills, ideas, and resources (as in citizen science, for example), can mobilize the full socio-economic potential and capacity of society. If many people are unemployed, have to do jobs that don't fit their skills, or

---

[f]http://www.oxfordmartin.ox.ac.uk/downloads/academic/The_Future_of_Employment.pdf

if they are excluded from socio-economic engagement, the competitiveness and well-being of a country is significantly reduced.

To unleash the good side of the digital revolution and new opportunities for everyone, we must provide useful and trustworthy information to everyone. In the same way as we have built public roads to promote the industrial age and public schools to fuel the service society, we need powerful public information systems and digital literacy to promote the digital era to come. Therefore, I propose to build a Planetary Nervous System that creates possibilities for pluralistic data use and opportunities for everyone to contribute to society and pursue flourishing lives [Gianotti *et al.* 2012]. The Planetary Nervous System would use the sensor networks behind the Internet of Things and potentially also the sensors in our smartphones (currently about 15) to measure the world around us and build a data commons together. The critical question is how this can be done in a way that respects our privacy and minimizes misuse as compared to the benefits the system would create. It is time to learn how to do this.

The Nervousnet project[g] has started to work on this. It aims to create an open and participatory information platform such as Wikipedia or OpenStreetMap, but for real-time data. In favor of security, scalability and fault tolerance, Nervousnet is based on distributed data and control. It will be run as a Citizen Web, i.e. built and managed by the users. This gives us maximum control over the data traces we produce. Each sensor can separately be turned on or off. External sensors (e.g. for smart home applications) can be added. Users can also decide what data to share and how frequently to record them. The shared data are anonymized, and they are deleted after a short period of time.

Nervousnet invites everyone to contribute to the creation of this powerful, but distributed and trustworthy information platform for the

---

[g]http://www.nervous.ethz.ch/

http://www.futurict.eu

https://www.youtube.com/watch?v=BKcWPdSUJVA

age of the "Internet of Everything".[h] It is an open platform that will allow developers to add own measurement procedures and Apps on top. These can be scientific applications, games, or business applications. This will allow everyone to provide data-driven services or products and establish own companies. In other words, Nervousnet could once be a global catalyst to create an information, innovation and production ecosystem that will produce new jobs and societal benefits. There is still a lot to be done though. We are currently working on end-to-end data encryption. We need to add multi-dimensional reputation, incentive and payment systems. We also plan to add a personal data store, as it was proposed by Sandy Pentland and others [Montjoye *et al.* 2014].

In perspective, Nervousnet will allow everyone to make better-informed decisions. It will offer five main functionalities. First, it will configure the sensor network to answer specific questions based on real-time measurements. For example, it will allow us to quantify the externalities of the interactions around us, which will make it possible to improve economic systems. Second, these measurements will be able to reveal the hidden forces underlying socio-economic change and other important intangible factors such as reputation and trust. This will fuel a better understanding of our complex, interdependent world, as it is now studied by Global Systems Science [Helbing 2013]. Third, the Planetary Nervous System will create awareness about the problems and opportunities around us. Fourth, it will enable self-organizing systems through real-time feedbacks such as self-organized traffic light controls, industry-4.0-kind-of production systems, or new solutions to socio-economic problems based on locally applied interaction mechanisms. So, 300 years after the invention of the invisible hand, we can finally make it work for us, by combining real-time measurements with suitable feedbacks, as advised by complexity science and enabled by multi-dimensional incentive and exchange systems. Finally, Nervousnet will allow one to build digital assistants supporting collective intelligence. This is needed to master the combinatorial complexity of our

---

[h]The Nervousnet app can be downloaded via Apple's app store and Google's play store. You can contact us at nervousnet@ethz.ch

increasingly interdependent world. So, an entirely new age with amazing new possibilities is ahead of us, fueled by information.

It is now within reach to build an information system that finally brings everything together: science, politics, business, and society. We can create self-organizing and self-improving systems with massively increased efficiency. The approach I propose is based on participation and compatible with democratic principles. It respects the autonomy of decision-making and supports free entrepreneurship, while considering externalities. Therefore, I also expect benefits for our environment and society. In particular, the information age may allow us to reduce the level of conflict, because information is an unlimited resource that offers endless creative possibilities. The digital economy is everything but a zero-sum game. Information can be reproduced as often as we like. To get more of it for us, we don't have to take it away from others. Furthermore, considering that money is just a coordination mechanism to organize the distribution of scarce resources, we can now build a better, multi-dimensional money and incentive system that rewards digital co-creation. So, what are we waiting for? Let's build the digital society together [Helbing 2015]!

References

Andris, C. *et al.* (2015). The Rise of Partisanship and Super-Cooperators in the U.S. House of Representatives, *PLoS ONE* 10(4): e0123507, http://journals.plos.org/plosone/article?id=10.1371/journal.pone.0123507

de Montjoye, Y.-A., Shmueli, E., Wang, S. S., and Pentland, A. S. (2014). openPDS: Protecting the privacy of metadata through SafeAnswers, *PLoS ONE*, 9 (7), e98790, http://journals.plos.org/plosone/article?id=10.1371/journal.pone.0098790

Diamond, J. (2011). *Collapse: How Societies Choose to Fail or Succeed*, Penguin, New York.

Frey, C. B., and Osborne, M. A. (2013). The future of employment: How susceptible are jobs to computerisation?, http://www.oxfordmartin.ox.ac.uk/downloads/academic/The_Future_of_Employment.pdf

Gianotti, F., Pedreschi, D., Pentland, A., Lukowicz, P., Kossmann, D., Crowley, J., and Helbing, D. (2013). A planetary nervous system for social mining and collective awareness, *Eur. Phys. J. Special Topics*, 214, 49-75, http://www.nervous.ethz.ch/, http://www.futurict.eu and https://www.youtube.com/watch?v=BKcWPdSUJVA

Helbing, D. (2013). Globally networked risks and how to respond, *Nature* 497, 51-59, https://www.youtube.com/watch?v=UHp0lV6ppQQ

Helbing, D. (2013). Economics 2.0: The natural step towards a self-regulating, participatory market society, *Evolutionary and Institutional Economics Review* 10, 1, 3-41, http://www.stefanlaemmer.de/

Helbing, D. (2015). *The Automation of Society Is Next: How to survive the digital revolution*, https://www.youtube.com/watch?v=KgVBob5HIm8&list=PLDmlT_Ptfv0fcMD29 kNKOIhV0yK9AhyQl

Kondor, I., Csabai, I., Papp, G., Mones, E., Czimbalmos, G., and Sándor, M. C. (2014). Strong random correlations in networks of heterogeneous agents, *J. Econ. Interact. Coord.*, 9, 2, 203-232

Kramer, A. D. I., Guillory, J. E., and Hancock, J. T. (2014). Experimental evidence of massive-scale emotional contagion through social networks, *Proc. of the National Academy of Sciences of the United States of America* 111, 8788-8790

Lämmer, S., and Helbing, D. (2008). Self-control of traffic lights and vehicle flows in urban road networks. *J. Stat. Mechanics*, 04, 04019

Lazer, D., Kennedy, R., King, G., and Vespignani, A. (2014). The Parable of Google Flu: Traps in Big Data Analysis, *Science 343*, 1203-1205, http://archive.wired.com/ science/discoveries/magazine/16-07/pb_theory

Lorenz, J., Rauhut, H., Schweitzer, F., and Helbing, D. (2011). How social influence can undermine the wisdom of crowd effect. *Proc. of the National Academy of Sciences* (PNAS), 108(28), 9020-9025

May, R. M., Levin, S. A., and Sugihara, G. (2008). Complex systems: Ecology for bankers, *Nature*, 451, 893-895

Medina, E. (2011). *Cybernetic Revolutionaries: Technology and Politics in Allende's Chile*, MIT Press, Cambridge, MA

Obbema, F., Vlaskamp, M., and Persson, M. (2015). China rates its own citizens – including online behavior, http://www.volkskrant.nl/buitenland/china-rates-its-own-citizens-including-online-behaviour~a3979668/ [25 April 2015]

Online Library of Liberty [Internet]. Immanuel Kant, Kant's Principles of Politics, including his essay on Perpetual Peace. A Contribution to Political Science (1784). http://oll.libertyfund.org/titles/kant-kants-principles-of-politics-including-his-essay-on-perpetual-peace/simple [7 Decemeber 2015]

Page, S. E. (2008). *The Difference: How the Power of Diversity Creates Better Groups, Firms, Schools, and Societies*, Princeton University

Rauscher, F. (2012). Kant's Social and Political Philosophy, *Stanford Encyclopedia of Philosophy*, http://plato.stanford.edu/entries/kant-social-political/

Shanne, H. (2014). *The Social Laboratory, Foreign Policy*, http://foreignpolicy.com/
    2014/07/29/the-social-laboratory/
Shi-Kupfer, K., and Stepan, M. (2015). Kontrolle über alles, *Zeit Online*, 15 July 15,
    http://www.zeit.de/politik/ausland/2015-07/china-plangesellschaft-xi-jinping
Tainter, J. A. (1990). *The Collapse of Complex Societies*, Cambridge University Press,
    Cambridge

Chapter 12

Future-Oriented Innovation:
How Affordances and Potentials can Teach us How to Learn
from the Future as it Emerges

Markus F. Peschl and Thomas Fundneider

Cognitive Science Research Platform & Department of Philosophy
University of Vienna, Universitätstr. 7, 1010 Wien, Austria
Franz-Markus.Peschl@univie.ac.at

This chapter is motivated by the question why so many innovations are driven by the past rather than by the future. It will be shown that this is due to our cognitive/biological conditions ("predictive mind hypothesis"). As a possible way out of these limitations, we will develop the concept of *future-oriented/Emergent Innovation*. The core idea is that the future can be understood as an affordance; we propose to compare the future itself as a kind of affordance offering us potentials that have to be identified/"sensed", cultivated, and finally realized. It is these potentials that enable us to "*learn from the future as it emerges*". We will show how such an approach can bring forth innovations that are not only (radically) new, but that are also sustainable, thriving, and fit into existing structures. Finally we develop implications from such an understanding of innovation for organizations and education. We show that a completely new set of skills, mindsets, and attitudes as well as a kind of personal transformation (or perceptual and cognitive patterns) is necessary for realizing it.

1. Introduction

1.1. *Innovation as being driven by the past?*

Although innovation is – ideally – concerned with novelty, the future, and shaping what is not there yet, it seems that most of the classical approaches in this field rely on a strategy that is based on *extrapolating the past into the future* (e.g., Fagerberg *et al.* [2006], Tidd [2006] and many others) rather than being driven by the future. In other words, looking more closely reveals that most approaches are mainly determined by making use of already existing concepts and by improving and developing them further (e.g., as happens in incremental innovation [Christensen *et al.* 2008; Ettlie *et al.* 1984]). In other cases, creativity techniques are the source for novelty e.g., by combining existing elements or by applying brainstorming, out-of-the-box thinking, or design thinking approaches [Brown 2008; Paulus *et al.* 2012] leading to more or less radical (and successful) innovations.

From a cognitive (science) perspective, such a "conservative strategy" of relying on past experiences and concepts is not surprising. Recent approaches in cognitive science [Clark 2013; Hohwy 2013] as well as in neuroscience [Mumford 1992] show that our mind works like an "experience-driven prediction machine": The basic idea of this so-called *predictive coding* approach to cognition is that perception is not primarily a (passive) bottom-up process transmitting signals from the sensory systems to higher cognitive areas and thereby create a high-level model of the world; rather, it can be shown that it is to a large extent an active *top-down* process of *projecting* internal hypotheses about the future states of the world in a cascade of predictions to the sensory systems. In other words, the brain generates hypotheses about future states of the world/sensory systems that are then "tested" in the interaction with the environment. As a consequence, the predictive coding/mind approach serves as an explanation why applying the rather conservative strategy of extrapolating the past into the future is so prevalent in the field of innovation. As cognition is primarily concerned with maintaining established stable interaction patterns with the environment (compare also a constructivist perspective on cognition

[Maturana 1970; Varela *et al.* 1991]), the case of generating *new* knowledge or patterns of interaction is rather the exception.

Hence, if innovation is supposed to be primarily future-driven/oriented, we have to overcome these limitations of a strategy that primarily extrapolates past experiences into the future. The goal is to not only adapt to changes in the environment by applying (and slightly changing) existing solutions, but to *(co-)create new niches and (pro)actively participate in shaping the future*. That is why, in this chapter we propose to shift our attention towards a regime of innovation that is rooted in a process of *"thinking/learning from the future as it emerges"* (compare Scharmer [2007: 52]). As has been shown in Peschl and Fundneider [2013] such an approach is concerned with *perceiving and actualizing future potentials* rather than projecting and improving/changing past experiences. Hence, we have to focus on what it means to perceive future potentials. We will show that there is a close relationship between perceiving future potentials and the concept of *affordance* [Gibson 1986]. In fact, we propose to compare the future itself as a kind of affordance and, having established that, look at future-oriented innovation through the glasses of affordances.

1.2. *Outline*

Section 2 gives a short introduction on the concept of affordances and shows how they are related to the anticipation of the future. Whenever we are dealing with the future and its anticipation we are confronted with *uncertainty* as well as with *opportunities*. If we are interested in a future-oriented understanding of innovation, it will be shown that we are dealing with a form of uncertainty about a future that is not only unknown, but unknowable.

Based on these considerations, we will develop the idea of understanding the *future as affordance* and how such a perspective can lead to sustainable and thriving innovation. Section 3 shows that this can be achieved by applying the concept of potentials and developing an understanding of what it means to "learn from the future as it emerges". This leads us to the notion of *Emergent Innovation* in which it is possible to bring forth innovations that are not only (radically) new, but that are also sustainable, thriving, and fit into existing structures.

Finally, section 4 draws some conclusions and elaborates implications for the fields of innovation, organizations, and education. Furthermore, it will be shown that such a future-oriented form of innovation not only an abstract process, but also implies and requires *personal transformation*.

2. On Affordances and Anticipating the Future

2.1. *Affordances and the perception of future potentials*

As has been shown above, assuming a future-oriented notion of innovation implies that we have to take a closer look at the process of *perceiving future potentials*. In this context the concept of *affordances* turns out to play a crucial role.

Following a situated/embedded/extended [Clark 2008; Clark and Chalmers 1998] as well as a constructivist perspective on cognition [Maturana 1970], one of the major goals of a cognitive system consists in establishing stable interaction patterns with its environment. Cognition is not so much about representing the world as accurately as possible, but to act successfully in the environment so that its resources are used in a way that the autopoietic structure/homeostatic equilibrium can be maintained. At this point the notion of *affordances* [Gibson 1986] comes into play: "An affordance [...] is a resource that the environment offers any animal that has the capabilities to perceive and use it. As such, affordances are meaningful to animals: They provide opportunity for particular kinds of behavior. Thus, affordances are properties of the environment but taken relative to an animal" [Chemero 2003: 182].

In such a perspective, the environment is not primarily a set of particular properties (e.g., shape, color, material, etc.) that is perceived and processed by the cognitive system. Rather, it can be seen as a structure providing or *offering opportunities for future/potential patterns of behavior*. These opportunities are exactly what is of interest in the context of a future-oriented innovation. Innovation is about creating and implementing new interaction patterns by making use of existing environmental structures in a novel manner and/or shaping these structures in such a way that they might turn out to be beneficial for the organism (or a community of organisms, market, etc.).

If we assume an "affordance perspective", we will see that future states themselves can be seen as affording specific new (not predictable) behaviors and, thus, innovations. As will be shown in the sections to come, there is a co-dependence between cognition, behavioral/interaction patterns and (potential/future) environmental states. These elements are linked via the concept of affordance. The challenge is to provide cognitive mechanisms and strategies that are capable of *anticipating* these patterns and states.

2.2. *Anticipation of the future*

In a way, affordances are always about future or potential behavioral patterns. Thus, the aspect of anticipation is included in almost any kind of innovation process. Whenever we are innovating, we intend to change an aspect of our environment and we are in the process of anticipating some aspect of the future. In other words, we are using (knowledge about) the future already in the present moment in order to achieve a (hopefully) desired future state by anticipating both this future state and the necessary means for reaching this state. R. Poli describes anticipation as follows [2010a: 770]: "Generally speaking, anticipation concerns the capacity exhibited by some systems to tune their behaviour according to a model of the future evolution of the environment in which they are embedded." In this context, Poli points out the importance of a "model of the future". In general, such a "model of the future" is a specific kind of knowledge that may assume various forms, such as an intuition, an idea, theory, a belief, guess, prediction, projection, etc.

However, what is common to most of these kinds of knowledge is the following key premise of anticipatory systems: „future states may determine present changes of state" [Poli 2010a: 770]. This is opposed to the classical Newtonian systems thinking in which future states are not allowed to affect present changes of a system. This difference is also crucial for innovation as these processes are ideally *led primarily by a (desired or perhaps not [yet] exactly known) future state*. Their intention is to change a future state of the system and/or to create a new system or artifact in a not yet (fully) determined or created eco-system.

From a philosophical perspective, this leads us directly to a very old concept, namely the concept of the *final cause* (e.g., Aristotle [2007]) as opposed to the efficient cause (compare also Mitleton-Kelly [2007]) that is prevalent in a Newtonian perspective. Really new systems cannot be predicted in the classical Newtonian manner (exactly, because they cannot be derived in a mechanistic/deductive manner), but they emerge in an act of (co-)creation. The final cause is the driving force (although it might also co-emerge [Mitleton-Kelly 2007]) that "pulls" the whole design/innovation process (towards its future/destination).

Poli expresses this in the context of anticipation as: "Future actions are interpreted according to an 'in-order-to' structure, whilst past actions are interpreted according to a 'because' structure. In-order-to motives are components of the action: they shape the action from within. By contrast, because-motives require reflective acts upon already taken decisions. This structure helps explain why we perceive actions as free according to in-order-to-motives and as determined according to because-motives" [2010b: 10].

2.3. *Uncertainty and opportunities in an unpredictable world*

The "in-order-to" structure implies that the process of tapping *opportunities* comes into focus, as opportunities – by definition – are not yet realized and can be realized "in-order-to" bring about a specific state in a system. As is pointed out by Sarasvathy *et al.* [2003], opportunities are the other side of the coin of uncertainty. In an unpredictable complex world opportunities can be neither explicitly recognized nor discovered, because we are confronted with "true uncertainty" (i.e., "a future that is not only unknown, but unknowable" [Sarasvathy *et al.* 2003: 144]). Rather, these opportunities have to be *created* through an abductive process [Sarasvathy *et al.* 2003: 146].

Hence, future-oriented innovation and

[...] entrepreneurial activity, in particular, is not to be modelled as discovery of that which is 'out there.' Such activity, by contrast, *creates* a reality that will be different subsequent on differing choices. Hence, the reality of the future must be shaped by choices yet to be made, and this reality has no existence independent of these choices. With regard to a 'yet to be created' reality, it is surely confusing to consider its emergence in terms of the discovery of 'overlooked opportunities' [Buchanan and Vanberg 1991: 178].

If future-oriented innovations can neither be recognized nor discovered, but have to be created, we will have to take a closer look at the strategies of how this process of creation can be realized. It is in this context that the concepts of affordance and anticipation having been discussed above play a crucial role.

3. Future-Oriented Innovation: Handling the Future as Affordance

3.1. *Two paradoxes in radical innovation*

The future allows for, offers, and affords opportunities for specific behavioral actions (possibly leading to [new] (innovation) artifacts). If we are concerned with innovation, we do not know exactly what could/should be these future behavioral actions (and the resulting new artifacts) in most cases, however. In a way, we find ourselves in a twofold (intertwined) paradoxical situation:

(1) Open/flexible vs. constraining character (of the environment): This dimension concerns the flexibility of the environment and its openness to changes, or, in other words, the qualities concerning opportunities in environmental structures. As we have seen, opportunities are always connected with various levels of uncertainty. These uncertainties concern the level of openness of opportunities towards change, i.e., the polarity lies in the ambivalence that an opportunity acts as an affordance in a twofold manner: (a) on the one hand, it offers specific possibilities to (inter-)act with a specific aspect of the environment in the sense of constraining the interaction possibilities or "using" it in a specific manner; (b) on the other hand, the environmental structures might be rather open to be changed in the sense of "inviting" the cognitive system to "collaborate" with or operate on them in a not yet determined (creative) manner. As an example think of the process in

which a sculptor shapes a raw block of stone: This material represents an opportunity. On the one hand, it is more or less open what sculpture will be carved out that block of stone; on the other hand, both the qualities and characteristics of the material (stone) and the applied tools (as well as the level of creativity of the sculptor) limit/constrain the possibilities of possible shapes. In a way, that is very similar to the situation, we are in when we are innovating. Another example is Kauffman and Felin's thought experiment of possible uses of a screw driver [Felin *et al.* 2014; Kauffman 2014].

(2) Novelty vs. connectedness/intelligibility/transferability to existing structures ("Anschlussfähigkeit"): on the one hand innovative behavior or artifacts should be novel or even radically new. On the other hand, there is the requirement that the level of novelty is not so "far out" that nobody can understand it or cope with it any more. This polarity concerns the ability of the cognitive system (or market) to "understand" and cognitively accept what this completely novel artifact is about or how it could be useful (for instance, for a possibly not yet known task). This is very close to what Krippendorff discusses about the paradox concerning novelty in the process of design and making sense of novelty [1989: 9]: "[…] making sense always entails a bit of a paradox between the aim of making something new and different from what was there before, and the desire to have it make sense, to be recognizable and understandable." Think, for instance, of innovations that were "far too early", such as Apple's "Newton" in the 1990s: neither technology (low quality in handwriting recognition, not enough computational power, display, low quality in UX design, size/weight, etc.) nor the user and the market (no mobile market yet, there was neither an ecosystem nor a clear idea, how this device could be used in an efficient manner at this time, etc.) were "prepared" for or could connect properly to this innovation.

How could we possibly solve these issues and twofold paradoxes? Future seems to afford specific opportunities; some of them are viable and some of them are not (yet) viable. It is a question of coming up with the "right" innovation, in the right time, and in the right place/context.

Plus, despite fitting into the right context, this innovation should be profoundly novel. In terms of Greek mythology, we are searching for the "καιρός" (kairos): having its roots in Greek mythology and rhetoric, kairos refers to doing the right thing in an opportune, fortune, and fitting moment. The aspect that is relevant for our context of innovation is that, if one finds such a moment and the "right" idea, it does not take too many resources and energy to come up with a successful/impactful (radically new) innovation, as the opportunity almost by itself affords and provides the right circumstances leading to a successful acceptance of the innovation.

3.2. *Potentials, latents, and adjacent possibles*

Future can be handled as affordance: it is like a door-handle that implicitly offers not yet known potential patterns of behavioral interaction. From an ontological perspective, this "unknown future" can be seen as follows: any phenomenon, entity, system, or object is unfolding its own becoming/behavioral dynamics according to its inner workings and its interactions with the environment over time. This means that most phenomena or objects are not completely determined in their dynamics (in the sense of that its future states are not completely predictable). This applies especially to complex systems. This perspective has its roots in, for instance, Aristotle's metaphysics [Aristotle 2007] and draws on the concepts of potentia/potency and actus/actuality or, as Kauffman [2014: 4ff.] calls them, (adjacent) possibles/res potentia and actuals/res extensa; contrary to actuals, possibles are open to develop in various ways and directions that are partially intrinsic to this phenomenon/object and partially dependent on environmental stimuli, influences, or changes. These external dependencies and possibilities appear to the cognitive system as implicit affordances [Chemero 2003; Gibson 1986].

R. Poli [2006] introduces the concept of latents and potentials in this context:

'Categorical openness' means that the entity is only partially determined, some of its aspects are still hidden. Better: some of its determination may be latent. The difference between being hidden and being latent can be clarified as follows:

hidden components are there, waiting for proper triggers to activate them. On the other hand, latent components do not exist at all in the entity's actual state [Poli 2006, 77-78].

The interesting and challenging point is to (a) identify these latent possibilities and (b) to cultivate them in a non-imposing manner so that they can develop into "interesting" and sensible innovations. This can be achieved by following a dynamics having its foundation in the concept of adjacent possibles: "New Actuals create adjacent possible opportunities in which new Actuals arise in a continuous unprestatable co-creation" [Kauffman 2014: 6].

The interesting question for the context of innovation is how it is possible to identify these potentials and how to make use of them in order to bring about new and thriving solutions and innovations.

3.3. *Future-oriented innovation as learning from the future as it emerges*

For future-oriented innovation, the really interesting challenge is to not only react and adapt to changes and problems, but, above that, to *actively co-create/co-evolve new environments*, problem spaces, and *shape* the future in a *sustainable and thriving manner*. "Co-evolution needs to be distinguished from adaptation, which is a one-way process, when the entity adapts to changes in its environment. While co-evolution happens, when the interacting entities co-evolve with their broader ecosystem" [Mitleton-Kelly 2007: 118].

This involves highly sophisticated skills and capacities on an individual/cognitive, designerly, as well as organizational level: e.g., being able to become aware of, reflect, redirect and reframe one's patterns of perception and cognition [Depraz *et al.* 2003; Scharmer 2001, 2007], being able to identify latent or hidden potentials [Poli 2011], or dealing with self-transcending knowledge [Kaiser and Fordinal 2010; Scharmer 2001]. In other words, being able to bring forth sustainable radical innovations that are not primarily based on the projections from the past into the future, but that are grounded in a process of "learning from the future as it emerges" [Scharmer 2007: 52]. We refer to this process as *Emergent Innovation* [Peschl and Fundneider 2008, 2013].

How can this be achieved? Our cognition and symbolic capabilities enable us to intellectually deeply penetrate the environment in order to achieve a profound understanding of the potentials that are not yet realized in a particular part of the (internal or external) environment; i.e., potentials or latents [Poli 2006, 2011] that are already there, however hidden or not yet developed, that need to be discovered, developed, and cultivated in order to emerge in the future. Compared to the classical approaches and practices to innovation this is a rather different strategy. It is partially based on Scharmer's [2007] Theory-U and does not primarily follow the classical approach of trial-and-error, variation, selection, and adaptation in order to bring forth change, novelty, and/or innovation; it rather makes use of *deep knowledge about the core* of the object of innovation (OOI) and its potentials in order to "learn from these potentials/future-states as they emerge". In other words, these potentials offer a (hidden) pointer towards the future possibilities that might emerge. For the innovation process, learning from these potentials means to make use of this future knowledge in order to initiate an appropriate change already in the present moment leading potentially to this desired change.

This approach is coherent with the concept of adjacent possibles [Felin *et al.* 2014; Kauffman 2014; Koppl *et al.* 2014], in which actuals create a niche for new opportunities that might emerge, if the context(s) of these niches change(s). Our approach goes one step further, however: as we propose to identify the core of these potentials and cultivate them further in an enabling environment, the resulting innovations/actuals are not "random" as it is the case, for instance, if creativity or brainstorming techniques [Kelley 2004; Paulus *et al.* 2012] are applied. I.e., instead of creating "far-out" or completely "out-of-the-box" niches/innovations, the Emergent Innovation process proposes to base innovation on a profound/deep knowledge of the *future potentials of the core of the OOI*. This leads to changes that fill the classical gap and paradox of radical innovations (see above): they fit and connect into the existing environment/context of the OOI in a sustainable manner (because they have their root in the core of the OOI) and they are at the same time fundamentally new (because they tap yet unrealized potentials of the core of the OOI).

If we start understanding innovation as such a process of "co-creating a future by learning from the future as it emerges", we could be one step closer to bringing about (more) innovations that could really matter.

4. Conclusions

We have seen that cognitive systems are heavily driven by past experiences ("predictive mind hypothesis" [Clark 2013; Hohwy 2013]) due to their biological/neural conditions and architecture. As an implication, this fact seems to be a major obstacle for coming up with radically new innovations. As a way of overcoming this obstacle we have introduced the concept of *future-oriented innovation* or *"Emergent Innovation"* [Peschl and Fundneider 2008, 2013]. In this context we have seen that the notion of affordance plays an important role: future can be understood as affordance. An environmental state offers/affords a set of possible future states and it is the task of the cognitive system to explore and actualize them. In such a perspective these future states can be seen as *potentials* that are actualized by the cognitive system's (creative) behavior. The challenge for our question of future-oriented innovation is to create such behaviors (possibly leading to innovation artifacts) that are both radically new and at the same time meet the requirement of being sustainable and intelligible. We have shown that an approach of "learning from the future as it emerges" [Scharmer 2007] could be a possible way out. The idea is to understand the very core and essence of the object of innovation in order to cultivate its future potentials. This ensures that both (radical) novelty and intelligibility are guaranteed.

What are some of the consequences for such a future-oriented approach to innovation?

For the quality of innovations in general: As has been shown, due to the connection to the core/essence of the OOI, such innovations have a high probability of being sustainable in the sense of offering/unfolding a thriving dynamics for their users and environments. In other words, *"innovations that matter"* and that do not only meet the requirements of novelty, but also of being a *responsible and sustainable innovation* (e.g., meeting, for instance, the criteria developed by Stilgoe *et al.* [2013: 1570ff.]: anticipation, reflexivity, inclusion, and responsiveness).

For organizations: Following Hamel [2009: 92], we are led by the question "What needs to be done to create organizations that are truly fit for the future?". One of his "moon shots for management" concern fundamental issues, such as coming back to the roots of an organization by identifying, cultivating, and working for a "higher purpose", or building on philosophical and interdisciplinary principles that go far beyond mere efficiency. As has been shown above, these are some of the core activities that are necessary for establishing a company that has a future-oriented approach in its DNA. In concrete terms, this means, for instance: (i) the management has to leave behind a mechanistic plan-and-control attitude and replace it by an *enabling attitude* opening up the space for autonomy, novelty, and emergence by establishing a balanced framework of constraints and facilitating processes/structures (compare also the concept of Enabling Spaces; e.g., Peschl and Fundneider [2012, 2014]. (ii) Understanding the very core of one's organization (and its products, services, and business models) and – starting from there – to develop and cultivate untapped potentials (instead of chasing already outdated trends). (iii) Taking the future seriously; i.e., going beyond the projection and adaptation of past successes and develop a mindset and culture of deeply diving into and exploring future potentials.

For education: One of the reasons why it is so difficult to establish a future-oriented approach to innovation lies in the fact that we are cognitively and biologically not prepared to do that (see predictive mind hypothesis above). Our educational systems are another reason for that. Most of our training, be it in science and/or economy, is mainly focused on analytical and past-oriented skills and competencies. As we have seen, future-oriented innovation requires a completely different set of skills and mindsets: epistemic skills of openness, reflection, observation skills, deep understanding, a high level of empathy, designerly and creative ways of thinking and approaching things (going far beyond "design thinking"; e.g., Brown [2008]), dealing with various levels of uncertainty, a sense for potentials and adjacent possibles [Kauffman 2014; Koppl *et al.* 2014], prototyping skills, etc. Most classical educational programs do not offer such a portfolio; it seems that it is not yet well understood by curriculum designers, what are necessary future (educational) requirements for such a hyper-dynamical and rather unpredictable economy and society. Peschl *et al.* [2014] have developed a study program in which students experience such a personal and organizational innovation process by being trained in these skills and attitudes (both theoretically and practically). The important point in this program lies in the fact that this innovation process is not primarily about the resulting innovations and technical skills, but about a deep *personal transformation*; i.e., a change in epistemic attitudes, in value systems, and in mindsets. Only if that happens, future managers and leaders will be capable of leaving behind a mechanistic approach to innovation and allow them to deal with an uncertain future in an open and sovereign manner.

4.1. *Thinking through becoming and making – innovation as personal transformation*

As a consequence of what has been developed, this section concludes with some remarks on the necessity of the intertwinedness of life and innovation.

Taking seriously what has been said so far about future-oriented or Emergent Innovation, has one more implication: normally, it is assumed that a cognitive system gives shape to its environment in a more or less creative process by externalizing his/her ideas/knowledge to the world. Somebody or a team has an idea and externalizes this knowledge by operating on and shaping an aspect of the material structure of the world (resulting in an innovation artifact). Assuming an approach to innovation that "learns from the future as it emerges", partly reverses this image. As is also suggested by Ingold [2013] or Roth *et al.* [2016], we have to rethink the whole process of designing or creating an innovation or a piece of art: there is a *co-dependence* between the dynamics and the becoming of the cognitive system and the environmental/material structure that is presumably shaped by it.

The claim is that such processes (of innovation, creating art, architecture, etc.) cannot be understood only in the way of minds as giving form/shape to matter, but that there is a process of *co-development/*

co-shaping going on between the cognitive system and the matter that is shaped. *Two streams of becoming are intertwined and shaping each other over time*: on the one hand, mind shapes the environment according to its possibilities, affordances, and the cognitive system's knowledge/ ideas by creating/making (innovation) artifacts. On the other hand, the environment (e.g., the innovation artifacts) shapes the cognitive system's mind/knowledge. This does not only happen *after* the creation process is finished, but it is happening *continuously during* this process of making ("thinking through making"). In other words, it is not only that the results/completed artifacts shape the cognitive system's mind, but that it is shaped already during interacting with the world and its potentials of being shaped/formed. This is in line with the extended approach to cognition [Clark 2008; Clark and Chalmers 1998; Menary 2010], a cybernetic/system's approach to design [Glanville 1998, 2007], or to Schön's [1992] reflective conversation with materials in a design situation.

This reveals a new aspect about our process of future-oriented/ Emergent Innovation: this approach to innovation is no longer an abstract and detached (from real life) activity. Rather, it has a direct impact on the process of making, creating, and becoming: it involves a kind of personal transformation concerning one's patters of perception and thinking/ knowing, mindset, attitudes, and one's even values and life. It is a process of co-shaping between the cognitive systems *and* the environment's affordances and future potentials.

References

Aristotle (2007). *Metaphysics*. http://classics.mit.edu/Aristotle/metaphysics.html [2 April 2011]

Brown, T. (2008). Design Thinking. *Harvard Business Review*, *86*(6), 84-93

Buchanan, J. M., and Vanberg, V. J. (1991). The market as a creative process. *Economics and Philosophy*, *7*(2), 167-186

Chemero, A. (2003). An outline of a theory of affordances. *Ecological Psychology*, *15*(2), 181-195

Christensen, C. M., Kaufman, S. P., and Shih, W. C. (2008). Innovation killers. How financial tools destroy your capacity to do new things. *Harvard Business Review*, *86*(1), 98-105

Clark, A. (2008). Supersizing the mind. *Embodiment, Action, and Cognitive Extension,* Oxford University Press, Oxford, New York

Clark, A. (2013). Whatever next? Predictive brains, situated agents, and the future of cognitive science. *Behavioral and Brain Sciences, 36*(3), 1-73

Clark, A. and Chalmers, D. (1998). The extended mind. *Analysis, 58*(1), 7-19

Depraz, N., Varela, F. J. and Vermersch, P. (2003). *On becoming aware. A pragmatics of experiencing,* John Benjamins Publishing Company, Amsterdam / Philadelphia

Ettlie, J. E., Bridges, W. P., and O'Keefe, R. D. (1984). Organisational strategic and structural differences for radical vs. incremental innovation. *Management Science, 30*(6), 682-695

Fagerberg, J., Mowery, D. C. and Nelson, R. R. (Eds.). (2006). *The Oxford handbook of innovation,* Oxford University Press, Oxford

Felin, T., Kauffman, S. A., Koppl, R., and Longo, G. (2014). Economic opportunity and evolution: beyond landscapes and bounded rationality. *Strategic Entrepreneurship Journal, 8*(4), 269-282

Gibson, J. J. (1986). *The ecological approach to visual perception* (new), Psychology Press. Taylor and Francis Group, New York

Glanville, R. (1998). Re-searching design and designing research. *Design Issues, 15*(2), 88-91

Glanville, R. (2007). Try again. Fail again. Fail better: the cybernetics in design and the design in cybernetics. *Kybernetes. The International Journal of Systems and Cybernetics, 36*(9/10), 1173-1206

Hamel, G. (2009). Moon shots for management. *Harvard Business Review, 87*(2), 91-98.

Hohwy, J. (2013). *The Predictive Mind,* Oxford University Press, Oxford

Ingold, T. (2013). *Making. Anthropology, Archaeology, Art and Architecture,* Routledge, Abingdon, Oxon, New York, NY

Kaiser, A., and Fordinal, B. (2010). Creating a ba for generating self-transcending knowledge. *Journal of Knowledge Management, 14*(6), 928-942

Kauffman, S. A. (2014). Prolegomenon to patterns in evolution. *BioSystems, 123*(2014), 3-8

Kelley, T. (2004). *The art of innovation. Lessons in creativity from IDEO, America's leading design firm,* Profile Books, London

Koppl, R., Kauffman, S. A., Felin, T., and Longo, G. (2014). Economics for a creative world. *Journal of Institutional Economics, 2014,* 1-31

Krippendorff, K. (1989). On the essential contexts of artifacts or on the proposition that "Design is making sense (of things)." *Design Issues, 5*(2), 9-39

Maturana, H. R. (1970). Biology of cognition, in: Maturana, H. R., and Varela, F. J. (eds.), *Autopoiesis and cognition: the realization of the living,* DReidel Pub, ordrecht, Boston, 2-60

Menary, R. (Ed.). (2010). *The Extended Mind,* MIT Press, Cambridge, MA

Mitleton-Kelly, E. (2007). The emergence of final cause, in: Aaltonen, M. (ed.), *The third lens. Multi-ontology Sense-making and Strategic Decision-making*, Ashgate Publishing, Adlershot, 111-124

Mumford, D. (1992). On the computational architecture of the neocortex. II The role of cortico-cortical loops. *Biological Cybernetics, 66*, 241-251

Paulus, B. P., Dzindolet, M., and Kohn, N. W. (2012). Collaborative creativity. Group creativity and team innovation, in: Mumford, M. (ed.), *Handbook of Organizational Creativity*, Academic Press, San Diego, CA, 327-357

Peschl, M. F., Bottaro, G., Hartner-Tiefenthaler, M., and Rötzer, K. (2014). Learning how to innovate as a socio-epistemological process of co-creation. Towards a constructivist teaching strategy for innovation. *Constructivist Foundations, 9*(3), 421-433

Peschl, M. F., and Fundneider, T. (2008). Emergent Innovation and Sustainable Knowledge Co-creation. A Socio-Epistemological Approach to "Innovation from within". In M. D. Lytras, J. M. Carroll, E. Damiani, Tennyson, D, Avison, D and Vossen, G. (Eds.), *The Open Knowledge Society: A Computer Science and Information Systems Manifesto* (Vol. CCIS (Communications in Computer and Information Science) 19, Springer, New York, Berlin, Heidelberg, 101-108

Peschl, M. F., and Fundneider, T. (2012). Spaces enabling game-changing and sustaining innovations: Why space matters for knowledge creation and innovation. *Journal of Organisational Transformation and Social Change (OTSC), 9*(1), 41-61

Peschl, M. F., and Fundneider, T. (2013). Theory-U and Emergent Innovation. Presencing as a method of bringing forth profoundly new knowledge and realities, in: Gunnlaugson, O., Baron, C., and Cayer, M. (eds.), *Perspectives on Theory U: Insights from the field*, Business Science Reference/IGI Global, Hershey, PA, 207-233

Peschl, M. F., and Fundneider, T. (2014). Designing and enabling interfaces for collaborative knowledge creation and innovation. From managing to enabling innovation as socio-epistemological technology. *Computers and Human Behavior, 37*, 346-359

Poli, R. (2006). The ontology of what is not there, in: Malinowski, J., and Pietruszczak, A. (eds.), *Essays in Logic and Ontology (Poznan Studies in the Philosophy of the Sciences and the Humanities, vol. 91*, Rodopi, Amsterdam/New York, 73-80

Poli, R. (2010a). An introduction to the ontology of anticipation. *Futures, 42*(7), 769-776

Poli, R. (2010b). The many aspects of anticipation. *Foresight, 12*(3), 7-17

Poli, R. (2011). Steps toward an explicit ontology of the future. *Journal of Future Studies, 16*(1), 67-78

Roth, W. M., Socha, D., and Tenenberg, J. (2016). Becoming-design in corresponding: re/theorising the co- in codesigning. *CoDesign, 12*(1). http://dx.doi.org/10.1080/15710882.2015.1127387 [27 January 2016]

Sarasvathy, S. D., Dew, N., Velamuri, S. R., and Venkataraman, S. (2003). Three Views of Entrepreneurial Opportunity, in: Acs, Z. D., and Audretsch, D. B. (eds.),

Handbook of entrepreneurship research, Kluwer Academic Publishers, Dordrecht, NL, 141-160

Scharmer, C. O. (2001). Self-transcending knowledge. Sensing and organizing around emerging opportunities. *Journal of Knowledge Management, 5*(2), 137-150

Scharmer, C. O. (2007). *Theory U. Leading from the future as it emerges. The social technology of presencing.* Cambridge, MA: Society for Organizational Learning.

Schön, D. A. (1992). Designing as reflective conversation with the materials of a design situation. *Research in Engineering Design, 3*(3), 131-147

Stilgoe, J., Owen, R., and Macnaghten, P. (2013). Developing a framework for responsible innovation. *Research Policy, 42*(9), 1568-1580

Tidd, J. (2006). *A review of innovation models* (No. Discussion Paper 1). London: Imperial College. http://web.iaincirebon.ac.id/ebook/indrya/Bandura/inovasi/innovation_models.pdf [29 October 2014]

Varela, F. J., Thompson, E., and Rosch, E. (1991). *The Embodied Mind: Cognitive Science and Human Experience*, MIT Press, Cambridge, MA

Chapter 13

Interactive Articulation and Probing of Processes:
Capturing Intention and Outcome
for Coherent Workplace Design

Christian Stary

Department of Business Information Systems - Communications Engineering
University of Linz
Altenbergerstraße 69, 4040 Linz, Austria
Christian.Stary@jk.at

The development of organizations, and thus socio-technical systems, is increasingly driven by its members. They focus on modelling business processes in order to have a point of reference and intermediary representation that can be implemented by information and communication technologies. While modelling, stakeholders articulate knowledge about their work. It requires socio-cognitive effort and is influenced by the method and notation used for modelling. Subject-oriented Business Process Management (S-BPM) claims and aims to provide a natural way for articulation due to its modelling notation. Although it needs only a few symbols to describe business processes and the notation allows for direct execution of validated models, so far it has not been taken up by practice, neither management nor operation. However, stakeholders could profit most when utilizing the S-BPM capability to dynamically design processes. In this chapter, the coherence of articulating knowledge on work tasks with representing this knowledge in terms of executable models is revisited. Proposing an intentional approach, task-specific behavior of stakeholders is framed by its triggers, such as individual intention, and its expected effects, in particular its outcome. This framing can be done on arbitrary levels of granularity, depending on a stakeholder's perspective and/or level of competence or insight.

1. Introduction

Once an organization needs to reconfigure or even re-invent itself continuously due to volatile settings, its stakeholders need to develop capabilities for organizational agility [cf. Worley *et al.* 2010; Kirchmer 2013], anti-fragile or resilient behavior [cf. Abdullah *et al.* 2013; Boin *et al.* 2013; Hamel *et al.* 2013; Tseitlin 2013; Lampel *et al.* 2014]. Business process models play a crucial role in this context, as they allow representing task-relevant behavior both, as-it-is, and as stakeholders envision it [cf. Jeston *et al.* 2008; El Kharbili *et al.* 2010; Weske 2011]. In case these models can be executed [cf. Sambamurthy *et al.* 2003; Overby *et al.* 2006; Ngai *et al.* 2011; Kim *et al.* 2012] behavior specifications can be experienced directly [cf. Fleischmann *et al.* 2012].

However, informed and qualified modeling, and thus designing the organization of work still seems to be a challenging task [cf. Fowler *et al.* 2007; Klaus *et al.* 2007; Kolb *et al.* 2015]. In-depth studies to that respect refer to the social context of IT adoption and use, and thus to stakeholders and their interactions [cf. Korpelainen *et al.* 2013]. Accordingly, process elicitation, modeling, and probing should be guided by direct recall, avoiding errors, incompatibilities, and inconsistencies grounded in articulation and representation [Harman *et al.* 2015].

Subject-oriented Business Process Management (S-BPM) has been developed to provide natural means for articulation due to its modelling notation. Although it needs only a few symbols to describe the behavior of involved stakeholders or systems, and the notation allows for direct execution of validated models, recent field studies reveal the enduring stakeholder need for expert and tool support when articulating and representing process-relevant information [cf. Fleischmann *et al.* 2015]. Hence, in the following we revisit the S-BPM approach with respect to articulating task-relevant behavior and creating semantically valid models. Section 2 introduces the S-BPM concept, its notation and use when applied in a well-informed way. Section 3 provides a contextual articulation scheme for stakeholders enforcing the contextual understanding of tasks – activities are framed by triggers and intended effects. Section 4 concludes the chapter, wrapping up its objectives and the opportunities provided by the articulation scheme when coupled with execution for probing of processes from a stakeholder perspective.

2. Notation as a Driver

The S-BPM approach [Fleischmann *et al.* 2012] roots in the observation that humans usually use standard semantics of natural language, comprising subject, predicate, and object, when describing how they act in a business process. According to S-BPM's modeling notation and procedure the subject is the starting point for describing a situation or a sequence of activities. The activities correspond to predicates that operate on business objects. Resulting models describe subject behavior, including its message-based interaction occurring in the socio-technical environment.

An S-BPM model is an abstract description (encapsulation) of behavior. A subject either represents a person acting in a given situation (not necessarily in a functional role given by organization), or a thread in a technical environment. A person or an IT component termed actor instantiates a subject. A specific actor may execute the behavior of different subjects and *vice versa*, different actors may execute the same behavior, as defined by a subject. These executions are mutually independent. Assigning an actor to a subject is part of implementing a subject.

The (diagrammatic) notation of the S-BPM modeling language comprises 5 symbols. It is based on process algebra. Its formal semantics allows for automated code generation. Hence, validated subject-oriented process descriptions are executable without further transformation and enable seamless roundtrip engineering.

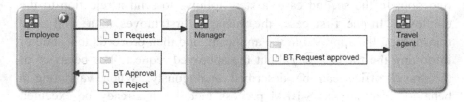

Fig. 1. Structure of a process (BT = Business Trip): Subject Interaction Diagram SID.

The subject-oriented description of a process starts with the identification of process-specific roles or task-bundles, i.e. the subjects, and the messages they exchange between them (see Subject Interaction Diagram SID in Fig. 1). When sending messages, required data is transmitted from sender to receiver via simple parameters or more complex business objects if required. In a refinement step, the modeler describes which activities and interactions the subjects have to perform in a certain sequence in the course of process execution. In this way, the behavior of individual subjects is specified, termed Subject Behavior Diagram (SBD). For each subject such a diagram has to be created, e.g. using tools like UeberModel (http://www.i2pm.net/interest-groups/ueber-model/home). In addition, business objects need to be defined giving the data structures relevant for interaction (message exchange) with other subjects.

The SBD in the left part of Fig. 2 corresponds to a refinement of the subject Employee in Fig. 1 (left side). It shows the order in which an employee sends and receives messages, or executes internal actions (functions), including respective states. The initial state is a function state for the employees completing their business trip request. The state transition 'Fill in BT Request done' leads to a send state in which an employee sends a request to the subject Manager, before entering the receive state, denoting the applicant's waiting for the manager's response. In case a rejection message is received, the process comes to an end. In case of approval received from the manager, the trip is made on the agreed date, and the business trip application process is completed.

The behavior of the subject Manager is complementary to that of Employee (see right part of Fig. 2). The manager waits in a receiving state for a request from the subject Employee. After receiving one, he/she switches to the state of decision, leading either to the approval or rejection. In the second case, a state follows to send a rejection to the employee. In the first case, the manager first moves to a send state transmitting the approval to the applicant, and then proceeds to a state of informing the travel agent about the approved request. The behavior of the travel office can be described analogously. When validating a behavior diagram the S-BPM process model can already be executed using a corresponding engine, such as UeberFlow (http://www.i2pm.net/interest-groups/ueber-flow/home).

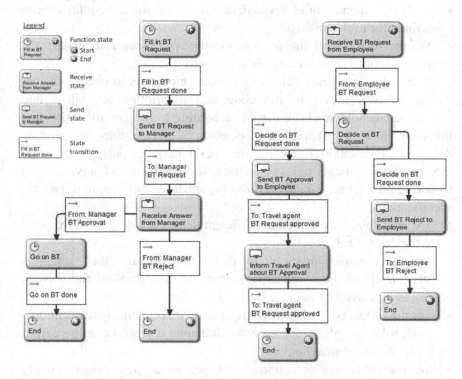

Fig. 2. Behavior of the subject Employee (left) and the subject Manager (right).

In the course of validation, a process model is reviewed according to the strategic aspects of a process not only with respect to risks, but also with respect to assigned responsibilities, such as process owners. A process owner needs to pay particular attention to the coherence of the adjunct evaluation system of the organization. When reviewing the process model process owners, in accordance with the actors of each step address several issues, laying ground for successfully implementing a process specification:

- Is the process flow in the model clearly defined (sequence of sub-steps and activities within the sub-steps)?
- Are the responsibilities (organizational units, roles, people) clearly defined for each sub-step?
- Are the relations of the process to other processes and thereby the necessary interfaces adequately described?

A specific task when validating process models is to check whether the given conventions of modeling and description are taken into account. Stakeholders check models according to their qualification and involvement in the represented operation. Thereby, they are able to detect representational errors, in particular, inconsistencies and incomplete specifications. They check for each subject a variety of topics, again relevant for successfully instantiating and executing process specifications:

- Are the subjects described in sufficient detail, and do they correspond to the desired roles?
- Are the required inputs, such as information, and their suppliers (organizational units, roles, people) sufficiently detailed and correct, i.e., as perceived by the involved stakeholders?
- Are the produced results (outputs) and their recipients (organizational units, roles, people) sufficiently accurate and correct, i.e. as perceived by the involved stakeholders?
- Are the sequences of actions to be performed in a subject clearly defined?
- Do work instructions (e.g. checklists, guidelines) for the execution of activities exist in each sub-step, and, if yes, are they part of the model?
- Are they sufficiently intelligible, so that concerned actors could work accordingly?

In the course of validation stakeholders also check business objects, such as the business trip data, that are exchanged between subjects:

- Do the business objects and their structures contain all attributes relevant for task accomplishment?
- Are operations defined on each business object?

For execution a complete interaction pattern between subjects is sufficient. It consists of a defined start and set of end states and corresponding send-receive pairs. Figure 3 exemplifies the MetasonicFlow (www.metasonic.de) user interface for stakeholders when executing an SBD. The model is displayed on the left side including a marked state in the middle indicating the status of execution when probing, and the interactive state concerning the flow is presented on the right side. After running instances of each subject a business process has been probed completely.

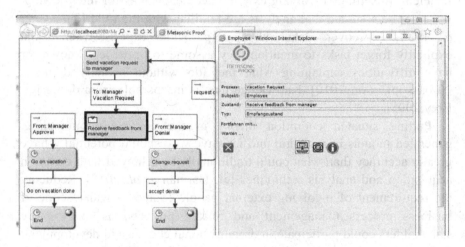

Fig. 3. Sample Probing of subject behavior Employee.

3. Contextual Representation as a Driver

In this section we first provide insight in capturing situations stakeholders face or are part of when accomplishing tasks. It lays ground for situated S-BPM articulation and probing. Then we detail the framing of activities with situation-specific information, both on triggering them, and on effectuation. Triggers can be events (externally set) or intentions (stakeholder-specific) in combination with input data to be processed, whereas effectuation is represented through output in terms of data or states, and the outcome, i.e. the (intended) effect of a certain activity or a set of actions.

3.1. *Situatedness*

The most authentic articulation and representation of situations can be assumed to stem from stakeholders experiencing these situations. In contrast to elicitation techniques involving analysts or facilitators, in the proposed self-contained articulation setting stakeholders do not have to rely on information provided by analysts, rather on the structure prepared for them. In settings involving external people, such as for interviewing, it cannot be assumed that analysts are familiar with the field [Parsaye *et al.* 1988]. Moreover, stakeholders, in particular experts, when asked explicitly forget tasks to mention they assume to be widely known, or have difficulties explaining what they do without actually doing it [Grosskopf *et al.* 2010]. Knowledge thus is inseparable from doing [cf. Brey 2005].

Putting situated cognition theory in the context of modeling, generated models in a natural and intuitive way should potentially have greater accuracy than what could traditionally be achieved with common acquisition and analysis techniques [cf. Harman *et al.* 2015]. Reducing the requirement of involving external people enables a wider scope of business process management and related projects, as many more stakeholders could participate in organizational change and development. S-BPM is focusing on parallel processes, thus its models can be created simultaneously after agreeing on communication interfaces.

An underlying concept in this context seems to play agency: According to Himma [2009] the

> idea of agency is conceptually associated with the idea of being capable of doing something that counts as an act or action. As a conceptual matter, X is an agent if and only if X is capable of performing action; breathing is something we do, but it does not count as an action. Typing these words is an action, and it is in virtue of my ability to do this kind of thing that, as a conceptual matter, I am an agent. [...] Agents are not merely capable of performing acts; they inevitably perform them (in the relevant sense). [...] The very concept of agency presupposes that agents are conscious [19].

Reflecting this understanding reveals the way of involvement in a situation when humans are acting or interacting. It underpins the requirement to devote design effort to human issues to the same extent developers spend for technical ones. The recognition of user modeling can be considered such an endeavor [cf. Brusilovsky 2002]. Situatedness is awareness about its world, comprising communities, organizations, societies or other contingent systems of systems, and its capability to induce changes on it [cf. Campos *et al.* 2009].

> The essence of situation awareness lies in the monitoring of various entities and the relations that occur among them. Since the properties of relations, unlike the properties of objects, are not directly measurable, one needs to have some background knowledge (such as ontologies and rules) to specify how to derive the existence and meaning of particular relations [Matteus *et al.* 2005].

Consequently, system development, concerning cognition, organizations, social or technological systems, should be driven by different systemic perspectives and lead to architectures allowing dynamic changes [cf. Rolland *et al.* 1999]. Situatedness of development processes is a key issue in software and method engineering communities, such as BPM [cf. Barwise *et al.* 1981]. Prescriptions, either from the user interaction or the task handling perspective, need to be adapted to the situation at hand, allowing for systems dynamics in the course of task or interaction processes.

Most important, we need to recognize that actors are embedded in situations. In cognitive science actors (there agents) are considered as *embodied* and interactively *situated* in worlds [Dobbyn *et al.* 2003]. When analyzing the meanings attached to these terms a set of conditions for situatedness and embodiment can be derived, based on the conclusive assumption that external representational schemas are required for adaptation. While virtual agents in virtual worlds are considered neither situated nor embodied, awareness of evolving goals, various modalities for interaction and task accomplishment procedures could lead to a rich repertoire of interactions.

Embedded actors could develop individual points of view, relative to their starting position work spaces, and have a capacity to develop a dedicated interaction space. None of these capabilities are possible without representational capacities, such as the S-BPM notation. Model-based approaches to cognitive support system have taken this view, both on the representational and processing level [cf. Stary 2000] while relating them to cognitive constructs [cf. Eberle *et al.* 2010]. On one hand, mutual relationships between user properties and interaction styles can be captured in terms of cognitive characteristics. On the other hand, rules for dynamically tuning task accomplishment and interaction can be kept in dedicated representation schemes, such as adaptation models. Such capabilities could open up a new era of stakeholder-driven engineering, in particular relevant in times of volatile settings.

The problem with this contextual information is that it cannot be encoded with standard data. While experts may be able to explain what they do, they are unable to easily provide context to that information [Brown *et al.* 1989]. It is suggested that the only way to accurately teach this information is to first provide its context – a practice commonly used during apprenticeships [Lave 1988]. From this, theories of explicit memory (sometimes referred to as tacit knowledge) have emerged as knowledge that cannot easily be conveyed to other people. To retrieve this information, it is easiest to use a simulation-based approach for memory recall [Rubin 2006], such as enabled by S-BPM models.

The quest for contextual representation when capturing task- or role-specific behavior in certain situations requires contextual design of articulation support. We suggest to frame activity-relevant information with context, thus providing a certain structure for articulating work behavior and probing support [cf. Stary *et al.* 2015]. As shown in Figure 4 it consists of

(1) *Trigger and incoming information*: Hereby we distinguish pragmatically and semantically relevant information (context) from syntactic structure (input). At least the context should be given when a learning/change task chain is started.

(2) *Functional processing information*: It specifies not only the function in terms of activities to be set, but rather the role in which a task is performed. In this way, the context can be represented more accurately compared with purely functional specifications.

(3) *Effect and deliverables*: Again, we distinguish pragmatically and semantically relevant information (outcome denoting the effect of using a feature) from the syntactic structure (output). At least some outcome should be generated once a learning/change task chain is completed.

For each task-relevant behavior a separate representation, a so-called activity brick, should be generated by stakeholders.

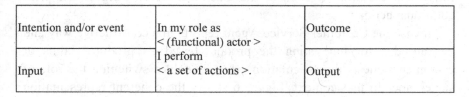

Intention and/or event	In my role as < (functional) actor >	Outcome
Input	I perform < a set of actions >.	Output

Fig. 4. The articulation scheme containing trigger, role-specific action, and effect.

3.2. *Triggering and effectuating behavior*

In this section we exemplify the framing of role-specific actions, triggering and effectuating behavior. The data are based on initial field tests of the articulation scheme and allow demonstrating the benefit of the approach for scoping subjects. The example shown is taken from a service provider in the field of software development.

Figure 5 shows the case when a stakeholder in the functional role of customer service agent articulates how a product claim from a customer is framed. The input is a product claim, e.g. when a product does not meet a customer requirement. The intention is to help the concerned customer, until he/she is satisfied. The output of this activity is either a hint how the requirement has already been met or a change request for product development, in case it could not be met so far.

Help customer	In my role as Customer	Customer is satisfied
Product claim	Service Agent I handle a product claim.	Hint or change request

Fig. 5. Customer service actor behavior handling customer product claims

From an S-BPM perspective this representation constitutes a particular subject which behavior can be detailed in creating an SBD. Although in the course of articulation the functional role (customer service agent) provides an intuitive entry point, the subject should be labeled more accurately product claim customer handling, as it is very likely that the work agenda of the Customer Service Agent comprise additional actions.

In case the Customer Service Agent reports in a constructive way and has an idea for innovating the product based on product claims or customer requests the articulation scheme enables switching the role of stakeholder in that context. Figure 6 shows the coherent representation for that case.

Innovate product	In my role as Customer Service Agent I re-formulate the product claim towards innovative featuring.	Product changes
Product claim from customer		Idea ticket

Fig. 6. Scoping another subject – Idea Provider.

The consequences for process modeling are substantial, since the SBD for handling a product claim as a customer service agent shapes a functional role handling subject, communicating with the customer and product department. The Idea Generator subject allows not only reducing the complexity when the workplace of a service agent is described, but rather develop a product improvement or organizational learning procedure that could serve as pattern across domains. The latter model could serve as input for the change manager to implement product innovation processes after the proposal has been collectively reflected. For a complete task chain, and thus business process specification, each output of an activity needs to correspond to an input of an adjacent activity. Then the details are specified in an SBD and can be executed as demonstrated above.

3.3. *Procedure*

Looking at procedural issues when setting up contextual representations, the crucial question is the how to articulate intention. Grice [1969] has already investigated the relationship between meaning and intention of utterers. From Böhm's research [1997: 69] we can conclude that meaning constitutes sensemaking for humans, as it needs to be seen intertwined with the functional context of a person and the goals this person is trying to achieve individually.

Sheeran [2002] has studied possible gaps between behavior and intention. Looking for psychological variables to 'bridge' possible intention–behavior gaps the author's meta-analysis of meta-analyses has led to a conceptualization of intention–behavior discrepancies. Four groups of variables, namely behavior type, intention type, properties of intention, and cognitive and personality variables, could be clustered as they moderate intention–behavior relations. As SBDs contain a task description according individual mental models, any verbalization of intention respects the stakeholder personality and cognitive model of a situation. As the intention type is not essential when articulating triggers of actions, each stakeholder can describe in the intentional context of the action (set) at hand the way he/she perceives it.

Hug *et al.* [2012] have referred to intentions in the context of process engineering. Rather than detailing how to facilitate stakeholder articulation with respect to intentional behavior,

> the intentional level is used to guide engineers through IS processes by dynamic choices. Each time an intention is achieved the model suggests the next steps that can be enacted and new ways to achieve them. The resulting IS development process is adaptive and flexible as it is dynamically constructed. [Hug *et al.* 2012: 204]

We will see below, for establishing intentional fit of activities this input is valuable.

When articulating business processes the completeness of work procedures can be checked according to the following steps:

1. Identification of activity bricks
   a. Start with variety of activities related to functional role
   b. Rephrase behavior for labeling subjects according to intention
   c. Enrich SID accordingly
   d. Detail SBD
2. Compatibility check
3. Generate chain(s).

In step 1 all activity bricks should be described. In step 2 the fitting of activity brick needs to be checked, since, e.g., not all product claims might be compatible to product development activities, and vice versa. At least the output/input relations need to be checked. In step 3 compatible activity bricks can be combined to form chains of activities (expressed in SIDs). There may be more than a single option for accomplishing a certain task. A typical case is making an innovative feature proposal for a product.

4. Conclusion

Developing an organization being able to adapt to changes dynamically requires stakeholder capabilities to design business processes. They represent task-relevant behavior both, as-it-is, and as-it-could-be. For informed and qualified modeling stakeholders require dedicated support, both when articulating process knowledge, and sharing it with others. We have developed a contextual procedure for subject-oriented business process modelling, as, albeit the easy-to-grasp notation, stakeholders still need support when constructing process models.

The presented scheme should help identifying self-contained behavior due to the explicit context representation when articulating knowledge on work tasks. The scheme frames activities by triggers (incoming side) and intended effects (outgoing side). Of particular help in Subject-oriented Business Process Management is the capability to execute validated models, as stakeholders can experience without further transformation what they have specified in the various subject models.

Future research will focus on empirical field tests and the integration of the scheme with organizational development tasks leading to architectures that fit to the stakeholders' perception and articulation of work tasks. In such a framework work tasks are being assigned to micro-features that are also framed by socio-technical context elements [cf. Stary *et al.* 2015].

References

Abdullah, N. A. S., Noor, N. L. M., and Ibrahim, E. N. M. (2013). Resilient Organization: Modelling the Capacity for Resilience, *Proc. International Conference on Research and Innovation in Information Systems* (ICRIIS), IEEE, New York, 319-324

Barwise, J., and Perry, J. (1981). Situations and Attitudes. *The Journal of Philosophy* 78, 668-691

Boin, A., and van Eeten, M. J. (2013). The Resilient Organization, *Public Management Review*, 15(3), 429-445

Böhm, W. (1997). *Entwürfe zu einer Pädagogik der Person*, Julius Klinkhardt, Bad Heilbrunn

Brey, Ph. (2005). The Epistemology and Ontology of Human-Computer Interaction, *Mind & Machines*, 15, 383-398

Brown, J. S., Collins, A., and Duguid, P. (1989). Situated Cognition and the Culture of Learning. *Educational researcher* 18(1), 32-42

Brusilovsky, P. (2002). Domain, Task, and User Models for an Adaptive Hypermedia Performance Support System. *Proc. IUI'02*, ACM, 23-30

Campos, J., Lopez-Sanchez, M., Rodriguez-Aguilar, J. A., and Esteva, M. (2009). Formalizing Situatedness and Adaption in Electronic Institutions. *Proc. COIN 2008*, LNAI 5428, 126-139, Springer, Berlin

Dobbyn, Ch., and Stuart, S. (2003). The Self as Embedded Agent, *Minds & Machines* 13, 187-201

Eberle, P., Schwarzinger, Ch., and Stary, Ch. (2010). User Modeling and Cognitive User Support: Towards Structured Development, *Univ. Access InfSoc*, doi: 10.1007/s10209-010-0210-z

El Kharbili, M., and Keil, T. (2010). Bringing Agility to Business Process Management: Rules Deployment in an SOA, in: *Emerging Web Services Technology Volume III*, Birkhäuser, Basel, 157-170

Fleischmann, A., and Stary, Ch. (2012). Whom to Talk To: A Stakeholder-Perspective on Business Process Development, *Univ. Access InfSoc*, doi: 10.1007/s10209-011-0236-x)

Fleischmann, A., Schmidt,W., Stary, C., Obermeier, S., and Börger, E. (2012). *Subject-oriented Business Process Management*, Springer, Berlin

Fleischmann, A., Schmidt, W., and Stary, Ch. (eds.) (2015). *S-BPM in the Wild – Value creating Practice in the Field*, Springer, Berlin

Fowler, J. J., and Horan, P. (2007). Are Information Systems' Success and Failure Factors Related? An Exploratory Study, *Journal of Organizational and End User Computing*, 19 (2), 1-22

Grice, H. P. (1969). Utterer's Meaning and Intention, *The philosophical review*, 147-177

Grosskopf, A., Edelman, J., and Weske, M. (2010). Tangible Business Process Modeling Methodology and Experiment Design, in: Rinderle-Ma, S., Sadiq, S., and

Leymann, F. (eds.), *Business Process Management Workshops, Lecture Notes in Business Information Processing*, vol. 43, 489-500, Springer Berlin Heidelberg

Hamel, G., and Valikangas, L. (2013). The Quest for Resilience, *Harvard Business Review*, 81(9), 52-65

Harman, J., Brown, R., Kannengiesser, U., Meyer, N., and Rothschädl, Th. (2015). Model while you do. Engaging an S-BPM Vendor on Process Modeling in 3D Worlds, in: Fleischmann, A., Schmidt, W., and Stary, Ch. (eds), *S-BPM in the Wild – Value creating Practice in the Field*, Springer, Berlin

Himma, K. E. (2009). Artificial Agency, Consciousness, and the Criteria for Moral Agency, *Ethics and Information Technology*, 11, 19-29, doi: 10.1007/s10676-008-9167-5

Hug, C., Deneckère, R., and Salinesi, C. (2012). Map-TBS: Map Process Enactment Traces and Analysis, in: Proceedings *Sixth International Conference on Research Challenges in Information Science (RCIS)*, IEEE, 1-6

Jeston, J., and Nelis, J. (2008). *Business Process Management. Practical Guidelines to Successful Implementations,* 2nd edition, Elsevier, Oxford, UK

Klaus, T., Wingreen, S., and Blanton, J. B. (2007). Examining User Resistance and Management Strategies in Enterprise System Implementations, in: *Proc. ACM SIGMIS CPR Conference on Computer Personnel Research*, 55-62

Kim, G., and Suh, Y. (2012) Building Semantic Business Process Space for Agile and Efficient Business Processes Management: Ontology-Based Approach, in: *Business Enterprise, Process, and Technology Management: Models and Applications*, 51

Kirchmer, M. (2011). What has Jazz to do with MPE?, *High Performance Through Process Excellence*, ch.11, Springer, Berlin, 159-169

Kolb, J., Rudner, B., and Reichert, M. (2015) Gesture-Based Process Modeling Using Multi-touch Devices, *Int. Journal of Information System Modeling and Design* 4(4), 48-69

Korpelainen, E., and Kira, M. (2013). Systems Approach for Analysing Problems in IT System Adoption at Work, *Behaviour & Information Technology*, 32(3), 247-262

Lampel, J., Bhalla, A., and Jha, P. P. (2014). Does Governance Confer Organisational Resilience? Evidence from UK Employee owned Businesses, *European Management Journal*, 32(1), 66-72

Lave, J. (1988). *The Culture of Acquisition and the Practice of Understanding*. Institute for Research on Learning Palo Alto, CA

Ngai, E. W., Chau, D. C., and Chan, T. L. A. (2011). Information Technology, Operational, and Management Competencies for Supply Chain Agility: Findings from case studies, *The Journal of Strategic Information Systems*, 20(3), 232-249

Overby, E., Bharadwaj, A., and Sambamurthy, V. (2006). Enterprise Agility and the Enabling Role of Information Technology, *European Journal of Information Systems*, 15(2), 120-131

Parsaye, K., and Chignell, M. (1988). *Expert systems for experts*, Wiley, New York

Rolland, C., Prakash, N., and Benjamen, A. (1999). A Multi-Model View of Process Modelling, *Requirements Eng.* 4, 169-187

Rubin, D. C. (2006). The Basic-systems Model of Episodic Memory. *Perspectives on Psychological Science* 1(4), 277-311

Sambamurthy, V., Anandhi, B., and Varun, G. (2003). Shaping Agility through Digital Options: Reconceptualizing the Role of Information Technology in Contemporary Firms, *MIS Quarterly* 27(2), 237-263

Sheeran, P. (2002). Intention-behavior Relations: A Conceptual and Empirical Review. *European Review of Social Psychology*, *12*(1), 1-36

Stary, Ch. (2000). TADEUS: Seamless Development of Task-Based and User-Oriented User Interfaces, *IEEE TA-SMC* 30, 509-525

Stary, C., Krenn, F., Lerchner, H., Neubauer, M., Oppl, S., and Wachholder, D. (2015). Towards Stakeholder-Centered Design of Open Systems: Learning from Organizational Learning, in: *Proc. of the European Conference on Cognitive Ergonomics 2015*, ACM, New York, 26

Tseitlin, A. (2013). The Antifragile Organization, *Communications of the ACM*, 56(8), 40-44

Weske, M. (2012). *Business Process Management. Concepts, Languages, Architectures*, 2nd ed., Springer, Heidelberg

Worley, C. G., and Lawler, E. E. (2010). Agility and Organization Design: A Diagnostic Framework, *Organizational Dynamics*, 39(2), 194-204

Chapter 14

Simulated Education and Illusive Technologies

Yagmur Denizhan

Electrical and Electronics Engineering Department,
Bogazici University
34342 Bebek, Istanbul, Turkey
denizhan@boun.edu.tr

Massive policies that are blind to individuals and their true needs compel the educators, as well as the pupils and students, to imitate true functioning. And when imitations are tolerated for the sake of pragmatic concerns, disregarding the essence and long-term goals of the process of education, education is tacitly replaced by its simulated version. However, simulated education supported by some advanced technologies turns out to be particularly destructive for students, who have a genuine capacity for becoming prospective developers of technology. This constitutes a rather unexpected corrective feedback to a system gone astray.

1. Introduction

Sustainability, as a favourite subject of today's discussions, is addressed in relation to various phenomena, but almost always with some connection to technology. Here, I want to examine the sustainability of technological development itself in correlation with the development of human individuals, particularly of those who are prospective developers of technology. Towards this end, I will try to identify some feedback relations between automation, ICT, growth-based market economy, social and technological policies on one hand, and mental development and education of engineering students on the other hand.

While doing so, I will rely on my observations as a professor of electrical and electronics engineering at a distinguished university of my country, as well as those of my colleagues at other engineering departments. Turkey has a midway position between developed countries and many developing countries in various respects, including education and social policies. The changes and course of affairs that I have observed in my country have probably occurred a few years earlier in developed countries, while some developing countries are still on the way of experiencing them. But based on the feedback from colleagues in other countries I am convinced that the issues I am going to address here are largely shared by the globalised part of the world.

2. Recent Pictures from the Engineering Education Scene

What made me first ponder on the intricate relation between technology and the general mentality was the sudden emergence of a new type of student behaviour in my sophomore class in 2007 or 2008: as a response to the comprehension questions I asked during the lectures many students were producing answers without understanding the content of the question, instead resorting to statistical clues, just as an Artificial Intelligence algorithm would do. As I pointed out in an earlier publication, "in the subsequent years the students' tendency to miss the essence of education and to seek simple algorithmic routes to success continued" [Denizhan, 2014].

Furthermore, there is also a general shift in the studying habits of students towards what used to be the approach of reluctant students of earlier times: provisory memorisation of procedures instead of comprehension of concepts. This can be best observed in recent graduate admittance interviews and PhD qualifier exams where students, when asked to explain a concept, exclusively respond by giving the algorithmic description of an operation that involves this concept.

As an academic advisor I also observe – almost parallel to these behavioural changes – a general rise in the prevalence of some psychological problems like *strong dependence on external appreciation, insufficient self-confidence*, and *rapid loss of motivation under failure*.

While these symptoms persisted and became commonplace during the many years that followed their sudden emergence, more recently some unprecedented types of error started to appear in the exam papers and home works:

A new category of error, which I want to name *primitive imitation*, mostly appears in the form of responses produced on basis of sheer visual pattern matching. For example, a statistically significant number of computer engineering sophomore students, who were given an assignment that requires a graphical representation, have delivered results which were apparently prepared as a very primitive imitation of the graphics they have found via a Google visual query giving the name of the representation method as keyword. Their answers not only had no relation to the specific assignment but also exhibited complete illiteracy with regards to the underlying symbolism; e.g. directional graphs without arrows. This demonstrates how far the system allows the students to proceed without acquiring even the basic logical mentality.

Another new category of error, which I call *groundless ingenuity*, refers to attempts of producing ingenious correlations without being aware of conceptual jumps. The knowledge of students who make this type of errors seems to consist of a collection of rules, regularities and methods, rather than constituting a hierarchically organised structure.

These mental and behavioural changes are of course consequences of a variety of factors, including economic, socio-political and technological ones. In [Denizhan 2014] I have primarily focused on performance-based evaluation and incentive policies, and here I will briefly summarise how they may influence the cognitive and mental development of learners. But beyond that, I will investigate the impact of advanced technologies together with their economic connections on the formation of engineering students, who are supposed to be the prospective developers of these very technologies.

3. Cognitive Development and Beyond

In order to analyse the impacts of these factors on the mental development of human beings, let us envisage human comprehension as a complex dynamic edifice that rises level by level towards higher abstraction. At the fundament of the mental edifice lies the reliable ground of embodied knowledge, i.e. a more basic edifice that starts at birth with the most basic instincts (like sucking) and gains new levels during the subsequent years' cognitive development. As a matter of fact, the rise of the mental edifice can be considered as an extension and a later stage of the earlier process of cognitive development. At any stage the rise of the edifice proceeds as a sequence of emergent leaps, a process vividly described by Alexandre Borovik [Borovik 2014] in the context of mathematics:

"The crystallisation of a mathematical concept (say, of a fraction), in a child's mind could be like a phase transition in a crystal growing in a rich, saturated – and undisturbed – solution of salt. An "aha!" moment is a sudden jump to another level of abstraction. Such changes in one's mode of thinking are like a metamorphosis of a caterpillar into a butterfly."

Such a leap is typically accompanied by joyful emotions and enthusiasm, providing the overall process with an inherent positive feedback mechanism, a self-perpetuating drive, which makes up the *internal motivation* of the learner. This can be best observed in toddlers, who – charmed by the appeal of gaining autonomy, as well as by the immediate joy of the leap–strive obsessively for new cognitive skills. But this healthy course of affairs asks for adequate external conditions, and therefore, the encounter with external conditions needs to be mediated by more competent or experienced fellow human beings, who can discern the state of the child and offer the necessary protection and support at the right dose. This is the kind of assistance referred to as *scaffolding* by the Vygotskian school of developmental psychology, which also emphasises that the child should be exposed to tasks which it can achieve (at least with some help) at its present developmental level, i.e. that the tasks are within the potential *zone of proximal development*.

Only adequate scaffolding can provide the child with *self-confidence* and *confidence in the holding environment* and sustain its *internal motivation*.

At early stages, where the sensitivity is highest, adequate scaffolding is safeguarded by the strongly coupled and strictly regulated physiological dynamics of the mother and the infant. But in the course of the years not only the physiological regulation on the primary caregiver(s) gradually fades out but also other human beings enter the scene, who act – at best – under the lesser regulation of the society. At this point pedagogical competence on behalf of teachers and educators can make a difference in gaining the child's trust in the education system.

Beyond cognitive development the mental development continues via transfer of knowledge from human to human. The ideal and most natural scenario for this transfer occurs in the form of a personal interaction between a willing learner and a person who has a solid grasp of the subject of interest, i.e. who has once personally experienced the "jump to a higher level of abstraction" associated with this subject. This case is a rather trivial extension of the scaffolding activity of primary caregivers during the basic cognitive development of the child. Under such conditions, the teaching person will naturally tend to assist the learner to make a transition similar to his/her own experience, and towards this end will adjust his/her interventions according to direct observations of and discernments about the learner. In this scenario performance testing may be meaningful and necessary as an indirect means of assessing the state of comprehension of the learner (if direct observation does not provide sufficient information) or as a means of providing self-confidence to the learner about the acquired skills. Nevertheless, the most common usage of performance testing aims at certifying the efficiency of the learning/teaching activity in the eye of third parties, which is already a serious departure from the ideal natural scenario of knowledge transfer.

And as we move further away from this natural scenario, performance testing gains undue importance, and eventually starts to jeopardise the process of learning, as I will try to explain in the next section.

Particularly problematic is the case of institutionalised mass education, where the personal interaction between teacher and learner is substantially reduced. Relatively successful examples of earlier practices show that educational success (i.e. achievement of educational goals that go beyond immediate pragmatic targets) in mass education largely depends on the sensibility and pedagogical competence of teachers and educators, who manage to keep a close watch on the developmental course of the learners, try to compensate for the system's blindness to individuals, and keep up the self-confidence of the learners, as well as their confidence in the education system. Obviously, such functioning is possible as long as the number of learners a teacher has to take care of remains within reasonable bounds.

But due to various economic, demographic, social and political factors the number of learners has grown disproportionately as compared to that of the teachers. As a result, practical concerns like scalability or standardisation started to dominate the pedagogical ones and automation of education became inevitable. The first and foremost component of education to be automated was the process of assessing the learners' state of comprehension.

Together with the advancement of digital computers the employment of multiple-choice tests in large-scale admission exams of schools and universities became an integral part of the education system and started to play a decisive role in the lives of many people. As such, these tests immediately assumed the role of a barrier in front of a huge flow, a bottleneck where candidates are ranked and decimated according to their ability of selecting the most plausible one among several alternative answers for a huge number of questions within a limited time.

Exams in the classical form are obviously better than multiple-choice tests. But when used for the same purpose as a race of answering a huge number of questions within limited time, they equally encourage employment of methods that by-pass true knowledge and comprehension. Memorisation of short-cut procedures to answer questions of specific types is certainly the most harmless one among these methods.

Whether multiple-choice or not, such tests obviously mark a radical departure from the natural scenario of learning because, while serving as a versatile method of automated performance assessment, they do not provide reliable information about the actual state of comprehension of the examinee. And more importantly; given the decisive role of the tests and the fact that these short-cut methods are not in conflict with "the rules of the game", they cannot even be regarded as a lie about one's state of comprehension. Indeed they are considered as completely legitimate strategies and are encouraged by parents and teachers.

Provided that the examinee would return to the natural mode of studying that is driven by internal reward mechanisms, one-time employment of a pragmatic strategy to jump a practical hurdle would not be a great issue. For many generations the large-scale high-school and university admission exams have constituted only temporary and contextual exigencies, and passed without leaving behind a permanent behavioural change. The symptoms I have mentioned in Section 2 did not manifest themselves until a breaking point was reached, which seems to be correlated with the introduction of *performance-based control policies* in various domains of social life, as pointed out in [Denizhan 2014] with reference to the 2nd episode of a documentary series by Adam Curtis [Curtis 2007]. These liberal policies, which prescribe that employees are given performance targets and set free to accomplish them any way they want, are a social application of the cybernetic feedback principle renowned for "hitting the targets". However, as described in detail in [Denizhan 2014], usage of these policies with highly set targets and high competitive pressure as a means of instigating the employees to ever increasing performance led to the very opposite. Under harsh survival pressure they were incited to invent means of imitating the achievement of targets, very much like the pupils and students, who under harsh exam conditions resort to short-cut methods of answering questions without understanding them. Thus, imitation became a routine practice.

Although authorities must have long noticed these practices, performance-based control policies were never abandoned, just as the massive admission exams are still part of the education system in spite of the well-known short-cut methods.

Authorities in charge of educational affairs, while admitting that the tests are not necessarily optimal, argue that they still provide useful information about the overall capacity of the examinees, and that there is no other practical way of evaluating and ranking so many candidates. Imitations' being tolerated for the sake of such pragmatic concerns disregarding the essence and long-term goals of the process of education means that education is tacitly replaced by its simulated version.

4. Simulation and its Discontents

Seen from the perspective of cognitive development and development of the personality, being forced to achieve externally set performance targets (which aim at economic growth, rather than the development of the individual) is likely to induce the very opposite of what is intended by Vygotskian pedagogy. Furthermore, it makes a huge difference at which stage one is exposed to such policies:

When encountered at an adult age (as is the case with the civil servants shown in [Curtis 2007]), having to chase the receding horizon of targets that are systematically kept beyond reach (outside the zone of proximal development) typically generates *resentment, anger* or *ambition* instead of *confidence in the holding social system*, and may turn the person into a frustrated servant, a reactionary rebel or a selfish careerist, who would readily imitate output performance, when needs be.

Yet the next generation (the generation of my students) is born into these conditions that entail imitation as a routine strategy to cope with a social environment that does not care about and does not support the individuals' self-actualisation. The outcome of such an early encounter is typically *helplessness* and feelings of *insufficiency* rather than *self-confidence, submission to the system* rather than *confidence in it*. These children grow up to become individuals (and possibly educators), who are largely *dependent on externally set rules* rather than being capable of *autonomous reasoning*. Deprived of self-confidence and confidence in the holding environment, which are the sources that foster *internal motivation*, they are doomed to depend on *external gratification mechanisms*. This last point closes the vicious circle and renders necessary the very policies that lead to the extinction of internal motivation. And once internal motivation disappears in a society, external means of reward and punishment becomes indispensable to keep things going.

But there is an even more dramatic change that comes with the generations that is born into this set-up. Since they have nothing to compare with, imitation constitutes for them the default mode, the normal way of functioning, which makes them part of the simulated education system. Pupils and students of these new generations know no other way of studying than learning how to answer specific type of questions, no comprehension beyond the ability of generating functioning operations, no knowledge beyond know-how. And as long as the education system appreciates their output performances and allows them to proceed to further levels, they are nourished by this external gratification and develop an *illusion of success and mastery* instead of the solid self-confidence built on the reliable fundament of embodied knowledge. Obviously, the same applies also to teachers and educators who are born into this system. For the lack of any other reference they mostly fail to recognise that something is utterly wrong in the education system, where pupils and students can formally climb up the stairs without actually being elevated to these levels, and can be caught up in the *illusion of a functioning system* as long they receive good scores from accrediting agencies. And when some course subjects, which indispensably require true comprehension, constitute a threat for the sustenance of the joint illusion of all stakeholders -teachers and learners alike- these subjects are simply removed from the curricula with the pretext that "today such tedious tasks don't need to be performed by human beings, instead pupils and students should be taught how to operate the computers that will perform these tasks". (What is again being dismissed here is the fact that the primary goal of assigning tasks within the realm of education is to incite a mental leap to a higher level of comprehension and abstraction, and not finding the answer.)

Keeping up the joint illusion is a full-time job for a system that is built on it. But more crucially, it is also indispensable if the gap between the present state and the point of departure from the solid reality is too wide to allow a soft-landing

5. The Aid of Technology

In the sustenance of the joint illusion, like in any other fields of human endeavour, technology assumes an important supportive role. For example, without the complicity of advanced communication and computer technologies, the previously mentioned students who have resorted to *primitive imitation* (i.e. tried to accomplish the assigned engineering problem via simple visual imitation of graphical patterns) could not have even attempted such an endeavour. But more importantly, without the aid of advanced technologies they could not have kept up long enough (that is, until the sophomore class of computer engineering at a distinguished university) the illusion that this could be a functioning method for solving complex problems and that engineering education consists of tasks that can be handled with basic cognitive skills and practical intelligence.

Today, computer-aided education is celebrated as an indicator of quality at all levels – from kindergarten to university –, unfortunately without distinguishing between tools and programs that support and scaffold cognitive and mental development on one hand, and those that generate only an illusion of competence and command on the other hand.

At this point, I want to coin a concept that addresses a specific aspect of mediating technologies: *illusiveness*, i.e. a qualitative measure of how much illusion a mediating technology generates in the minds of its users. Depending on the domain of usage, illusiveness may or may not be a desirable property. But it is clear that technologies designed to be illusive have to be promoted with proper warning, taking into consideration all of its implications for the functioning of the society, and making sure that they are used consciously and cautiously. Unfortunately, such diligence has been exercised neither in connection with technologies of automated performance assessment, nor with performance-based social policies (which is a technology par excellence), nor with computer tools.

In that respect, contemporary ICT devices equipped with extremely *illusive user interface technologies* deserve special attention. The user-friendly interfaces of advanced ICT gadgets translate even sophisticated operations into basic sensorimotor tasks like clicking, shifting, dragging and dropping, and into basic cognitive tasks like pattern matching. Never before have technology users been so perfectly "protected" from the complexity of the underlying phenomena and absolved from the exigency of having some comprehension about them. Market dynamics unleashes masses of cheap ICT gadgets with illusive interfaces upon the plastic brains of young children. While these toys become parents' favourite means of keeping the children occupied, whole generations are raised without being sufficiently exposed to the challenging stimuli of the real world that would have compelled the emergence of new cognitive abilities. Instead, gadgets with illusive user interfaces give children a *false sense of self-confidence*, eventually attract many of them to professions of prospective technology developers and assist their progress even during the first years of their higher education by translating relatively sophisticated tasks into the language of a lower cognitive level, creating in the students the illusion of mastery and autonomy in the respective domains. Meanwhile, illusive assessment technologies (particularly multiple-choice tests, but also more classical performance assessment methods) conceal from the educators (and from the students themselves) the students' lack of true comprehension for a long while.

The simulated education system, which bestows a favour on those who "do not waste time and energy" with efforts towards true comprehension, is particularly destructive for students, who are driven with the self-gratification of comprehension and have a genuine capacity for becoming prospective developers of technology. In the capacity of an academic advisor I often have to observe such students sinking into a depression, being alienated from engineering, and possibly escaping to other fields (mostly humanities or arts) where they hope to find more room for autonomous development and self-actualisation.

On the other hand, those who stay are the ones who accept becoming operators carrying out ready-made recipes, i.e. becoming standardised and replaceable building blocks of the industrial apparatus – replaceable by the many graduates that pour out of the factories of simulated education, or eventually replaceable even by computers.

6. Conclusion

My criticism of the present course of technology and education may be running the risk of being dismissed as a radical anti-technological stance or a romantic yearning for a lost paradise. However, my purpose is not to condemn technology, nor to dismiss the possibility that it can be efficiently employed to address the needs of an overcrowded and largely destabilised world. If designed with the proper purpose, ICT devices could be perfect aids for scaffolding children and youngsters in their cognitive and mental development, and for leaps to higher levels of comprehension.

But for such usage to be possible, first we have to give up the present habit of hailing technology as a generic saviour, irrespective of its character, and helplessly holding on to every short-time remedy. Only then we can state clearly the basic criteria that will allow a distinction between admissible and non-admissible strategies and tools, and apply them systematically to steer technological progress.

The present route of technology is characterised by an obstinate effort to delay the inevitable consequences of short-sighted and palliative policies that have caused and continue to cause great sociological, psychological, ecological and economic damages. It is not the only possible route but an outcome of the self-ordained dynamics of growth-based market economy that is blind to individuals and their true needs. Having once taken this direction, technology – together with all other components of social life, particularly education – is drifting away from the natural and sustainable route of human progress, and is increasingly engaged in sustaining by all means the illusion that we can indefinitely continue this way. And this uncontrolled drift is declared to be progress.

"Progress" at the expense of satisfaction, happiness and self-actualisation of humans can at best be an instance of black humour of the kind "The operation was successful, but we have lost the patient". If science and technology cannot devise methods of soft-landing the system on a real and sustainable ground, irrepressible consequences will sooner or later arrive and ensure the landing, not necessarily very softly. It is rather meaningful that among the diverse scenarios that predict an ultimate feedback upon this uncontrolled drift, mostly in the form of an ecological or economic disaster, a smaller scale but crucial feedback arrives from the human component: the most promising engineering students who blow as a safety fuse of the system.

I interpret this as a reminder about the unique role of education and see in it the possible soft spot where the vicious circle of illusion can be broken. This provides me with plenty of inspiration about how to reach for the resentful bright minds spitted out by system of simulated education, and how they can be regained for true human progress. This is and will be my source of motivation as an educator and academic advisor until the day the last genuine component of education, the direct human interaction, is replaced by its simulation.

References

Borovik, A. V. (2014). Calling a spade a spade: Mathematics in the new pattern of division of labour. arXiv:1407.1954 [math.HO]

Curtis, A. (2007). *The Trap: What Happened to our Dreams of Freedom.* BBC documentary film

Denizhan, Y. (2014). Performance-based control of learning agents and self-fulfilling reductionism, *Systema* 2 no. 2, 61-70

Chapter 15

The Service and Disservice of Information Overload:
Ways To Cope

Robert K. Logan

Physics Department & St. Michael's College, University of Toronto
60 St. George Street, Toronto, ON, Canada M5S 1A7
logan@physics.utoronto.ca

The service and the disservice of information overload have been a part of the human experience from the very beginning of our existence. Overcoming the problems associated with information overload has led to breakthroughs in communication and information processing including the emergence of speech, writing, mathematical notation, science, computing, the Internet and the World Wide Web. Possible ways of dealing with information overload are suggested including the importance of context and feed forward, the notion of the compact library, and the need for a general systems or multidisciplinary approaches to education, research, commerce and the formulation of public policy.

1. Introduction

One of the effects of living with electric information is that we live habitually in a state of information overload. There's always more than you can cope with.

– Marshall McLuhan

Information overload paradoxically provides both service and disservice. It creates both problems and opportunities. The service of information and the disservice of information overload are obvious. Information, the difference that makes a difference (Bateson) is essential for survival. Too much information, however, overwhelms their recipients who are then unable to identify the information that is most critical for the realization of their objectives and hence their well being.

The service of information overload is less obvious. It occurs through a reversal of cause and effect whereby information overload leads to new possibilities in an effort to cope with the glut. The effect of the disorientation due to information overload becomes the cause of coping mechanisms to deal with the information overload and hence the emergence of new patterns of organization. We will show that these new patterns of organization that emerged were in fact new forms of communication and information processing that provided structure and patterns to what had previously been a situation of information overload.

The first structure for organizing information overload was speech or oral communication, which was followed in turn by writing, mathematics, history, law, science, the printing press, computing, the Internet, Web sites and search engines. Each new mechanism for dealing with an information overload created a new source of information overload, which in turn led to a still newer coping mechanism and through recursion led to the evolution of language and new forms of communication and the organization of knowledge. The structure of remedies for information overload that led to new forms of communication and information organization is that of a spiral or the *corso ricorso* structure introduced by Vico in his Scienza Nuova (New Science) and the tetrad structure of McLuhan's Laws of the Media in which each technique for dealing with information overload flips into a new form of information organization and eventually a new form of information overload.

2. The Emergence of Speech

The first information overload that humans experienced was the experience of living in large groups to take advantage of the technology of the control of fire. The hominins, like Neanderthals that pre-dated fully human *homo sapiens*, made use of fire but not quite at the same level as the human that replaced them about 40,000 years ago. It is known that Neanderthals made use of fire when they were lucky enough to encounter it in nature due to a lightning strike or a volcano but it is believed that they were unable to make use of fire to the same extent as humans.

Fire use would have provided a significant advantage for the human population and may indeed have been an important factor in the overall collapse or absorption of the Neanderthal population," according to Anna Goldfield, a doctoral candidate in archaeology at Boston University [...] [www.livescience.com/50532-neanderthals-died-no-fire.html].

Many people believed that Neanderthals used small fireplaces but were unable to use fire in a systemic manner," said Paola Villa, an archeologist at the University of Colorado Boulder and one of the authors of the study [...] [http://www.thestar.com/life/2011/03/16/neanderthals_not_so_dumb_when_it_ca me_to_fire_study.html].

One of the consequences of the mastery of fire control was that humans began to live in larger groups to take advantage of the benefits of fire. "The size and distribution of archaeological sites shows that Neanderthals spent their lives mostly in small groups of 5-10 individuals (compared to 20-30 individuals for Cro-Magnon humans)" [en.wikipedia.org/wiki/Neanderthal_behavior].

Living in large groups to take advantage of the benefits of fire such as warmth, the increase of the sources of food and their preservation, and protection from animals led to an information overload that humans had to deal with as the number of potential conflicts and the need to coordinate the activities of a group rose exponentially with the number of players. The information overload or complexity of early human life could no longer be processed at the pre-lingual perceptual level of hominin life.

The [information] overload of interacting with many people and carrying out more sophisticated activities led to the need for better communications to better co-ordinate social transactions and co-operative activities such as the sharing of fire, the maintenance of the hearth, food sharing, and large scale co-ordinated hunting and foraging [Logan 2007: 54].

The hominid brain could no longer cope with the richness of its life based solely on its perceptual sensorium. In the information overload and chaos that ensued, I believe, a new abstract level of order emerged in the form of verbal language and hence conceptual thinking [Logan 2007: 42].

Percepts represent the direct impressions of the external world, which are apprehended through the senses. Concepts, on the other hand, are abstract ideas that result from the generalization of particular examples of perceptual experiences. Concepts allow one to deal with things that are not immediately sensed in either the space and/or the time dimension. If our first words were concepts, then language allowed us to represent things that are remote in space or time. The mechanism that allowed this transition to take place was speech. Spoken language is both a form of communication as well as an information processing system. The emergence of speech represented the actual transition from percept-based thought to concept-based thought and information processing. The spoken word was the actual medium or mechanism by which concepts were first expressed or represented. Concepts are absolutely essential for planning because they allow for abstraction and in particular allow consideration of things displaced in both space and time. This explains the fact that humans are the only animals that are capable of both conceptual language and planning.

The initial concepts of humans were, in fact, the very first words of their spoken language. Each word served as a metaphor and strange attractor uniting all of the pre-existing percepts associated with that word in terms of a single word and, hence, a single concept. All of one's experiences and perceptions of water, the water we drink, wash with, cook with, swim in, that falls as rain, that melts from snow, that we find in rivers, ponds, lakes and oceans were all captured with a single word, water, which also represents the simple concept of water.

Living in large groups to take advantage of the benefits of fire created an information overload that spoken language was able to resolve through spoken language and the planning and co-ordination that it permitted. The exact date of this transition is not known but estimates range from 50 to 100 thousand years ago. This dating is consistent with the displacement of Neanderthals by *homo sapiens* 40,000 years ago as the human ability for speech led to their superior organizational abilities.

I have suggested that spoken language and abstract conceptual thinking emerged at exactly the same time as the bifurcation from the concrete percept-based thinking of pre-lingual hominids to the conceptual-based organization of information [2007]. This transition, an example of punctuated equilibrium, could have been the defining moment for the emergence of the fully human species *homo sapiens*.

3. The Emergence of Writing and Mathematical Notation

With the emergence of agriculture and the information overload that ensued, the spoken word and the human capacity for memorization encountered limits as to how much data could be processed and preserved. As a result, writing systems and numerical notations emerged, which allowed the amount and type of data being stored to expand exponentially. The invention of writing and mathematical notations had a tremendous impact on the informatic capacity of human language, thought and organization. Written records gave rise to new forms of classification, analysis, and other forms of information processing. Once again we will see how information overload led to new developments in communication and information processing.

The first forms of notation to deal with information overload emerged in the fertile crescent between the Tigris and Euphrates rivers where a system of three dimensional clay accounting tokens representing agricultural commodities was invented 10,000 years ago to serve the administrative function of the government. These clay tokens were first deciphered by Denise Schmandt-Besserat [1978, 1992]. She showed that these tokens were the forerunner of writing and mathematical notation. The agricultural system in Sumer depended on the construction of irrigation systems that were administered by priest/accountants. They collected produce from the farmers and redistributed the produce to the irrigation workers. The clay tokens representing different agricultural commodities such as wheat, emmer, oil and lambs were given to the farmers as receipts for their tributes.

This system of notational tokens operated more or less unchanged for 5000 years until circa 3000 BCE when the tokens were placed inside clay envelopes and the tokens were first pressed into the wet clay envelopes so that the contents of envelope could be determined without breaking open the clay envelope. After 100 years of using this system it suddenly occurred to administrators of this system that they did not need to put the tokens in the envelope. All they needed to do was press the tokens into a clay tablet. Written notation began as a back of the envelope development. As the quantities of agriculture commodities transacted increased with the emergence of Sumerian city-states another innovation was introduced. Rather than stamping the same token multiple times the tokens representing the large and small measure of wheat were used to represent the numbers ten and one respectively. They operated like the Roman numerals X and I. To distinguish the impressions of the wheat tokens used as numbers from the measures of actual wheat agricultural quantities were no longer stamped into the clay using the three dimensional clay tokens but the outline of the impression they would make were inscribed in the clay using a wooden stylus. This resulted in the simultaneous appearance of signs representing numerals (mathematical notation) and signs representing words (writing).

This is how the information overload in Sumer gave rise to writing and mathematical notation. The idea of writing and mathematical notation spread rapidly to other agricultural based societies in the old world throughout the Middle East, Europe, India and China. Quite independently of this development a system of writing and mathematical notation arose in the new world of the Western Hemisphere with the Mayans, Olmecs, Zapotecs, Teotihuacanos, Mixtecs, Tarascans and Aztecs in Mexico and the Incas in Peru all of whose economies were based on agriculture. A similar development among hunting and gathering societies never occurred.

The Mexican system of mathematical notation was quite sophisticated as they invented a symbol for zero, a development that was missed by the Ancient Greeks and the Romans but developed by Hindu mathematicians 2000 years ago and was picked up by Arabic mathematicians and did not arrive in Europe until the 11th Century through the contact of European and Arabic merchants.

4. The Emergence Of Science

Another form of information overload for young people occurred, namely the learning of the skills of reading, writing and arithmetic. It was for this reason that formal schools were organized dating all the way back to Sumer 5,000 years ago. In order to teach these skills teachers began to collect information for their lesson plans and from this activity scholarship and eventually science emerged.

Within its [the school's] walls flourished the scholar-scientist, the man who studied whatever theological, zoological, mineralogical, geographical, mathematical, grammatical, and linguistic knowledge was current in his day, and who in some cases added to the knowledge [Logan 2007: 2].

Science emerged as organized knowledge to deal with the information overload created by the use of writing by teacher/scholars. One of the cognitive tools that these teachers created that was essential for science was classification that writing made possible. Classification is one of the most effective ways of dealing with information overload. The methods and findings of science are expressed in the languages of writing and mathematics, but science may be regarded as a separate form of information processing because it has a unique way of systematically processing, storing, retrieving, and organizing information, which is quite different from the way information is organized using either written text or mathematics alone. Science is not just knowledge about or a description of nature but rather it is knowledge organized in a special way so that results can be generalized and new information can emerge or be easily collected from the existing knowledge base that science has created. Once again with science we see how an information overload has led to the emergence of a new form of information organization.

The ability to create written records and organize information allowed for the emergence of history, literature, philosophy, codified law and the social sciences as well. None of these human endeavors flourished to the same extent in oral societies because of the limitations of human memory. With the written record the information overload that these fields of human thought gave rise to could be preserved and expanded upon.

One of the impacts of science over the centuries was the complexification of science-based technology and as a consequence the rapid increase in population. A new level of information overload emerged in the late 19th Century. The United States government called upon Herman Hollerith who had developed an electromechanical tabulating device to help with the gathering and processing of information for the 1890 US census. Data was entered onto cardboard cards by punching holes in them much like the computer cards of the mainframe computers of the 1950s through the 1970s. The cards were placed on the tabulating machines in which pins were impressed on the cards. Those pins that made it through the holes in the card completed an electric circuit and the information represented by the punched hole was tabulated. The machines were quickly adapted to a number of other commercial activities. In 1911 Hollerith sold "his Tabulating Machine Company to financier Charles Flint for US $2,312,100, and the company became part of Flint's Computing-Tabulating-Recording Company. In the 1920s, C-T-R evolved into IBM" [www-03.ibm.com/ibm/history/ibm100/us/en/icons/tabulator]. Once again information overload led to a new development, in this case, automated tabulating machines and eventually in the 1940s to computers. And as they say the rest is history, a well-documented history.

Mainframe computers evolved into minicomputers and then to personal computers and from here to networked computers and then the Internet, the World Wide Web and search engines. Along the way each development led to an information overload that stimulated the next development. With personal computers there was so much information to share that the Internet took off. The information overload of the Internet led to the World Wide Web and from there to Web 2.0, social media and search engines, a virtual cascade of online information processing developments.

5. The Spiral Structure of How Information Overload Led to the Evolution of Information Processing

Each new development in human communication from the emergence of speech to that of the Internet, the Web and Google follows a similar patterns of an information overload giving rise to a new communication/information processing development which in turn gives rise to a new information overload and so on and so forth. This structure of historical development parallels Giambattista Vico's *corso* and *ricorso* as developed in his Scienza Nuova (New Science) in which a society experiences growth followed by a collapse followed by a repeat of the pattern ad infinitum. It also parallels McLuhan's Laws of Media [1988] in which each new human artifact enhances some function, obsolesces a former way of carrying out that function, retrieves something from the past and then flips into a complementary form. The process of information overload followed by a remedy in the form of a new information medium or technique followed by another information overload will continue as long as humans live on this planet and evolve their technology.

Here is an example of how McLuhan's Laws of Media (LOM) reflect the spiral evolution of language and information processing. Every LOM identifies what human function the artifact enhances, what previous way of achieving that function that it obsolesces, what it retrieves from the past and what, when pushed to its limits, it flips into. This series of LOM show the spiral structure of speech, writing, schools, science, computing the Internet and the Web.

LOM: The spoken word
- enhances thought and communication,
- obsolesces mimetic communication (i.e. communication by gesture, hand signal, body language and non-verbal communication),
- retrieves inner thought, and
- reverses into written communication.

LOM: The written word
- enhances the storage and organization of information and abstract thought,
- obsolesces the spoken word as the principal medium of storage,
- retrieves memory of things past, and
- reverses into the need for formal education or schools.

LOM: The teachers in schools
- enhance creation of new information and its organization,
- obsolesce apprenticeship training,
- retrieve the knowledge structures of the oral age, and
- pushed to their extreme flip into science

LOM: Science
- enhances the production and organization of knowledge,
- obsolesces magic and superstition,
- retrieves the shaman, and
- reverses into computing.

LOM: Computing
- enhances the storage and organization of information,
- obsolesces books,
- retrieves libraries, and
- reverses into the Internet and the Web.

6. Addressing the Problems of Information Overload

McLuhan's observation that "one of the effects of living with electric information is that we live habitually in a state of information overload", applies with even greater validity with digital information.

> Humankind has stored more than 295 billion gigabytes (or 295 exabytes) of data since 1986, according to a new report based on research by scientists at the University of Southern California... USC report calculates the amount of stored data grew by 23% a year between 1986 and 2007. The scientists also concluded that 2002 should be considered the beginning of the digital age because it was the first year digital storage capacity overtook total analog capacity worldwide [www.computerworld.com/article/2513110/data-center/scientists-calculate-total-data-stored-to-date--295--exabytes.html].

McLuhan's suggestion for dealing with information overload is pattern recognition: faced with information overload, we have no alternative but pattern-recognition.

While details are sometimes important, not all details are crucial. In this age of information overload one cannot expect to keep track of all the details of the many branches of knowledge. Having a general idea of the overall pattern of human knowledge, however, is indispensable in the digital age in which there are so many overlaps in the various domains of knowledge. This is why in our book *The Future of the Library: From Electric Media to Digital Media* [Logan and McLuhan 2016] McLuhan and I recommended the creation of a compact library that summarizes human knowledge in a collection of not more than 500 to 2,000 books.

What today's reader, faced with book glut and information overload, requires is not access to all information but, rather, guidance to that information, i.e. an up-to-date guide to the literature [...] Holistic patterns and guides are the only way of dealing with the overload, and not ever more efficient ways of collecting, storing and accessing information.

Information overload is due to the runaway of the left side of the brain, which focuses on the fragmented and specialized. The holistic, pattern-recognizing facility of the right side of the brain was pushed down by print and permitted the takeover of the left-brain. With the speed-up of electric communication patterns re-emerge and the right brain reasserts itself, creating the need for the compact library. The left-brain perceives figure while the right brain provides the ground without which the figure is meaningless. The compact library would provide the ground in which the meaning of the book as figure would emerge. Because the ground is continually changing, so are the meanings of books, and therefore the up-date of the compact library is essential or else one loses the sense of where it's at. The figure-ground library, the compact library, is a radical form of education [Logan and McLuhan 2016, bold removed].

The problem of information overload is not only the glut of information in the books in our libraries and online on the Internet but also the attitude of the users of information that are mesmerized by the sheer quantity of information in their field and because of their desire to keep up with all the details of their field they lose sight of the context of the specialized information they are focused on.

The problem of information overflow or book glut does not result alone from the sheer number of volumes created by the printing press, but also from specialists [...] The effects of specialism are to fragment knowledge into isolated and specialized compartments [...] The awareness of information overload is a result of the effects of our new electric and digital media, which create pattern recognition through information speed up. As information and knowledge in a specialized field increased beyond the capacity of an individual, the field fragmented further into more specialized areas. This mechanism of sub-dividing and narrowing the areas of knowledge one feels responsible for, allowed the specialist to cope with the information explosion [...] The fragmentation and explosion of knowledge practiced by the specialist are the products of the mechanical age of industrialization and mass production. This is no longer possible with electric and digital media. Our world is imploding [Logan and McLuhan 2016].

The educational needs of the world are changing as a result of information glut. We live in a complex world of high technology and intractable social problems. At one and the same time we must confront the effects of exploding population, diminishing resources, information glut, and over-specialization. We face dangers of imminent famine, a poisoned environment, runaway inflation, economic decline, large-scale unemployment, structural poverty, pervasive alienation and malaise, political breakdown, nuclear proliferation, political terrorism and global warming. Coping with information overload by taking a general systems or multidisciplinary approach to education, research, commerce and the formulation of public policy is the only way to deal with these challenges. It is not how much you know but how relevant what you know is to the problems we face and how what you know relates to what others know vis-à-vis these problems.

References

Logan, R. K. (2007). *The Extended Mind: The Emergence of Language, the Human Mind and Culture*, University of Toronto Press, Canada

Logan, R. K., and McLuhan, M. (2016). *The Future of the Library, From Electric Media to Digital Media*, Peter Lang, New York

Schmandt-Besserat, D. (1978). The earliest precursor of writing, *Scientific American 238*

Schmandt-Besserat, D. (1992). *Before Writing: Vol. 1. From Counting to Cuneiform*, University of Texas Press, USA

Kramer, S. N. (1959). *Life Begins at Sumer*, Doubleday Anchor Books, USA

McLuhan, M., and McLuhan, E. (1988). *Laws of Media: The New Science*, University of Toronto Press, Canada

Part III

Meaningful Technology?

Chapter 16

Islam Between Inclusion and Exclusion: A (Decolonial) Frame Problem

Syed Mustafa Ali

Computing and Communications Department, The Open University
Walton Hall, Milton Keynes MK7 6AA, UK
s.m.ali@open.ac.uk

In this chapter, the 'Frame Problem' in AI is mobilized as a trope in order to engage the 'question' concerning the inclusion and/or exclusion of Islam (and Muslims) from European – and, more broadly, 'Western' – society. Adopting a decolonial perspective, wherein body-political, geo-political and theo-political concerns are centered, the meaning and applicability of categorical dichotomies such as 'religion' and 'politics' and their relationship to the historical entanglement of 'religion' and 'race' in the formation of the modern world are interrogated in the context of understanding the nature of the relationship between Islam and Europe/'the West'. It is argued that the tendency within Western liberal democratic discourses to (1) frame the problem of Islamophobia and 'the Muslim question' in terms of misrepresentation – that is, misinformation, disinformation and 'distortion' of the flow of information – and (2) frame the issue of "Islam and Europe/'the West'" in terms of inclusion and/or exclusion of the members of a 'religious' minority into a post-modern, post-Christian/'secular' polity circumvents disclosure of the violent historically-constituted structural background or 'horizon' against which such 'options' are generated. The essay concludes by sketching some possible decolonial responses to this critical and existentially-problematic state of affairs.

1. Introduction

In the field of artificial intelligence (AI), the Frame Problem refers to the problem of 'knowing what stays the same as actions occur in a changing world'. According to Lormand [1999],

> The original frame problem appears within the situational calculus [a logical formalism wherein] there are "axioms" about changes conditional on prior occurrences ... Unfortunately, because inferences are to be made solely by deduction, axioms are needed for purported *non*changes ... Without such "frame axioms", a system is unable strictly to deduce that any states *persist*. The resulting problem is to do without huge numbers of frame axioms potentially relating *each* representable occurrence to *each* representable nonchange. [326]

Some philosophers of mind have argued that the scope of the frame problem is broader than that of a specific formalism or representation: for example, according to Daniel Dennett, it relates to the problem of knowing "how to ignore information *obviously irrelevant to one's goals*", while John Haugeland understand it as the problem of "how to keep track of *salient side effects* without constantly checking for them" [Lormand 1999: 326].

Another way of thinking about why the frame problem arises draws on phenomenological insights into the relationship between formal representations and a non-representational *background* of embodied and situated knowledge about the natural world and cultural practices against which such representations are interpretable – a 'horizon' which provides "the condition of the possibility of determining relevant facts and features" [Dreyfus 1992: 36]. I want to suggest that this line of thinking is fruitful for thinking about contemporary social problems including issues of social inclusion and exclusion.

It is my contention that 'frame problems' of a similar nature – that is, those having to do with the persistence of a tacit background or 'horizon' against which phenomena become interpretable – are ubiquitous in spheres of human action – social, political, economic, ethical, cultural, religious and otherwise – when viewed from a critical perspective, that is, in terms of a consideration of power relationships. By adopting a decolonial perspective wherein body-political (who is speaking), geo-political (from where) and theo-political (to what end) concerns are centered, and informed by a recognition of what Heidegger referred to as the 'ontological difference' between beings (things, phenomena etc.) and being as a 'horizon' for understanding (or making intelligible) such beings, it becomes possible to expose and thereby interrogate the historical structure of the tacit systemic background which provides the condition of the possibility of understanding how and why 'the Muslim question' is – must be – framed as a choice between inclusion and exclusion.

I begin by sketching the political ontology of the modern world – *what* it is and *how* it came to be – from a decolonial perspective. Traveling backwards in time (and space), I draw attention to the historical entanglement of 'race' and 'religion' in the violent constitution of modernity, and the formative role and historical sedimentation of structural anti-Islamism in the constitution of European identity. I then go on to briefly comment on the relationship between the modern world and the Islamicate – that is, the social and cultural complex historically-tied to Islam as a civilizational matrix – in terms of how the colonial and imperialist discourse of Orientalism, the contemporary phenomenon of Islamophobia, and recurrent debates over a purported 'Clash of Civilizations' can be understood as ontic manifestations of anti-Islamism.

I maintain that framing the 'question' concerning the inclusion and/or exclusion of Islam (and Muslims) from European – and, more broadly, 'Western' – society in such terms masks (occludes, conceals) the ontology – nature, structure, boundaries etc. – and historicity of the systemic background or 'horizon' against which the binary 'options' of inclusion *into* and exclusion *from* Europe/'the West' emerge; rather than focusing on how the demarcating boundary between European/Western identity ('self') and non-European/non-Western – specifically, Islamic/Muslim – difference ('other') is historically co-constituted and reproduced by power-relationally differentiated actors, the issue is framed in terms of a choice of where to position – or be positioned – in relation to this boundary, the ontology of the latter having been tacitly naturalized, that is, de-politicized.

I conclude by briefly sketching some possible decolonial responses to this critical and existentially-problematic state of affairs.

2. World-Making

My point of departure in exploring the 'frame problem' associated with questions of inclusion and inclusion vis-à-vis Islam and Europe (or, more broadly, 'the West') is a consideration of how the modern world came to be. These two terms – 'modern' and 'world' – necessitate a certain amount of unpacking. Drawing upon a sociological and phenomenological account such as that presented by Berger and Luckmann [1966], it might be argued that a 'world' is a socially-constructed reality into which people find themselves 'thrown' and which they shape through various kinds of action, both individual and collective. However, this way of thinking about 'world' tends to obscure certain fundamental considerations relating to the site and operation of power and its role in bringing forth such a reality – that is, 'poietically' constituting the being (or ontology) of a world. Heidegger [1995] might have been correct in asserting that the stone is world-less, the animal is poor in world, and the human is world-forming, yet what such an articulation omits to consider – intentionally or otherwise – is the asymmetric wielding of power by different agents (bodies), differently located in time (history) and space (geography), in relation to such world-forming action; in short, Heidegger's world-forming 'human' is a universalizing abstraction that masks differential power relationships. Furthermore, and central to my argument, it is a levelling abstraction that masks (conceals, occludes) a tacit Eurocentrism.

Following the lead of psychiatrist, phenomenologist and seminal decolonial thinker, Frantz Fanon [1986], I want to argue that when thinking about, speaking of, and acting in the 'modern world', we need to understand the latter as 'The World' – that is, *the* global hierarchical system of domination, whose dominant core lies in 'the West' and whose subaltern periphery is constituted by 'the Rest' [Hall 1992], which emerged as a historically-unprecedented phenomenon during what has come to be known as the long *durée* of the 16th century. While broadly concurring with the claims of decolonial scholarship vis-à-vis the uniqueness and historical onset of 'The World', I shall attempt to nuance its genealogy and ontology with a view to informing the central issue at hand, viz. the question of inclusion and exclusion of Islam (and Muslims) in relation to Europe (and 'the West').

2.1. *Naming 'The World'*

In addition to 'the West' and 'the Rest'– and the 'West' can include 'Eastern' constituents such as Japan (a case of the exception *confirming the rule*) – 'The World' goes by many other names articulated with increasing intensity, clarity and visibility in the contemporary era: coloniality of power [Quijano 1992], racist culture [Goldberg 1993], global white supremacy [Mills 1997], the modern racial world system [Winant 2004], the Orientalist world system [Samman 2008] and the colonial matrix of power or modernitycoloniality [Mignolo 2011] among others. What is common to all such 'namings', if only in terms of a Wittgensteinian shared family resemblance, is the centrality of *race* as a unifying principle in their articulation. Before proceeding, it is necessary to briefly clarify what I mean by race/racism.

2.2. *Two conceptions of race/racism*

While it is beyond the scope of this essay to review the different ways in which race/racism can be and has been conceptualized, two formulations can be usefully contrasted, both of which frame race/racism as real yet not natural (in the sense of biologically 'given') and as involving naturalization (in the sense of depoliticisation) of systemic hierarchical exclusion. Where they differ is in terms of their range of applicability: the first, due to Mills [1997], is analytical in orientation and views race/racism as a socially-constructed reality that can, in principle, be trans-historically (and trans-geographically) located; the second, due to Hesse [2004, 2007], is postcolonial/decolonial in orientation and views race/racism as a series of Eurocentric material assemblages that emerge in a specific context, viz. European colonial expansion during the long durée of the 16th century. While Mills' framework appears less parochial, arguably this is at the expense of its conceptual abstractness. This point is significant since some commentators such as Hobson [2012] insist that a distinction can and *should* be made between racism and Eurocentrism, including the latter in its colonial and imperial manifestations, and that racism should be tied to its 'scientific' conceptualization in late 19th century Europe, its historical origin as a term in the 1930s, and its material expression in the Jewish Holocaust under Nazi Germany. However, Hesse [2004, 2011] contests this move, arguing that conceptualizing race in biological terms and in an exclusively *European* context results in anti-Semitism being placed in the analytical foreground of race discourse, while non-European – that is, colonial – formations of race are tacitly moved into the background. In what follows, I have recourse to a decolonial conception of race/racism.

2.3. *Decoloniality basics*

According to Wallerstein [2006: 1], "the history of the modern world-system has been in large part a history of the expansion of European states and peoples into the rest of the world", commencing with the so-called Columbian "voyages of discovery" in 1492 CE which resulted in the emergence of a capitalist world-economy.

Decolonial thinking takes its lead from Wallerstein's world-systems theory yet modifies it by re-conceptualizing analysis of the world system from the (Southern/Non-European) margins/periphery rather than the (Northern/European) core. Crucially, however, this decolonial 'shift' retains the centrality of the long durée of the 16th century in conceiving the formation of this system, but frames it as a 'colonial matrix of power' in which race, rather than capital, functions as an organizing principle structuring a number of entangled hierarchies including, but not limited to, the epistemic, spatial, sexual, economic, ecological, political, spiritual and aesthetic [Grosfoguel 2011].

2.4. *The architecture of modernity/coloniality*

Decolonial interrogation of the contemporary world system readily exposes the 'dark underside' [Mignolo 2011] of Western modernity as a racist colonial order. One way of conceptualizing the architecture of this system is in terms of the "three pillars of white supremacy", viz. (1)

slaveability/anti-Black racism, which anchors capitalism; (2) genocide, which anchors colonialism; and (3) Orientalism, which anchors war – pillars which are held to be "separate and distinct, but still interrelated" – more specifically, intersecting [Smith 2010]. While useful as a way of exploring the entangled logics constitutive of the modern/colonial world, Smith's framework is problematic insofar as positing each of these sub-systemic phenomena as co-constitutive 'pillars' points to a tacit assumption of synchrony and ontological parity/structural isomorphism which is contradicted by appeal to the historical record; in addition, and as I will later argue, Smith's identification of the third pillar as 'Orientalism' is inaccurate as a term designating the paradigmatically antagonistic nature of Western engagement with the Islamicate world. Hodgson [1974: 59] defines 'the Islamicate' as that which is associated with the 'civilizational complex' grounded in and emerging from Islam, yet not necessarily characterized by fidelity to Islam in any doctrinal or 'confessional' sense; it should be noted, however, that Hodgson's characterization of Islam as a 'religion' is problematic insofar as the latter has a European genealogy and generalizing it so as to apply it to non-European traditions points to a certain Eurocentric universalism at work [Asad 1993; Cavanaugh 2014].

Against Smith, I want to argue that a more accurate depiction of the architecture of modernity/coloniality conceives it in terms of the temporally-hierarchical 'sedimentation' and/or 'nesting' of various forms of structural violence; such hierarchy is non-reductive in the sense that 'lower level' – that is, historically earlier – phenomena inform and limit, but do not determine those at 'higher' levels – that is, historically later. (I should like to suggest that such 'nesting' and 'informing' points to computational or *algorithmic*, and informational conceptions of systemic racism as explored in [Ali 2013, 2015, 2016].) This position resembles that of Hesse [2007] who maintains that rather than being necessarily correlated with the presence (or absence) of material markers on the body,

> Racialization [is] embodied in a series of onto-colonial taxonomies of land, climate, history, bodies, customs, language, all of which became *sedimented* metonymically, metaphorically, and normatively, as the assembled attributions of race [emphasis added]. [658-659]

In short, while embodiment, in the broad sense of materiality (or physicality), is a necessary condition for race, such embodiment can assume – and, historically, *has* assumed – different forms including – and crucially, for my argument – forms that are religious, philosophical, 'scientific' and cultural or civilizational [Blaut 1992].

2.5. *Entanglements of 'Race' and 'Religion'*

Granted the racial constitution of the modern world – or rather, modernity/coloniality – what bearing does this have on the 'question' concerning Islam (and Muslims)? While Islam is only problematically construed as a 'religion', is it perhaps not even more problematic to consider Islam in terms of race/racism? Against this view, a critical race theoretical tendency within an emerging body of scholarship associated with critical approaches to the study of religion insists that 'race' and 'religion' are structurally intertwined. According to Lloyd [2013: 80],

> Race and religion are thoroughly entangled, perhaps starting with a shared point of origin in modernity, or in the colonial encounter. If this is the case, religion and race is not just another token of the type 'religion and,' not just one approach to the study of religion among many. Rather, every study of religion would need to be a study of religion and race.

Crucially, recent decolonial scholarship, for example, that of Maldonado-Torres [2014a, 2014b] building on the work of Wynter [2003] and others, has begun to engage such considerations, pointing to the decisive role played by 'religion' in lead up to the 'Big Bang of Race' – that is, the emergence of world-systemic modernity/coloniality – commencing with the Columbian voyages of European expansion in 1492 CE.

2.6. *Decoloniality otherwise*

While endorsing the overall thrust of an approach that considers 'race' and 'religion' as entangled, and while broadly concurring with the decolonial framing of this entanglement as presented by Wynter,

Maldonado-Torres and others, I suggest that this account needs modifying along at least three lines.

Firstly, it must interrogate more thoroughly how the entanglement of 'race' and religion is informed by distinctions such as that between 'the religious' and 'the secular' or 'the political', and the Eurocentric nature of the genealogies of such binaries by engaging with and incorporating the insights of other critical approaches to the study of religion including those of Asad [1993, 2003], Casanova [2008] and Cavanaugh [2014]. In this connection, consider the following statement by Cavanaugh in the context of discussing "the myth of religious violence":

> The idea that religion has a peculiar tendency to promote violence depends on the ability to distinguish religion from what is not religion – the secular, in other words. [However,] there is no *essential* difference between religious and secular ... These are invented categories, not simply the way things are [and] these categories were invented in the modern West ... The myth of religious violence promotes a dichotomy between *us* in the secular West who are rational and peacemaking, and *them*, the hordes of violent religious fanatics in the Muslim world. *Their* violence is religious, and therefore irrational and divisive. *Our* violence, on the other hand, is secular, rational, and peacemaking. And so we find ourselves regrettably forced to bomb them into the higher rationality. [Cavanaugh 2014: 487]

Which points to the second modification based on the question of the relative significance of the anti-Islamic component – or 'pillar' – in the formation of the modern/colonial world. Maldonado-Torres [2014a] concedes that:

> The expansionist view of a *holistic and systemic Christendom* that we see in the eleventh and twelfth centuries cannot be properly understood without reference to the first two Crusades (the first from 1095 to 1099, the second from 1146 to 1149) and the struggle against imperial Muslim power [emphasis added]. [643]

However, he then goes on to describe the racial world system emerging in the long *durée* of the 16th century, commencing with the Columbian voyages, as effecting a 'rupture' of the "theological-racial episteme" [648] which existed previously in the medieval era, and its replacement by an anthropological/racial episteme [651] which he ties to a process of Western secularization; in short, "*homo religiosus* begins to be displaced by *homo politicus* and *homo economicus*" [652]. I am inclined to consider the idea of a 'rupture' problematic insofar as it suggests a break with the past whereas I want to argue for continuity through change based on the phenomenon of historical *sedimentation* of structural relations referred to earlier. In short, I want to argue for the taking up into and *persisting* of the old at the core of the new which is crucial in terms of how we think about the ontological background or 'horizon' of 'The World'. On this point, consider the following statement of Mastnak [2004] who might be understood as strongly contesting the view that there is anything approaching a symmetry between the different components – or 'pillars' – contributing to the forging of modernity/coloniality:

> Lumping together the Saracen with the Jew or Cathar or, later, with an African animist or an Inca priest – as all 'different' and 'inferior' because they refused "the universal and rational message of Christianity" – may make a point against 'European denigration of the other' [yet] such an approach does little to elucidate the nature of power in Western Christendom and the role of the image of the Saracen in articulating that power. In my view, *the image of the Muslim alone was integral to the articulation of power in the Christian West* [emphasis added]. [571]

Thirdly, and building upon the preceding two points, there is a need to consider how anti-Islamism functions in and *as* a background or 'horizon' informing debates that were arguably of decisive significance in the discursive emergent construction of 'race' such as that which took place at Valladolid during 1550-1551 CE between Bartholome De Las Casas and Juan Gines de Sepulveda [Mastnak 1994a]; in this connection, it is not insignificant that the fall of Constantinople to the Ottomans in 1453 CE revived Crusading activities in Europe [Hamdani 1981].

In summary, while concurring with decolonial scholars such as Sylvia Wynter [2003], Nelson Maldonado-Torres and others regarding the systemic particularity (specificity, uniqueness) of the 'Big Bang of Race', I suggest that the conditions for the possibility of rendering this 'bang' intelligible require excavation of a previously-ignited anti-Islamic 'gunpowder trail' leading up to the 'powder keg' that ultimately explodes globally as race via European colonial expansion.

3. Anti-Islamism

Understanding the nature of the modern/colonial world system – a system predicated on a violent binary hierarchy of Europeanness and non-Europeanness [Hesse 2004] or 'the West' and 'the Rest' [Hall 1992]

– is essential for understanding the paradigmatic background 'horizon' against which categories such as 'religion' and 'politics' and orientations such as 'religious' and 'secular' emerge, are framed and set in hierarchical opposition; for example, the modern liberal democratic West presents itself as secular/political and rational in contrast to a religious and irrational 'Muslim' – rather, Islamicate – world. This is significant since excavation of the site of 'religion' reveals it as, among other things, a modern/colonial category which has been used to domesticate (privatize, depoliticize) the Islamicate [Asad 1993; Moosa 2009; Cavanaugh 2014]; in this context, contemporary Islamism signifies the re-emergence of Islam in the public sphere – that is, the *re*-politicization of Islam [Sayyid 1997]. I suggest that in Western contexts, this 'ghostly' reappearance of what can be shown to be an old and familiar *enemy* is registered in familiar terms, viz. as perceived threat and projected Orientalist misrepresentation manifesting in contemporary form as Islamophobia, rhetoric about an alleged 'clash of civilizations', and debates about the inclusion/exclusion of Islam (and Muslims) from Western society. I maintain that the foundations of such phenomena are pre-modern/pre-colonial, deeply sedimented and require excavation.

3.1. *Anti-Islamism as ontological*

While decolonial scholars rightly point to the 'colonial moment' of the long *durée* of the 16th century inaugurated by the Fall of Granada in 1492 CE, and the commencement of the Eurocentrically-framed 'voyages of discovery' as initiating indigenous genocide, systematizing anti-black racism and bringing the modern/colonial world into being along structurally-hierarchical lines, the phenomenon of structural/systemic anti-Islamism dates back much earlier – arguably to the launch of the Crusades in 1095 CE. As Hamdani [1979: 39] states, "the year 1492 is an important milestone ... Yet its birth in a medieval crusading milieu is most often underrated, if not totally forgotten." I suggest that while decolonial scholars such as Maldonado-Torres have not *forgotten* the crusading milieu, they *have* underrated its importance vis-à-vis thinking about modernity/coloniality, and that this underrating is due to a mistaken conception of the *paradigmatic* relationship between

Christendom and 'Islamdom', that is, the spatial-political abode of the Islamicate. For example, Maldonado-Torres [2014a] claims that

> In the twelfth century, Christian conceptions of the 'Saracens' were more than anything else *defensive reactions* against the power and prestige of the Arab–Muslim Empire [such that] Christian kingdoms began to articulate their internal unity on the basis of religion and language [emphasis added]. [644-645]

However, historian Tomaz Mastnak has called such 'defensive' accounts into question by examining how Christian, and subsequently European, political identity was formed through an antagonistic negative dialectical relationship with the Islamicate [Mastnak 1994b, 2002, 2003, 2004, 2010]. On his view, Christian 'reactions' of the kind referred to by Maldonado-Torres were motivated less by an *actual* existential threat from an aggressive and expansionist Islam [Mastnak 2004], and far more by a *perceived* and projected threat manufactured by a rising papal 'secular' power in the 11th century concerned with 'exorcising' – that is, externalising – violence from within Christendom by redirecting it towards a constructed antagonistic 'Other', thereby forging a 'Crusading Peace' [Mastnak, 2002]. According to Mastnak [1994b: 3],

> Europe as a unity that [emerged from Christendom and] developed a 'collective identity' and the ability to orchestrate action [...] was, as a rule, articulated in relation to Muslims as the enemy [...] [Crucially,] European identity was formed not *by Islam* but, predominantly, *in the relationship* [...] *to Islam.*

Mastnak rightly points out that what is being targeted here is not so much Islam as a religion in the sense of a doctrine or theology – although such framings readily feature in pre-European discourses within Western Christendom [Daniel 1960; Blanks and Frassetto 1999; Tolan 2002; Arjana 2015] – but rather Islam as a socio-political order, notwithstanding the problematic application of the term 'religion' to Islam for reasons mentioned earlier, and concerns about the separability or otherwise of 'religion' from 'politics'/'the secular'. It is important to note that the opposition/antagonism at work here between Christendom and Islamdom is not trans-geographical in nature, but fundamentally Eurocentric, 'Western' or 'Occidental' [Penn 2015].

However, what is most important to point out, insofar as it bears on the ontological sedimentation thesis argued for herein, is that such anti-Islamism transcends later *internal* conflicts within Europe such as the

Thirty Years War between the Catholic papacy and Protestant separatists – a conflict which resulted in the Treaty of Westphalia in 1648 CE and, ultimately, the formation of a global interstate system [Bulliet 2015]. What this means is that, once it has been *produced* as a means by which to unite Christians and facilitate the formation of Europe, anti-Islamism does not disappear with the resumption of internal Euro-Christian conflict, but persists, albeit *reproduced* in new guise; formerly it was the Saracen, then the Moor, and then the Turk, yet what remains the same across such changes is the threat of an antagonistically-viewed Islamicate 'Other'. I suggest that this points to the existential facticity of a *historically-essential* relationship, one that *persists* – thereby pointing to a frame problem – through various transformations or 'iterations', viz. Christendom, Europe, 'the West'.

Incorporating the arguments of Mastnak into a decolonial perspective suggests that the 'Big Bang of Race' needs to be positioned – and considered – in relation to a prior 'Big Bang of Religion' which occurred in the pre-modern/pre-colonial era and involved the sedimentation of anti-Islamism in a European identity that informed and inflected the onset of systemic racialization. Commenting on the 'legacy system' effects of this prior 'bang', Mastnak [2002: 346] states that

> As an ideal and as a movement, the Crusades had a deep, crucial influence on the formation of Western civilization, shaping culture, ideas, and institutions. The Crusades set a model for 'expansionist campaigns against non-Europeans and non-Christians in all parts of the world.' The ideas, iconography, and discourse associated with the Crusades made a profound imprint on 'all Christian thinking about sacred violence' and exercised influence long after the end of actual crusading. They continued to play a prominent role in European politics and political imagination. In fact, the crusading spirit has survived through Modernity well into our own postmodern age.

3.2. *Anti-Islamism as ontic*

If this line of argument is correct and the ontological background or 'horizon' of 'The world' should be understood in terms of a historically-sedimented structure incorporating an anti-Islamicate 'core', what does this mean in terms of how to think about anti-Islamicate phenomena such as 18th and 19th century Orientalism, contemporary neo-Orientalism underpinning a purported 'clash of civilizations', and the discriminatory practice of Islamophobia? Should these be understood as simply "more of the same" crusading activity? Allen [2010] considers such a position to be problematic insofar as it evinces a trans-historical retrospective projection which fails to engage contextual factors – social, political, economic, cultural etc. – particular to the contemporary era.

While recognizing the markedly different nature of the contemporary era in contrast to pre-modernity, I am inclined to think that arguments for a radical difference mask/occlude the foundational role of anti-Islamism in the constitution of racial modernity/coloniality vis-à-vis ontological considerations. Rather than thinking in terms of *identity* and/or *difference* between anti-Islamism, on the one hand, and Orientalism and Islamophobia, on the other, I suggest we are dealing with phenomena situated on different 'sides' of an 'ontological difference', such that one cannot be reduced to yet also not separated from the other; following Heidegger [1969], I suggest we are dealing with a case of identity and difference being 'the same' in the sense of belonging together. On this basis, I suggest that Orientalism, Islamophobia and other related phenomena are best understood as ontic phenomena, manifestations of a historically-sedimented anti-Islamicate foundational component to the ontological background or 'horizon' that is 'The World'; such phenomena constitute instances of a 'dislodging' of such sediment to the surface of 'The World'.

4. Beyond the 'Between'

Granted the persuasiveness, if not correctness, of my decolonial interrogation of the "question concerning Islam", wherein the 'choice' between inclusion and exclusion of Islam (and Muslims) into Europe (and 'the West' more broadly) has been shown to conceal the ontological background 'horizon' of a world – 'The World' – foundationally-constituted through a historically-sedimented antagonistic anti-Islamism, where does this leave us? If the modern/colonial world system is indeed a violent global systemic hierarchy, then perhaps some form of 'counter-violence' is necessary to bring 'The World' to an end and replace it with another, different and hopefully better world. Insofar as Islam, Muslims and the Islamicate might refuse to engage 'The World' in terms of the 'choice' between inclusion *into* it or exclusion *from* it, the possibility of contributing to bringing forth a world beyond 'The World' arises. How might this be achieved? What form(s) might such 'counter-violence' take?

One possibility is to have recourse to rhetoric and argumentation. For example, Almond [2013] presents five strategies for deconstructing the idea of 'Europe' by undermining the notion that it is a self-contained space – a key assumption underlying the 'Clash Thesis' – and which might be extended to 'The World': (1) Re-origination (alienating Europe's origins); (2) re-configuration (splitting it into alternative topographies); (3) provincialization/de-universalization (reducing it to just another language game); (4) fissuring through internal Othering (revealing its internal differences); and (5) strategies of commonality (showing how many of its features spill over into adjacent cultural spaces). It should be noted that Almond ultimately remains sceptical about the success of any such purely discursive move.

Another possibility that presents itself is concrete, 'physical' violence, a continuation or resumption of the violent decolonization process that Fanon describes in *The Wretched of The Earth* [1968], albeit on a possibly trans-national or post-national basis. It is important to contrast this kind of violence with the allegedly nihilistic violence associated with groups such as Al-Qaeda and, more recently, IS (Islamic State). Commenting on the phenomenon of Al-Qaeda, Abou El Fadl [2002] described them as "orphans of modernity", and that "far from being authentic expressions of inherited Islamic paradigms, or a natural outgrowth of the classical tradition, these are thoroughly a by-product of colonialism and modernity", their vision of Islam being self-defined in opposition to 'the West' as a constructed antithesis. Insofar as the reactionary violence of IS/Al-Qaeda is dialectically-constituted, it might be argued that it constitutes an ontic phenomenon which operates according to the logic (or 'grammar') of an occluded ontological background 'horizon' of violence that engendered both 'the West' and, derivatively, its illegitimate and violent abandoned post-colonial offspring. On this basis, both the violence of 'the West', by which is meant here the 'coalition of the willing' in the international system dominated by Europe and the US, and that of Al-Qaeda and its successors needs to be placed on the same side of an 'ontological difference' and opposed through a commitment to ontological 'counter-violence'. Such decolonial violence, taking its lead from Fanon is targeted at the logic of 'The World' and its entangled hierarchical structure as captured in the maxim "'The World' must *end* so that the earth (and its people) can *mend*." I should like to add that should such a path be adopted, it must be informed by a commitment to what Delkhasteh [2007], drawing on the thought of Iran's first elected President AbolHassan Banisadr, describes as 'de-violentization', viz.

> The implementation of policies, which can lead to decreasing and eventually eliminating violence: of individuals towards themselves, towards each other, and towards the environment. Although this doctrine prioritizes pacifism, it also recognizes the possibility that controlled and limited use of 'defensive violence' may be necessary in order to neutralize 'aggressive violence' if the conditions for its total elimination are not in place ... Pacifism in its absolute terms rejects the use of violence irrespective of circumstances, while the doctrine of de-violentization is based on the belief that power will not be neutralized without resistance.

However, perhaps the most interesting possibility, and one that arguably speaks most to the possibility of a Muslim refusal of the choice between inclusion into or exclusion from Europe, 'the West' and 'The World' understood ontologically and with respect to the decolonial framing of this problem, is that presented by Asad [2012], albeit framed in the context of a principled opposition to statist politics:

> For Muslims the possibilities of 'political Islam' may lie [in] the practice of public argument, and in a struggle guided by deep religious commitments that are both narrower and wider than the nation state ... It presupposes openness and readiness to take risks in confronting the modern state that the state (and party politics) cannot tolerate. This politics may confront the liberal state by opposing particular policies through civil disobedience, *or even by rising up against an entire political order* ... This is not politics in the Schmittian sense of a confrontation between 'friend' and 'enemy,' but in the sense of trying to *force* unregarded *questions* into the public domain as defined by the liberal state [emphasis added]. [84-86]

References

Abou El Fadl, K. (2002). The Orphans of Modernity and the Clash of Civilisations, *Global Dialogue*, 4(2)

Ali, S. M. (2013). Race: The Difference That Makes a Difference, *tripleC*, 11(1), 93-106

Ali, S. M. (2015). Orientalism and/as Information: The Indifference That Makes a Difference. *DTMD 2015: 3rd International Conference*. In: ISIS Summit Vienna 2015 – The Information Society at the Crossroads, 3-7 June 2015, Vienna, Austria. http://dx.doi.org/10.3390/isis-summit-vienna-2015-S1005

Ali, S. M. (2016). Algorithmic Racism: A Decolonial Critique. *10ᵗʰ International Society for the Study of religion, Nature and Culture Conference*, 14-17 January, Florida, USA

Allen, C. (2010). Contemporary Islamophobia Before 9/11: A Brief History, *Arches Quarterly*, 4(7), 14-22

Almond, I. (2013). Five Ways of Deconstructing Europe, *Journal of European Studies*, 44(1), 50-63

Arjana, S. R. (2015). *Muslims in the Western Imagination*, Oxford University Press, UK.

Asad, T. (1993). *Genealogies of Religion: Discipline and Reasons of Power in Christianity and Islam*, John Hopkins Press, USA

Asad, T. (2003). *Formations of the Secular: Christianity, Islam, Modernity*, Stanford University Press, USA

Asad, T. (2012). Muhammad Asad, Between Religion and Politics, *Islam & Science*, 10, 77-88

Berger, P., and Luckmann, T. (1966). *The Social Construction of Reality: A Treatise in the Sociology of Knowledge*, Pelican, London

Blanks, D. R., and Frassetto, M. (1999). *Western Views of Islam in Early and Medieval Europe: Perception of Other*, Palgrave Macmillan, UK

Blaut, J. M. (1992). The Theory of Cultural Racism, *Antipode: A Radical Journal of Geography*, 23, 289-299

Bulliet, R. W. (2015). The Other Siege of Vienna and the Ottoman Threat: An Essay in Counter-Factual History, *ReOrient* 1(1), 11-22

Casanova, J. (2008). Eurocentric Secularism and the Challenge of Globalization, *Innsbrucker Diskussionspapiere zu Weltordnung, Religion und Gewalt* 25, 1-18

Cavanaugh, W. T. (2014). Religious Violence as Modern Myth, *Political Theology*, 15(6), 486-502

Daniel, N. (1960). *Islam and the West: The Making of an Image*. One World, UK

Delkhasteh, M. (2007). The Doctrine of De-Violentization in Islam: An Alternative to Christian Pacifism? Available at http://iranian.com/posts/the-doctrine-of-de-violentization-in-islam-an-alternative-to-chr-35169 (accessed 03/08/2014)

Dreyfus, H. L. (1992). *What Computers Still Can't Do: A Critique of Artificial Reason*, MIT Press, USA

Fanon, F. (1968). *The Wretched of The Earth*, Grove Press Inc., USA

Fanon, F. (1986). *Black Skin, White Masks*. Pluto Press, UK

Goldberg, D.T. (1993). *Racist Culture: Philosophy and the Politics of Meaning*, Blackwell, USA

Grosfoguel, R., and Mielants, E. (2006). The Long-Durée Entanglement between Islamophobia and Racism in the Modern/Colonial/Capitalist/Patriarchal World System, *Human Architecture: Journal of the Sociology of Self-Knowledge*, 1, 1-12

Grosfoguel, R. (2011). Decolonizing Post-Colonial Studies and Paradigms of Political Economy: Transmodernity, Decolonial Thinking, and Global Coloniality, *Transmodernity: Journal of Peripheral Cultural Production of the Luso-Hispanic World*, 1(1), 1-37

Hall, S. (1992). The West and The Rest: Discourse and Power. In *Formations of Modernity*. Edited by S. Hall and B. Gieben. Polity Press, Cambridge, 275-331

Hamdani, A. (1979). Columbus and The recovery of Jerusalem, *Journal of the American Oriental Society*, 99(1), 39-48

Hamdani, A. (1981). Ottoman Response to the Discovery of America and The New Route to India, *Journal of the American Oriental Society*, 101(3), 323-330

Hay, D. (1957). *Europe: The Emergence of an Idea*, Edinburgh University Press, UK

Heidegger, M. (1969). *Identity and Difference*. Translated and with an introduction by J. Stambaugh, Harper & Row, USA

Heidegger, M. (1995). *The Fundamental Concepts of Metaphysics: World, Finitude, Solitude*. Translated by W. McNeill and N. Walker. Indiana University Press, USA

Hesse, B. (2004). Im/Plausible Deniability: Racism's Conceptual Double Bind, *Social Identities* 10(1), 9-29

Hesse, B. (2007). Racialized Modernity: An Analytics of White Mythologies, *Ethnic and Racial Studies* 30(4), 643-663

Hesse, B. (2011). Self-Fulfilling Prophecy: The Postracial Horizon, *The South Atlantic Quarterly* 110(1), 155-178

Hobson, J. M. (2012). *The Eurocentric Conception of World Politics: Western International Theory*, 1760-2010, Cambridge University Press, UK

Lloyd, V. (2013). Race and religion: Contribution to symposium on critical approaches to the study of religion, *Critical Research on Religion*, 1(1), 80-86

Lormand, E. (1999). *The MIT Encyclopedia of The Cognitive Sciences*. Edited by R. A. Wilson and F. C. Keil. MIT Press, USA

Maldonado-Torres, N. (2014a). AAR Centennial Roundtable: Religion, Conquest, and Race in the Foundations of the Modern/Colonial World, *Journal of the American Academy of Religion*, 82(3), 636-665

Maldonado-Torres, N. (2014b). Race, Religion, and Ethics in the Modern/Colonial World, *Journal of Religious Ethics*, 42(4), 691-711

Mastnak, T. (1994a). Fictions in Political Thought: Las Casas, Sepulveda, the Indians, and the Turks. *Fit vest / Acta Phil*, X V (2), 127-149

Mastnak, T. (1994b). Islam and the Creation of European Identity. *CSD Perspectives. Centre for the Study of Democracy*, Research Papers, Number 4, University of Westminster Press, UK

Mastnak, T. (2002). *Crusading Peace: Christendom, the Muslim world, and Western Political Order*, University of California Press, USA

Mastnak, T. (2003). Europe and the Muslims: The Permanent Crusade? In *The New Crusades: Constructing the Muslim Enemy*. E. Qureshi and M. Sells (Eds.), Columbia University Press, USA, 205-248

Mastnak, T. (2004). Book review of John V. Tolan, Saracens: Islam in the Medieval European Imagination, *Speculum*, 79(2), 568-571

Mastnak, T. (2010). Western Hostility toward Muslims: A History of the Present. In *Islamophobia / Islamophilia: Beyond the Politics of Enemy and Friend*. A. Shyrock (Ed.), Indiana University Press, USA, 29-52

Mignolo, W. D. (2011). *The Darker Side of Western Modernity: Global Futures, Decolonial Options*. Duke University Press, USA

Mills, C. W. (1997). *The Racial Contract*. Cornell University Press, USA

Moosa, E. (2009). Colonialism and Islamic Law. In *Islam and Modernity: Key Issues and Debates*, Edited by M. K. Masud, A. Salvatore and M. van Bruinessen. Edinburgh University Press, UK, 158-181

Penn, M. P. (2015). *When Christians First Met Muslims: A Sourcebook of the Earliest Syriac Writings on Islam*, University of California Press, USA

Quijano, A. (1992). Colonialidad y modernidad/racionalidad (1989), reprinted in *Los conquistados. 1492 y la población indgena de las Américas*, Edited by H. Bonilla, Tercer Mundo Editores, Equador, 437-448

Samman, K., and Al-Zo'by, M. (2008). *The Orientalist World System*. (eds.) Paradigm Publishers, USA

Sayyid, S. (1997). *A Fundamental Fear: Eurocentrism and the Emergence of Islamism*, Zed Books Ltd, UK

Smith, A. (2010). Indigeneity, Settler Colonialism, White Supremacy. *Global Dialogue*, 12(2)

Tolan, J. V. (2002). *Saracens: Islam in the Medieval European Imagination*, New York, USA

Wallerstein, I. (2006). *European Universalism: The Rhetoric of Power*. The New Press, USA

Winant, H. (2004). *The New Politics of Race: Globalism, Difference, Justice*. University of Minnesota Press, USA

Wynter, S. (2003). Unsettling the Coloniality of Being/Power/Truth/Freedom: Towards the Human, After Man, Its Overrepresentation – An Argument, *CR: The New Centennial Review*, 3(3), 257-337

Chapter 17

Rewiring the Islamic Net:
Creating an Alternative to the Online Propaganda
of IS (Islamic State)

Rüdiger Lohlker

Oriental Institute, University of Vienna
Spitalgasse 2-4, 1090 Vienna, Austria
ruediger.lohlker@univie.ac.at

The Islamic State (IS) is (in)famous for its professional propaganda on the Web. Attempts to create narratives to counter the narratives of IS utterly failed up to now. The project presented intends to construct an alternative hegemony restricting the online space of IS and its claim to be the sole representative of Islam.

1. Introduction

IS has emerged as an important player in contemporary propaganda warfare online. The expert production of videos, graphic files and propaganda magazines represents a new stage of jihadi propaganda.

The professional feeling of this propaganda entices an audience raised in the new visual culture of the entertainment industry, be it television, films, gaming or the Web, to an interest in IS leading in some cases to a migration to Syria/Iraq joining IS – or staying outside but becoming a kind of fan of IS and the fan culture emerging since 2014.

IS on-line propaganda has proved to be resilient to any attempts to close it down. E.g., closing down Twitter accounts created two related movements of IS propaganda: creating new accounts with user names not related to concepts used before (caliphate, muhajir etc.) and changing to new platforms, e.g., *telegram, shortwiki* and others.

Behind the visual aspect of IS propaganda an intense discussion on Islamic religious issues is to be found. IS is trying to create a discourse fostering a new brand of Islam strongly linked to the idea that violence is the only means for the revival of Islam nowadays and the way to make (IS-)Islam dominant globally. This religious discourse is to large extent immunized against external critique [Lohlker 2016]. This religious discourse is highly flexible and resilient and can only be limited in its attractivity by the existence of alternative representations of Islam not affected by any relation to IS theology. This dimension of IS propaganda has been ignored to a large extent by any study of the phenomenon called IS.

Leaving aside the usual understanding of IS propaganda as networked on-line activity that may be disturbed by paralyzing as many nodes of the network as possible, another new approach may be helpful to understand the resilience of IS on-line.

Magnus Ranstorp assessed, that networks shifted into a

polymorphic structure or design with multiplicity of nods or pods swarming towards a mission or resurrecting shortly before or after an operation. More fundamentally it allows survivability through a constant virtual presence with no real or tangible physical centres of gravity and in constant stealth mode and ideological motion. Having simply an online presence confers a certain degree of legitimacy which they otherwise would not have. It also allows them to resurrect and reconfigure at any time [Ranstorp 2007].

Recent research revealed the importance of "so-called 'disseminator' accounts, which are run by sympathetic individuals who sometimes lend moral and political support to those in the conflict" [Carter *et al.* 2014].

The role and strategic importance of these sympathizers is crucial for the resilience of IS. These sympathizers are usually called media mujahedeen. The resilience of IS has emerged over the last two years as jihadist groups have moved from broadcasting content via a few 'official' accounts to a dispersed network of media mujahedeen. These supporters of jihadist groups who disseminate propaganda content online operate through a dispersed network of accounts, which constantly reconfigures. This marks a shift away from the broadcast models of mass communication which characterizes radio- and television broadcasting, to a new dispersed and resilient form (inspired by 'peer-to-peer' sharing); the user-curated "Swarmcast" [Fisher 2015: 4].

Interpreting the production, distribution and dispersal of Jihadist digital content as an emergent element of netwar, provides a conceptual framework through which strategic and system-wide assessments of Jihadist digital activities can be developed. Specifically, it can explain how the actions of individual members of the media mujahideen aggregate into system-wide structures and behaviours for the purpose of content distribution. [...] This ability to act without explicit direction is also the reason why the Swarmcast can survive the loss of prominent nodes and accounts by constantly reorganising, just as a flock of birds reorganises in light if attacked by a predator. The notion of Swarmcast combines the understanding of emergent properties of complex systems observed in nature with an emphasis on information-age technology with the irregularisation of conflict, alternate operational structures, and the connection between physical and Internet based battlefields. In the Swarmcast model there is no longer a clear division between the audience and a content producer in control of the means through which to broadcast content to that audience. Instead, once content is produced and released, it is often the distributing network of media mujahideen, rather than the original producer, that ensures continuing content availability [Fisher 2015: 6].

The evolution of the dispersed swarmcast structure is not limited to follower/following relationships on social media but can also be observed in the content sharing behaviors of social media users. A case study of Twitter activity between January and March 2013 provided evidence of the emergence of new jihadist social media strategies and the dispersed networks distributing content. This study has demonstrated how Jabhat al-Nusra (JaN), a Syrian jihadi group opposing IS, used Twitter to disseminate content, and the type of content they shared. The analysis of a JaN hashtag in 2013 provided two specific findings, first, social media provided a means for "official" channels to engage in active communication with sympathizers, and, second, the study concluded that Twitter functions as a beacon for sharing short-links to content that is dispersed across numerous digital platforms.

Today's social media zeitgeist facilitates emergent behavior producing complex information-sharing networks in which influence flows through multiple hubs in multiple directions. Network analysis of tweets containing the same tag, [...] during spring 2014 showed that users have continued to interact using the tag and that the network has remained distributed and resilient [Fisher 2015].

This applies to IS' use of Twitter accounts, too.

Speed is another crucial element of Jihadi online activities as is agility:

For example, trailers for the ISIS-released Flames of War video could easily be found on YouTube. A single posting of the trailer was watched over 750,000 times and the average duration was over one minute for the 1 minute 27 second trailer. The full version was also easily available via the agile, multiplatform release. For example, a version of Flames of War with Russian subtitles was posted on Vimeo and played over 13,000 times, while another version available on LiveLeak has been viewed 5,500 times. At least two versions of the full HD download were available on Gulfup and had been downloaded 21,550 and 5,600 times respectively. Another version of the video was hidden in the e-books section of Archive.org and had been downloaded over 12,000 times. Further versions were also available from 180upload.com and Mediafire.com, while references to the film are still shared on Twitter using both Arabic [...] and English [...] tags [Fisher 2015].

Although the variety of platforms used by the propaganda of IS have increased and new ones emerged the over-all structure of the jihadi swarmcast is still discernable. Any new channel used to disseminate IS material is instantly distributed across the already existing swarm of accounts.

2. Counter-Narratives and Hashtags

Attempts to counter this propaganda by, e.g., producing video content telling the viewers that IS is representing a perversion of Islam, Islam is to be seen and practiced in a peaceful way have failed to a large extent. The online campaigns run by part of Anonymous also give ample proof that these attacks do not have a lasting impact.

Attempts to flood #tags used IS accounts celebrating the Paris attacks with anti-IS-messaged only had a limited impact.

Recent research by the research group *Human Cognition* is able to show that even after the intense online reactions to the Paris attacks in November 2015 IS communication run by the media mujahedeen demonstrates its ongoing speed and resilience.

IS clusters were not paralyzed at all still being able due to is dispersed structure to reach out to other clusters. Anti-IS activity did not affect the IS clusters. So anti-IS activism of this kind may have a positive 'we are acting'-effect on the users producing this content but no effect related to IS.

INFORMATION SHARING NETWORKS

SPEED, AGILITY, RESILIENCE

The information dissemination around the Paris attacks demonstrates the ongoing speed and resilience of the Media Mujahedeen (members of IS media outlets and global supporters).

Despite efforts to flood tags used by IS and the Media Mujahedeen, IS supporters were still able to communicate and disseminate information rapidly.

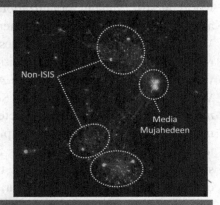

Non-ISIS

Media Mujahedeen

ANALYSIS PROVIDED BY HUMAN COGNITION

http://BLACKLIGHT.GLOBAL

Fig. 1. Information Sharing Networks. (http://BLACKLIGHT.GLOBAL)

The IS video clusters demonstrate this none-effect: the first IS video (Kirkuk 'province' of IS) praising Paris attacks was published November 16. 12 more in Arabic with partially French subtitles and titles have been published since Nov. 25 video calls on U.S. to send ground troops and praises the size of caliphate. A close video dissemination analysis shows that different users are important at different times – but crucially – that the information is shared through a rolling group of users where there is an ongoing churn of users joining the group and then drift away over time (Fig. 1).

3. VORTEX

Taking into account this failure of any attempts to counter IS propaganda directly, a new strategy seems to be necessary. The "Vienna Observatory 'of applied Research on Extremism and Terrorism" (VORTEX) aims at doing this.

VORTEX is a project of a research group at the University of Vienna doing research on online Jihadism for many years now and cooperating with the LibForAll-Foundation (Jakarta, Winston-Salem etc.) and the world largest Muslim organization, the Nahdlatul Ulama (NU), with around 70 million followers and members.

The profile of NU may be described as a mass organization well rooted in a regional Islamic tradition that is totally different from the varieties of Islam dominant in the Arab world, esp., those influenced by Wahhabism and Salafism. This Southeast Asian Islam, called *Islam nusantara*, shows some characteristic traits. It is based on an understanding of Islam that is pluralistic within Islam and tolerant towards other world-views, favors democracy as a way of organizing a state, rejects the idea of an Islamic religious state and adheres to the idea of a secular nation state. This characterization of *Islam nusantara* is an ideal type but aptly describes the idea of what this Southeast Asian variety of Islam tries to be.

NU will provide the necessary man- and woman-power to start to build an alternative representation of Islam on the Web able to compete with the IS and other extremist representations of Islam on a 24/7 basis in Arabic targeting the most important symbolic capital of IS and other Islamic extremists: the ability to publish Arabic language content understood as being more authentic than other forms of Islam since it is the language of the Quranic revelation. The production of NU will feed into the strategies and structures developed in the context of VORTEX and will be swarmcasted on the Web.

To give an example of the activities of NU we may look into the recent release of a film on Islam Nusantara. Mustofa Bisri, the spiritual leader of NU, said on the occasion of the release:

> According to the Sunni view of Islam […] every aspect and expression of religion should be imbued with love and compassion, and foster the perfection of human nature.

> This message of tolerance is at the heart of the group's campaign against jihadism, which will be carried out online, and in hotel conference rooms and convention centers from North America to Europe to Asia. The film was released Thursday at

the start of a three-day congress by the organization's youth wing in the Central Java city of Yogyakarta. [...]

"We are directly challenging the idea of ISIS, which wants Islam to be uniform, meaning that if there is any other idea of Islam that is not following their ideas, those people are infidels who must be killed," said Yahya Cholil Staquf, general secretary to the N.U. supreme council. "We will show that is not the case with Islam." [Cochrane 2015]

The idea behind VORTEX is to take into account that a sustainable competition with religiously legitimated extremism has to be built on a thorough religious understanding that is competing with, e.g., the IS version of Islam: pluralistic religion vs. religious totalitarianism, tolerance accepting the other vs. exclusivism negating the other, democratic law-making by humans vs. so-called law of God, secular nation state vs. Islamic state.

The ultimate aim of VORTEX is to reclaim the Web from extremist propaganda.

References

Carter, J. A., Maher, Sh., and Neumann, P. R. (2014). *#Greenbirds: Measuring Importance and Influence in Syrian Fighter Networks*. ICSR, London (via icsr.info)

Cochrane, J. (2015). From Indonesia, a Muslim Challenge to the Ideology of the Islamic State, *New York Times*, November 26, 2015 (via nytimes.com)

Fischer, A. (2015). Swarmcast: How Jihadist Networks Maintain a Persistent Online Presence, *Perspectives on Terrorism*, 9, 3-20 (via terrorismanalysts.com)

Lohlker, R. (2016). *Theologie der Gewalt: Das Beispiel IS*. Facultas, Vienna

Ranstorp, M. (2007). The Virtual Sanctuary of al-Qaida and terrorism in an age of globalization, in: Eriksson, J., and Giacomello, G. (eds.), *International Relations and Security in an Age of Globalization*, Routledge, London and New York, 31-56

Chapter 18

Reproducibility, Media and Communication

Tomáš Sigmund

Department of System Analysis, University of Economics in Prague
nám. W. Churchilla 1938/4, 130 67 Praha 3, Czech Republic
tomas.sigmund@gmail.com

This article presents two contradictory perspectives on the development of reproducible media. It starts with W. Benjamin's idea on the progressive character of new media and confronts it with Adorno's rather pessimistic view expressed in his concept of media industry. Then it finds parallels in the current evaluation of social media by J. Surowiecky with his idea of the wisdom of crowds and J. Lanier's idea of digital Maoism. The article concludes these contradictory perspectives can have validity as mutually dependent only.

1. Introduction

There is no doubt media influence communication of information. One of the famous expressions of this fact can be found in M. McLuhan's famous sentence "the medium is the message". The development of new media in the 20th and 21st century changed our society and culture. New devices, Facebook, Google and other inventions have become part of our lives.

Since the beginning of the 20th century the availability of information for the wide public allowed by the new media has drawn attention. Hand in hand with it goes the use and misuse of the ease of communication. I will analyze the optimistic and pessimistic perspectives on reproducible media. We can learn something from both of them, but none of these approaches can be taken on its own as it considers just one part of the complex problem.

2. Walter Benjamin

W. Benjamin in his famous article *The Work of Art in the Age of Mechanical Reproduction* [1968] draws attention to the fact that the ways art was produced in the beginning of the 20th century differs from the way it was produced in the previous periods. The main difference consists in the mass reproduction techniques that deprive works of art of their aura. Benjamin was influenced by the development of photography and by the rise of totalitarian ideologies in the 30s. He observed that reproducibility of arts is the consequence of the development of mass production.

Reproducibility of art has been known for a long time as the examples of stamping, woodcuts, engraving etc. show, but it was not until the invention of photography and later film that reproduction was accelerated with minimal effort. It means Benjamin analyses predominantly the influence of photography and film on art and the social consequences of that. Benjamin focuses on the physical medium underlying every artwork. This element was often neglected in the history of art, treated as neutral matter, but Benjamin considers it very important for understanding the content and so prefigures McLuhan's analysis condensed in the famous sentence "medium is the message". Medium has for Benjamin a specific grammar, irrespective of the artist's intention [Taylor and Harris 2008: 18].

Benjamin draws attention to the dominance of the original over its copies in its here and now in the past which he also calls the aura of the work of art. Aura is related to distance of the recipient from the artwork. With reproduction and independence on context the distance from the artwork gets smaller. Faithful copies remove the aura of the original because they make the identification of the original's place in the tradition impossible. In the digital sphere the original and the copies cannot be discerned and can be placed in any context that makes the identification of here and now impossible. Benjamin considers photographs of real artworks, not photography as such, but his ideas can be easily applied to the digital photography and any digital content. It is infinitely reproducible and context-free.

Benjamin makes clear our perception has changed with the mass reproduction. Freeing art from the tradition and rituals to which it was bound leads to its free use and so to the emancipation of man. L'art pour l'art developed and art has been used in politics, too. Exhibition value of art was bound to the development of film and photography. In films the spectators take the position of the camera and lose the personal contact to the artwork. That stresses the exhibition value and suppresses the cult value. The mass character of film and photography is expressed in the fact that everybody can make films and everybody can be in the film. Reality is perceived through instruments, distance decreases, details increase. The experiences related to art's perception were simplified and made mass-related. Pleasure, joy have been considered art's appraisals.

The characteristics of photograph and film are that they increase sensual impressions. That makes the work of artist and scientist similar. We get more visual impressions and they are more clear and distinct. With photography and film we see things we did not see before, the visual language has been developed. The modes of perception have changed and the public wants to be distracted by shocking images. Distraction of works of art shows people are interested in them and proves that the new perspective on things became so automatic that man can adopt it even in the state of distraction.

The negative effects of the loss of aura are in Benjamin's view caused by the capitalist structure of the society. Its extreme was achieved in the fascist ideology that allowed masses to express themselves, but in an extremely alienated mode only. Politics was aestheticized by fascism, but it will be replaced by communistic politicization of aesthetics. In the communist society self-realization of man and his activities, his free development and participation in society's life would be allowed. That means W. Benjamin was optimistic in relation to the mass reproduction. He believed the availability of artworks and free possibility to produce art would lead to liberation and emancipation of man.

The opposite view is represented by T. Adorno who had a pessimistic view of modern media; he praised the classical types of art production and saw in it – not in the easily reproducible content – an instrument for man's liberation.

3. Theodor Adorno

Adorno's theory of mass media was developed in the context of Frankfurt School and their critical theory project. The Frankfurt School continued in Marx's position and reacted on the fact that the development of capitalist societies did not correspond to Marx's predictions. That is why they focused more on the integrating role of culture for societies. W. Benjamin was also associated with the Frankfurt School since 1923 when the Institute for Social Research was founded, which later became home to the Frankfurt School. He became acquainted with T. Adorno there. They had conversations with one another and exchanged many letters. Adorno was influenced by Benjamin's method, but also disagreed with him in many matters. Benjamin was not dialectical enough for him.

Benjamin focused on the relationship between politics and art. Art became reproducible to get rid of aura and to express and support the emancipation tendencies in the society. He believed the new technologies would allow for a new form of culture made by and for the masses. Adorno focused in contrast to Benjamin on the independence of art from politics and its misuse in politics in the form of culture industry.

Adorno argued with Horkheimer in their book The Dialectic of Enlightenment [1969] that the media industry paralyzed any political activities of men by offering them easy satisfaction of their needs and amusing them. Their media theory can be considered a refutation of Benjamin's hope. In their opinion, media released from the aura imprisoned people in a sophisticated technological version of false consciousness [Taylor and Harris 2008: 63]. Industrial capitalism has developed an ideology promoted by mass media. Artworks lost their independence and became economic goods that have economic, not aesthetic value. Aesthetics became function of the goods and was determined by the advertising and selling function. The culture industry serves as an instrument of integration and governance. Production regulates consumption and so integrates all consumers. Knowledge produced in the culture industry serves the instrumental objective of governing and ruling the masses. An example can be the marketing principles that give to the marketing specialists power over the audience.

Knowledge produced in culture provides principles of understanding the world and when properly designed it can be used to integrate and rule the population.

The current social order defines in Adorno's view what is possible in terms of its limits. Instrumental reason prevailing since the enlightenment transformed media into instruments reinforcing commodity values. Media thus reinforce what was previously contained in them as notions like pseudo-events, spectacle, hyperreality, celebrities, reality TV etc. confirm. Societies concentrate too much on the technological means they have at their disposal and forget to think about their cultural ends. Cultural products tend to standardization and homogeneity. Unfortunately, today events like product placement, sponsoring, advertising, branding etc. prove how far the totalizing tendencies have led.

The culture industry supports according to Adorno false needs in people who replace the true striving for freedom, creativity and real happiness. People influenced by the culture industry and its advertising instruments succumb to commodity fetishism that claims commodities have human and social values and so can be bought for money. People praise things according to their price, not their value. All media have a generally similar tone and produce standardization and only seeming individualization that is based on accidents, not on real differences. People are told by the media industry that the consuming way of life is the only possible and the critical aspect of media gets lost. Hesitation, doubts, social life disappear and seem inappropriate.

The governing social order has in Adorno's opinion not been threatened by media development; on the contrary it has been fortified. Man's freedom has not been strengthened, but rather impoverished. Culture industry has fortified the status quo. People prefer passive satisfaction to self-realization and system change. Media concentrate on sentimental kitschy products and disregard difficult ambiguous critical artworks that lead to questioning the status quo.

If we consider the power fashion has and the spread of globalization focusing on the satisfaction of basic human needs and pleasure, we will find mass culture very similar to Adorno's picture. The economic interests need not be concealed any more, media openly present their economic objectives. The traces of spontaneity become absorbed by scouts and imitators and become part of the culture industry. It has no chance to resist. Classical music is used for sound tracks, novels are simplified and filmed into cartoons. Any difference is subordinated. There is no room for the consumer to classify, producers have already classified for him. Effects dominate over content, the obvious over the hidden, details over main features, virtuality over reality. Life resembles films, no more space for imagination is left.

Culture industry so reduces individuals to consumers and supplies them with banal shallow content. The culture industry has in Adorno's perspective a structural nature and only a structural critique (not a critique of an individual artwork) can change something. Adorno stresses the inherently manipulative character of low art. High art can be misused for manipulation, too, but it was not originally created for that purpose. Adorno did not discover the fact that art was produced for money, its new idea was that the formal possibilities of art were outlined within the society structurally governed by commercial concerns.

Adorno stresses in contrast to Benjamin the negative role of entertainment and distraction. Entertainment is used to relief the burden of capitalist violence. So art blocks the tension that is for Adorno characteristic of higher types of art. The tensions express contradictions within the socio-historical environment from which they arise. These contradictions on the other hand provoke contradicting interpretations. The complete resolution of the conflicts and contradictions would require a transformation of society to which in his opinion higher art leads.

Ideas analogical to the above mentioned two streams (Benjamin and Adorno) were expressed in relation to social networks that represent a new development of media. Although they are not so sophisticated and profound – they consider the effects of media predominantly – they implicitly follow similar lines of thought.

4. Collective Intelligence

J. Surowiecky [2005] claims social media are in an equal position to traditional media. They spread information very quickly among general public. The first time the equal position was proven was the 2004/2005 tsunami in Southeast Asia. Videos and blogs reported on the situation sooner than newspaper and TV stations. Mainstream media used social media as a source. The motivation of social media journalists is not profit, but sharing their story, getting attention of the fans, readers and listeners. The general public was active in the process of getting, analyzing and spreading information.

Surowiecky claims a group can be in some instances more intelligent than the most intelligent of its members. Group formation is enabled by the social network that is based on the availability of information for its members. They can freely create and use information and so creatively contribute to the emergent content. Surowiecky's book *Wisdom of the crowd* [2005] is based on numerous case studies and anecdotes where his claim was confirmed. A typical example he uses is Galton's experiment in which the weight of ox was better estimated if individual guesses were averaged than if the weight was estimated by any group member or an expert. Surowiecky's examples of group intelligence can be classified into categories like cognition (market judgment and evaluation which is faster and more precise than an expert's assessment), coordination (people naturally coordinate their behavior in the traffic, in using public spaces etc.) and cooperation (people trust one another on the market without a central control). For the formation of a wise crowd diversity of opinions, independence, decentralization and aggregation is necessary. However, in many cases the crowd produces bad behavior. The reasons for that are too much homogeneity in the crowd, centralization, isolation and division of information, imitation of crowd members and unsuitable emotionality.

The advantages of network society are not limited to the crowd phenomena. E.g. in the game industry there were some attempts to use game players in solving real issues, but within the game environment. The advantage people have in comparison to computers is recognizing patterns [Mohammadi 2014].

Surowiecky does not claim group thinking is always better than an individual judgement, but there are cases where this synergetic effect of mutual interaction works well and new qualities appear. As he writes, "The idea of the wisdom of crowds is not that a group will always give you the right answer, but that it will consistently come up with a better answer than any individual can provide" [2005: 235-236]. The emergence of new quality is enabled by the interaction and communication of the group members and for that the easily reproducible content is a necessary condition. So Adorno's worries about the prevalence of low culture has not been quite confirmed with the development of new media. The economic interest does not prevail completely. However, the situation in the current medial society is not only positive

5. Anonymous Collectivism

Jaron Lanier points out to the fact that blogs, wikis and social networks repeat very often the opinion that has been once formulated and support standardization. It is difficult to have an individual opinion as the power of the group is very strong. The members of social networks want to belong to the group and that is why they repeat the group's opinions. For Surowiecky's principle of crowd intelligence to work the members of the crowd are critical.

The idea of collective intelligence has been attacked by many thinkers. J. Lanier thinks the aim of social networks is to destroy one's intelligence and support anonymous collectivism. He even calls the online collectivism "digital Maoism". An example can be the speculative bubble, i.e. crowd craziness that causes that prizes of the shares go up or down. Group fanaticism led to the support of Nazism, communism, religious fanaticism etc. There is no reason to think that digital revolution would lead to a change in the thinking of crowds.

Lanier criticizes in his One-Half a Manifesto [2000] a situation when computers become masters of life. The computing power increases, but the performance of computers increases slowly only. The problem with computers consists in their inability to be creative. If we succumb to them, we lose the potential plurality of perspectives on the world.

In his Digital Maoism [2006] Lanier criticizes the situation in the cyberspace where we consider just one source of information like the Wikipedia authority, where the relation to the real author and the sophistication of his ideas is lost, where the source of information creates a false sense of authority behind the information, where the information source produces mainstream beliefs and where information is manipulated by anonymous editors behind the scene. All these approaches create some sort of totalitarianism.

With the spread of social media and big data, the potential for manipulation and totalitarian tendencies increased. Big data analysis has been used in presidential elections, in commercial applications, marketing and other areas of human life. They use the common human features like the willingness to help, altruism, reciprocity, empathy, respect for authority, group specific features (e.g. group identity) and individual features (stereotypes, submission, prosocial behavior etc.), and manipulate man's behavior using techniques of social engineering.

People using Internet lose control of their data that become available for unexpected purposes. The easy reproducibility of information makes the referents of the information vulnerable to manipulation. It can be traced down on the social network users who freely repeat the dominant opinions, but also on the customers who are influenced by personalized advertising, search results and suggestions.

Which of these contradictory perspectives is so the right one? I think both of them. It is difficult to imagine a world where man could do nothing else but pursue his self-realization and emancipation. There will always be something necessary, manipulative, violent. But we must criticize it and try to get out of the manipulation in order to open space for something new. This is a never-ending process, but its regulative idea calls for fulfilment here and now. Technology including new media technology has a dual face. Both of its sides are contradictory, but mutually dependent at the same time.

6. Dual Face of Technology

The dual face of technology manifests itself in the fact that the critique of the negative influence of technology will provide space for the appearance of its opposite effects which will later appear negative from another perspective, too. Arnold [2003] claims that technology including network media has a dual face: on the one hand it supports the purpose for which it was designed, constructed and used, but on the other hand ironically it provides unintended effects that lead in the opposite direction. To provide some examples we can mention antibiotics that were originally invented to provide protection against bacteria and pathogens and to reduce diseases. In the course of time they made pathogens stronger and our health weaker. Air conditioning cools down the inner environment, but increases external temperatures. The linear logic of cause and effect does not work here. ICT that abolished distance among community members created an environment where almost everybody is at the same distance [Heidegger 1969]. Cooper [2002] states that our increased ability to assert oneself is at the expense of one's quality and maturity.

If we look at the effects of new media, we can generalize the results of Arnold who analyzed the effects of mobile phones. His analysis is not instrumental, he accepts technology and stays away from it – he evaluates it critically.

The first appreciated quality of new network technologies is their mobility: they are small, can operate without cable connection to the Internet, have many functions and do not bind its user to a specific environment. He can move without losing the ability to work. On the other hand, because technology allows unanimous identification of the device, it also fixes its user to itself and the user is always available. He has no free time. New technologies allow independence, one can travel, be in contact with many friends and colleagues, but technologies require at the same time that everybody has got it and has a compatible type and operating system. The communication at distance may cause isolation and vulnerability, one communicates, but the partner is at a distance, the interaction is limited etc. The information is available, but without context, simplified, without warranty. The bridging of distance to others or to information is ostensible only. And using communication technology means I am in the same position as other users, I am part of their community, but still isolated and at a distance. People who are physically close become distant in their ideas – they communicate with somebody who is not present, solve issues which are not related to their physical context etc. But they can be closer to more urgent issues or to people to whom they otherwise would not be able to communicate. Modern technologies also break the difference between close and distant friends as everybody is at the same distance. On the other hand, that may be helpful and allow finding new friends or deepening the relations that may be developed in reality. People get new senses (hear at long distance, remember big amounts of data due to their online databases etc.), but can be accessed, analyzed, influenced as well. The boundaries between private and public, free and charged, available and busy, important and not important is more fixed as the signal can be coded, the switched off device cannot be from a distance switched on, without password the access is not possible, but more benevolent at the same time as login information can be stolen, code can be broken etc. The idea of new technologies is to save time, help their users, do some work for them, but they waste their time with their games, competitions, supply of functions etc.

7. Conclusion

A. Ross [2014] says that if Adorno saw today's cultural landscape he would be grimly satisfied to see his worst fears realized. Pop culture is prevailing and almost hegemonic, celebrities and media stars dominate the media, the mega rich live their unreal lives, traditional types of art like opera, poetry etc. are uncool and undesired; pop is ruling.

Internet supports unification and false freedom, the hope that abundance of mainstream products would lead to interest in non-mainstream products has not been fulfilled. Culture seems to be monolithic and just a few companies like Google, Amazon, Facebook etc. govern the taste of the consumers. Search engines with their hints ("Did you mean…") suppress unusual searches and freedom. Lists, rankings and likes guide people's attention. Neglecting would mean expulsion from the social group.

On the other hand, however, Benjamin's view has not been completely wrong. The modern culture and new media support the idea of equal rights and ban on discrimination. The situation of minorities seems to be better than in the past. The idea of collective intelligence has helped in some instances and people can learn from the experience of many others.

Even under suppression or maybe because of it new voices appear. S. Hall [1980] distinguishes four types of encoding/decoding a message. The first one is the dominant code where the encoder expects the decoder to decode the message in the same way it was encoded. "When the viewer takes the connoted meaning full and straight and decodes the message in terms of the reference-code in which it has been coded, it operates inside the dominant code" [Hall 1980: 136]. The second one is the professional code. "It serves to reproduce the dominant definitions precisely by bracketing the hegemonic quality, and operating with professional coding which relate to such questions as visual quality, news and presentational values, televisual quality, 'professionalism' etc." [136]. The third type of coding is the negotiated code. "It acknowledges the legitimacy of the hegemonic definitions to make the grand significations, while, at a more restricted, situational level, it makes its own ground-rules, it operates with 'exceptions' to the rule" [137]. And for us the most important is the fourth type of coding called oppositional coding or globally contrary code. "It is possible for a viewer perfectly to understand both the literal and connotative inflection given to an event, but to determine to decode the message in a globally contrary way" [138]. The receiver understands the common interpretation of the message, but uses a different code to decode it and so breaks it through. Hall questions the idea of a fixed meaning determined by the sender, transparency of the message and passivity of the audience.

Hall and Whannel [1964: 276] characterized teenage culture as a contradictory mixture of the authentic and the manufactured – an area of self-expression for the young and lush grazing ground for the commercial providers. Commodification of subculture does not exclude authenticity. Distortion is part of the system. In this he comes closer to Adorno's conception of artwork as contradictory and provoking reaction. Commodification is never absolute and its conflicts with higher values provoke reactions. Adorno however did not find that feature in lower types of art.

To extend that idea a little further we may say that full presence of something is impossible for man. Man always needs some instruments to access reality. They show him reality, but distort it at the same time, hinder direct access to it. Media are both obstacles and instruments. We even do not have direct access to the media as they are a background for the presented content and as soon as they would be subjects of our investigation they would lose its background character and would get a different background (e.g. that for which they were originally background). From that it follows we can never be sure about the media effects. We do not know how they will be interpreted, what effects they will have. In order to be as close to reality as possible we should support plurality of interpretations and opinions. Media will always provide some space for them.

What we must keep doing is to criticize the current understanding of the world in order not to get caught in one of its aspects. The ideas of the critiques of new technologies are grounded, but their result, that they uncover the only substance of technology is not, their critique just opens space for various aspects technology can have. If we criticize from one perspective another character will become manifest, because technology has a dual face.

References

Arnold, M. (2003). On the phenomenology of technology: the "Janus-faces" of mobile phones, *Information and Organization*, 13, 231-256

Benjamin, W. (1968). The Work of Art in the Age of Mechanical Reproduction, in: Arendt, H. (ed.), *Illuminations*, London, Fontana, 214-218

Cooper, S. (2002). *Technoculture and critical theory: in the service of the machine?*, Routledge, UK

Hall, S. and Whannell, P. (1964). *The Popular Arts*, Hutchinson, UK

Hall, S. (1980). Encoding / Decoding, in: Hall, S., Hobson, D., Lowe, A., and Willis, P. (eds.), *Culture, Media, Language: Working Papers in Cultural Studies, 1972–79*, Hutchinson, London, 128–138

Heidegger, M. (1969). *Discourse on thinking*, Harper & Row, USA

Horkheimer, M. and Adorno, T. W. (2002). *The Dialectic of Enlightenment*, Stanford University Press, USA

Lanier, J. (2000). One-Half a Manifesto, https://edge.org/conversation/one-half-a-manifesto [13 July 2015]

Lanier, J. (2006). *Digital Maoism: The Hazards of the New Online Collectivism*, http://edge.org/conversation/digital-maoism-the-hazards-of-the-new-online-collectivism [10 December 2015]

Mohammadi, D. (2015) How online gamers are solving science's biggest problems, *The Guardian*, http://www.theguardian.com/technology/2014/jan/25/online-gamers-solving-sciences-biggest-problems [5 May 2015]

Ross, A. (2014) Walter Benjamin, Theodor Adorno, and the critique of pop culture. *The New Yorker, The Naysayers*, September 15, 2014

Surowiecki, J. (2005). *The Wisdom of Crowds*, Anchor Books

Taylor, P. A. and Harris, J. L. (2008). *Critical theories of mass media: Then and now*, McGraw Hill/Open University Press, UK

Chapter 19

Governance from Below and Democratic Rebuilding
in Times of Crisis

Asimina Koukou

University of Vienna, Universitätsring 1, 1010 Wien, Austria
Bertalanffy Center for the Study of Systems Science
Paulanergasse 13, 1040 Vienna, Austria
asimina.koukou@bcsss.org

This chapter discusses the reasons of the European crisis, by examining the failures of the EU institutions to bring the citizens closer to the EU, the impacts of neoliberal ideology on politics and the effects of the media in the division of the publics. Lastly, it discusses the role of social movements in the transformation of society and the rebuilding of democracy.

1. Introduction

The EU has entered its seventh year of recession, keeping unemployment and poverty rates at a high level. The enforcement of harsh austerity policies, by international organizations as a measure of crisis management, has given rise to public discontent and rage against authorities and institutions on national and European levels. Under these circumstances, social movements emerge in order to condemn the existing governing structures and struggle for more equality and democracy.

This chapter examines the reasons why the European crisis has emerged and explores the ways through which European society self-organizes in order to rebuild democracy. The topic is examined through the lens of Evolutionary Systems Theory (EST) that dates back to the General System Theory (GST) of Ludwig von Bertalanffy. Evolutionary

Systems Theory (EST) [Hofkirchner 2013: 55-59] examines simultaneously both the dialectic of old and new and the dialectic of parts and whole, which "together constitute the evolutionary context" of reality [Fleissner and Hofkirchner 1996]. In particular, EST investigates the evolution of society through time (diachronous aspect), by drawing attention to the processes occurring during social formation in combination to the new social conditions that alter the dynamics of modern societies. At the same time, it concentrates on the structural evolution of an entity (synchronous aspect) that "can give rise to something new, which may eventually gain autonomy and reverse the situation by shaping the old entity" [ibid.]. The latter looks at the organization, structural relations (internal and external), and cognitive and collaborative abilities of entities that contribute to the current state of society.

EST applies the principle of self-organization, which is a process that brings order in any system through the interactions between the parts. It is a way through which evolutionary systems change, maintain or reshape themselves. In other words, it is a process in which "human actors and social structures are mutually related and produce each other" [Fuchs 2003: 23]. The principle of self-organization is based on the principle of 'unity-through-diversity' [Bertalanffy 1968; Hofkirchner 2013: 58] which needs to inform our nowadays society.

This work will present how unity could emerge in the European system through diversity, conflicts, marginalization and fragmentations. The first section presents the historical failure of European Commission to connect EU institutions with European citizens through a series of 'a-political' official documents. In the second section it is argued that the existing economic model is accountable for the European crisis, as it focuses on economics at the expense of politics. In the third section the reporting of the crisis and Europe by the media is examined, and in particular its contribution to the division of the publics. In the last section, social movements are at the epicenter of discussion, as political, collective actors that could bring novelty and change in European democracy.

2. Historical Evolution of EU Policies on Citizens' Participation

Within the years, EU bodies have introduced several policy documents and democratic innovations to reinforce participation, transparency, accountability and legitimacy.

Having the negative Danish referendum as a starting point, the EU institutions took measures to improve their performance and decrease the gap between them and the European public. Thus, on 25 October 1993 the Commission, Parliament and the Council adopted an *inter-institutional declaration on democracy, transparency and subsidiarity*. The objectives of this agreement were to make the EU decision-making processes transparent and the official documents accessible to the citizens, as well as increase public's trust in the institutions. This effort was followed by the *White Paper on European Governance*, published by the Commission on 25 July 2001, proposing "opening up the policy-making process to get more people and organizations involved in shaping and delivering EU policy" [Commission 2001a: 3]. In order to achieve this, the EU should strengthen the "Community method" [8], by promoting "better involvement and more openness, better policies, regulation and delivery as well as global governance and refocused institutions" [4-5]. In particular, the Commission emphasized on the need of the institutions and member states to "communicate more actively with the general public on European issues" [11] as well as shape "more effective and transparent consultation" [15]. In fact, on June 2001 the Commission recognized the need to bind citizens closer to Europe by releasing a *framework for cooperation on the information and communication policy of the European Union* [Commission 2001b]. This strategy aimed at creating new forms of cooperation among states, national governments, local actors and civil society, so as "all would have their word to say". In the meantime, the European Commission from 2001 to 2004 adopted three communications[a] on information and

---

[a]The three communications were: i) Communication on a new framework for cooperation on activities concerning the information and communication policy of the European Union – COM(2001) 354, ii) Communication on an information and communication

communication, which were never implemented as their main emphasis was on financing the campaigns and not on reinforcing dialogue. EU policies gave priority on improving "the quantity, quality and accessibility of information on EU issues" [Michaelidou 2008: 349], rather on democratic participation. Thus, the European Commission's official documents reduced their discussion to information processes as being the only motives towards the development of citizens' participation in EU matters.

A change in the Commission's strategy can be spotted in the *Action Plan to improve communicating Europe* published in July 2005, where it was stated that "communication is more than information" [Commission 2005a: 3]. For the first time the European Commission stressed the necessity for creating a dialogic relationship between EU institutions and the citizens as well as "going local". The outcome of consultation on the aforementioned action plan was the *Plan D for Democracy, Dialogue and Debate* [Commission 2005b], which aimed at developing a range of tools that could be utilized to obtain feedback directly from the public and generate in this way a real dialogue on European policies. The need for making the EU institutions more democratic and closer to citizens was more than imperative.

Despite the steps taken to increase communication between EU and citizens, the gap between them continued to exist. According to *Eurobarometer 63* and *64*, trust in the European Commission fell significantly during the first half of 2005 (46%). The result remained the same in the second half of the year, with a significant rise in the proportion of citizens who tended not to trust this institution (from 21% to 33%). Same observations were made for the European Parliament as well. Although 51% of citizens still had trust in the European Parliament [Eurobarometer 64], the percentage of people who did not trust the institution has increased by 3 points during 2005 (from 31% to 34%). As a response to that, the Commission signed the *White Paper on a European Communication Policy* [Commission 2006] intending to create

---

strategy for the European Union – COM(2002) 350 and iii) Communication on implementing the information and communication strategy for the European Union – COM(2004) 196.

a strong public sphere that would found on media and new technologies (Internet) in order to empower the citizens, increase their active participation and enhance cooperation among them across all levels (local, national, European). Such initiative would allow the function of new forums for civic debate and 'virtual meeting places' through the use of new channels for communication on European issues. Once again, the focus of the document was reduced to information and in particular the information shared with the public through the use of the Internet. New technologies were regarded as the main tool for more inclusion of citizens in the public sphere and enhancement of public debates on EU issues.

Building on the previous White paper, the Commission's document on *Communicating Europe in Partnership* [Commission 2007a] came to assure a coherent and integrated communication between the different EU institutions and member states. The objective of this communication was not only to inform the public on European issues but also to give them the voice to be heard and make an influence. Special reference was made to education and active citizenship, but as Michaelidou [2008: 351] states the argument of the 'democratic deficit' is not provided at all and "the main responsibility for 'communicating Europe' to its citizens is still left with the member states". As a follow-up, the document on *Communicating about Europe via the Internet – Engaging the citizens'* from December 2007 introduced the idea of using the Internet not only as a source of information but as a political/democratic tool for bringing the people closer [Commission 2007b: 5]. A first development was the EUROPA website which functioned as "a one-stop shop for information and interactivity" [Lodge and Sarikakis 2013: 174]. The *Communicating Europe through Audiovisual Media* strategy [Commission 2008a] came as complementary to the Internet strategy. The goal was to create a European Public Sphere through the use of audiovisual media. The Commission clearly referred to a range of actions that would facilitate the coverage of EU affairs and the engagement of people in a properly informed and democratic debate on EU policies [11]. This communication would allow media professionals to create networks of channels and broadcasters in EU content.

The *Debate Europe – building on the experience of Plan D for Democracy, Dialogue and Debate* [Commission 2008b] that was launched in April 2008 envisaged empowering citizens "by giving them access to information so that they may be in a position to hold an informed debate on EU affairs" [Commission 2008b: 4]. This could be realized through "virtual and face to face communication, deliberative consultation and polling, country-level, cross-border and pan-European consultations" [ibid.]. For the first time the European Commission marked the role of participatory democracy on EU-related issues at local, regional, national and cross-border level. The Action would reinforce civil society initiatives with the form of citizens' consultations in each country, the formulation of proposals at European level as well as local actions and projects aiming at specific needs (schools, festivals, conferences, public spaces, Internet debates and so on) [Commission 2008b: 48].

The most important step towards participatory democracy was taken on April 2012, when the European Commission introduced the *European Citizens' Initiative (ECI)*, a new tool that would give permission to one million of EU citizens to make their voices heard in Brussels by proposing legislation to the Commission. The conditions for implementation of the ECI were defined by the *Regulation on the Citizens' Initiative* [2011], adopted by both the European Parliament and the Commission in February 2011. This initiative would encourage citizens' participation and engagement in the EU's political life. Despite its recent appearance, it has been criticized for being undemocratic and being unable to provoke "bottom up deliberation or even top down communication" [Bouza 2011: 25]. The ECI has also been accused for having design problems as well as empowering "well-organised and resourceful groups" [ibid.: 34].

In summary, the body of documents produced by the Commission in the course of our recent history was "one of a-political persuasion, of engaging the Commission in communicating positive messages about European governance in an anodyne, nonprescriptive, nonpartisan a-political way. This overly simplistic view overlooked the role of national parties (at all levels) and that of social movements" [Lodge and Sarikakis 2013: 176]. The Commission appeared to be undecided on whether to take an informational or a participatory direction of action. The query then whether the European Commission really desired to create a strong connection between the public and the institutions is reasonable. Undoubtedly, the evolution of the policy documents reveals that the EU bodies forgot their final aim and goal in the course of history.

3. The Current State: The European Crisis

The global financial crisis began to have severe impacts on Europe in 2008, after the collapse of the US bank Lehman Brothers. As more and more companies declared bankruptcy, this caused severe consequences to the European real economy. What had initially started as a financial crisis now became an economic crisis until in some EU countries the detrimental effects caused a sovereign debt and deficit crisis [Lapavitsas 2012: 6; Della Porta 2015: 32]. Under these circumstances, several southern European countries (Greece, Italy, Spain, and Portugal) – even countries beyond the Eurozone, such as the UK – came at the epicenter of the economic turbulence, as they were unable to pay their public debt. The latter refers to the money owed by governments to their creditors, often borrowed "to pay for construction of infrastructures and public buildings, but also to pay for government costs when tax revenues do not provide sufficient income" [Picard 2015: 14]. In order to cope with the debt crisis, international organizations imposed harsh austerity measures – "cutting wages, reducing public spending and raising taxes, in the hope of reducing public borrowing requirements" [Lapavitsas 2012: 7] – to peripheral countries as measures of crisis management. While these measures pointed at reducing the deficit, the rates of poverty and unemployment as well as social inequalities and injustices reached their zenith. Additionally, austerity policies strengthened the "political dependency" of nation-states from "core capitalist states as well as international organizations" and reduced their "welfare provisions" such as public education, health, social care [Della Porta 2015: 27]. At the same time, the dramatic rise of populism across Europe as well as the outrageous reactions to the refugees crisis have put at stake both European values and democracy.

According to the economists the current crisis is attributed to monetary and fiscal policies. In particular, the political economist Carlo Panico [2010] ascribed the crisis to the defects of the institutional organization of the European Monetary Union (EMU). Likewise, Paul Krugman,[b] in an article published in New York Times in January 2011, pointed out that "the architects of the euro, caught up in their project's sweep and romance, chose to ignore the mundane difficulties a shared currency would predictably encounter – to ignore warnings, which were issued right from the beginning, that Europe lacked the institutions needed to make a common currency workable". The well-known economist Joseph Stiglitz [2012, 2014a, b] has accused the ECB for putting "the interests of the banks well above that of the Greek people" and the unstable market processes "embedded in a flawed set of institutional arrangements and policy frameworks" as being responsible for the crisis. In the same vein, Costas Lapavitsas stressed that the crisis was caused due to "the bad performance the institutions of the Eurozone and mostly the central bank" [2012: 69] manifested. Stiglitz [2014a, b] argued that structural and institutional reforms on the euro were needed to overcome the crisis. But is this really the solution to the problem?

Neoliberalism is the economic paradigm that prevails in our society and it is based on the liberalization of the markets, the privatization of public goods and deregulation. The current crisis is the product of this model, which according to Harvey [2005:46]

> proposes that human well-being can best be advanced by liberating individual entrepreneurial freedoms and skills within an institutional framework characterized by strong private property rights, free markets, and free trade. The role of the state is to create and preserve an institutional framework appropriate to such practices. The state has to guarantee, for example, the quality and integrity of money. It must also set up those military, defense, police, and legal structures and functions required to secure private property rights and to guarantee, by force if need be, the proper functioning of markets. Furthermore, if markets do not exist (in areas such as land, water, education, health care, social security, or environmental pollution) then they must be created, by state action if necessary. But beyond these tasks the state should not venture. State interventions in markets

---

[b]Krugman, P. (2011), Can Europe be Saved? Retrieved on 12 March 2013 from: http://www.nytimes.com/2011/01/16/magazine/16Europe-t.html

(once created) must be kept to a bare minimum because, according to the theory, the state cannot possibly possess enough information to second-guess market signals (prices) and because powerful interest groups will inevitably distort and bias state interventions (particularly in democracies) for their own benefit.

In other words, free market was seen as the supreme good of modern society that could contribute to the creation of wealth and the improvement of humans' living standards. The power of the market is strengthened because the state guarantees institutionally the realization of its practices. Harvey points out that neoliberalism has a monopolistic and absolute right at the expense of human rights and entitlements Indeed, it is the 'counterrevolution' imposed from above that finally brought "immense wealth to a few at the expense of the many" a distinctive feature of our times [Harvey 2005: 162].

The act of 'enclosure', through "which corporations pluck valuable resources from their natural contexts, often with government support [...] and declare that they be valued through market prices" [Bollier 2014a: 37], is identical of the expansionary politics of free market in natural and human resources. For Karl Polanyi [1957: 41] the enclosures of fields and commons are regarded as "a revolution of the rich against the poor." This argument contradicts Polanyi's theoretical statement that the market economy was not inseparable from the state and they both co-existed in market society under the influence of two organizing principles. The one was 'economic liberalism', "aiming at the establishment of a self-regulating market, relying on the support of the trading classes, and using largely laissez-faire and free trade as its methods". The other was the principle of 'social protection' "aiming at the conservation of man and nature as well as productive organization, relying on the varying support of those most immediately affected by the deleterious action of the market – primarily, but not exclusively, the working and the landed classes – and using protective legislation, restrictive associations, and other instruments of intervention as its methods" [1957: 138]. The market society and the economy should complement social relations [Chakravartty and Sarikakis 2006: 9]. A fully liberalized system gives rise to social disintegration and environmental destruction, by converting all elements of social life to commodities. When the market disconnects from the social context then crises emerge, like the one we are experiencing in Europe today. This detachment from the people is accountable for the annihilation of 'man's relationships' and 'natural habitat' [Polanyi 1957: 48]. Therefore, the enforcement of harsh austerity measures by international organizations to the most vulnerable members of the Eurozone, depicts how distant economic actors are from ordinary citizens.

For Costas Douzinas, neoliberalism has turned politics into the administration of economics [Douzinas 2013: 29]. Everything is subjected to the logic of markets. Economic institutions set the rules of the game and their actions seem to serve the interests of the most powerful countries. It is inevitable to rescue from this situation unless a change in the existing economic model is realized. Likewise, Naomi Klein [2007, 2015] contends that markets and state work together at the expense of natural resources, labor force and human rights. She regards neoliberalism as a "hidden", hegemonic ideology that imposes its power over the people and makes efforts to put all social relations under the protection of the markets. The hegemony of neoliberalism is better imposed in a society, when crises occur. Klein [2007: 6] cites Friedman, who stated that

> only a crisis – actual or perceived – produces real change. When that crisis occurs, the actions that are taken depend on the ideas that are lying around. That, I believe, is our basic function: to develop alternatives to existing policies, to keep them alive and available until the political impossible becomes politically inevitable

The current state in Europe illustrates the gap between the elites and the people. It reveals an antagonistic and competitive relationship among the poor and the rich, the Southern and Northern countries of Europe. The discussion revolves around the enforcement of austerity measures and public debts, omitting to refer to human values and social welfare. The absence of solidarity and reciprocity provokes huge fragmentations and divisions in the population. Apart from that it puts peace and democratic values at stake. Colin Crouch [2004] has stated that 'we are living in a post-democracy'. Post-democracy is still a democracy, but the power is not in the people anymore, but in the elites (political and economic). European states are only interested in achieving high economic standards undermining the politics. Europe is at a crossroads of its historical development and it needs a leap in quality. Do the media prepare the conditions for this transition or not?

4. Reporting Europe and its Crisis

Most of the information we have today about risks, disasters and crises comes from the mass media. The media create and distribute the news from the senders (e.g. governments, policy officers, stakeholders) to the receivers (public). In broad terms, the media are responsible for attracting citizens' attention, criticizing the dysfunctional policies of the authorities and contributing to social change. In a well-functioning democratic polity, the media are considered to be the 'Fourth Estate', a term that is attributed to Edmund Burke, a British politician, who said that "there were three Estates in Parliament, but in the Reporters Gallery yonder, there sat a fourth Estate more important far than they all", as quoted by Thomas Carlyle's book *Heroes, Hero Worship, and the Heroic in History* [2008: 222]. The media are supposed to serve as 'guardians' and 'watchdogs' of the public interest. Their role is to act "free from government control and influence" [Kiran 2000: 88] and exercise control over the authorities [Norris 2016: 16], by criticizing their decisions, laws and policies. By revealing corruption and illegal activities, the media promote objectivity and build a trustful relationship with the citizens [Bennett 1990]. Besides, the media are the bond between the governors and the governed, create the 'public sphere' and act as arenas of public debate [Habermas 1989]. The media serve as 'forums' of participation where pluralism is promoted and diverse voices are heard [Fraser 1989; Livingstone and Lunt 1994]. Based on equal rights and free access, all citizens are allowed to contribute to the development of public opinion. In addition, the media shape the public agenda and "focus public attention on a few key public issues" [McCombs 1972:2003]. They also determine what issues are "important" and make them salient by providing what is "noticeable, meaningful, or memorable to audiences" [Entman 1993: 53]. The reason of highlighting specific issues is to "raise awareness of social problems" and "make people more responsive to social needs" [Norris 2016: 16].

However powerful the media are, many scholars criticize and accuse them of acting as 'guard dogs' and not as 'watchdogs', meaning that they become part of the 'power oligarchy' in the system [Donohue 1995]. The media are blamed for giving legitimacy to the elites, establishing and creating deliberately false ideas, beliefs and choices to things for social attention [Bell 1975]. They are used to manufacture public "consent", becoming in this way a mouthpiece of political and economic elites [Chomsky and Herman 2002]. Furthermore, there is common sense that the media are used by governments as tools for propaganda and fulfilment of their interests [Butsch 2007: 2]. Media are also blamed for being driven by profit motives, instead of informing the public and enabling public discussion. From the above, media are turned to be captives of "the state and/or commercial corporations" [ibid:8]. Journalists, governments and market dominate them, having as a consequence the creation of passive audiences. Dahlgren [2005] sees the media as vertical channels between citizens and the government, a top-down process that limits social dialogue and direct interaction.

In the case of the European crisis, the media play a crucial role in conveying the issues, conditions, discourses, and solutions about the European 'problem' (which shift from the fate of euro and the Eurozone to questions of policy, democracy and constitution). Since the outbreak of the crisis, there has been a growing interest in academic research with regard to the role of the media in times of crisis. Scholars have raised questions regarding the ways the media frame the crisis and Europe as well as its implications for the existence of a European Public Sphere (EPS) and identity.

Triandafyllidou *et al.* [2009], through a diachronous-historical analysis, highlighted "a highly diversified set of 'national' conceptualizations of Europe". In pre-1989 crises, they encountered that the media became a "national filter of perception of Europe", whereas after the fall of the Berlin Wall their conceptualization of Europe did not change significantly. For Triandafyllidou *et al.* [2009: 267] the EPS can be characterized as European, only because national media were located in Europe. When the discussion comes to the international coverage of a specific crisis, such as the Greek one, then a stereotypical representation of the crisis is observed. The media usually focus on the problematic

Greek economy, the potential 'metastasis' of the crisis in the rest of the European continent and the internal pathologies of Greek politics such as corruption, bureaucracy, nepotism, tax evasion [Tzogopoulos 2011, 2013]. However, the dysfunctions of the Greek state and its political system are also the dominant narrative in Greek press, as presented by Hara Kouki [2014: 16] in her work *European Crisis Discourses: the case of Greece*. The aforementioned work examined the dominant discourses concerning the euro crisis in five countries and their findings showed a de-politicization both of the crisis and the European institutions [2014: 79]. The paper suggests that Europe must be politicized in a way that alternative voices can be heard.

Other empirical research has demonstrated that crisis reporting 'accentuated polarization' especially in terms of Europe, the European Union, issues of legitimacy and the future of European integration Sarikakis [2012a, 2013, 2016]. Furthermore, this analysis confirmed a relation between the press and the elites, as well as a clear division between 'us' and 'them'. Similarly, Mylonas [2012] acknowledges that the discourses produced by the media are 'highly ideological', reproducing the neoliberal discourse and expressing the interests of the capitalist class. Thus, the media in times of crisis are seen as the tools for the cultivation of a neoliberal understanding of society that preserves conflicts, contradictions and divisions. To sum up, the academic research indicates that the information produced and diffused by the media with respect to the euro crisis is one-sided and biased. By reporting only one side of the story, they magnify hostility and fear towards the 'other'. This leads to a further division between the member states, the rise of extreme-right parties and anti-immigrant rhetoric. The media do not serve as social institutions any more, instead they are connected to the elites by interwoven webs of relations. As a consequence, the powerful classes "control the channels which provide information" [Fuchs and Hofkirchner 1999]. Thus, truth is deliberately hidden, aiming at uncritical and irrational publics. The vision of Robert Schuman and Jean Monnet for a united Europe as a remedy to nationalism, seems to collapse nowadays and the media play the most crucial role in this breakdown.

5. Overcoming the Crisis

It is apparent that European society faces constraints within the structure of the EU, which impede the system to evolve. These constraints oppose to human agency taking the form of limitations to democratic policy-making and participation as well as undermining of human values and rights. Those who possess a powerful position make decisions and take measures for the citizens, without literally including them in the process. Thus, the structure does not give enough significance to the whole, as a consequence citizens' dissatisfaction and distrust arises.

According to GST, a system is more than the sum of its parts [Bertalanffy 1968]. In order the system to function properly, interactions between the structure (institutions) and the agency (individual or collective agents, states) of the European society need to be established. Human interactions take place at the agency level and are responsible for the social relations emerging at the structural level and hereupon the latter is emergent to the micro level and exerts to it a downward causation. The macro level in this way "plays the role of the *Third*", which "establishes and mediates the relation between two other things" [Hofkirchner 2014b: 59]. It is a mode of reflexivity that needs to be established in order to create a good society.

The European crisis has shown that society is in need of a change, a transition that would contribute to the emergence of a new supra-system that would compose of conscious, communicative and cooperative actors. The current social movements seem to assist in the realization of this goal. Through their self-organization which is a "creative activity of the system in the course of which novelty is produced [...] and marks a difference in the development of the system" [Hofkirchner 2013: 169], social movements build new alternative structures and networks for the benefit of the people, especially those who are affected by the crisis, live under the poverty line and are incapable of paying their taxes, mortgages and bills. The following section refers to *governance from below*, a political process through which diverse claims are expressed, communicative spaces are created and new democratic and participatory processes are exercised.

5.1. *Governance from below*

Since the beginning of the crisis, anti-austerity movements have gained momentum across the European continent. In 2011, Spanish and Greek people occupied the squares Puerta del Sol in Madrid and the Syntagma square in Athens respectively, calling the people to protest against austerity politics and claim for a democratic rebirth, equality, justice and dignity [Tsaliki 2012; Simiti 2014; Della Porta 2015]. The *indignant citizens movement* expressed in the streets of both countries, gave the opportunity to the people to reconsider their lives and react against the dominant power structures. Thus, movements such as the Greek *we don't pay* (initially against the highway tolls), *without middlemen* (against the market intermediaries) and the *anti-gold mining movement/Skouries movement* (against ore mining for the protection of the environment), as well as the Spanish *Stop Desahancios Platform* (against eviction), the British *NHS social movement* (against the privatization of health system) and the Romanian *Save Rosia Montana movement* (against the Rosia Montana mining project) emerged and constitute some identical examples of citizens' struggles for the commons (common goods). The *commons* refer either to natural goods and material resources (forests, water, air, electricity) or social and cultural resources (public buildings, education, health) that are owned, shared and used in common [Rilling 2009: 1; Bollier 2014ab]. Claims for the commons arise when people feel that they are excluded from "social distribution and [are] invisible to political representation" [Douzinas 2013: 96]. Consequently, people create alternative platforms in which they make their own rules and decisions on how to manage and govern their common resources, resisting to the organized political and economic interests. According to Negt and Kluge [1993: 60] this is a new *public* that comes from below, from the proletariat as an alternative to the bourgeoisie, from the minorities as a response to the authorities that control everything. Negt and Kluge give emphasis on the ability of the workers (labor movement) to self-organize and resist "against their bourgeois enemy." Thus, in this work, the term *governance from below* refers to the political process of resistance that comes from the marginalized and peripheral groups of society in an effort to challenge the existing dominant power, as well as oppose inequalities and injustices. *Governance from below* is a new way of political collective action that gives the opportunity to alternative voices not only to be heard but also be constituent part of social life.

Generally speaking, most of the rebellions, uprisings, protests, social movements and occupations start with an act of resistance and disobedience. The state is supposed to assure the rule of law, guarantee citizens' security and protect human rights. Nevertheless, sometimes "policies and laws violate the principles of equal liberty or basic rights", as a consequence disobedience arises [Douzinas 2013: 92]. Disobedience is "a sign of moral conscience" [89], meaning that people comprehend that the "established power" oppresses their sense of justice and naturally they react to this. For Nancy Fraser [2005: 5], social justice means 'parity of participation'. Justice consists of three principles: the one is the principle of distribution that is equivalent to economic equality. This principle is realized if people "have the resources they need in order to interact with others as peers" [ibid.]. The second is the principle of recognition that refers to cultural differences. This principle is met if "status inequality or misrecognition" is ruled out. The third is the principle of representation that is linked to democratic accountability and is fulfilled if criteria of social belonging and decision rules are established. Combining all the principles together, one can say that Fraser's justice can be accomplished, if citizens own the resources and the 'status order' as well as have equal voice in public deliberations and fair representation in policy-making. In other words, social justice is achieved through a combination of redistribution, recognition and representation claims. "No redistribution or recognition without representation" can exist in society today [Fraser 2005: 17]. According to Fraser, all claims are mutual and irreducible to each other. Currently, the claims of anti-austerity movements and citizens' networks overlap. Apart from economic claims, citizens request for more justice and democracy. Their agenda is not one-dimensional, on the contrary it consists of demands that cover all aspects of human life and democratic participation, ranging from struggles for work, health, food, education, water, public buildings and environment to fights against fascism.

The novelty of our today social movements is their networked and decentralized character [Negri and Hardt 2005; Castells 1997, 2007,

2011, 2012]. Different people from diverse backgrounds come together and designate an "open and expansive network in which all differences can be expressed freely and equally, a network that provides the means of encounter so that we can work and live in common" [Negri and Hardt 2005: xiv]. These networks are based on communication, collaboration and effective relationships [ibid: 66]. With the support of Internet and new technologies, new citizen networks, communities and identities are built that connect local and global in a given time [Castells 2007]. Digital technologies have altered the way human societies operate, self-organize and exercise counter power. For Castells [2007] counter power expresses the interests of the subordinate groups that come "to challenge and eventually change the power relations institutionalized in society". By describing the communicative strategy of the Zapatistas, Castells pointed out that both the Internet and the media were used as tools to spread the movement's message across the world and organize other networks of solidarity initiatives as well. In the era of crisis, the Internet creates the necessary condition(s) for the transformation of the organization of society ("self-organization") through the establishment of new communicative spaces that can be online or offline spaces of communication.

The term communicative space has its origins in Jürgen Habermas and refers to a social space generated by communicative action. For Habermas [1981: 86] *communicative action* is

the interaction of at least two subjects capable of speech and action who establish interpersonal relations (whether by verbal or extra-verbal means). The actors seek to reach an understanding about the action situation and their plans of action in order to coordinate their actions by way of agreement. The central concept of interpretation refers in the first instance to negotiating definitions of the situation which admit of consensus.

Communicative action goes hand in hand with the *ideal speech situation*. The latter refers to a condition in which all individuals who have the competence to speak and act, can participate in discourse. Apart from that, they are equal to provide their rational arguments and also to question the validity of their interlocutors' claims. In this dialectic way, truth is reached as well as prejudices and errors are dissolved [Habermas 1981]. The ideal speech situation creates the appropriate background for all participants to express equally their views and make their 'inner nature' transparent. The process of reaching mutual understanding and sharing of perspectives establishes the conditions for self-organization.

All self-organized movements, solidarity networks and citizens' cooperatives that exist in Europe today, function as communicative-social spaces. From the gatherings in public squares to the assemblies in the neighborhoods, citizens are free to participate, express their views, exchange opinions and provide solutions on issues of common interest. 'Assembly' (in Greek: 'Agora') is the place where the people come together for the realization of a particular purpose. These places are 'open to everyone' [Sitrin and Azzellini 2014; Della Porta 2015: 186-191], meaning that they give free access to the wider public. All people are equal to participate. In these communicative spaces the inclusion of marginalized groups is promoted. They are spaces that acknowledge human diversity and heterogeneity and they permit the 'untold', 'unrecognised' and 'unarticulated' to be articulated [Sarikakis 2012b]. In general, they are spaces within which 'reflexive' deliberations take place [Archer 2007: 3-4]. With the use of rational, reflexive and critical arguments, people 'make their way through the world'. They share their knowledge and personal experiences and find ways to build new communities – communities in which people "organize and coordinate structures to govern their own lives" [Sitrin and Azzellini 2014: 19]. In these communities real collaboration and social relationships are performed. Under these conditions, several community cooperatives (social kitchens, social clinics, self-organized environmental groups) that provide food-aid, medical care, household supplies and so on are constructed. All these are alternative forms of political participation that intend to make the citizens' actions known with the hope that they will transform society. Apparently, EU citizens struggle to regain control over their resources as well restore their dignity and pride.

The *governance from below* could operate as catalyst in strengthening deliberative and participatory democracy in society. Citizens' activities emphasize both the 'discursive quality of democracy' [Della Porta and Mattoni 2012] (namely the use of rational arguments, the realization of consensus and the defense of the commons) and the equal, inclusive and transparent participation of citizens in political actions. Therefore this work suggests that *governance from below* could serve as the infrastructure for a democratic society and the communicative medium through which the beliefs and values of the people could be transmitted to the top-down governance. Governance from below could serve as a model for the participatory design of the whole society.

5.2. *A future vision for Europe*

A new system in Europe is possible, as long as the efforts of the agents are grounded on a specific balance of cognition, communication and cooperation (the Triple-C Model of Evolutionary Systems Theory) [Hofkirchner 2013]. These three principles are mutually influenced and they constitute the practical steps for governing our world today. This study indicates that the way social movements work in Europe resembles this Triple-C Model. Social movements have experimented alternative solutions and new governance models within the crisis, which indicate what exactly society needs in order to make progress. The lessons learned by the social movements should not be disregarded, instead they should guide the actions of all humans for bringing better impact to the whole society as well.

Humans, nowadays, are in need of self-organizing by the way of a new mode of reflexivity [Hofkirchner 2014a.]. According to Margaret Archer [2007: 4], reflexivity is "the regular exercise of the mental ability shared by all normal people, to consider themselves in relation to their (social) contexts and vice versa". Social movements have managed to view the world and its problems from the position of the *other*. They have taken into consideration the Third, namely they view the world from a meta-level [Hofkirchner 2014a]. In the current crisis, that idiotism [Hofkirchner 2014a], competition and antagonisms [Hofkirchner 2015] prevail, all actors – individual and collective – would need to think about the European society as a whole and not as parts (states, citizens). In order to accomplish this, each of them would need to adopt "meta-reflexives", which means that they should be critically reflexive about their internal conversations and then be critical about the system in which they live in [Archer 2007]. By being critical both to themselves (personal intentions) and the way society works today, they would be able to pave the way for better communication among them.

Social movements have made visible the conditions under which *communication* can take place effectively and assure better solving to problems. Thus, humans would envision a society in which true deliberation and participation could occur, a society in which all could co-exist harmonically, without the one acting at the expense of the other. This presupposes the development of deep respect and meaningful understanding for the 'different'. People need to understand that they share the same land and live under the same conditions of crisis.

Lastly, people would have to build strong relations of *cooperation*, because collaboration (and not inactivity) leads a system to evolution. Teamwork presupposes the sharing of common goals, beliefs and intentions, as well as a sense of 'we'. This presupposes the application of the system theoretical principle "unity through diversity" [Hofkirchner 2013], which denotes that humans unite in working together for the commons, despite their differences. The commons operate as the Third [2014b: 62-64], as the causal power that relates individuals together. The commons create a reciprocity that dissolves all the supposed oppositions existing in a society.

Therefore, change in European society is not determined only by structural factors, historical transitions or technological developments, but is the combined outcome of individual or collective actions, knowledge, consciousness, communication, cooperation and willingness to change ways of life and values. What is needed today is to establish a dialectic relationship between social movements and society. Social movements can shape society, and in turn society can shape social movements. Both of them need to be considered as being reciprocally influenced and connected. Besides, both social movements and social change can occur in societies, they can flow together, they influence one another and, thus, bring new potentials and chances for development.

To put it differently, a strong relationship of cooperation needs to be established between the *governance from below* and the governance from above. This will lead European society to the transcendence to a new meta-level. It is not only about challenging authorities, but proposing alternative solutions to them as well. The bottom-up activities could energize the debate to rethink the system and rebuild Europe. It is about opening a fruitful dialogue, in which states and institutions could cooperate with the citizens for the common goods. People need to realize that the interplay of all social actors and forces is accountable for a better society and sustainable democracy.

References

Archer, M. (2007). *Making our Way through the World: Human Reflexivity and Social Mobility*, Cambridge University Press, Cambridge

Bell, D. (1975). The End of American Exceptionalism, *The Public Interest*, Fall 1975, 193-224

Bennett, W.L. (1990). Toward a Theory of Press State Relations in the United States, *Journal of Communication*, 40 (2), 103-125

Bollier, D. (2014a). *Think like a Commoner. A Short Introduction to the Life of the Commons*, New Society Publishers, Canada

Bollier, D. (2014b). The Commons as a Template for Transformation. *Great transition Initiative*, February 2014, 1-14

Bouza, G. L., (2011). Anticipating the Attitudes of European Civil Society Organisations to the European Citizens' Initiative (ECI): Which Public Sphere may it Promote?, *Programme of the College of Europe, Cahiers de Recherche Politique de Bruges*, No 24/February, Bruges, 23-51

Butsch, R. (2007). *Media and Public Spheres*, Palgrave-Macmillan, Basingstoke UK, New York USA

Carlyle, T. (2008). *Heroes and Hero Worship*, Project Gutenberg Edition

Castells, M. (2007). Communication, Power and Counter-power in the Network Society, *International Journal of Communication*, 1, 238-266

Castells, M. (2011). A Network Theory of Power, *International Journal of Communication*, 5, 773–787

Chakravartty, P., Sarikakis, K. (2006). *Media Policy and Globalization*, Palgrave Macmillan, New York

Chomsky, N., Herman, E. (2002). *Manufacturing Consent*, Pantheon, New York

Commission (2001a). *European Governance - A White Paper*, COM(2001)428

Commission (2001b). *A New Framework for Co-operation on Activities Concerning the Information and Communication Policy of the European Union*, COM(2001)354

Commission (2002). *Communication on an Information and Communication Strategy for the European Union*, COM(2002) 350

Commission (2004). *Communication on Implementing the Information and Communication Strategy for the European Union*, COM(2004)196

Commission (2005a). *Action Plan to Improve Communicating Europe by the Commission*, Brussels

Commission (2005b). *The Commission's contribution to the period of reflection and beyond: Plan-D for Democracy, Dialogue and Debate*, COM(2005)494

Commission (2006). *White Paper on a European Communication Policy presented by the Commission*, COM(2006)35

Commission (2007a). *Communicating Europe in Partnership*, COM(2007)568

Commission (2007b). *Communicating about Europe via the Internet- Engaging the citizens*, SEC(2007)1742

Commission (2008a). *Communicating Europe through Audio-visual Media*, SEC(2008), 506/2

Commission (2008b). *Debate Europe-building on the experience of Plan D for Democracy, Dialogue and Debate*, COM(2008) 158 final

Crouch, C. (2004). *Post-democracy*, Polity Press, London

Dahlgren, P. (2005). The Internet, Public Spheres, and Political Communication: Dispersion and deliberation, *Political Communication*, 22, 147-162

Della Porta, D., Mattoni, A. (2012). Cultures of Participation in Social Movements, in: Delwiche, A., Henderson, J.J. (eds.) *The Participatory Cultures,* Routledge, London, 170-181

Della Porta, D. (2015). *Social Movements in Times of Austerity*, Polity Press, UK

Donohue, G.A. (1995). A Guard Dog Perspective on the Role of Media, *Journal of Communication*, 45(2), Spring 1995, 115-132

Douzinas, C. (2013). *Philosophy and Resistance in the Crisis*, Polity Press, UK

Entman, R. M. (1993). Framing: Toward Clarification of a Fractured Paradigm, *Journal of Communication*, 43(4), 51-58

Eurobarometer 63 (July 2005). *Public Opinion in the European Union*, http://ec.europa.eu/public_opinion/archives/eb/eb63/eb63.4_en_first.pdf

Eurobarometer 64 (December 2005). *Public Opinion in the European Union*, http://ec.europa.eu/public_opinion/archives/eb/eb64/eb64_first_en.pdf

European Parliament and the Council of EU (March 2011). Regulation (EU) No 211/2011 of 16 February 2011 on the Citizens' Initiative, L65-1, http://eur-lex.europa.eu/LexUriServ/LexUriServ.do?uri=OJ:L:2011:065:0001:0022:en:PDF

Fleissner, P., Hofkirchner, W. (1996). Emergent Information. Towards a Unified Information Theory. *BioSystems*, 2-3 (38), 243-248

Fraser, N. (1989). *Unruly Practices: Power, Discourse and Gender in Contemporary Social Theory*, University of Minnesota Press, Minneapolis

Fraser, N. (2005). Reframing justice in a globalizing world, *New Left Review*, 36, 1-19

Fuchs, C., Stockinger, G. (2003). The Autocreation of Communication and the Re-Creation of Actions, in: Arshinov, V., Fuchs, C. (eds.) *Causality, Emergence, Self-Organisation*, NIA-Priroda, Moscow, 303-321

Habermas, J. (1989). *The Structural Transformation of the Public Sphere,* Polity Press, Cambridge

Hardt, M., Negri, A. (2004). *Multitude. War and Democracy in the Age of Empire,* The Penguin Press, New York

Hofkirchner, W. (2013). *Emergent Information A Unified Theory of Information Framework,* World Scientific, Singapore

Hofkirchner, W. (2014a). The Commons from a Critical Social Systems Perspective, *Recerca Revista de Pensament i Analisi,* 14, 73-91

Hofkirchner, W. (2014b). Idiotism and the Logic of the Third, in: Lakitsch, M. (ed.). *Political Power reconsidered. State Power and Civil Activism between Legitimacy and Violence,* Peace Report 2013, 55-75

Hofkirchner, W. (2015). Mechanisms at Work in Information Society, in: Archer M. (ed.), *Generative Mechanisms Transforming the Social Order,* Springer, Dordrecht, 95-112

Kiran, R.N. (2000). *Philosophies of Communication and Media Ethics: Theory, Concepts and Empirical Issues,* BR Publishing Corporation, London

Kouki, H. (2014). European Crisis Discourses: the case of Greece, in: Murray-Leach, T. (ed.), *Crisis Discourses in Europe Media EU-phemisms and Alternative Narratives,* Civil Society and Human Security Research Unit London School of Economics and Political Science, 16-20

Lapavitsas, C. *et al.* (2012). *Crisis in the Eurozone,* Verso, London

Livingstone, S., Lunt, P. (1994). The Mass Media, Democracy and the Public Sphere, in: Livingstone S., Lunt, P. (eds). *Talk on Television: Audience Participation and Public Debate,* Routledge, London, 9-35

Lodge, J., Sarikakis, K. (2013). Citizens in 'An Ever-Closer Union'? The Long Path to a Public Sphere in the EU, *International Journal of Media and Cultural Politics,* 9(2), 165-181

McCombs, M. (1972). The Agenda-Setting Function of Mass Media, *Public Opinion Quarterly,* 36 (2), 176-187

Michaelidou, A. (2008). Democracy and New Media in the European Union: Communication or Participation Deficit?, *Journal of Contemporary European Research,* 4 (4), 346-368

Negt, O. & Kluge, A. (1993). *Public Sphere and Experience: Toward an Analysis of the Bourgeois and Proletarian Public Sphere,* University of Minnesota Press, Minneapolis

Rilling, R. (2009). Beyond the Crisis: Empowering the Public!, *Rosa Luxembourg Foundation,* 5, 1-8

Sarikakis, K. (2012a). 'Crisis' – 'Democracy' – 'Europe': Terms of Contract? Framing Public Debates of the Crisis, *Workshop of the Austrian Research Association on the Financial Crisis of the 21st Century,* Österreichische Forschungsgemeinschaft

Sarikakis, K. (2012b). Securitisation and Legitimacy in Global Media Governance: Spaces, Jurisdictions and Tensions, in: Volkmer, I. (ed.), *Handbook of Global Media Research – Handbooks in Communication and Media,* Wiley-Blackwell, Malden

Sarikakis, K. (2016). Proteste in Europa. Die neuen Medien und die Wut des Publikums, in: Limbourg, P., Grätz, R. (eds.), *Geschlossene Gesellschaften? Beteiligungsprozesse, Medien und Öffentlichkeiten in Europa,* Steidl, Göttingen, 43-53

Simiti, M. (2014). Rage and Protest: The Case of the Greek Indignant Movement, *Hellenic Observatory European Institute,* Greese Paper 82, 1-44.

Triandafyllidou, A., Wodak, R., Krzyzanowski, M. (2009). *The European Public Sphere and the Media: Europe in Crisis?* Palgrave, London.

Tsaliki, L. (2012). The Greek 'Indignados': The Aganaktismeni as a Case Study of the 'New Repertoire of Collective Action', Transmediale Media Art Festival, Berlin

von Bertalanffy, L. (1968). *General System Theory: Foundations, Development, Applications,* George Braziller, New York

Chapter 20

Towards a Critical Understanding
of "Alternative Media":
Resistance, Technology and Social Change

Banu Durdağ

Faculty of Communication, Ankara University
06590 Cebeci, Ankara, Turkey
bdurdag@ankara.edu.tr

In today's world, characterized by rapid social changes, technology is being demonstrated as the driving force of history and as the key of a more participatory and democratic society. Both dominant and dissident groups are suffering a fetishized technology narrative. Contrary to this defect, the ignorance of technology as a non-human factor in the understanding of social change is another flaw. In order to overcome the pitfalls of both "technological determinism" and "social determinism", the study tries to offer a *dialectic materialist position* on the understanding of the relationship between technology and social change by examining *Çapul TV*. This non-commercial "alternative media" will be analyzed as a class effort to release emancipatory *praxes* in order to build "alternative" ways for communication. By this questioning the study aims to go beyond the narrow perspective that limits the issue to the role of "alternative usages" of information and communication technologies (ICTs) in "social movements", and to reach a critical understanding of "alternative media".

1. Introduction

With the emergence of new technologies, new concepts of "revolution" are introduced, such as "digital revolution" or "ICTs revolution". These conceptions not only capture the notions of the left but also camouflage the very social biases of technology. They reinforce the fetish character of technology and block clear analyses of the relationship between technology and social change. By enshrining technology as a revolutionary actor, social relations and social change are reified. This not only erodes the social and material meanings of revolution but also decouples social change from revolution, making people "to see revolution as an unrealized extreme as opposed to a daily possibility" [Gaines 1999: 87]. In contrast to such technological determinist perception of social change, excluding technology from the analysis creates an idealist account in which there is no room for non-human factors in the understanding of social change. Both "technological determinist" and "social determinist" extremes miss the complex nature of social change. Social change is a multifaceted and multi-stratified process composed of the dialectical relationship between human and non-human factors [Servaes and Hoyng 2015: 3]. In this respect, the study tries to offer a *dialectic materialist position* on the relationship between technology and social change in order to move beyond such extremes by examining *Çapul TV*[a] (capul.tv) which was established as a live Internet-based non-commercial TV channel at the very beginning of the Gezi Resistance in Turkey and became the permanent channel of other resistances around the country.

Even though, contemporary social movements appear as unorganized and spontaneous demonstrations and each one seems to have its own socio-historical context, neo-liberal antagonisms as the decisive triggering factor of those collective reactions cannot be disregarded. The study assesses the Gezi Resistance, which began in the last days of May 2013 at Taksim Gezi Park in Istanbul and spread around the country, as a *social rebellion moment* which made social change more visible by bringing collective, nation-wide reactions to neoliberal authoritarianism based on and motivated by Islamic conservatism. The Gezi Resistance

---

[a]Recep Tayyip Erdoğan, former prime minister, denounced the Gezi Resistance protesters as "çapulcu", literally looter in English. However, the protesters embraced this labeling and used it to describe themselves and express their support to the resistance. Önder Özdemir, one of the founders of *Çapul TV*, says that they wanted to take the domain name of capulcu.tv, instead of capul.tv ("çapul" means loot in English); however they missed it [Aydoğan 2014].

revealed a set of multifaceted emancipatory *praxes*. One of them is creating its own communication spaces/platforms by organizing various park forums around the country and using ICTs to produce and distribute its own information. *Çapul TV*, as one of those spaces/platforms, emerged as a prompt reaction to the ignorance of the resistance by Turkish mainstream media. Behind this prompt reflex there is more than ten years of non-commercial "alternative media" experience with a labor class focus, such as sendika.org (news website), live broadcasting of TEKEL workers' resistance[b] via sendika.tv and International Labor Film & Video Festival [Aydoğan 2014]. In this respect, the study examines *Çapul TV* as a class effort releasing emancipatory *praxes* in order to build "alternative" ways for communication. *Çapul TV* provides a suitable example both to explore the articulation of agency, technology and social change, and to discuss the existing hegemonic mode of communication and its counter-hegemonic "alternative". Besides, although it is a unique case and may seem impractical to be generalized, this uniqueness makes it a valuable example that gives hints for a democratic communication system.

In the second section, following this introduction, the study draws the main contours of a *dialectic materialist position* on the relationship between technology and social change with a communication focus inspired by Raymond Williams' works and Henri Lefebvre's understanding of *praxis*. By providing a critical understanding, this position can be a useful *analytical tool*. In the third section, the fundamental aspects of the Gezi Resistance are described. By this discussion, the dynamics of the resistance and what it revealed concerning the emancipatory possibilities of ICTs are aimed to tease out. Then, the study develops *dialectically related levels and sub-levels of analysis* for alternative media research by reviewing critical alternative media discussions. In the final section, these levels and sub-levels of analysis with a focus on the relationship between technology and social

---

[b]TEKEL was the state company of tobacco and alcoholic beverages and privatized gradually between 2008 and 2010. Thousands of workers laid-off due to the privatization, sparking strikes and protests. TEKEL workers occupied the streets of Ankara, the capital city, with their resistance tents, and lived under these tents for over 70 days.

change will be clarified by examining *Çapul TV*. By this examination, the study purposes to achieve a critical assessment of the relationship between technology and social change, and to reach a critical understanding of alternative media that demonstrates emancipatory potentials and existing limits of ICTs.

2. "A Dialectic Materialist Position" on Communication Technologies and Social Change

Different positions on the relationship between technology and social change lie on a spectrum from technological determinism to social determinism. These different positions are related to how technology, society and social practices are correlated with each other. Both extremes miss the complex and multi-stratified relationship between technology and social change. Within the limits of the discussion, a dialectic materialist position with a communication focus is offered in order to go beyond such misleading extremes. Drawing the main contours of a dialectic materialist position also requires a critical understanding of both communication technologies and social practices. Raymond Williams' conceptualizations can be taken as a starting point both to attain a critical understanding of communication and communication technologies, and to sketch out a critical comprehension of social practices. Williams puts communication at the hub of the material and symbolic (re-)production of social relations, and describes it as a process which makes "unique experience into common experience" [Williams 1965: 55]. Thereby the main purpose of communication is "the sharing of human experience" [Williams 1973: 32]. He highlights that "the process of communication is in fact the process of community: the sharing of common meanings, and thence common activities and purposes; the offering, reception and comparison of new meanings, leading to tensions and achievements of growth and change" [Williams 1965: 55]. The comprehension of "communication as a whole social process" [Williams 1965: 55] provides also an understanding of communication technologies as a process in which social relations are materialized, transformed and modified [De la Haye 1980: 55].

Williams rejects simple cause and effect explanations of technological determinism, but he also recognizes the hegemonic position of technological determinist thinking. He warns us against the resurgence of technological determinism that comes with every new technology [McGuigan 2015]. Additionally, he is against "the notion of a determined technology", which closes off all alternative meanings and dimensions of new technologies [Williams 2003: 133]. He rejects "the idea that technologies would necessarily be used in the precise ways envisaged by the developers" [Freeman 2002: 433]. He emphasizes that both communication process and communication technologies have "social complications" which are not totally predictable [Williams 1981]. There is a clear example of this: In the 19th century, religious and political authorities were "arguing that the poor must be able to read the Bible, as a means to their moral improvement, overlooked the fact that there is no way of teaching a man to read Bible which does not also enable him to read the radical press" [Williams 1981: 230-231]. Williams reminds us of the emancipatory potentials of communication technologies for a counter-hegemonic "alternative" communication system. Even those technologies are predominantly intended to fulfill the priorities of dominant groups.

His position on the relationship between technology and social change must be associated with his understanding on the notion of "determination" as "setting bounds or limits and exertion of pressure" [Williams 1985: 98-99]. This understanding makes possible his rejection of both technological determinism and the notion of determined technology. At this point, reminding Henri Lefebvre's definition for *determinism(s)* seems important in order to achieve a clear comprehension on the dialectic relationship between *mechanisms* setting bounds and *praxes*. Lefebvre [1982: 55] defines *determinism(s)* as follows:

> [They] are inherited from the past; they are forms, systems, structures that somehow survive more or less intact and have yet to be superseded or have as yet been only incompletely superseded: they continue to exert an active influence upon the present. Determinisms do not rule out accident, contingency, or creative efforts on the part of individuals and groups to do away with such survivals.

This framework allows us to understand social change as an interrelated and multi-stratified process including the factors of humans, their products, and existing social mechanisms that set bounds but can be transformed or demolished by social practices. Understanding of communication technologies and social change as a dialectically related whole makes possible to realize the existing contradictions, conflicts and tendencies. Such a position also sheds light on the complex nature of communication technologies as a social process in which the spectrum of technological possibilities are marked by the interests of dominant groups, but also can be formed by social struggle in order to reveal the emancipatory possibilities of these technologies.

3. The Gezi Resistance as a "Social Rebellion Moment"

The beginning of the social rebellion was in the last days of May 2013 at Taksim Gezi Park, which is one of the few green spaces left in the city center. On May 27th, with the entering of bulldozers into Gezi Park to uproot the trees in order to begin the construction of a new shopping mall (the main project is composed of the rebuilding of an Ottoman barrack with a new concept of shopping mall, and the construction of a mosque in Taksim Square), a group of activists began to defend the park. The brutal attacks of police to disperse the small-scale peaceful protest sparked nation-wide urban uprisings. Police constantly exercised abusive and excessive force by using tear gas, water cannons, plastic bullets and live ammunitions over the next months. By early July over 8,000 people were injured and during the resistance 14 people were killed by the police [TBB 2014]. Gezi Park is adjacent to Taksim Square that has a symbolic meaning for the Turkish left given that dozens of people died in May Day of 1977 at the square. The square was banned to May Day celebrations for decades with few exceptions. Nevertheless, unions' constant struggle to organize May Day in the square succeeded to force the Justice and Development Party (Adalet ve Kalkınma Partisi – AKP) government to open the square for celebrations between 2010 and 2012. But, in the eve of the resistance, the AKP government banned again the square for May Day under the pretext of construction in the square.

The increasing authoritarian and interventionist practices of the AKP government have two main interrelated axes intending to advance neoliberalism with an intensified Islamic conservatism. The first one is based on grabbing the commons in order to advance the capitalist accumulation. The project of constructing dams and hydroelectric power plants (HES) across the country, causing environmental and socio-economic destructions rather than providing sustainable energy, is one of the most known examples of this [Hürriyet 2014]. The project brought local resistances around the country, and they still struggle to reclaim the commons. The other axis is based on systematically imposing Islamic conservatism that is mainly used as an ideological tool to hide and boost the first one. The project composed of constructing the Ottoman barrack and a mosque in Taksim Square is one of the clear examples of such practices combining capitalist accumulation with the re-symbolization of collective meanings. In this respect, the Gezi Resistance was more than protecting the park. It was an outcome of the particular processes and mechanisms crystalized by neoliberal authoritarianism legitimized by Islamic conservatism.

Korkut Boratav defines the Gezi Resistance as a "mature class reaction". He underlines that it was a rebellion of "working-class", even though it did not display the common characteristics of "labour class movement". Protesters were skilled, educated workers and students, who will be a part of labor class or the reserve army of labor in the short-run, and they were opposing the consolidation of political power and bourgeoisie that grabs the commons [Boratav 2013]. Therefore, the Gezi Resistance was reactive in the sense that it was against the existing economic, social and political structure characterized by neoliberal authoritarianism. It was a backlash against the cooperation between political power and capital that penetrates directly into everyday life. Furthermore, it was an expression of the dissatisfaction with the understanding of political participation that is limited to elections. It was also proactive in the sense that it created "alternative" communication experiences. It was in fact a *social rebellion moment* that made social change more visible.

Turkish mainstream media ignored the resistance around the country, causing the questioning of its legitimacy. Mainstream media became unable to fulfill its most fundamental function, which is to give information to people, due to the complex relationships based on financial gain between the ruling party and the media owners. However, the resistance achieved to produce its own information and to distribute it. Gezi Postası as the non-commercial daily newspaper of the park, Gezi Radyo (radio channel), Revoltistanbul (Internet-based live stream channel) and direnisteyiz.org (news website) are among the examples of non-commercial "alternative" communication spaces/platforms of the resistance. Furthermore, from the outset of the resistance, activists were using social media such as Twitter and Facebook in order to share information and to mobilize people, just like in the Occupy Movement, the Arab Spring and the other recent social movements. *Çapul TV*, which was the only channel on air in Gezi Park, is the unique example of these spaces/platforms. Before delving into *Çapul TV* experience, there is a necessary question that needs to be answered: How a critical understanding of "alternative media" can be reached?

4. Questioning "Alternative Media"

In today's world characterized by rapid social changes, accelerated technological developments, and ever increasing social movements, an important dimension of the questioning of the relationship between technology and social change is the discussion of alternative media. Indicating non-commercial alternative communication spaces/platforms as one of the most important outcomes of the resistance make necessary to address this discussion. Although the notion of alternative media is popularized especially when a new communication technology is introduced or a social movement emerges, it sometimes can be inadequate to define different communication experiences and practices. This inadequacy can be associated with the responses of those questions: Alternative to what? Can everything different from the hegemonic media be described as alternative? Those questions must not be addressed separately from the already existing important issues related to ownership, organizational structure, decision-making process and the processes of production and distribution.

Williams describes four communication systems considering whether they are "controlled" or "free", and in this categorization composed of authoritarian, paternal, commercial, and democratic systems especially the first three are to some extent active in practice [Williams 1973: 116-124]. In the authoritarian system, in which a minority governs a society, communication is seen as a tool "to transmit the instructions, ideas, and attitudes of the ruling group" [Williams 1973: 117] in order to maintain and strengthen the existing social order. There are both direct and indirect controls by a system of censorship. The paternal system is also authoritarian but with a conscience that puts values and purposes in the first place rather than the maintenance of power [Williams 1973: 117]. Censorship is also extensively used both directly and indirectly in this system. "Where the authoritarian system transmits orders, and the ideas and attitudes which will promote their acceptance, the paternal system transmits values, habits, and tastes, which are its own justification as a ruling minority, and which it wishes to extend to the people as a whole" [Williams 1973: 118]. It has an explicit tendency to see the people as masses. The controllers of the system act as guardians who sometimes put the blanket over everything and sometimes permit a measure of controlled dissent as a relief-valve [Williams 1973: 118].

In contrast to the authoritarian and the paternal systems, the commercial system provides a certain amount of freedom that depends on market mechanism. Therefore, the main purpose of communication is to gain profit and extend the physical and symbolic conditions of capitalist exchange relations [Williams 1973: 118-119]. Additionally, this system based on capitalist production and distribution possesses certain exclusion mechanisms; for example, a cultural form or information that is unlikely to sell quickly and acquire a profitable return has no chance to be included [Stevenson 2002: 14]. Lastly, Williams sketches out the main aspects of a democratic model of communication system. A democratic communication must be against all forms of controls [Williams 1973: 120-123]. There must be right to transmit and right to receive as the basic rights for a democratic basis: It must be open to public discussion in order to contribute, challenge and review [Williams 1973: 120]. A democratic communication system must overcome the issues of skills/professionalism, commercialism and control [Williams 2005: 54]. Therefore, detaching the means of communication from the domination of capital and political power is a must for a democratic communication system.

Williams outlines the democratic model through the other existing systems, and puts it as an alternative to them. He notes that the debate should not be limited to the issues of control and freedom, but the whole range should be looked over in order to clarify detailed comparisons and future possibilities [Williams 1973: 124]. His description of democratic communication model still inspires the discussions of alternative media. Chris Atton realigns Williams' formulation and deepens it in order to reach a contemporary alternative media conceptualization [Atton 2006: 4, 9, 25-29]. According to Atton, alternative media should offer "the means for democratic communication to people who are normally excluded from the media production" [2006: 4]. He sets a typology of alternative media with six aspects as follows: The first one is related to content. It must be politically, and socially/structurally radical. The second is about form that should be enriched by varieties of presentations. The third concerns the using and introduction of new technological facilities into the production and reproduction processes. The fourth is about the distribution that should look for alternative ways, especially the anti-copyright ones. The fifth is about the transforming of social relations, roles and responsibilities, such as deprofessionalization, and the rearrangement of organization against hierarchical decision-making structures. The final one is about transforming the communication processes such as creating decentralized, horizontal networks [Atton 2006: 27]. Funda Başaran [2009: 408-409], who is a scholar, activist, and one of the founders of *Çapul TV*, critically reviews Atton's typology and reformulates the main aspects of alternative media by referring to Williams' democratic communication model and Harrold Innis' conceptualization of monopolies of knowledge. Her reformulation that is based on five criteria can be summarized as such: The first is about the linkage of alternative media with social movements. In this respect alternative media should aim to contribute to transforming society into a more democratic one. Secondly, alternative media should produce and distribute that knowledge that is excluded by monopolies of knowledge. The third is about being against hierarchy of professionalism. The fourth is related to the ability to afford costs. The last one is about struggling against the commercialization of communication.

Considering the common emphases of the discussion, and the dialectical position drawn in the previous section a critical understanding of alternative media can be achieved by specifying dialectically related levels and sub-levels of analysis for alternative media research:

(1) Organizational/Structural level:

    (a) Economic: It must be decapitalized/non-commercial. It must be based on voluntary labor and collective solidarity.

    (b) Decision-making: It must be collective and against centralized and hierarchical structures.

(2) Content level:

    (c) Quality of content: It must express the information of people who are excluded from the existing hegemonic media. It must be deprofessionalized, and politically/ideologically radical.

    (d) Production and distribution technics: It must be produced and distributed with alternative ways offered by different technological possibilities.

(3) Cognitive and Normative level:

    (e) Individual/Collective: Individual and collective content producers must be against professionalism and commercialism, and realize information, communication, and communication technologies as a field of class struggle.

    (f) Social: It must mobilize self-reflexivity in order to encourage revolutionary communication processes and to disclose transformational possibilities for a more democratic and egalitarian society.

In the section below, the study aims to clarify this critical understanding of alternative media by exploring *Çapul TV*. This examination can contribute to deepen these three levels and sub-levels, especially the cognitive and normative level, of analysis for alternative media research.

5. *Çapul TV* Versus *Penguins* of the Mainstream Media

Leading Turkish news channels, such as NTV and CNN Turk, kept silent and ignored the beginning and spreading of the resistance by airing documentaries about penguins, and cooking programs. Thus, penguin became the symbol of media's ignorance, as well as the logo of *Çapul TV*. This ignorance reminded people and activists on the streets that mainstream media is not just organized as a medium but predominantly structured as a capitalist enterprise. In Turkish mainstream media, there is not only self-censorship mechanism but also a heavy-handed control of the ruling party. It is not surprising that in a media based on capitalist accumulation, debates are easily depoliticized and information conflicting with the interests of market or political authority is readily excluded. However, *social rebellion moments*, as in the case of the Gezi Resistance, create small scale but significant ruptures in the hegemonic social order. The establishment of *Çapul TV* is one of them. In order to critically evaluate and draw the main aspects of *Çapul TV*, the section proceeds by a series of steps that are illustrated with the responses[c] of those questions: Alternative to what? How is *Çapul TV* economically organized? How are its decision-making and production processes structured? What are the qualitative and technical aspects of its content? How do the actors describe this experience and their positions? How do they include ICTs in this process?

Önder Özdemir and Başaran underline that *Çapul TV* is a part of the efforts for creating an "alternative media platform" which brings different but interrelated platforms together. These platforms are as such:

---

[c] Responses are based on the interviews with the founders and reporters of the channel, and the data collected through participant observation, and newspaper interviews of the channel founders. Interviews with the founders and volunteers of *Çapul TV* were made in the Alternative Media Workshop which was held within the *LaborComm-2015*, The 6th International Labor and Communication Conference, on May 09-10, 2015, in Ankara. The workshop brought together the voluntary reporters of *Çapul TV* and other volunteers of direnisteyiz.net, inadinahaber.org, seyrisokak.org, which were established during the resistance, and jiyan.org and sendika.org which have been existed long before the resistance.

sendika.org, sendika.tv, and International Labor Film & Video Festival, and sinematek.tv which is an open access digital cinema library – *cinémathèque*. Thereby, *Çapul TV* is based on this collectivity that brings together many volunteers, most of them have already had experience in organizing different alternative communication practices for many years. Ali Ergin Demirhan, one of the founders and voluntary reporters of *Çapul TV*, explains how they had the idea to establish the channel: "We decided to establish *Çapul TV* when we were at Gezi Park on June 3rd. We thought and discussed that there is a need for a medium that displays and expresses what is really happening in the park, and why those people are in the park" [Hürriyet 2014]. He adds, "We have already had experience on Internet-based live broadcasting. However, 3G platforms were inadequate to connect at the park because too many people were trying to connect from the same area. We looked for an alternative to connect properly, and decided to use satellite technology" [Hürriyet 2014]. Thus, *Çapul TV* started with live broadcasts with limited equipment, two cameras, two laptops, an audio mixer, gas masks[d] and a few microphones, on 6 June at Gezi Park until police attacked to clear of the demonstrators on 15 June. During this period, it reached an audience of over 1.5 million people and more than 80,000 social media followers, and its live broadcasts were also transmitted by several opposition satellite channels, such as IMC TV, TV 10, Hayat TV and Besta Nuçe [Hürriyet 2014]. It initiated the establishment of the Association of Alternative Media (Alternatif Medya Derneği – AMD). "Resistance journalism" trainings were organized by the cooperation of *Çapul TV* and the AMD [Aydoğan 2014]. Over two hundreds volunteers were trained in 15 different provinces of Turkey [Hürriyet 2014]. Now, *Çapul TV* continues to live broadcast via Internet from two permanent studios, in Istanbul and Ankara, and also from the streets. It has also more than ten unique periodic programs [Hürriyet 2014].

Demirhan states that *Çapul TV* was established as a reaction to the censorship and disinformation of the mainstream media [Evrensel 2014].

---

[d]During this period, the crew was under police attacks. They continued to broadcast by donning gas masks. To see some images, Çapul TV e-book http://alternatifmedya.org.tr/wp-content/uploads/2014/05/capultvkitap.pdf

He adds that even if there were no oppressive and reactionary environment, the structure of the hegemonic media already passivizes the public; hence, *Çapul TV* is not a simplistic attempt to surpass the censorship, but it is in fact an emancipatory medium that is disclosed by the revolutionary *praxes* of the people on the streets [Evrensel 2014]. Özdemir also emphasizes that *Çapul TV* is not either emulating the mainstream media or competing with them, but fighting against them [Aydoğan 2014]. Moreover, Özdemir and Başaran emphasize that "considering the traditional mass media, there is no possibility to create an "alternative"; because they have already become an absolute part of capitalist accumulation. Contrary to this, the struggle for ICTs keeps going on. Therefore, an alternative media can only be possible through these new technologies". Başaran adds that "these new technologies, especially the Internet, remain open to alternatives and provide ammunition to strengthen emancipatory possibilities, until they are entirely seized by market forces". In this regard, Başaran defines *Çapul TV* as an alternative media producing and distributing the information of the people who are excluded by the hegemonic one. Çağlar Özbilgin, one of the voluntary reporters of *Çapul TV* and sendika.org, also defines this experience as a part of class struggle that makes media one of the most important means of this struggle. He stresses that this experience manifests the possibility of creating an alternative.

Çapul TV is based on voluntary labor and collective solidarity. It is against commercialism; thus, there is no sponsorship or advertisement. After its first year of broadcasting, an international solidarity campaign was organized in order to cover technical needs and expenses such as rent and utilities. Özdemir states that they cover such expenses by solidarity campaigns, grants and donations through the legal basis of the AMD [Aydoğan 2014]. Demirhan [2014] explains the labor process of the channel as mobilizing skills and abilities of activists on a collective base. He stresses that "the commercial opposition media, which imitates the technical and formal aspects of the mainstream media, cannot satisfy the wage motivation of the employees with their limited resources when it is compared with the mainstream media" [Demirhan 2014]. Thus, the commercial opposition media cannot survive within such a harsh competitive environment. On the other hand, it is obvious that "the mainstream media avoids using its capabilities to uncover the issues or events conflicting its economic interests or interests of political power" [Demirhan 2014]. Therefore, in both cases commercial preoccupations limit the practices to form a democratic communication model. Voluntary labor as in the case of *Çapul TV* not only barricades alienation but also reveals emancipatory outcomes that cannot be realized by the wage labor system [Demirhan 2014; Çapul.TV, 2014: 6]. Voluntary reporters of the channel emphasize that *Çapul TV* is based on ideological and political motivation with a collective decision-making process rather than profit-led drive. Başaran adds that "of course, sometimes there can be a number of requirements needed to be managed by quick decisions. Or, there can be some situations in which some of us should take more duty. But, these are exceptional circumstances. *Çapul TV* is against hierarchical decision-making and production processes".

The content is also alternative concerning the quality and production/distribution technics that remove the barriers of professionalism. In technical sense, its content is composed of a variety of different production processes. It has three different but related content categories. Primarily it broadcasts resistances around the country, and forums in which people and activists discuss reforms and transformative actions. It not only becomes a voice of resistances but also displays police violence, and physical and ideological oppressions of the political power. Secondly, it broadcasts recorded images or videos, produced by volunteers around the country. Lastly, it broadcasts unique periodic programs with different contents from science to art, music to urban struggles, and law to youth. Additionally, the channel effectively uses social media. Volunteers announce the daily programs and share news, and information through the channel's social media accounts. But they also use social media platforms to produce and distribute different contents. For example, they use Periscope to live broadcast from streets in order to reach and inform much more people. It is obvious that those are commercial social media platforms accumulating capital by targeted advertising. But the point is that it is an effort to give and add those platforms an ideological/political shape and meaning in order to mobilize people. Demirhan [Evrensel 2014] says: "We try to build another form of making news that everyone can participate and contribute. We take into account the debates and demands of the Gezi Resistance as reference. The general interests and unifying agendas of social opposition are principal for us. We stand against chauvinistic and exclusionist contents". Başaran also indicates that the main aim of *Çapul TV*'s content is to make people excluded from the hegemonic media an active agent of politics. While mainstream media and commercial opposition media require the support of capitalist investment or political power for a permanent and qualitative broadcasting, *Çapul TV* makes possible to broadcast via Internet connection and mobile phones as everyday life technologies [Demirhan 2014]. Thus, its production and distribution technics are also alternative to both mainstream and other commercial media. When such technologies are inadequate to distribute the content, it looks for alternative ways offered by different communication technologies, just like in the case of using satellite technology to live broadcast. *Çapul TV*'s content, considering the quality and production/distribution technics, is free from direct or indirect control mechanisms and commercial concerns, and also free from the limits and mediation of professionalism.

The cognitive and normative aspects of *Çapul TV* experience strengthen its struggle to build and expand a democratic model of communication. The volunteers define themselves as activists. They emphasize that they are not just the witnesses of events but also the subjects of events. They describe what they are doing as a form of class struggle. One of them says, "It is a form of reaction shaped by self-awareness and self-consciousness. The government continues to use its police violence on the people presenting their demands for a democratic society in a peaceful way on the streets. We aim to inform people about what is really happening on the streets". The volunteers emphasize that "the point is that we do not record events or make news through the codes of professionalism. What distinguishes our journalistic practices from the mainstream media is our activism". Mustafa Aldemir, a software engineer and one of the volunteers of *Çapul TV*, says: "We actually are activists, [...] and we are doing journalism because the journalists are not doing their jobs. We believe that we should do it, someone should do it and because nobody else is doing it" [Mortada

2013]. Özbilgin describes what they are doing as illuminating the truth. He adds that "these experiences in the sense of achieving the knowledge of the truth have already been, and will always be. New ones will be articulated these accrued experiences. Our biggest strength is our struggle to achieve the knowledge of the truth". Demirhan [2014] states that using these experiences for a better future is their duty. They include ICTs in this process as a part of class struggle as well. One of the volunteers states that "communication technologies are not just medium but are the means of production; therefore, they are one of the most important and integral part of our struggle". Demirhan [2014] and Başaran emphasize that their purpose is to support and contribute to the *praxes* attempting to build a more egalitarian and democratic society.

6. Conclusion

Within the limits of the study, a dialectic materialist position is offered to put more stress on the complex and multi-stratified nature of the relationship between technology and social change. This position enables to define the Gezi Resistance as a *social rebellion moment* that makes small scale but significant ruptures in the existing social order, and to explore *Çapul TV* as one of the multifaceted emancipatory *praxes* of the resistance. This position also allows to critically reformulate the category of alternative media. Even though the conceptualization of alternative media has some weaknesses as was discussed, it can be analytically useful and effective to explore such media experiences through such a critical perspective. It is obvious that there are certain non-commercial opposition media practices within traditional mass media, and there will always be. But, in order to define a media practice as "alternative", as was crystallized in the *Çapul TV* experience, it must challenge the hegemonic one and offer transformational possibilities in the sense of self-reflexivity that might encourage revolutionary communication processes for a more democratic and egalitarian society. As was stated by Williams [1973: 19, 152] alternatives as a practice can be learned, and communication begins to struggle to learn. He reminds us that "we can change these models [of communication], when they become inadequate, or we can modify and extend them" [Williams 1973: 19]. *Çapul TV* is one of the examples of such practices characterized by collectivity, solidarity, non-commercialism, deprofessionalism, self-reflexivity and mobilization of the power of the information related to people excluded from the hegemonic media. It takes the media as a critical medium; therefore, it challenges the capitalist and commercial forms of media practices by struggling both for communication and communication technologies.

Çapul TV is not just alternative to mainstream but also to commercial opposition media considering organizational/structural composition, content, and cognitive/normative aspects of it. In this respect, it is a class effort releasing emancipatory *praxes* in order to create a democratic model for communication. Volunteers highlight that "it does not mean that we provide an alternative communication that is perfect and ultimate one. We call people to struggle for the right to communicate […] and *Çapul TV* represents an important stage of this struggle" [Çapul.TV 2014: 5-6]. Başaran also notes that "it should be recognized that the existing opportunities posed by ICTs are not certain. On the one hand there are profit-led decisions and practices dominating these technologies, and on the other hand there are struggles both on these technologies and their potentials in order to create alternative future possibilities. Thus, *Çapul TV* is a part of such struggles".

References

Atton, C. (2006). *Alternative Media*, Sage, London, California, New Delhi

Aydoğan, A. (2014). Çapul TV: Önder Özdemir, in: Kejanlıoğlu, D. B., and Scifo, S., (eds.), *Alternative Media and Participation. Cost Action ISO906*, http://www.costtransformingaudiences.eu/system/files/alternative%20media%20an d%20participation-19-02-14.pdf [21 December 2014]

Başaran, F. (2013). The resistance prevails! So the resistance's media as well!, http://www.sendika.org/2013/06/the-resistance-prevails-so-the-resistances-media-as-well-funda-basaran/ [19 June 2013]

Başaran, F. (2009). Alternative communication on Internet in Turkey, in: Sapio, B. (ed.), *The Good, the Bad and the Challenging, Proc. COST298*, 407-415

Boratav, K. (2013). A matured class based contumacy, http://sendika4.org/2013/06/kor
    kut-boratav-1-evaluates-the-gezi-resistance-a-matured-class-based-contumacy/ [14
    October 2015]

Çapul TV (2014). *The Media of Resistance: Çapul.TV*, (in Turkish). http://
    alternatifmedya.org.tr/wp-content/uploads/2014/05/capultvkitap.pdf [11 November
    2015]

De la Haye, Y. (1980). *Marx and Engels on the Means of Communication: The
    Movement of Commodities, People, Information and Capital*, International
    General, New York

Demirhan, A. E. (2014). The legacy of the Gezi is a guerilla media: Çapul TV, (in
    Turkish). http://sendika7.org/2014/06/gezinin-emaneti-bir-gerilla-medya-capul-tv-
    ali-ergin-demirhan/ [31 October 2015]

Evrensel (2014). The unifying force of the Gezi: Çapul TV, (in Turkish). http://www.
    evrensel.net/haber/86389/gezinin-birlestirici-gucu-capul-tv#.U6GJDhYbf34   [23
    September 2015]

Freeman, D. A (2002). Technological idiot? Raymond Williams and communication
    technology. *Information, Communication & Society*, 5(3), 425-442

Gaines, J. M. (1999). Political mimesis, in: Gaines J. M., and Renov, M. (eds.),
    Collecting Visible Evidence, University of Minnesota Press, Minneapolis, London,
    84-102

Hürriyet (2014). The format of space of looter has been developed, (in Turkish). http://
    www.hurriyet.com.tr/capulcu-meydani-formati-gelistirildi-26606002 [5 November
    2015]

Lefebvre, H. (1982/1966). *The Sociology of Marx*, Columbia University Press, New York

McGuigan, J. (2015). *Raymond Williams: A Short Counter-Revolution – Towards 2000
    Revisited*, Sage, London

Mortada, D. (2013). Çapul TV: Turkey's alternative to mainstream media. http://
    www.pri.org/stories/2013-06-21/apul-tv-turkeys-alternative-mainstream-media [12
    October 2015]

Servaes, J. and Hoyng, R. (2015). The tools of social change: A critique of techno-centric
    development and activism, *New Media & Society*, September, 1-17

Stevenson, N. (2002). *Understanding Media Cultures*, 2nd edn. Sage, London

Türkiye Barolar Birliği – TBB. (2014). Gezi Report, Türkiye Barolar Birliği Yayınları:
    Ankara, (in Turkish). http://tbbyayinlari.barobirlik.org.tr/TBBBooks/518.pdf [30
    September 2015]

Williams, R. (2005/1980). *Culture and Materialism*, Verso, London and New York

Williams, R. (2003/1975). *Television: Technology and Cultural Form*, Routledge,
    London and New York

Williams, R. (1985/1976). *Keywords*, Oxford University Press, New York

Williams, R. (1981). Communications Technologies and Social Institutions, in: Williams, R. (ed.), *Contact: Human Communication and its History*, Thames and Hudson, London
Williams, R. (1973/1962). *Communications*, Penguin, London
Williams, R. (1965/1961). *The Long Revolution*, Penguin, Harmondsworth

Chapter 21

Europe at the Crossroads:
The Dangers of Economizing on Democracy
and the Prospects of *Democratie Sans Frontières* [a]

Zoe Lefkofridi

*Robert Schuman Center for Advanced Studies, European University
Institute, Florence, Italy
Faculty of Sociology and Political Science, University of Salzburg,
Austria
zoe.lefkofridi@eui.eu; zoe.lefkofridi@sbg.ac.at*

This chapter discusses why democracy in the European Union is under
strain, by highlighting the causes of its malaise and the perils involved
in the way multiple crises facing the Union are currently handled. Also,
it discusses conventional channels of representation available to
Europeans and a novel instrument of participation, the European
Citizen Initiative and concludes with how transdisciplinary scientific
collaboration could help strengthen European democracy.

---

[a]This chapter is based on the keynote lecture I gave at the *International Society
for Information Studies' (IS4IS)* Summit entitled "The Information Society at the
Crossroads: Response and Responsibility of the Sciences of Information", that
was held at the Vienna University of Technology, 03-07.06.2015. My keynote
lecture was entitled "Europe at the crossroads: Is economizing on Democracy
the way forward?". The present chapter draws on the keynote, while also
incorporating subsequent developments such as the Greek Referendum of July
5, 2015 and the accommodation of war refugees.

1. The 'Problem' of Democracy in a Transnational Polity

This book is about social and technological problems that concern the future information society. The 'problem' dealt with in this chapter concerns democracy in the European Union (EU). To begin with, as 'problem' can mean many things[b], here I will combine the different uses of the word: a 'problem' is something that stands in front of us, a difficulty, a question demanding solution. Encompassing these variable meanings, this essay understands European democracy as a difficulty standing before us and as a question that demands solution.

To begin with, the democratization of the Union is imperative at this stage of the Union's development [see Schmitter 2000] but this became most evident with the crisis. *European* policy – that is, a common policy that aims at serving Europeans as a collective – can be neither *transnationally democratic* nor *democratically transnational* when the *political* (citizens' voices and party organizations) remain nationally bound while the *economic* (market) is transnationalized. In this chapter, I will argue that national parties have been gradually weakened as democratic actors that can shape policy in a transnational multilevel environment – they are literally unable to act unilaterally in all policy areas transferred to the EU level. However, as European integration caused their enfeeblement, national parties for decades functioned in denial of Europe; not only did they do very little to adapt to the new multilevel polity and policy environment but they also depoliticized debates about policies that were transferred to the EU level. The crisis brought about the sudden and unprecedented politicization of European policies, which led national parties to panic and retreat to nationalist discourse. In essence, Europe's unexpected politicization revealed

---

[b]In its original meaning, 'problem' is a product of the Greek verb $\pi\rho\circ\beta\acute{\alpha}\lambda\lambda\omega$ (before + throw/place). So a problem is 'something' that is put forward, proposed, or even projected. The word passed from Ancient Greek to Latin and from there to Old French: *problème* in the 14th century meant 'a question for solution' and in the 15th it meant 'difficulty'. Around the 16th century *problem* was used in English in its mathematical sense: a question that requires solution using logic and by combining data (information).

parties' failure to adapt to the political and economic system they themselves gradually built. This failure, in turn, is detrimental to the quality of representative democracy.

For representative democracy to function in a Europe without borders, citizens and parties should (be able to) mobilize *beyond borders*. A *"democratie sans frontières"* is a 'problématique' where politics, sociology, economics, information technology, communication and media studies could and should join forces. Though the present contribution is firmly based in the social sciences, and politics in particular, it acknowledges that there is no single method that can tackle all problems. As to identify solutions to the problem of European democracy, we need to work across disciplines, this chapter seeks to present the problems of European democracy in ways that research in other disciplines can be inspired to engage in the pursuit of solutions.

I will begin with the democratic deficits of the Union that during the crisis became apparent even to the layman European (section 2). I will then discuss the role played by national political parties and the importance of Europe's (de-)politicization, which to a large extent explains also the behavior of political leadership during the crisis (section 3). Yet, to fully understand the logic behind our leaders' incapability of providing democratic transnational governance during the crisis, we need to comprehend the complex channels of representation available to citizens in the EU system (section 4). In this context, a series of key questions are raised: Do the institutions in place manage to express and represent citizens' views and positions in EU policy making? Are citizens' preferences well represented at the key EU-level decision-making institutions? Does EU membership impact the capacity of member states to be responsive to citizens' demands? To provide some answers to these questions, I will present research findings on citizens' representation at the EU level and the impact of EU membership on policy responsiveness. I will then move beyond parties to discuss the problématique of transnational democracy in the EU from the perspective of the recently introduced European Citizens' Initiative (ECI) (section 5). In the concluding section (section 6), I will briefly mention some of the many ways a synergy of different disciplines could help strengthen transnational democracy.

2. EU Democracy in its Deepest Crisis?

Following the Second World War, a number of Western European political elites launched a peace project of cooperation in the coal and steel sectors. The project gradually expanded in scope and membership to become the European Communities (EC), and later transformed into a supranational political system, the EU. During the 1990s, the member states transferred more and more competences to the EU level in pursuit of common policies in an ever-wider range of policy areas (e.g. economy, trade, human rights, immigration, foreign affairs etc.).

Today, the EU shows signs of disintegration and its future look gloomy [Lefkofridi and Schmitter 2015; Schmitter and Lefkofridi 2016]. In the summer of 2015 we even witnessed the partial and erratic suspension of the Schengen agreement and the reestablishment of border controls between EU member states, which *de facto* undermined European integration. This was yet another piece of evidence that the project of cooperation and integration devised to cure the continent from nationalism, racism and antagonism between European states is going through tough times. Yet, the economic crisis in the Eurozone triggered by the outbreak of the global financial crisis (2008), and the *en masse* arrival of Syrian war refugees (2015), which eventually led to political crises in the EU, revealed that not only European unity and solidarity, but also representative democracy is under strain [Fasone *et al.* 2015].

Beyond eliciting soul-searching within the EU, the nature and duration of these multiple crises have exposed the Union's democratic deficits: during crisis management, the executive power and non-majoritarian, technocratic institutions often side-lined parliaments, citizens and democracy more broadly. Crucially, all this is in sharp contrast with the spirit of the latest EU treaty reforms and deliberations that date back to the Convention on the future of Europe (2001-3). Both the rejected draft Constitutional Treaty, and its subsequent, modified version – what came to be known as the Lisbon Treaty (2009) – sought to strengthen representative democracy and citizen participation in EU policymaking [for a detailed discussion, see Mayoral 2011]. Democrats all over Europe had welcomed the Lisbon Treaty as an unsatisfactory yet important step towards addressing the Union's deep democratic deficit, inter alia by strengthening parliaments at the national and European levels and introducing the ECI that opens up possibilities for transnational citizen mobilization and agenda-setting (see section 5).

Despite having previously committed to enhancing citizens' participation in, and control of, EU policymaking, during the crisis national party governments bestowed EU institutions with fiscal and budgetary powers without, however, giving citizens decision-making power for major polity and policy developments that affect their lives. That democracy was perceived as "irrelevant" to crisis management is most vividly illustrated by the results of two attempts to organize a referendum in Greece.

2.1. *The 2011 and 2015 referendum plans in Greece*

His European partners thought that Greek Prime Minister George A. Papandreou was completely out of his mind when in 2011 he announced his plan to hold a referendum[c] over the bilateral loan agreement between Greece and its lenders. Papandreou came to this idea because citizens had for months peacefully occupied the Syntagma (Constitution) Square located opposite the Greek Parliament and demonstrated in effort to be heard by their representatives. Like the very first democratic citizens at the ancient *agora*, protesters gathered to discuss political and economic issues in pursuit of alternatives to the government's policy direction that was presented as a one-way street. Not only was citizens' mobilization and protest ignored by EU partners, but Papandreou's long center-stage presence in Greek politics was also terminated; a technocratic government led by Lucas Papademos came to replace the elected cabinet, while the same happened in Italy with the appointment of a technocratic government presided by Mario Monti.[d] With the crisis being approached

---

[c]As Vassilopoulou and Halikiopoulou [2013] explain, that referendum would have functioned as a vote of confidence on his government, would have granted him a clear popular mandate for the adoption of further austerity measures and would have helped him avoid the prospect of early elections.

[d]Some observers [e.g. Roche 2011] view with suspicion the fact that Lucas Papademos (former ECB Vice President), Mario Monti (former Commissioner)

as a *technocratic* issue of fiscal consolidation, the solution could only come about by the "objective" technocratic rule that was not constrained by (domestic) electoral clienteles.

Four years later, when the Greek economy had shrunk by 25% and unemployment had risen to 25% (and youth unemployment to 50%), and Greeks had gone to the polls three times (in May and June 2012 and in January 2015), the announcement of a referendum on further austerity measures (which was indeed held on July 5, 2015) caused the rage of EU partners and brought the country's EU membership in jeopardy.[e] The Greek Radical Left-led Government (SYRIZA-ANEL) had been elected in January 2015 with debt relief as its key goal. Greek debt had grown unsustainable, and every bailout package was worsening the situation for the Greek society: the taxation imposed on Greek citizens in order to finance an ever growing debt, in combination with austerity measures (including the devaluation of labor) has had severe consequences for the society's survival [see Lefkofridi 2014].[f] Although this government, like all others before, conceded (ideological) defeat by accepting all creditors' terms about austerity measures in exchange of financial assistance, the creditors kept on refusing to put the debt issue on the negotiating table. The referendum was thus a 'last resort', panicky move, which was taken in a rush as the Greek government realized that EU partners were unwilling to satisfy any of the goals included in their electoral program.

The referendum was organized hastily and the wording of the question posed was complex; crucially, the referendum ended up causing bitter divides among Greek citizens – most notably among those who were in favor of Greek EU membership and of the European project as a

---

and Mario Draghi (current ECB President) previously worked at Goldman Sachs.

[e]For an illuminating analytical narrative, see [Tsebelis 2016].

[f]For example, a recent Report by the Director of the National Bank of Greece shows that: in 2011 the 21.4% of the Greek population lived below the poverty line, while 31% was at the threshold of poverty and thus also endangered of social exclusion; the amount of people living in households where none was employed increased by 53,7% between 2010-2011 [Bank of Greece 2013: 101-3].

whole: for instance, those who feared Grexit accused those who voted NO as being 'irresponsible', while those who envisioned a different Europe accused those who voted YES as being 'acquiescent'. Premier Tsipras' hopes that demonstrations in support of a Greek NO in various European cities and an overwhelming NO by the Greeks themselves would strengthen his negotiating position proved illusory. On the contrary, a punitive response would follow the decision of the Greek society – that six years in the crisis was watching its fabric being torn- to reject further austerity measures. This is not to say that Greeks had not been warned of what might follow, quite the opposite.

On the one hand, the EU's *nomenklatura* threatened with Grexit: the President of the Commission Jean-Claude Juncker (2015) followed by the President of the European Parliament Martin Schulz and the President of the Eurogroup Jeroen Dijsselbloem advised the Greek people not to put their country's EU membership at risk. The three Presidents' blackmailing statements were puzzling for anyone with good knowledge of the EU system, since a legal basis to justify Grexit was absent from the EU treaties. On the other hand, top American economists [e.g. Galbraith 2015, Krugman 2015, Stiglitz 2015] who assessed austerity as the *wrong policy direction* encouraged the Greeks to vote 'no' to more austerity that would bring their economy deeper into recession. At the same time, the majority of the IMF board that for years had not expressed a clear position on the Greek debt[g] insisted in publishing a report, which clearly stated that the Greek debt is unsustainable, four days prior to the Sunday vote [Reuters 2015].

Despite the NO's crushing victory, EU partners kept on rejecting the idea of debt relief, while the government of Greece did not put an end to austerity or in any way change the policy course dictated by its lenders. Rumors wanted an alleged report on Grexit[h] to have convinced the

---

[g]An IMF report issued in Summer 2013 discussed the sustainability of the Greek debt and admitted that the IMF made mistakes in the Greek case [The Wall Street Journal 2013]; it did not however recommend a change in policy direction.

[h]This report is supposed to be kept in a safe, for details, see URL: http://www.politico.eu/article/juncker-secret-grexit-report-bailout-exit-eurozone-greece/ (accessed 20.02.2016).

Tsipras government to back down from opposing austerity. Most crucially, during the final round of negotiations the German Finance Minister Schäuble ambushed the continent with a 'time-out' proposal. With this, the German government ignored both economic historians,[i] who reminded of how many times and how much Germany benefited from debt relief, and economists [e.g. Dany *et al.* 2015] who argued that Germany has benefited from the Greek crisis even if Greece would default on all its debt owed to the German government via different channels, e.g. the European Stability Mechanism (ESM), or the International Monetary Fund (IMF). Ignoring history, economics, and the referendum's result, the 'time-out proposal' designed for Greece constituted mainly a warning to the publics in Spain and Portugal, where national-level elections were forthcoming. In other words, Spaniards and Portuguese were well advised to refrain from electing populists that might oppose the austerity policies – if they did, their situation might worsen, like in the case of Greece. Ironically, however, the vindictive implications of the Greek referendum confirmed the arguments of Eurosceptics about how European integration may undermine democracy (see below, section 3).

2.2. *The perils involved in agoraphobic muddling-through*

During the crisis, citizens' demonstrations, referendums or electoral results that sought to bring about policy change were all in vain: policy change became 'impossible', despite the fact that policy failed blatantly. European decision-making and the politics of crisis management were – and remain – 'agoraphobic'[j]. The way national governments across the

---

[i]Here is a summary of what economic historian Albrecht Ritschl argued: http://www.lse.ac.uk/researchAndExpertise/researchImpact/PDFs/germany-hypocrisy-eurozone-debt-crisis.pdf (Accessed 20.02.2016).

[j]While *phobia* means fear, *agora* denotes the public space, the place of the assembly, where the citizens of the first democracy met to deliberate. The term agoraphobia is used in psychiatry to signify a state of anxiety caused in situations where the sufferer perceives the environment to be unsafe, or dangerous. I use it here to describe the way political elites reacted to the crisis: political leadership has been marked by such an anxiety; as I will explain below,

EU have been handling the crisis has revealed a great fear of the public and have, to the extent it was possible, denounced ideas of involving it in EU decision-making. The key driver of policy was not the citizens' but the markets' needs and desires. Not surprisingly, with the *"Market"* emerging as Europe's Holy Grail amidst the financial crisis, Europeans trust in democratic institutions declined – a manifestation of a growing distance between political elites and the masses on issues of EU policymaking. This growing distance is troublesome because the policy outcomes it produces are not very poor. The fact that the political leadership across the EU has proven unprepared for effective transnational governance is dangerous not least because it falls short of solutions to imminent economic problems that concern Europe as a whole – such as the skyrocketing unemployment that deprives young Europeans from a better future or the human degradation occurring in refugees' camps – phenomena that remind of obscure pages of European history.

Yet, how to pursue sound *European policy*, i.e. policy that reflects the policy views and advances the common interests of *European citizens*? Certainly not by pitting one *Volk* against the other and through blame-games – and yet, that is what political leaders in all EU member states have been doing, and this has resulted in ineffective, muddle-through policies for economy and migration. European solidarity is especially eroded by the fact that national party governments across the EU sympathize – in varied degrees – with the rhetoric of the Eurosceptic, nationalist and xenophobic Radical Right, whose electoral strategy and discourse entertains simultaneously the economic insecurities and the cultural fears of European publics.

Though it is widely known that the Radical Right owes its success to its tough stance on immigration, recent research reveals that it has devised a new, more dangerous strategy that involves also economic issues. Radical Right parties which used to hold liberal, pro-market positions on economic issues, have moved towards the left and now

---

the more Europe got politicized, the more unsafe the political leadership felt (in terms of losing power), and in panic, it retreated to the nationalist chauvinist discourse of the Radical Right.

support welfare state expansion; however, the pro-welfare agenda they promote is deeply tied to their populist-nationalist, anti-immigrant and exclusionist rhetoric [Lefkofridi and Michel 2017]. In this way, the Radical Right appealed to left-authoritarians, a specific group of voters that combined authoritarian views on sociocultural issues (e.g. immigration) with left-wing views on economic issues (e.g. welfare) [Kriesi *et al.* 2008; Lefkofridi *et al.* 2014]. In the absence of parties combining such views, this group was underrepresented [Thomassen 2012]. Though the size of this group varied across the EU, it was above 5%, which is the minimum threshold for parliamentary representation within the Union [Lefkofridi and Michel 2017]. Hence, the Radical Right sought to fill this vacuum and get the left-authoritarian votes. However, the combination of Eurosceptic- nationalist, and authoritarian positions with left-wing positions on economic issues is perilous due to its resemblance to nationalism-socialism – an ideology that assumed (cultural, moral and/or racial) superiority of some *Völker* over others, and caused the destruction of Europe in the 1930s.

It is therefore very worrisome that the rhetoric of "natives first" (at whatever cost, i.e. even if it means loss of human lives) employed by the Radical Right across Europe is – in varied degrees – embraced by mainstream parties, especially those of the center right, which fear losing votes. This kind of rhetoric is particularly dangerous during the current economic and refugee crisis that has put more pressure on European economies and welfare systems. Instead of uniting to protect European labor rights and standards of living, politicians engaged in antagonism and competition, pitting one Volk against the other. Instead of searching the causes of their problems in the regulation of the financial sector, the irresponsible behavior of banks or the fact that the multinational capital has the power to threaten governments to relocate their investment/industry to countries with lower wages and weaker labor rights, leaders in creditor states emphasized the cultural and moral differences (working and spending habits) between North and South and blamed the crisis on the lazy and corrupt Southerners. Now that Southern European economies are plunged by unemployment and Southern Europeans are forced to migrate to the North, while millions of war refugees also search for shelter in the EU, the Radical Right intensifies its chauvinist discourse and energizes the division between solidarity and diversity by accentuating the differences within Europeans, along with differences between European and non-European (e.g. Islamic) cultures. At the same time, the crisis is touching the rich North too, where public and private actors announce budget cuts and austerity measures. Refugees, but also Southern Europeans are willing to work for much less, and Northern companies are eager to hire them to save costs. These are very dangerous constellations – and European history is abundant with examples manifesting how nationalism, chauvinism and racism result in bloodshed and destruction.

In the case of the so-called "refugee-crisis", a united response of Europe would not only have allowed war refugees to find a safe shelter easily but it might also have been able to bring about peace in the troublesome region, so that these people would not have to flee in the first place. Unfortunately, however, this is not at all what happened. The first countries that loudly negated European solidarity were the newest European member states, with Hungary representing the hardest line on the accommodation of refugees. This course of action may have been expected by Hungary given that democracy (including respect for human rights) under the government of Victor Orbán has been seriously questioned already prior to the refugees' inflows. Recently, however, the Austrian government in cooperation with Slovenia and the Visegrad Four agreed to help the Former Yugoslav Republic of Macedonia to seal its border to Greece, where the refugees arrive by sea on a daily basis. This decision shifts the burden to the few EU member states (who recognize that war refugees have no home to return to and thus *must* be accommodated) and especially to their partner, Greece, which is the arrival point. The latter lacks the administrative potential to process these thousands of asylum applications, and the resources to accommodate or integrate all these people in need, also because of the economic crisis it has been experiencing since 2009.

As closing the borders does not stop the refugee's arrival to Greece via Turkey, this type of unilateral decisions turn a blind eye to the problem, instead of solving it; they do not just deny the humanitarian need of refugees but also the need for European solidarity. Due to the fact that the Visegrad Four have a short experience with both EU membership and democracy, their lack of sensitivity regarding the human rights' issues involved in the refugee crisis and their lack of solidarity towards the rest of the EU is, perhaps, less surprising. The decision of Austria to be the first to set an upper limit for refugees, however, has been heavily criticized not only because it violates both the 1951 Geneva Convention on refugees, and the EU's free movement of labor but also because it does not contribute to the solution of the problem. Yet, Austria is a perfect example to illustrate the power of the Radical Right.

On the one hand, Austrian policy is in part a response to German policy that in January 2016 refused entry to 2.000 refugees at its Austrian border. On the other hand, Austria is a rich but small country that has already received a large number of asylum applications (approximately 90.000 at the time of writing) and the Austrian government – that is composed of two parties (Christian Democratic ÖVP and Social Democratic SPÖ) that have been in decline during the last decades – feels under pressure. The key reason underlying the Austrian government's behavior is that recent polls show that the Austrian Radical Right (FPÖ) – one of the most successful Radical Right parties in Europe – scores around 33%, which means that every third Austrian would vote for it. In a desperate attempt to win (or an attempt not to lose more) votes, the mainstream, government parties embrace the Radical Right's hardline rhetoric on immigration. In this way, however, they risk further undermining European unity and legitimizing racist approaches to the refugee problem: protecting the comfort of the "natives" at any cost becomes the ultimate goal, even if this implies that the "others" will drown in the sea, or experience inhuman conditions.

The similarity of the Eurocrisis and the refugee crisis lies in the fact that political leaders' handlings demonstrate extreme short-sightedness: they tend to approach common problems as being "someone else's", and attempt to solve them unilaterally although EU countries are deeply interdependent. Yet, *why* are governing elites retreating to chauvinism and nationalism despite the fact that the problems Europe is now facing necessitate common, European solutions? Below I will argue that this is because although policy was becoming increasingly supranational, politics remained stubbornly national.

3. The Role of National Parties and Europe's Politicization

Europe's multiple crises did not just generate great conflict but they also 'forced' debates on thorny issues of European integration 'into the open': EU jargon like 'Grexit' or 'Brexit', 'no-bailout clause', 'Transfer Union', 'two-speed Europe', 'Dublin II' as well as questions about 'European values' moved beyond university lecture halls and parliaments and penetrated the national media and personal discussions around the continent. Perhaps the most positive among recent developments in Europe is that Europeans got thirsty for "European" news, about what EU officials and political leaders say or do [Poschardt 2015]. Because of the crisis, and through the crisis, there is ever more politicization of Europe, i.e. the mobilization of more and more EU citizens paying attention to the integration process and expressing a greater diversity of opinions about it. A question that arises is whether and to what extent the institutions in place, and in particular political parties, are able to "express" citizens' diverse opinions [Sartori 1976] and represent them in EU policy making.

3.1. *Europe's de-politicization*

The unprecedented degree of Europe's politicization through the ongoing crises is important because, despite increasing policy transfers to the EU level, and the empowering of EU-level institutions, EU policy and polity issues had, up until the crisis, been largely absent from national and EP election campaigns. National parties who structure competition in both national and European elections have deliberately kept Europe on their organizational and ideological periphery [Poguntke *et al.* 2007; Ladrech 2007]. Despite the transfer of sovereignty in so many policy areas, traditional party elites did not make an effort to transfer their organizations' "loyalty" to the EU level [Lefkofridi and Schmitter 2015]. This is because they – even those momentarily involved at the EU level – have been deeply entrenched and professionalized in terms of career expectations in their respective national regimes (and this has been a crucial complication for EU democratization, see Schmitter [2000]). Moreover, while national governments were eager to transfer competences in some policy areas (e.g. economy or environment), they were very reluctant in promoting cooperation in others, such as culture and education or the media. As a result, people's sense of belonging remained by and large bound within national borders and the building of a European identity was not actively pursued.

The politicization of Europe had been portrayed as a "sleeping giant" [Van der Eijk and Franklin 2004], or perhaps a giant that had been "sedated" by national parties purposely [Mair 2007]. Empirical research has convincingly demonstrated that national parties have shown few signs of adaptation to the EU environment in terms of their organizational structures [Poguntke *et al.* 2007], their electoral campaigns in European [Lefkofridi and Kritzinger 2008] and national elections [Pennings 2007; Kriesi 2007] as well as their policy positions [Lefkofridi 2015]. In sum, although EU membership changed dramatically the policy and polity environment of national parties, they did little to adapt to it – with severe consequences for citizens' representation in EU policymaking.

The only parties that sought to mobilize voters on issues of European integration have been the parties on the extreme poles [deVries 2007]. On the one hand, radical right parties accuse the EU of being undemocratic and insulated from national publics' preferences. In their view, domestic policy fails to respond to national publics *because* of the EU; to solve this problem, the radical right advocates the need to halt European integration, reinstate supremacy of EU law, and push for policy "spill backs" (e.g. natives' priority over immigrants, including fellow EU citizens) [Lefkofridi and Schmitter 2015; Lefkofridi and Michel 2017]. On the other hand, Euroscepticism from the radical left concentrates on the EU's neoliberal direction [Hooghe *et al.* 2002] that harms especially the poorer strata, who lack the resources (e.g. education) to survive the competition that the Single market fosters. Economic integration promotes liberalization and privatization in the domestic markets – including the marketization of health and social services; according to radical left Eurosceptics this comes at the expense of the policy preferences of the disadvantaged, the poorer strata's preferences.

In spite of these critical voices, mainstream national parties avoided engaging wholeheartedly with European integration based on the assumption that their national constituents were indifferent or ignorant about EU issues. When the Eurozone crisis and the accommodation of war refugees exacerbated the tension between meeting citizens' wishes and adhering to EU institutional rules and commitments [Alonso 2014; Schäfer and Streeck 2013], we witnessed mass mobilization and protest all around the continent. Many European citizens demanded European policy solutions that differed from those promoted by their own national governments. They took the streets to join demonstrations against austerity and the solutions pursued at the EU and national levels that increase inequality and hurt the middle and lower classes [Accornero and Pinto 2015; Beichelt 2014; Della Porta 2012]. A citizen-elite gap on EU level policy became also apparent when party leaders indulged in nationalist-chauvinist or even racist discourse, while large parts of European publics were welcoming refugees. Europeans' transnational mobilization and protest is evidence of their engagement with European integration and their deep concern about Europe's future policy directions [Schmitter and Lefkofridi 2016].

Although Euroscepticism has been increasing, it is misleading to interpret it as a sign of growing nationalism, chauvinism and racism among European citizens. Citizens are disappointed in the way political elites handle the economic and refugee crisis at the EU level, both of which were not distinguished by unity and solidarity. Hence, citizens' Euroscepticism should also be perceived as a healthy skepsis, a critical stance towards the current state of an otherwise great idea: Europe. As any scientist would proudly defend, *skepsis* does not only signify the rejection of Europe, but also the demand of alternatives to a failing, disintegrating Europe that indulges to its old sins – antagonism, racism and national chauvinism. In representative democracies, it is political parties who must express this skepsis by articulating clear alternatives and giving citizens real choices; it in this way that Europeans, and above all young Europeans, will regain confidence that a different Europe in peace and solidarity is possible [Collignon 2011].

Through the crises, European citizens realized that they are interdependent not just economically but also politically – as it became evident that no national party could unilaterally affect policy. Contrary to the citizens, however, political parties seem to be falling behind the curve. This is bad news for European democracy – not least because the "history and development of the European model of democracy has been closely associated with the history and development of political parties" [Bardi 1994: 357]. Given the centrality of political parties in all representative democracies constituting the Union, if parties are failing, party democracy in Europe and representation via parties is also failing. To understand the crux of the problem, we need to consider the extent to which citizens can influence EU policy making via the institutions in place. In the next section, we thus briefly discuss the channels available to European citizens in the transnational multilevel EU polity.

4.   Channels of Citizen Representation to the EU Level

How are citizens represented at the EU level? The EU polity provides citizens with two channels of representation in EU policy-making.

4.1. *The parliament*

First, there is a direct (supranational) channel, which operates through the selection of (national) party candidates to represent citizens at the European Parliament (EP). The EP is not just the only collective body whose composition can be determined directly by the European people, and the only supranational institution with a clear mandate of citizen representation; it is also the only supranational institution where citizens' representatives sit along party-ideological – instead of territorial – lines.

Yet, the actual architecture of the EP representation channel results in a "split-level" party system seeking to balance territorial and partisan competition [Lord 2004: 116]. Elections to the EP are organized at the national level: every five years citizens of national constituencies go to the polls to select among candidates for EP membership that are sorted in national parties. Although elections are nationally organized, the EP, acknowledged by the Single European Act (SEA) as the "indispensable means of expression" for "the democratic peoples of Europe", is organized along European (as opposed to national) party lines. In essence, citizens' "expression" is entrusted to political parties at the European level. So, after the election, the MEPs of each national party re-sort themselves into transnational political groups so as to make policy and (co-)decide on legislation that affects the EU citizenry as a whole. However, the weight of national political settings on party organization strategy and style of competition in EP elections (Europe's depoliticization discussed above) hindered the development of transnational parties [Bardi *et al.* 2010].

These in turn, have also influenced how scholarship viewed European politics. Despite that most contemporary policy problems within the EU demand European-level solutions, our conceptual and empirical understanding of democratic politics remains to a large extent also confined within national borders. For instance, previous studies of representation in the EP examine the linkage between citizens and either national parties [McEvoy 2012; Mattila and Raunio 2012] or their candidates to the EP [Thomassen and Schmitt 1997]. Though this research has revealed varied gaps between citizens and elites (e.g. on issues of European unification), it has relied solely on a national-level concept of democratic representation. Crucially, it has neglected the interaction between national parties and European level parties [McElroy and Benoit 2012, 2010, 2007]. This is problematic because the bond between citizens and national parties/candidates or even Members of EP (MEPs) tells us only one part of the story about the linkage between citizens and those legislating on their behalf at the EU level. The reason is that national parties can achieve very little by acting unilaterally: to affect policy outcomes they need to join forces with similar parties from other countries. So after the EP election, the nationally recruited MEPs join European political groups and, when voting on legislation, tend to align with them [e.g. Mühlböck 2012; Hix *et al.* 2009]. Hence, European level parties are vital to our understanding of citizen representation at the EU level.

The conceptual and methodological neglect of the multiple levels where citizen representation in EU policymaking plays out is a paramount obstacle to the understanding of how actors of democracy, namely citizens and political organizations adapt to processes of

European integration. Moreover, ignoring the multilevel structure of European policymaking leaves us with a blind spot regarding which actors are more or less successful in responding to the challenge of transnational democracy and why. Hence, to fully understand citizens' representation in EU policymaking we need to pay attention to the Union's "split-level" structure [Lord 2004; Schmidt 2009, 2006]: policy inputs and outputs occur at different levels of government. Our recent research [Lefkofridi and Katsanidou 2014] extends standard accounts of citizen representation in the EU by acknowledging the hierarchical relationships involved in the representational process at both theoretical and methodological levels. Recent research which acknowledged the multilevel nature of EP representation, revealed a completely different, much more positive picture: a pioneer study of multilevel representation in the EP prior to the crisis [Lefkofridi and Katsanidou 2014] showed that even when the electoral connection between citizens and European level parties was lacking, party organizations could still manage to channel citizens' views through the EP's split-level structure. This gives some hope regarding the potential of national parties to create common fronts at the EU level.

4.2. *The Council*

Second, there is the indirect (intergovernmental) channel of representation through the participation of their national governments in the Council (which meets in different formations depending on the issue at stake). The Council is a peculiar institution in that EU citizens can neither select nor outvote it as a whole if it fails them in the same way that state's governments are typically selected and voted out of power. In national elections citizens from each member state can elect small parts of the Council. Yet, the EU-level consequences of these national choices are not straightforward because, as mentioned above, European issues had never been an integral part of electoral campaigns. Hence, citizens are not aware of the European-level consequences of their national-level choices. As a consequence, there is no general debate about the policies citizens would like to see at the EU level and policy debates are often articulated as "national" conflicts [Collignon 2011]. Since the outbreak of the financial crisis national governments have often retreated to exclusive and state-centric calculations of interest often undermined decisions they themselves took at EU Summits [Barroso 2012].

Even worse, due to the conceptual and methodological neglect of the multiple levels where citizen representation in policy making should occur, and due to the fact that the Council is understood as representing states, not citizens, the linkage between the Council and the citizens that get affected by its policies is largely under-researched. However, the crisis has rendered the scholarly neglect unsustainable and a series of questions regarding the Council are raised: firstly, since the Council has been designed to represent member states, an important question is whether and how EU membership impacts these member states' capacity to respond to citizens' policy preferences in the domestic arena, as well as whether EU membership affects policy responsiveness to different income groups unequally; in other words, whether policy in EU MS tilts towards the preferences of the wealthy. These questions are all the more important on the face of rising Eurosceptic and populist parties on the right and the left poles of party systems across the EU. Since policies are transferred to the EU level, national governments' hands are "tied" and they cannot unilaterally 'undo' decisions taken by previous governments at the EU level [Mair 2007] – and this became most evident with the incapacity of the SYRIZA-led government to fulfill its electoral promises for changing policy direction. A pioneer study [Donnelly and Lefkofridi 2015] shows that while EU membership does not harm policy responsiveness to the public at large, if we consider the diversity of policy preferences within the public, we do find an income bias.

Secondly, the Council might have been originally designed to represent nation-states, but the outcomes of its decisions nowadays matter not only for some professional sectors but also for all Europeans citizens. Since no one can 'kick the rascals out' in case the Council's policies fail, the second important question that arises is the extent to which the Council is congruent with the European citizens who are affected by its policies, as well as which citizens in particular. To illustrate, the Council's policy reaction to the crisis has been austerity, in an effort to achieve fiscal consolidation; as budget cuts affect redistributive measures and the provision of social policy to the disadvantaged they predominantly hurt the poor, who are the most vulnerable. Recent research [Giger and Lefkofridi 2015] that examines the ideological congruence between the Council and different income groups shows that the Council is consistently on the right of both the rich and the poor during the period 2000-2012; moreover, while the ideological position of the rich is not overrepresented, the poor's position is consistently underrepresented in the Council.

By politicizing Europe to an unprecedented extent, the crisis has underlined that national political parties need to transnationalize policy debates and create common fronts in the context of both the Council and the EP; their willingness and capacity to collaborate closely and integrate determines the extent to which they can successfully pursue policy that reflects the wishes of their constituencies, which is a key function elected parties are expected to perform in representative democracies. This matters greatly for the functioning of party democracy in a transnational multilevel polity given that national parties are unable to act unilaterally and affect policy in areas of EU competence. The next section looks at the possibility for transnational democracy beyond parties, by briefly discussing the promises and pitfalls of the ECI.

5. Transnational Democracy beyond Parties? ECIs amidst Europe's Deepest Crisis

As stated in the introduction, the Lisbon Treaty (2009) established the European Citizens' Initiative (ECI) as an instrument that addresses citizens directly by allowing one million Europeans to submit a policy proposal to the European Commission. In theory, the ECI aims at citizens' engagement in legislative agenda-setting [European Commission 2011]. EU citizens can call on the Commission to propose legislation on a specific topic provided that this (a) concerns the implementation (and not amendment) of the treaties and (b) falls within the framework of Commission's powers. According to the European Commission the ECI provides "a singular opportunity to bring the Union closer to the citizens and to foster greater cross-border debate about EU policy issues, by bringing citizens from a range of countries together in supporting one specific issue" (European Commission 2010: 3). In other words, the ECI is present as an unprecedented experiment of transnational democracy with potential to contribute to the Europeanization of the public sphere. This, in turn, is vital for European integration because the public sphere enables participation in collective choice; allows the (re-)production of the 'social imagery', i.e. gives Europe shape (by imagining it in specific ways) and constitutes a medium of social integration, a form of social solidarity, as well as an arena for debate [Calhoun 2003; see also Habermas 1998]. The (re-)production (and even transformation) of a European social imagery and the advancement of social integration are particularly important in the context of the current crises of the Eurozone and the accommodation of war refugees, during which we have witnessed not just antagonistic behavior between member states but also nation-bashing, recourse to cultural stereotypes as well as increasing political extremism and chauvinism.

However, the limited scholarship on the ECI remains largely skeptical regarding the potential of the ECI to reinvigorate democracy in the Union. On the one hand, the ECI is welcomed as an infusion of participatory democracy in a largely top-down integration process. On the one hand, it presents citizens with tremendous difficulties. Once registered, an ECI must gather the support of one million EU citizens (who are entitled to vote) from at least seven member states; and there is a minimum number of signatures to be collected in each of these seven states. Although this should be more feasible in the era of advanced computer-mediated communication [e.g. della Porta and Mosca 2005] compared to fifty, or even fifteen years ago, it remains a Herculean task. Even worse, the timeframe for signature collection is currently set to twelve months, thus posing significant time constraints to campaigning and collecting signatures "offline" (that includes face-to-face communication), as opposed to online campaigning (via virtual public spaces). Also, ECI initiators encounter translation costs so as to appeal to linguistically diverse publics, as well as data protection problems. Most crucially, the ECI relies on a weak concept of participatory democracy: unlike national-level initiatives, it does not lead to a popular vote. The Commission, who is obliged to consider and respond to each submitted proposal and respond to successful proposals within three months, is *not* bound to act. So, in terms of impact, the ECI resembles the petition to the European Parliament but implies a much more cumbersome process [de Witte *et al.* 2010; Starskaya and Çagdas 2012]. One would expect that few citizens would bother to even start an ECI.

But despite all these hurdles, and the fact that its official launch in April 2012 occurred amidst the deepest crisis of European integration, fifty-one requests have thus far been made to the Commission. Eighteen were rejected during the stage of registration on the grounds that they concerned matters falling outside the framework of powers of the Commission. Thirty-three citizens' initiatives were launched: five are still in the process of signature collection, while twenty-eight have already concluded it after having gained the support an estimated six million citizens. However, only three managed to meet the signature thresholds required within the specified twelve-month period to be submitted to the European Commission for consideration. Given increasing Euroscepticism and Europeans' declining trust in conventional democratic institutions at national and EU levels, these attempts are impressive also because they manifest the mobilization of wider and wider publics paying attention to the integration process and expressing a greater diversity of opinions about it. This, in turn, is further evidence of the politicization of Europe [Schmitter and Lefkofridi 2016].

6. Instead of Conclusion: Can Science Foster Transnational Democracy?

What began as a peace project to prevent hostility among European states (that had led to the destruction and bloodshed of the two World Wars) developed into an unprecedented experiment in transnational democracy. This experiment has thus far failed because, despite increasing policy transfers to the EU level, the key democratic actors (parties and citizens) who were deeply entrenched in, and bounded by, their national regimes have been unwilling and/or unable to mobilize transnationally. This was not obvious to the layman until the crisis, which politicized European policies that had been kept in the dark; it revealed the interdependence of European peoples and the fact that no country can provide solutions to common problems by acting unilaterally. It also uncovered the incapacity of the political leaders to provide for transnational democratic governance.

The antidote to their current retreat to nationalism, chauvinism and racism is the strengthening of those channels that could allow the European demos "in the making" [Nicolaidis 2013] to get involved in EU policy making, such as pan-European parties, movements, and initiatives. Most recently, Europeans who have been actively involved in the organization of European Citizens' Initiatives together with politicians and intellectuals from all around the continent established the "Democracy in Europe Movement (DIEM) 2025[k]" – a movement that is critical of the current state and direction of the Union and demands its democratization. Although its future is unknown, the birth of this movement constitutes further evidence that Eurosceptics may in fact include a much bolder vision of the EU than that of the (allegedly) pro-European elites who succumb to nationalist-chauvinist discourse due to vote optimization strategies.

A question that is raised is whether science and technology can help European democracy. I reply with a resounding YES. The synergy of different disciplines can help elites get more in touch with what citizens want and communicate to citizens which policy directions are possible; it can also help citizens express their views more often and more clearly by simplifying their participation in politics. While political science can help structure and organize policy debates and present alternatives, information technology, communication and media studies can help improve the linkages between elites and citizens.

One example of how science and technology already helps democracy are the so-called Voting Advice Applications (VAAs) which are redefining the communication between political parties and citizens. By providing citizens with valuable information on the positions of parties, they enable them to make informed choices in elections [for a discussion and methodology see Garzia and Marschall 2014; Gemenis 2015]. The provision of this information, in turn, enhances citizens'

---

[k]The official website of the movement is http://diem25.org/

electoral participation. Another way of improving citizens' democratic participation is making the procedures easier and faster through the use of modern technology (e-voting, see Trechsel [2007]). A similar approach could be adopted in the case of the ECIs: they could be put on an easy to use pan-European electronic ballot, where all Europeans could – in a few seconds – express their support or opposition to a number of proposals originating by their fellow Europeans.

Furthermore, given that contemporary society is familiar with social media, e-fora functioning in multiple languages could be established so as to enable citizens' transnational networking and their cooperation across borders in order to advance common causes, like online petitions and initiatives. In the same way, information technology could also help parties' transnational cooperation. For instance, building on and updating the information provided by VAAs on party positions, parties could connect to like-minded parties in other countries and could quickly establish points of agreement and disagreement. Moreover, using smartphone applications, parties could better connect to European citizens to inform them about important issues and ask them to feed back to them.

In sum, a transnational democracy is possible and provided that there is political will, it could soon materialize with the help of science and technology. The question is whether the current leadership of Europe will opt for transnationalising democracy or re-nationalizing European policies and further weaken the European project, as the Radical Right advocates.

References

Accornero, G., and Ramos Pinto, P. (2015). 'Mild mannered'? Protest and mobilisation in Portugal under austerity, 2010–2013. *West European Politics*, 38 (3), 491-515

Alonso, S. (2014). You can vote but you cannot choose: Democracy and the sovereign debt crisis in the Eurozone, *Estudio/Working Paper 2014/282*, Instituto Mixto Carlos III.

Bank of Greece (2013). *Director's Report for 2012*. Athens, Bank of Greece, 02.2013, http://www.bankofgreece.gr/BogEkdoseis/ekthdkth2012.pdf [4 March 2014]

Bardi, L. (1994). Transnational Party Federations, European Parliamentary Groups and the Building of Europarties, in: Katz, R. S., and Mair, P. (eds.), *How Parties*

Organize: Change and Adaptation in Party Organizations in Western Democracies, Sage, London

Bardi, L., Bressanelli, E., Calossi, E., Gagatek, W., Mair, P., and Pizzimenti, E. (2010). How to Create a Transnational Party System. A study prepared in the framework of the European Union Democracy Observatory for the European Parliament (AFCO Committee). *EUDO Observatory on Political Parties & Representation (OPPR).*: European Parliament, Brussels

Barroso, J. M. D. (2012). Speech at the European Parliament Plenary Debate on the European Council 28-29.06 Plenary session of the European Parliament, Strasbourg, 3 July 2012, European Commission SPEECH 12/518

Baubök, R., Cayla, P., and Catriona S. (2012). Should EU Citizens Living in *Other Member States Vote There in National Elections?* EUI Working Papers RSCAS 2012/32

Beichelt, T. I., Hahn-Fuhr, F., Schimmelfennig, F., and S. Worschech (2014). *Democracy Promotion and Civil Society in Post-Socialist Europe*, Palgrave Macmillan, London

Bouza Garcia, L., Cuesta Lopez, V., Mincheva, E., and Szeligowska, D. (2012). The European Citizens' Initiative - A First Assessment, *Bruges Political Research Papers* 24/2012

Calhoun, C. (2008). Social Science for Public Knowledge, in: Eliaeson, S., and Kalleberg, R. (eds.), *Academics as Public Intellectuals*, Palgrave, London, 299-317

Calhoun, C. (2003). The Democratic Integration of Europe: Interests, Identity, and the Public Sphere, in: Berezin, M., and Schain, M., (eds.), *Europe without Borders: Re-Mapping Territory,Citizenship and Identity in a Transnational Age*, Johns Hopkins University Press, Baltimore

Collignon, S. (2011). The Role of Parties in the European Union, 8 June 2011, *Social Europe*, https://www.socialeurope.eu/2011/06/the-role-of-parties-in-the-european-union/#_ftn2 [12 February 2016]

Dany, G., Gropp, R., and von Schweinitz, G. (2015). Germany's Benefit From the Greek Crisis, IWH Online- Leibniz Institut für Wirtschaftsforschung Halle, http://www.iwh-halle.de/d/publik/iwhonline/io_2015-07.pdf [12 February 2016]

della Porta, D. (2012). Critical trust: Social movements and democracy in times of crisis, *Cambio*, 2, 33-43

della Porta, D., and Mosca, L. (2005). Global-net for Global Movements? A Network of Networks for a Movement of Movements, *Journal of Public Policy*, 25 (81), 165-190

De Vries, C. E. (2007). Sleeping giant: Fact or fairytale? How European integration affects national elections, *European Union Politics*, 8(3), 363-385

Donnelly, M., and Lefkofridi, Z. (2015). Regional Integration & Policy Responsiveness. Paper presentation at Research Workshop *"Beyond the Democratic Deficit: Political Representation & Differential Policy Responsiveness in the European*

Union", 14-15 May 2015, Robert Schuman Centre for Advanced Studies, European University Institute; Florence

Efler, M. (2006). *European Citizen Initiative: Legal Options for implementation below the constitutional level*, Democracy International, Berlin

European Commission (2011). *Guide to the European Citizens' Initiative*, Publications Office of the European Union, Luxembourg

European Commission (2010). *Proposal for a regulation of the European Parliament and of the Council on the citizens' initiative*. Brussels, COM (2010) 119 final

Habermas, J. (1998). *The Inclusion of the Other. Studies in Political Theory*, in: Cronin, C., and de Greiff, P. (eds), MIT Press, Cambridge, MA

Garzia, D., and Marschall, S. (2014). *Matching Voters with Parties and Candidates: Voting Advice Applications in Comparative Perspective*. ECPR Press

Gemenis, K., (2015). An iterative expert survey approach for estimating parties' policy positions, *Quality & Quantity*, 49(6), 2291-2306

Hix S., Noury A., and Roland G. (2009). Voting Patterns and Alliance Formation in the European Parliament, *Philosophical Transactions of the Royal Society*, 364, 821-831

Hix, S., Noury, A., and Roland, G., (2006). Dimensions of politics in the European Parliament, *American Journal of Political Science*, 50(2), 494-520

Hooghe, L., Marks, G., and Wilson, C. J. (2002). Does left/right structure party positions on European integration?, *Comparative political studies*, 35(8), 965-89

Kaufmann, B. (2012). *The European Citizens' Initiative Pocket Guide*, Green European Foundation, Luxembourg

Kaufmann, B., Lamassoure, A., and Meyer, J. (eds.) (2004). *Transnational Democracy in the Making*, IRI Europe Handbook, Amsterdam

Kriesi, H. (2007). The role of European integration in national election campaigns, *European Union Politics*, 8(1), 83-108

Kriesi, H. Grande, E., Lachat, R., Dolezal, M., Bornschier, S., and Frey, T. (2008). *West European Politics in the age of globalization*, Cambridge University Press, Cambridge

Ladrech, R. (2007). National political parties and European governance: the consequences of 'missing in action', *West European Politics*, 30(5), 945-960

Lefkofridi, Z. (2014). From Bad to Worse? Reflections on the Crisis in Greece and in Europe, *Austrian Journal of Political Science- Österreichische Zeitschrift der Politikwissenschaft*, 2, 217-228

Lefkofridi, Z. (2015). National Political Parties and EU Policy Developments: the Case of Greece prior to the Crisis, *Journal of Modern Greek Studies*, 32(2), 287-311

Lefkofridi, Z., and Kritzinger, S. (2008). Battles fought in the EP arena: Developments in National Parties' Euro-manifestos, *Austrian Journal of Political Science*, 37(3), 273-96

Lefkofridi, Z., Wagner, M., and Willmann, J. (2014). Left-Authoritarians and Policy Representation in Western Europe: Electoral Choice across Ideological Dimensions, *West European* Politics, 37(1), 65-90

Lefkofridi, Z., and Katsanidou, A., (2014). Multilevel representation in the European Parliament, *European Union Politics*, 15(1), 108-131

Lefkofridi, Z., and Schmitter, P.C. (2015). Transcending or Descending? European Integration in Times of Crisis, *European Political Science Review*, 7(1), 3-22

Lefkofridi, Z., and Michel, E. (2017). The Electoral Politics of Solidarity, in: Banting, K., and Kymlicka, W. (eds), *The Strains of Commitment: the Political Sources of Solidarity in Diverse Societies,* Oxford University Press, forthcoming

Lord, C. (2004). A Democratic Audit of the European Union, Macmillan, London

Mair, P. (2007). Political Opposition and the European Union, *Government and Opposition*, 42/1, 1-17

Mattila, M., and Raunio, T. (2006). Cautious Voters and Supportive Parties: Opinion Congruence between Voters and Parties on the EU dimension, *European Union Politics*, 7/4, 427- 449

Mattila, M., and Raunio, T. (2012). Drifting Further Apart: National Parties and their Electorates on the EU Dimension, *West European Politics*, 35(3), 589-606

Maurer, A., and Vogel, S. (2009). *Die Europäische Bürgerinitiative: Chancen, Grenzen und Umsetzungsempfehlungen*, Stiftung Wissenschaft und Politik, Berlin

Mayoral, J. A. (2011). Democratic Improvements in the European Union under the Lisbon Treaty: Institutional changes regarding democratic government in the EU, *European Union Democracy Observatory,* Robert Schuman Centre for Advanced Studies, European University Institute

McElroy, G., and Benoit, K. (2007). Party Groups and Policy Positions in the European Parliament, *Party Politics*, 13(1), 5-28

McElroy, G., and Benoit, K. (2010). Party Policy and Group Affiliation in the European Parliament, *British Journal of Political Science*, 40, 377-398

McElroy, G., and Benoit, K. (2012). Policy Positioning in the European Parliament, *European Union Politics*, 13(1), 150-167

McEvoy, C. (2012). Unequal Representation in the EU: A multi-level Analysis of Voter-Party Congruence in EP Elections, *Representation*, 48(1), 83-99

Mühlböck, M. (2012). National versus European: Party Control over Members of the European Parliament, *West European Politics*, 35(3), 607-631

Nicolaïdis, K. (2013). European demoicracy and its crisis, JCMS: *Journal of Common Market Studies*, 51.2, 351-369

Pennings, P. (2006). An empirical analysis of the Europeanization of national party manifestos, 1960-2003, *European Union Politics*, 7(2), 257-270

Poguntke, T., Aylott, N., Carter, E., Ladrech, R., and Luther, K.R. (eds.) (2007). *The Europeanization of national political parties: power and organizational adaptation*, Routledge

Poschardt, U. (2015). Die Krise macht uns jetzt zu wahrhaften Europäern, *Die Welt*, 3 July 2015, http://www.welt.de/debatte/kommentare/article143520903/Die-Krise-macht-uns-jetzt-zu-wahrhaften-Europaeern.html [7 July 2015]

Reuters (2015). Exclusive: Europeans tried to block IMF debt report on Greece: sources. http://www.reuters.com/article/2015/07/03/us-eurozone-greece-imf-idUSKCN0PD 20120150703 [3 July 2015]

Roche, M. (2011). La "franc-maçonnerie" européenne de Goldman Sachs. *Le Monde*, 15 November 2011, http://www.lemonde.fr/crise-financiere/article/2011/11/15/lafra-nc-maconnerie-europeenne-de-goldman-sachs_1603875_1581613.html [28 August 2012]

Sartori, G. (1976). *Parties and Party Systems: A Framework for Analysis*, Cambridge University Press, Cambridge London New York and Melbourne

Schäfer, A., and W. Streeck (2013). *Politics in the Age of Austerity*, Polity Press, Cambridge

Schmidt, V. A. (2006). *Democracy in Europe: The EU and National Polities*, Oxford University Press, Oxford

Schmidt, V. A. (2009). Re-Envisioning the European Union: Identity, Democracy, Economy, *Journal of Common Market Studies*, 47, 17-42

Schmitter, P.C. (2000). *How to Democratize the European Union--and why Bother?* Rowman & Littlefield

Schmitter, P. C., and Lefkofridi Z. (2016). Neofunctionalism as a theory of disintegration, *Chinese Political Science Review*, 1, DOI: 10.1007/s41111-016-0012-4.

Starskaya, M., and Çagdas, Ö. (2012). Analysis of the Online Collection Software provided by the European Commission for the European Citizens' Initiative, *Working Papers on Information Systems, Information Business and Operations* 01/2012, Department für Informationsverarbeitung und Prozessmanagement, WU Vienna University of Economics and Business, Vienna

The Wall Street Journal (2013). *IMF concedes it made mistakes on Greece*. June 5, 2013. http://www.wsj.com/articles/SB10001424127887324299104578527202781667088 [10 July 2015]

Thomassen, J. (2012). The blind corner of political representation, *Representation*, *48*(1), 13-27

Thomassen, J., and Schmitt, H. (1997). Policy Representation, *European Journal of Political Research*, 32(2), 165-184

Trechsel, A. H. (2007). E-voting and electoral participation, in: *The Dynamics of Referendum Campaigns*, Palgrave Macmillan, UK, 159-182

Tsebelis, G. (2016). Lessons from the Greek Crisis, *Journal of European Public Policy*, 23 (1), 25-41

Van der Brug, W. and Van Spanje, J., (2009). Immigration, Europe and the 'new'cultural dimension, *European Journal of Political Research*, *48*(3), 309-334

Van der Eijk, C., and Franklin, M.N. (2004). Potential for contestation on European matters at national elections in Europe, in: Marks, G., and Steenbergen, M. (eds), *European integration and political conflict*, 32-50

Vasilopoulou, S., and D. Halikiopoulou (2013). In the Shadow of Grexit: The Greek Election of 17 June 2012, South European Society and Politics, 18(4), 1-20

Chapter 22

Constructive News:
A New Journalistic Genre Emerging in a Time of Multiple Crises

Uwe Krüger

Institut für Kommunikations- und Medienwissenschaft, Universität Leipzig
Burgstr. 21, 04109 Leipzig, Germany
uwe.krueger@uni-leipzig.de

In recent years, a nascent trend called "Constructive News" resp. "Solutions Journalism" has become visible in Western societies. These stories – often presented in a positive, encouraging tone of "good news" – show examples where people are working toward solutions for social problems. We can grasp this phenomenon theoretically with regard to the news values theory, and we see two different factions of journalistic protagonists: one system-inherent (with social entrepreneurship as the main field of coverage, claiming to be unpolitical, neutral observers) and one system-critical (coming from social movements and seeing themselves as change agents on the path to a degrowth society). I argue that this new journalistic genre can have opportunities on a micro level (for the psychological well-being of individuals) and on a meso level (for the prosperity of media organizations) as well as on a macro level (for social progress). Also, I discuss criticism and problems of "Constructive news", especially a proximity to public relations and lobbying, and ideological traps by defining the respective problem and its causes.

1. Conception of a Genre

"Mainstream media has a bias for bad news. We're missing half of the world's stories." This slogan signaled the start of the Solutions Journalism Network 2012, a self-described independent non-profit organization in New York that is committed to changing journalism, or more specifically, to changing the selection of news and the focus or direction of journalistic research. The organization's website presents "Best Practice" examples of solutions-oriented journalism, including stories such as "How Cincinnati revitalized police-community relations" (showing how the city has improved relations between the police and citizens after extended civil unrest), "Interrupting violence in Brooklyn" (on an initiative to mediate conflict and provide "peer counselors" for problematic cases) or "An Afghan success story: fewer child deaths" (through a joint project of the Afghan Ministry of Health and the non-governmental organization Save the Children).[a]

That which the Solutions Journalism Network attempts to propagate and legitimize is not simply "good news," the likes of which appear in sappy Christmas editions of the *BILD* newspaper, in the *Huffington Post* "Good News" section among saccharine videos of animals and children or in the economic section "Gute Nachricht (Good News)" in the gratis Swiss newspaper *20 Minuten*, with its reports of soaring pension fund revenues or booms in the Swiss housing market. The organization defines its subject so:

> Solutions journalism is rigorous and compelling reporting about responses to social problems. It investigates and explains, in a critical and clear-eyed way, examples of people working toward solutions. It focuses not just on what may be working, but *how* and *why* it appears to be working, or alternatively, why it may be stumbling [italics in original].[b]

Aside from celebrity gossip and economic success stories, this definition (news coverage of attempts to solve *social* problems) excludes other topics as well, including technology journalism about *technical* innovations and inventions, or service-oriented journalism that give consumers orientation and advice [Eickelkamp 2011].

The organization makes the case for journalists to direct their attention not only to problems and social wrongs, but also to the people and projects that are striving to change them (i.e., "solution providers").

---

[a]http://solutionsjournalism.org/examples/

[b]http://solutionsjournalism.org/about/solutions-journalism-what-it-is-and-what-it-is-not/

In this way, it aims at a transformation or completion of the criteria that determine journalistic news selection and topic emphasis.

The central approach to explain the selection of news is the news value theory, which attributes the selection and emphasis of news decisions to the internal content characteristics of events and topics, the so-called news factors. The classic news factors, which have been cited in journalism textbooks since the 1930s, are considered to be immediacy, prominence, unusualness, conflict, significance (consequences) and proximity. Using empirical evidence, communication scientists from Scandinavia and Germany, among others, have further developed this catalog since the 1960s. Contemporary catalogues of news factors include a series of event characteristics with negative connotations, such as "controversy," "aggression/conflict," "damage/failure [Beiler 2013]." The proponents of solutions-oriented journalism are now attempting to shift the focus of journalists in another (or: additional) direction. The aim is to establish a new news factor, one that can be referred to as "problem-solving" or "attempted problem-solving" and is related to known news factors such as "benefit/success" [Schulz 1976; Staab 1990] or "progress" [LaRoche *et al.* 2013].

The idea for the genre gains clarity when one considers terms that have been used to describe the same or similar ideas. The journalistic startup company *Sparknews* in Paris, for example, speaks of *impact journalism*, because coverage of successfully implemented projects (should) inspire recipients to act and thus have an effect or impact on society. Ute Scheub, a freelance journalist in Berlin and founding member of the *taz* newspaper, prefers the term *heartening journalism* [Scheub 2016]. The Canadian journalist David Beers, who operates the solutions-oriented news site The Tyee, calls it *future-focused journalism*, explaining: "If muckraking (investigative reporting – UK) asks 'What went wrong yesterday, and who is to blame?' then future-focused journalism asks 'What might go right tomorrow and who is showing the way?'" [Stack 2008: 405].

Still other protagonists refer to *constructive journalism*, a term that we use synonymously for solution-oriented journalism in the following. It is used by the Danish TV-journalist Ulrik Haagerup [2014] who significantly increased the percentage of solution-oriented stories in the evening TV news show of the public broadcast in Denmark and wrote an influential book about that process [Haagerup 2014], by the Constructive Journalism Project in London (est. 2014), the project "Peace Counts" with its director Michael Gleich and by the Transformational Media Initiative (TMI). Even the term *transformation journalism* continues in this direction [Ronzheimer 2013], although in this case, it specifically has to do with journalism that aims to support a "major transformation" to a more sustainable economy, often overlapping with environmental and sustainability journalism.

Solutions journalism or constructive journalism also shares certain commonalities with the concept of *peace journalism,* which is pursued, among others, by the aforementioned "Peace Counts" project [Prinzing 2010] and can be traced back to the Norwegian peace researcher Johan Galtung. According to Galtung [1998: 7], peace journalism, in its support of nonviolent transformation of conflict by providing conflict-sensitive coverage, is – as opposed to "war and violence journalism" – not "victory-oriented," but rather "solution-oriented." As a result, peace journalism can be seen as a subset of solutions journalism in that the construction of "social problems" necessarily includes conflict, violence and war.

2. Historical Development and Protagonists of the Genre

2.1. *Robert Jungk as pioneer*

The German futurologist and publicist Robert Jungk (1913-1994), one of the greatest masterminds of the global environment and peace movement and inventor of "future workshops," can very well be considered the first practitioner and theorist of constructive news. Shortly after World War II, in the year 1948, he founded a news service in New York called the *Good News Bulletin*, a "concentration of good news packed into a few folded pages and sent to newsrooms and universities once a week" with an initial circulation of 150 copies. In terms of content, he especially illuminated the works of various subsidiaries of the newly founded UNO,

WHO, Unesco and Unicef, evidently relying on their respective public relations offices for material [Jungk 1993: 238-239].

A long life was not in the cards for the project, however. Although the media response was positive, the search for financiers met with little success. After the death of his mother temporarily took a toll on his motivation, Jungk gave up the project. Nevertheless: "From then on, 'Good News' appeared without my help every week in the 'Saturday Review.' The endeavor was therefore not entirely in vain [Jungk 1993: 240]."

As a publisher, Jungk continued to distribute tokens of good news with books such as "51 Models of the Future – A Catalog of Hope" (1990) or "Dolphin Solutions '93. The Year of Creative Answers" (1993), for which he relied on the archives of Jakob von Uexküll, the founder of the Alternative Nobel Prize (Right Livelihood Award) and the initiator of the World Future Council [Benking 2013].[c] To the editors of *taz* newspaper, which arose in the aftermath of the social movements of the 1970s, he once even advised "not to forget the coverage of successful projects and positive alternatives" [Scheub 2016]. In 1988, he gave a presentation regarding his fundamental concepts on this subject during the Carl-von-Ossietzky-Days at University of Oldenburg. In it, Jungk [1990: 203] established a connection between constructive news and investigative reporting:

> I believe that the 'investigative journalism' of today and the future – trained in the spirit of Ossietzky [a German journalist and pacifist who received the Nobel Peace Price and died in 1938 after being tortured by the Nazis], persistently contradictory, constantly revealing new secret evidence of the secretive intentions of the powerful – also has another duty that has not yet been recognized, but is becoming increasingly urgent: He or she [...] must not simply maintain a defense

---

[c]Coming from Jungk, we can draw a historical line of "spreading good examples" not only via news journalism but also via more durable media like books and databanks. In addition to Jakob von Uexküll's Right Livelihood Award, notable works in this category include earlier projects such as the "Idea Bank" from Norwegian Kjell Dahle, founded in the early 1970s; the "Encyclopedia of World Problems and Human Potential," started in 1972 by Anthony Judge and James Wellesley-Wesley (continued today as an online databank, among other forms); and the Institute for Social Inventions, established by Nicholas Albery in 1985.

against the evil or the threatening; instead, they should turn their vigilance and clear-sightedness toward the often quiet, still barely perceptible beginnings of other civilizations that are emerging in many places already, not just in the Federal Republic of Germany, but in almost all countries of the world.

With this, Jungk [1990: 204-205] was referring to "social inventions and experiments that attempt to educate differently, work differently, live differently, build differently, produce new energy differently, inform differently," and he praised "the divergent, the divulging, the press that describes new ways and methods – from the increasingly numerous alternative city magazines to the *taz.*" For, as he put it, "They bring new trace elements of truth, hope and enthusiasm to the often dry, vitamin-less fare other news agents provide."

2.2. *Development since the 1990s*

A solution-oriented approach first became a topic of the theoretical debate during the "Peace journalism" controversy of the 1990s and 2000s [Hanitzsch 2007]. During this time, the project "Peace Counts" (founded in 2002) was establishing itself by documenting the work of civil conflict managers in crisis zones. In the 1990s, media journalists in the USA observed a boom in solution-oriented journalism: A variety of regional and national newspapers and magazines began offering article series and columns such as "Silver Bullets" or "What Works"; publications and news agencies such as *Hope* magazine or *Yes! A Journal of Positive Futures* were founded [Benesh 1998]. The quarterly magazine *Yes!* proved especially successful: Between 1998 and 2013, the publication reports its subscription numbers had surged from 5.500 to 40.000. The bi-monthly *Solutions Journal*, established in 2010, catered to more refined tastes with a combination of popular and scientific news articles that had been chosen through a peer-selection process.

David Bornstein, who had made a name for himself through his research on microloans and the Grameen Bank of the Bangladeshi Nobel Peace Prize winner Muhammad Yunus, founded the aforementioned Solutions Journalism Network in 2012 as a lobby organization that collected and published "Best Practice" examples from the genre, awarded research grants, offered workshops and presentations and developed higher education curricula. Bornstein is also the founder of the solutions-oriented news portal dowser.org (now takepart.com) and co-author of the blog "Fixes" in the *New York Times* (since 2010). The *Washington Post* started a similar column in 2012 called "The Optimist."

Nevertheless, this scene in the USA remains small and largely separate from the large media concerns. This description applies to other countries, as well – with the exception of Denmark, in which the Executive News Director of the public broadcaster DR, Ulrik Haagerup, has managed to significantly increase the portion of constructive news in the last several years [Haagerup 2014]. Even in Germany, solutions journalism is scarcely present in big media, aside from a couple columns in *Geo* ("Werkstatt Zukunft/Workshop Future") or *National Geographic* ("Das gute Beispiel/The good example" "und Genial gedacht/Bright idea"), a short-lived "Constructive News Offensive" from *Spiegel Online* in August 2015 and the works of a few authors for the weekly *Die Zeit*. The alternative daily *taz* had proven only a temporary home for solutions-oriented journalism: Next to three thematic "good news" editions of 2009/2010, it played a participatory role in the first *Sparknews*-initiated "Impact Journalism Day" (since 2013, *Sparknews* has organized an annual "Impact Journalism Day," in which newspapers from around the world publish an issue with mainly solutions-oriented stories); and a weekly double-page feature called "Progress" was created in April 2013. After one and a half years, however, the section was cancelled due to internal disagreements on the usefulness of constructive news [Krüger and Gassner 2014: 23]. Aside from the established media, many new magazines with a focus on constructive news have appeared since 2010, including the alternative business magazine *Enorm* and *Oya*, a cooperative "culture-creative magazine about alternative thinking and living." There have been solutions-oriented new portals on the Internet since 2010, including visionews.net ("Success stories on peace, environment and gender justice from around the world," published by Ute Scheub), klimaretter.info ("the magazine for climate and energy transition"), perspective-daily.de (with paid content) and the charity-operated futurzwei.org with its "Stories of Success," filed away under the "Future Archive."

In addition to the previously mentioned journalists' office *Sparknews* (Paris, founded 2011 by Christian de Boisredon) and the Organization Reporters d'Espoirs (founded in 2003, likewise by de Boisredon), protagonists in other European countries are the quarterly newspaper *Positive News* in Great Britain, ("the world's first positive newspaper," founded in 1993, circulation of 50,000 copies, with offices in Spain, Hong Kong, Argentina and the US) as well as the web portals De Correspondent (Netherlands, since 2013), noticiaspositivas.net (Spain, since 2002) and mutmacherei.net (Austria, since 2011).

Empirical studies remain lacking for an analytical differentiation of the diversity of the protagonists and publications. A certain divide nevertheless stands out between two ideological factions: On one side are those from the social movements or political left and green alternative scenes, who in Germany are often influenced by Robert Jungk and who search for solutions mainly in the civil grassroots initiatives apart from the political elite, governments and corporations. They question the capitalist system and view themselves as active co-creators of a more or less targeted transition toward a degrowth society or sustainable economy; typical topics of coverage are regional currencies, solidary agriculture, transition towns, decentralized and green energy supply, or repair cafés. They refer to themselves as "change agents" (Ronzheimer) or "midwives for eco-social innovation" (Scheub). They reject an objectivity standard for journalists, considering such a norm unrealistic, ideological or senseless [Krüger and Gassner 2014: 25; von Lüpke in Fleck 2012: 83]; instead, the journalist's professional role should include a sense of advocacy on behalf of lesser known actors with less resources and in favor of certain political goals (in the sense of a fundamental social-economic transformation).

On the other side are journalists like David Bornstein and Christian de Boisredon, who seem unaffiliated with any sociopolitical movement, revere the objectivity standard and view solutions journalism as inherent in the current system. They often first become introduced to the topic through their observation of social entrepreneurship – Muhammad Yunus' microfinance bank proved to be a formative experience for both Bornstein and de Boisredon – and they let themselves be supported by corporations and the super-rich (the Solutions Journalism Network relies, *inter alia*, on funding from the Bill and Melinda Gates Foundation and the Rockefeller Foundation; *Sparknews* was initially established using funds from the French water corporation Veolia Eau). Some are members of the organization Ashoka ("Home of the Changemaker"), which connects social entrepreneurs around the globe and whose supporters include business consultant McKinsey. Christian de Boisredon and Michael Gleich are Ashoka Fellows, Keith Hammonds of Solutions Journalism Network previously worked for Ashoka and Ashoka sponsored a conference on Solutions Journalism in Canada in 2013.

Consequently, the hypothesis could be ventured that the range of protagonists can be divided into a (system-inherent) "Ashoka-faction" and a (system-critical) "Jungk-faction". This would require further examination through protagonist surveys and content analyses of their respective outputs.

3. Supposed Benefits and Opportunities of the Genre

Scouring through the mission statements of relevant organizations in addition to essays, interviews and statements from protagonists reveals three aspects in which constructive news can prove useful:

(1) for the psychological well-being of producers and recipients (i.e., it can have positive effects on the micro level for an individual),

(2) for the economic success of media outlets (i.e., it can have positive effects on the meso level for a media organization) and

(3) for the development of society (i.e., it can have positive effects on a macro level).

3.1. *Micro level: Psychological well-being of journalists and recipients*

Cofounder of the *taz* Ute Scheub [2016: 197] describes her journey toward constructive news or heartening journalism so: "For more than twenty years, I have tried to castigate social wrongs in the *taz*, which inevitably led me to report mostly on bad news. I increasingly noticed how this tendency settled like a black dust on my soul and stripped my soul of its energy. (…) Other journalists I knew well became numb after a while or responded with increased cynicism." Similarly, freelance journalist Geseko von Lüpke says: "When I just look at the sewers or the destruction or the suffering or despair, then I get burnt out myself" [in Fleck 2012: 89]. Today, Ute Scheub prefers to "activate rather than depress" her readers [Krüger and Gassner 2014: 25]. The Solutions Journalism Network points in the same direction and asserts that constructive news "can make listeners feel powerful, less likely to tune out and less apathetic or cynical about the problem."[d]

Empirical evidence for this assertion can be found in various studies. According to a survey [Kuhlmann *et al.* 2014: 16] on "topic apathy", recipients often turned away from media themes when the "topic […] contains problems that are very difficult to solve." An online experiment of 710 English-speaking adults found that when each person was given an example of a classic, negative news story and a positive one, the classic story had a negative effect on the individual's overall emotional appraisal, and that many more positive news stories are likely needed to counter-balance the negative emotional effects of the classic story [Gyldenstedt 2011].

Another experiment from Curry and Hammond [2014: 2] of 755 American adults showed that when presented with articles on three social problems, some with a suggested solution and some without, the readers of the solutions-oriented articles consequently felt more "inspired" and "optimistic". It should be taken into account that the Solution Journalism Network shared joint responsibility for this study as a lobby organization; further independent research would be ideal to substantiate the results.

Medical research provides clues about the corresponding neurophysiological effects: People who witness events portraying an extraordinary level of kindness tend to experience an increase in levels of empathy, trust and empowerment [Zak 2012] through the release of the "love hormone" oxytocin. It remains to be verified, however, whether this effect also applies to being witness to events that are relayed through the media.

---

[d]http://solutionsjournalism.org/about/why-solutions-journalism/

3.2. *Meso level: Economic success of media outlets*

Constructive news also appear to offer certain benefits and opportunities for media companies to improve their potential economic prosperity. The *taz* has experienced success in this area using three solutions-oriented special editions in the years 2009 and 2010: Two of the three issues sold 5-10 per cent more copies at newsstands than the average, and the first was even the most-sold issue of the *taz* of the year [Krüger and Gassner 2014: 23]. Similarly, the French daily *Libération* achieved its top seller of the year 2012 with the special issue "Le Libé des solutions", inspired by *Sparknews* founder Christian de Boisredon [Krüger and Gassner 2014: 22].

The CEO of the Solution Journalism Network, David Bornstein, points to the successes of the *Deseret News*, a regional newspaper in Utah, with a higher percentage of solution-oriented coverage as a result of the Network's consultancy work. He provides evidence for this with a self-commissioned case study: Accordingly, solutions-oriented stories resulted in more pageviews for the *Deseret News* website and a higher distribution on Facebook and Twitter than problems-oriented stories [Noack *et al.* 2013: 8]. A study of the online distribution of *New York Times* articles lends additional corroboration for this phenomenon in showing that positive articles were more widely distributed than negative [Berger and Milkman 2011]. However, the relationship between the evoked emotions and distribution behavior proved to be more complex. For instance, content that was able to evoke strong emotional responses was more likely to go viral whether the response was positive (such as awe) or negative (anger or fear).

Ultimately, the success of the media depends at least partly on its image among recipients. Thirty years ago, Haskins and Miller [1984] had already found a positive correlation between good news and image. In an experiment, the two varied the portion of negative and positive news reports in a newspaper and asked participants to then give their opinions. The result: Newspapers with more "good news" received more positive assessments and were seen as more objective and more useful to society. In light of the current skepticism and distrust that plagues the media in Germany [Krüger 2016] as well as in other countries [Ladd 2012], in addition to constant accusations from users that media coverage is not objective enough, it seems solutions-oriented journalism may offer a way to correct this impression. On an additional note: The experiment also showed that, when the portion of good news in a newspaper increased, so too did participants' willingness to pay for a subscription.

3.3. *Macro level: Social progress*

Many of the involved parties stress the social benefits aspect of constructive news. Well-researched reports of successful – or failed – projects might serve as a guide for others. "People must learn about credible examples of responses to problems in order to become empowered, discerning actors capable of shaping a better society." Harald Welzer, a German researcher in social psychology and director of the non-profit foundation Futurzwei, said this about the organization's collection of "Stories of Success": "For us, it's about portraits of 'the first mover,' or, to use more traditional terms, it's about role models. One can imitate them" [Grefe and Thadden 2012].

Likewise, science journalist Manfred Ronzheimer echoes this sentiment about the social importance of transformational journalism: "In this way, the transformation journalist becomes a social service provider, a journalistic agent of change for the Major Transformation, instead of a paid hack for a profit-oriented commercial media system" [Ronzheimer 2013: 123]. Freelance journalist Geseko von Lüpke sees in this his responsibility "to serve as a death-bed escort for a ruined system and as a midwife for a new culture." His goal is to "identify the 'islands of the future'" that have formed in the global civil society and to network them [Fleck 2012: 89-90].

These are the rationales the scene's primary actors provide, and which could theoretically be further expounded upon. A social evolution theory, as sociologist and philosopher Jürgen Habermas outlined in the 1970s, may lend itself to the task. Coming from Luhmann's theory of social systems, Habermas claimed that individual learning processes precede social development "so that social systems, as soon as their structurally limited steering capacity is overburdened with inevitable problems, are able to fall back on a surplus of individual [...] learning capacities and utilize them for the institutionalization of new levels of learning" [Habermas 1976: 136].

In this way, an avant-garde of individuals learns a skill first, and then the society learns from them ("to raise the steering capacity to another level") [Habermas 1976: 133]. Habermas neglects to answer the question, however, of *how* the knowledge, ideas or skills of these pioneers spread in society. In archaic cultures this was doubtless achieved through word-of-mouth communication or visual inspection; in modern cultures it is presumably mostly via the media – through constructive news, for instance (Fig. 1).

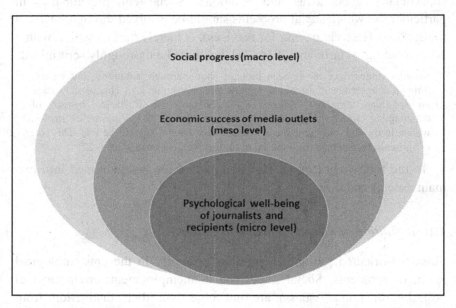

Fig. 1. An "onion model" of the Genre's supposed opportunities (source: author)

4. Critical Reflection: Problems and Risks of the Genre

Having previously described the benefits and opportunities associated with the genre, it remains to take a critical stance. One common critique of Solutions Journalism is its seemingly natural proximity to public relations (PR) and lobbying: "Dealing in solutions also tends to move the journalist from informer to advocate, which is tricky territory" [Stray 2012]. On the other hand, such closeness is not inevitable; instead, it depends on the individual journalists' understanding of their role and the quality of their work (see section on journalistic quality and PR).

The strongest criticism of Solutions Journalism to date comes from Kathrin Hartmann, a German freelance journalist and author who has conducted her own research on fighting poverty through micro-financing and developed a much more skeptical stance than Bornstein and de Boisredon. She claims that constructive news tends to mask the complex causes that often underlie social injustices and advocate for only superficially good ideas and solutions. Social entrepreneurship, in particular, by which social problems should be resolved through business transactions (i.e., via paying for services), is merely "privatization with a social coating" [Hartmann 2014: 26] that must be thoroughly scrutinized:

> Social changes have never been brought about through 'solutions', but instead through enlightenment, discourse, protests and opposition. [...] This concentration on solutions ultimately follows the neoliberal maxim 'tackle instead of complaining' and turns the idea of saving the world into a mosaic of stories, which, in the end, only give the appearance that everything will be fine. This sort of anti-enlightenment is the opposite of journalism. [Hartmann, 2014, 27]

In the following section, Hartmann's critique is subdivided into two main aspects and discussed.

4.1. *Definition of the problem and its causes*

Solutions-oriented journalism presides primarily in the epistemological realm of problems. Social issues (be it unemployment, environmental pollution or homelessness) are not objective; their distinction from complex contextual occurrences is a matter of perception and interpretation. People identify and define problems under the influence of their values and attitudes, basic assumptions, experiences and interests. Social problems, therefore, are constructs resulting from negotiation processes in society. Since these defined problems or complexes of problems never have only one cause but are instead multi-causal, the suggested solutions themselves cannot be uncontroversial [Stray 2012]. Rosen [2012] phrases it so: "It is hard to say what the problem is, to define it clearly or to tell where it stops and starts. There is no 'right' way to view the problem, no definitive formulation. The way it's framed will change what the solution appears to be." Indeed, the concept of "frames" is useful to get the point. Frames are interpretive patterns in which people focus their attention on a certain aspect of the often confusing reality and thereby reduce its complexity. According to the classical definition provided by Entman [1993], frames consist of four elements: problem definition, causal interpretation, moral evaluation and treatment recommendation. It follows, then, that the suggested solutions or treatment recommendations depend on how one defines the problem and which causes or responsibilities one attributes to it.

This is where a portion of Hartmann's critique resides. The more narrowly a topic is framed and the fewer the causes that can be attributed to it, the easier it is to present an idea or an initiative as a solution. Hartmann [2014: 27] gives a negative example of a story about the project water.org, sponsored by the food and drink corporation PepsiCo, intended to motivate people in poor countries to invest in their own water supply and sanitation via micro-financing – an intrinsically capitalist solution that promotes the privatization of water and negates the agreement between all UN member states that clean drinking water and sanitation accommodations are a basic human right and thus should be guaranteed by the government. In general, it appears a large number of the Best Practice examples on the Solutions Journalism Network website highlight projects that fight the consequences of poverty (e.g., an NGO helps youth from poor families apply to college) without addressing the poverty problem as a political task. The implication here is that it is the responsibility of the individual to escape from poverty.

This form of solutions journalism stands, in the words of Downs [1972: 39], in "the great American tradition of optimistically viewing most obstacles to social progress as *external* to the structure of society itself. The implication is that every obstacle can be eliminated and every problem solved *without any fundamental reordering of society itself,* if only we devote sufficient effort to it" [italics in original]. Ultimately, Hartmann's criticism asks if constructive news blend out the systemic causes of problems, thereby excluding suggested solutions that are critical of the system and putting forth merely a (system-innate) doctoring of symptoms in the guise of solutions.

4.2. *Journalistic quality and the border to PR*

A second aspect of Hartmann's critique can be categorized under the term "journalistic quality" and the distinction to PR.

The quality of journalism is defined differently among communication scientists [Beck *et al.* 2010: 16ff.]. With the integrative approach from Arnold [2009] there has in the meantime been a catalogue of various quality criteria established, including diversity, balance, relevance, credibility, independence, research, criticism and neutrality. The Solutions Journalism Network stresses that it is not about advertising for protagonists or suggested solutions (as heroes, wonder weapons or silver bullets); important instead are thorough non-partisan research, source diversity, evidence and data.

Hartmann [2014: 27] refers to Bornstein's interactions with Muhammad Yunus and micro-financing as a negative example, criticizing that "to date there has not been a single serious study that verifies the poverty-reducing effect", instead pointing to many victims of micro-financing that have fallen deeper into poverty. According to Hartmann, Bornstein only mentions critical studies "at most as an afterthought."

Exactly how the topic of micro-financing should be appraised cannot be determined here, though it can be asserted that Hartmann's critique does not delegitimize or discredit the idea of constructive news. Rather, it addresses the subject on the level of "journalistic quality", for an impartial investigation on micro-financing as a possible solution to the problem of poverty must adequately include critical studies. In the case of microloans having primarily detrimental effects on the borrower, these results should be unsparingly represented. It would not be so much a form of "good news", then, but enlightening solutions journalism, and the next generation of those struggling against poverty could take the results into account.

Ideally, over the course of this process – activists attempt to solve a problem, accompanied by critical solutions journalists – one would simultaneously probe the possible systemic causes of the respective problems (some of which may indeed only be overcome through protest and opposition).

What if, however, there are no critics for certain projects or innovations? Reiner Metzger, Vice-Chief Editor of the *taz*, envisions this problem: "A journalist travels to Afghanistan to the minesweeper, and everyone thinks the project is super. There is no test to verify the percentage of mines that are cleared" [Krüger and Gassner 2014: 25]. "And how is one supposed to criticize the organizations that operate village markets and shops in tiny communities, where people still meet in these times of supermarkets and scattered work opportunities?" [Metzger 2014]. One possible answer is to engage with the project more extensively than usual and to accompany the protagonists and involved parties for a longer time period. Such prolonged documentation produces real benefits for the recipients, since they are better able to grasp the way a certain solutions approach operates and can be less reliant on statements from activists and involved parties.

5. Conclusion

"But where the danger is, the saving powers also grow", as a saying from German lyric poet Friedrich Hölderlin goes – and where permanent crises are, at least there grows also the desire of many journalists and recipients to find solutions, perhaps even redemption through journalism. It may be significant that the term "Solutions Journalism" first appeared [Benesh 1998] during the world-political turn of eras in 1989/90 and that now – a time in which financial depressions, the Syria and Ukraine crises, refugee catastrophes, terrorism, climate change and soil degradation have all become disheartening, permanent companions – more and more journalists and media, even if largely separate from the big publishing houses and broadcasting stations, are interested in setting their sights on a better future.

There is an apparent division between the two factions of solution-oriented journalists: on the one hand, the actors from the social movements, who consider fundamental changes in the social and economic system as necessary, want to support corresponding grassroots initiatives and have abdicated the classical journalistic ideal of objectivity; on the other, the friends of social entrepreneurship, who have in principle no objections to capitalism and no qualms about having governments or corporations as solutions-providers or sponsors. This preliminary classification remains to be empirically examined, revised and supplemented.

Constructive news does not necessarily have to do with "good news" – a thorough investigation on the effects of certain solution approaches and program could come to an exceedingly negative conclusion and would nevertheless be more useful to society than a story that is purely PR, one that barely scratches the surface and whose primary goal is to give recipients a temporary feeling of well-being. In this way, it is prudent to discuss the quality of the currently observable mix of Solutions Journalism and "good news," in order to differentiate between socially valuable reporting on solutions and the misleading, misinformative well-being coverage. Undoubtedly, today's practice cannot be the distribution of unverified press releases from UN relief agencies anymore, as Robert Jungk once did, since meanwhile even these organizations have strong interests in their respective markets.

It would be sensible to create a code of ethics for solutions-oriented journalism. This could build upon the initiative "Media Doctor Environment" from the Technical University of Dortmund, which has compiled criteria for good environmental journalism. As the initiative appropriately asserts: "The article should not propagate seeming solutions that are not effective against the elimination or avoidance of environmental problems, but serve advertisement more than the environment."[e]

References

Arnold, K. (2009). Qualitätsjournalismus, *Die Zeitung und ihr Publikum*, Konstanz
Beck, K., Reineck, D., and Schubert, C. (2010). *Journalistische Qualität in der Wirtschaftskrise*. Konstanz

---

[e]http://www.medien-doktor.de/umwelt/bewertungen/die-kriterien/

Beiler, M. (2013). *Nachrichtensuche im Internet. Inhaltsanalyse zur journalistischen Qualität von Nachrichtensuchmaschinen,* Konstanz

Benesh, S. (1998). The rise of solutions journalism, in: *Columbia Journalism Review,* March/April, 36-39, http://www.sequilibre.com/herramientas/CJR%20-%20The%20Rise%20of%20Solutions%20Journalism,%20by%20Susan%20Benesh.htm

Benking, H. (2013). The origins of spreading good examples. http://benking.de/futures/sOrigins_Spreading_GoodExamples-new-May-2013.html

Berger, J., and Milkman, K. L. (2012). What makes online content viral? *Journal of Marketing Research,* 49(2), 192-205

Curry, A. L. and Hammons, K. H. (2014). The power of solutions journalism. Engaging News Project and Solutions Journalism Network. http://engagingnewsproject.org/enp_2014/wp-content/uploads/2014/06/ ENP_SJN-report.pdf

Downs, A. (1972). Up and down with ecology - the "issue-attention cycle.", *Public Interest,* 28(summer), 38-50

Eickelkamp, A. (2011). *Der Nutzwertjournalismus. Herkunft, Funktionalität und Praxis eines Journalismustyps,* Cologne

Entman, R. (1993). Framing. Toward clarification of a fractured paradigm, *Journal of Communication,* 43(4), 51-58

Fleck, D. C. (2012). *Die vierte Macht. Spitzenjournalisten zu ihrer Verantwortung in Krisenzeiten,* Hamburg

Galtung, J. (1998). Friedensjournalismus: Was, warum, wer, wie, wann, wo? in: Kempf, W., and Schmidt-Regener, I. (eds.), *Krieg, Nationalismus, Rassismus und die Medien,* Muenster, 3-20

Grefe, C. and Thadden, E. (2012). Stiftung Futurzwei: Wir sind nicht nett, *Die Zeit,* No. 4, 20.1., http://www.zeit.de/2012/04/Harald-Welzer

Gyldensted, C. (2011). *Innovating news journalism through positive psychology.* University of Pennsylvania. http://repository.upenn.edu/cgi/viewcontent.cgi?article=1024&context=mapp_capstone

Haagerup, U. (2014). *Constructive news. Why negativity destroys the media and democracy – and how to improve journalism of tomorrow,* Rapperswil

Habermas, J. (1976). *Zur Rekonstruktion des Historischen Materialismus,* Frankfurt on Main

Hanitzsch, T. (2007). Situating peace journalism in journalism studies: A critical appraisal, *Conflict and Communication Online,* 6(2), http://www.cco.regener-online.de/2007_2/pdf/hanitzsch.pdf

Hartmann, K. (2014). Erlösungsjournalismus, *Message,* 16(1), 26-27, http://www.message-online.com/archiv/message-1-2014/leseproben/erloesungsjournalismus/

Haskins, J. B. and Miller, M. M. (1984). The Effects of Bad News and Good News on a Newspaper's Image, *Journalism Quarterly,* 61(1), 3-13

Jungk, R. (1993). *Trotzdem. Mein Leben für die Zukunft.* Munich

Jungk, R. (1990). *Zukunft zwischen Angst und Hoffnung. Ein Plädoyer für die politische Phantasie.* Munich

Krüger, U., and Gassner, N. (2014). Abschied von den Bad News, *Message*, 16(1), 20-25, http://www.message-online.com/wp-content/uploads/SoJ. pdf

Krüger, U. (2016). *Mainstream. Warum wir den Medien nicht mehr trauen.* Munich

Kuhlmann, C., Schumann, C., and Wolling, J. (2014). "Ich will davon nichts mehr sehen und hören!" Exploration des Phänomens Themenverdrossenheit. In *Medien & Kommunikationswissenschaft*, 62(1), 5-24

Ladd, J. M. (2012). *Why Americans hate the media and how it matters*, University Press, Princeton

LaRoche, W., von Hooffacker, G., and Meier, K. (2013). *Einführung in den praktischen Journalismus. Mit genauer Beschreibung aller Ausbildungswege Deutschland, Österreich,* Schweiz, New edition, Wiesbaden

Metzger, R. (2014). In eigener Sache, *taz* from 10.4/5.2014, 12

Noack, M., Orth, J., Owen, B., and Rennick, S. (2013). A transformational journey. Adopting solutions journalism at Utah's Deseret News. http://solutionsjournalism. org/wp-content/uploads/2013/11/Deseret-News-Case-Study.pdf

Prinzing, M. (2010). The project Peace Counts – a promoter of real change or mere idealism? In: Keeble, R., Tulloch, J., and Zollmann, F. (eds.), *Journalism, War and Conflict Resolution*, Oxford, 257-269

Ronzheimer, M. (2013). Vom Nullthema in den Mainstream. Die Rolle der Medien in der Transformation, *Politische Ökologie*, 133 ("Baustelle Zukunft. Die Große Transformation von Wirtschaft und Gesellschaft"), 118-123

Rosen, J. (2012). Covering Wicked Problems, Keynote address to the 2nd UK Conference of Science Journalists, June 25 at The Royal Society, London. http:// pressthink.org/2012/06/covering-wicked-problems/

Stack, M. (2008). Media and Schools, in: Mathison, S., and Ross, E. W. (eds.), *Battleground: Schools.* Vol. 1: A-K, 400-406, Westport

Scheub, U. (2015). Medien sollen Hoffnung machen! Positive statt negative Schlagzeilen. In: Kreibich, R. & Lietsch, F. (eds.). Zukunft gewinnen! Die sanfte (R)evolution für das 21. Jahrhundert – inspiriert vom Visionär Robert Jungk. München, 196-198

Schulz, W. (1976). Die Konstruktion von Realität in den Nachrichtenmedien, *Analyse der aktuellen Berichterstattung*, Freiburg und Munich

Staab, J. F. (1990). *Nachrichtenwert-Theorie. Formale Struktur und empirischer Gehalt,* Freiburg and Munich

Stray, J. (2012). The hard part of solution journalism is agreeing on the problems. Blog entry from 05.15.2012. http://jonathanstray.com/the-hard-part-of-solution-journalism-is-agreeing-on-the-problems

Zak, P. J. (2012). *The moral molecule: The source of love and prosperity*, Boston

Chapter 23

Media and Information Technology
in Ten Years' Time:
A Society of Control Both from Above and Below,
and from Outside and Inside

Jörg Becker

Institut für Politikwissenschaft, Philipps Universität Marburg, Germany

Every technology has two immanent functions: rationalisation and control.

In the turbo-capitalism of an information economy IT and the mass media control people a) from above, in an authoritarian way (class struggle and social hierarchy), b) from below, in an internalised way (participation as a join-in trap), c) from within (psychological self-colonisation) and from without (voluntariness and flexibility as necessary turbo-capitalist virtues).

1. Introduction

Theodor W. Adorno, Max Horkheimer and George Orwell, all of them politically well reputed left-wing intellectuals each with his very own independent intellectual edifice, came to the same conclusions at the same time about German Fascism. The philosophical fragment *Dialectic of Enlightenment* of 1944 [Adorno 2002], the novel *Animal Farm* of 1945 [Orwell 1946] and the novel *Nineteen Eighty-Four* of 1949 [Orwell 1949] – all deal with the same theme, namely, the totalitarian surveillance state from which there is no escape, in which those rebelling against the reign of violence, once they have been successful in their rebellion, impose a more brutal rule than their predecessors, in which the Ministry of Truth monitors the past, a state-imposed newspeak replaces everyday language, and the War Ministry is renamed the Peace Ministry.

Here human barbarianism seems to be the civilisational consequence of an enlightenment that is always understood merely instrumentally.

But reality still always provides the best satires. Since Edward Snowden's revelations about the all-embracing surveillance practices by the NSA of all global electronic communications, democracy has ceased to exist. When there is no longer a case-by-case review, when anticipation replaces the legal judgement of an established criminal act, when there is no longer an assumption of innocence, when no communicative private sphere exists anymore and when courts decide in secret and without the possibility of appeal, then the state based on the rule of law is dead. To use the term surveillance democracy is to already play it down somewhat.

2. Above and Below

For about the past 150 years of industrial capitalism, it has been a societal inevitability of the development of productive forces that new technologies can no longer be differentiated according to a good or bad use of them. Günther Anders realised this as early as 1956, when he remarked about television that, "No means is only a means" [Anders 1980: 99]. A new technology is no longer neutral, when being already subject to the patterns of profit maximisation and instrumental exploitation in the process of their genesis. It always comes from above and is always used to stabilise power. Things were different once upon a time, and Johannes Gutenberg is a good example of this.

His invention around 1450 of moving letters for printing books was not only technically innovative, but, above all, socially innovative. It was an invention by the urban bourgeoisie in its struggle against church and aristocracy. Through the dissemination of the Bible in book form and through Martin Luther's translation of the Bible into German in 1520, these two bourgeois revolutionaries robbed church and aristocracy of their written, Latin monopoly over knowledge, and with that, of their hegemony over the interpretation of God and the world. It was a successful struggle from below against above by means of a new communication technology. Things have changed since.

When German radio broadcasting was born in 1923, it was state, centralist and liable to charges – it went hand in hand with the prohibition to produce radio broadcasts by private people, especially against the Rote Funker movement; it was also a restriction of the technical features of their terminal devices. And the step from an Internet previously subsidised by the state and the military to a public infrastructure in 1994 ran parallel to the criminalisation of hackers, who only shortly before that had been lauded as computer pioneers.

Nothing is more suitable for illustrating the concept of state control of the social behaviour of its citizens than the history and organisation of television. German television was born as state television twice. First, on the occasion of the Fascist Olympic Games in Berlin in 1936, and again in 1952. It was kept firmly in the hands initially of the state and then of public administration until all the TV infrastructures – i.e., transmission, distribution, social conditioning an adaptation into the everyday life of the viewers – were so well developed that in 1984 they could be given over to private companies to maximise their profits without those company having to pay a single cent for the thirty years of advance payments of public money.

Moreover, an apparently only technical aspect is of decisive importance for the birth of German television in 1952. It would have been possible at that point in time, and in purely technical terms, to opt for a technical implementation of Bertolt Brecht's political theory of radio in 1927/1932, namely, as a two-way medium [Brecht 1967]. It would have been technically possible in 1952 to develop the new medium of television not as a network with one broadcaster and many receivers, but as a network with a feedback channel allowing recipients to participate technically. Needless to say, such a concept could not appeal to the politically strong control concept of a centralised Adenauer state, which disseminated propaganda from above to below only, and had plans for both a new propaganda ministry and state television.

Since the privatisation of the German television landscape, in which, with a certain time lag, the public TV stations have adapted to the programming of private TV stations, television can be defined as the sell-off of different target groups to the advertising industry. In this sales process, programme content is just the free lunch. And as the consumer goods industry transfers its advertising costs to the consumer products, the user thus pays indirectly a TV charge for the programmes of the private TV stations. So this economic model approximates to a licence to print money both for the private TV stations and for the consumer goods industry.

In the early 21st century, socialisation in the industrial countries means above all media socialisation. The mass media, as socialisation agencies, make an essential contribution to the fact that during their social learning processes the members of society can fulfil all sorts of social norms and role expectations. Integration is a concept that can scarcely be separated from socialisation. The mass media are the most important agencies for an integration of social communication. Here the "entertaining" free lunch of television takes first place – in Germany at an average of four hours of broadcasting time per day in 2014. Given the average life expectancy of 80 years in Germany, this corresponds to about ten years of life consuming TV 24 hours a day.

The social control exerted by television is precarious in many ways. On the one hand, a socialisation shift form primary experiences to secondary, meaning media, experiences, promotes an increase in alienation. On the other hand, the content of media programming turns out to be ethically questionable and dysfunctional as regards a democratic public domain. As early as 1980, the so-called father of Latin American communication research, Luis Ramiro Beltrán, in his book *Comunicación Dominada* [Beltrán 1980] outlined the following twelve elements as the basic norms in what TV offered in most countries: individualism, elitism, racism, materialism, adventurism, conservatism, conformism, defeatism, belief in fate, fixation on authority, romanticism and aggression. Sexism is surely a further element that can and has to be added to these.

The great increase in TV channels since the early 1980s due to cable and satellite television has led to an intensification of these thirteen basic media offers, but not to a pluralisation of content and opinion. In that period of time the number of TV channels in Germany increased from two public channels to meantime 150 private television stations. And a sobering experience is that the increase in the number of TV channels has not led to a richer content, but to a multiplication of the same. Noam

Chomsky coined a linguistically apt and catchy term for the social function of television in the title of his book and film *Manufacturing Consent* (1988/1992) and in the concept of *consent without consent* [Chomsky 1996] which he took over from the English sociologist Anthony Giddens.

Information control is particularly difficult to define when it takes place with the apparent agreement of those being controlled. It is here precisely that the idea of the control society that Gilles Deleuze outlined in his book *Pourparlers* [Deleuze 1990] comes into play: those being controlled feel well under that control; they enjoy and internalise it. In the field of television, this internalised control can be seen clearly in the series Big Brother, which started in the Netherlands in 1999. In that series, for 24 hours 24 cameras registered the life of so-called volunteers in a closed apartment. At regular intervals the viewing public – by means of a telephone ballot and the Internet – forced one of the participants to leave the apartment, to end the game. Do the TV viewers control the game? What is the difference between players and viewers? Which of them is more cynical?

If up until the 1980s a social control by the mass media was a result, impact and function of desired political action by state and government, this was put an end to by the de-regulation of the mass media under the banner of neo-liberalism. The policy of de-regulation was, and still is, a self-decapitation of politics, a transfer of the mass media to the exclusive social control of the market.

The favourite argument that these deliberations are inadmissibly generalised, given that there is the one or other good TV programme, overlooks two things. One, the exception still proves the general rule. Two, this argument fails to understand the role which culture has played for some time now for turbo-capitalism. In his book *The Transformation of Democracy* [1967] Johannes Agnoli was able to clearly outline and analyse the fact that culture, especially where it is critical of the system, is only granted a playground because its critique is merely a cultural one, with no economic dimension. Where there is no systemic critique of turbo-capitalism, a repressive tolerance will allow many a critical cabaret show, many a politically cheeky song and many a *Heute Show*.

3. Outside and Inside

In view of the triple technological convergence of information technology with telecommunication and television, which, as a troika, have long since overtaken the automobile and chemical industries as a driving force in the economy, Gilles Deleuze's concept of the control society applies in two ways. Control from below and from within takes place more through mass television; control from above and from without more through IT technologies.

The control of information by military and intelligence services is anything but a new phenomenon. In this context, the reason Oliver Cromwell gave for a state monopoly in 1657 is notorious: "The postal service will be one of the best means of uncovering and resisting dangerous and despicable attacks against the commonwealth" (quoted after Becker 1989: 17). In other words, and drawing attention to the dialectics of freedom and force: the state promotes free communication so as to be better able to control it.

Since the NSA scandal, we know that current IT technologies have brought with them an incredible qualitative increase, particularly in the field of information control (which, by the way, few social scientists would have considered possible). The following is a list of just ten remarkable facts, connections and processes, which affect all policies to do with work, everyday life and capital:

- It is common knowledge, meantime, that the NSA controls the whole of telephone and the whole of Internet communication worldwide (both connection data and content). Currently, in Utah, the NSA is building the world's largest data centre for storing a quadrillion text pages so as to be able to register and store global electronic communication of a period of 100 years. Moreover, the NSA is working on a so-called quantum computer that can decipher all encryptions. The Federal German Intelligence Service, BND, cooperates with the NSA at different levels.
- In the high frequency trading done on the financial markets, just a few milliseconds, sometimes even nanoseconds, decide on the financial success or failure of a money transaction. The international finance market is thus out of control.

- In the future Industry 4.0, the so-called internet of things, information processing is already indispensable, resulting in a total tracking, i.e., a trail tracking of all movements, actions and services. This automated wave of industrialisation will drastically increase both the structural unemployment that already exists, as well as the productivity growth and the profits of enterprises. And 3D printings will confront us with changes in productivity and security, the impacts of which we can scarcely oversee due to their complexity.

- Wi-Vi, a radio device developed by the Massachusetts Institute of Technology, can observe through walls.

- The American chain of shops called Macy's with a special technology can recognise each client entering the shop by means of a corresponding App on his or her smart phone; it can follow that client around and link what it records with his or her user Internet behaviour. Marketing specialists call this consumer DNA.

- Supermarkets that use cameras with a software developed by the Denmans company can not only observe their clients, but also assess how they are thinking and feeling with seven so-called primary emotions: anger, derision, repulsion, anxiety, joy, sadness and surprise.

- By linking communication data with biometric data for face recognition, the state has the possibility of surveying its complete population.

- So that home appliances can communicate with one another and new markets be tapped thanks to the usage data gained, Google has bought up companies that produce smoke alarms and thermostats.

- By means of speech-commands, Amazon can enable its loudspeakers installed in private apartments to record all conversations taking place in those apartments.

- Amazon has taken out a patent on an algorithm that sends a package before anyone has ordered it. Linking the usage data of Amazon clients is heading, according to Amazon, in the direction of what it calls anticipatory dispatch.

These are just a few examples, but their social message is the same everywhere: legal concepts such as the right to informational self-determination guaranteed by the constitution, data protection, a private and intimate sphere, will become historical residual categories in a global neoliberal economy with less and less regulated free spaces for doing whatever. And anyone who thought the NSA scandal was a welcome occasion for making international relations more transparent and democratic was mistaken in many ways.

Firstly, digital capitalism illustrates the existing, still unchecked global dominance of the US. Not only did Henry Kissinger, on a secret visit to China in 1970, agree with Deng Xiaoping on the construction of two US communications intercept stations in the Chinese province of Xinjiang which were active up until the 1990s – to give just one scarcely known example of the range of US American supremacy – US American Internet giants like Google, Microsoft, Amazon, Apple, IBM, General Electric or Cisco dominate the global cyber world.

What is more, the network supplier Cisco is another highly interesting example of the intricate and contradictory US-Chinese cyber-relations. While the US State Department, in its ritualised annual report on the state of human rights, laments the violation of those human rights in the Chinese Internet, the US Cisco company sells the Chinese government the filter software for monitoring the political content on the Chinese Internet (with the cognizance of the US American secret services, needless to say).

Secondly, the NSA scandal is a welcome occasion for the Europeans, and especially the Germans, to expand their own digital infrastructure for eavesdropping, intercepting and controlling. Currently a gigantic dynamism can be observed in the apparently competitive world between the USA and the EU. To put it cynically: the German Intelligence Service or BND is benefitting from Edward Snowden's revelations.

Thirdly and finally, the NSA scandal is also an occasion for serious concern, even resignation in that no treaty could successfully prompt the USA to end its global cyber controls through the NSA, for the simple reason that apart from the USA no other country would be technically in a position to be able to verify such an American termination of activities.

It is possible, however that these forms of external control are much less drastic in their social consequences than the different forms of self- and internal control. I would just like to list three of these:

- The structure and organisation of social media such as Facebook are characterised by the fact that they seem to rely on the voluntariness of their users. Like the lovemark philosophy of the Saatchi & Saatchi advertising agency or the smiley philosophy of the US American advertising graphic artist Harvey Ball in the 1960s, here too it is a question of the maximum number of "followers" and "likes". Facebook users, deeply rooted in the so-called Californian ideology (a hippies' concept of freedom plus the high-tech industry's capital interests), voluntarily and continually disseminate hundreds of private and intimate data about their person throughout the digital universe. They are not worried by the fact that these data form the basis of digital marketing and control strategies of Facebook. However, refusal strategies towards Facebook come to nothing. The global attractiveness of Facebook is already so strong that a digital public sphere is only possible by participating in it. It goes without saying that the public sphere of Facebook differs from that of Jürgen Habermas [Habermas 2008]. It is a private commercial public domain that functions according to the General Terms of Trade of the market-monopolist Facebook.

- Equally complicated is the "voluntariness" of the digital dissemination of health data by medical insurance companies. A user – the insurance branch calls him or her a self-optimiser – "voluntarily" measures his pulse with a body sensor, the number of steps taken daily, and other sporting activities. If he or she "voluntarily" transfers theses health data to their medical insurance company, they are rewarded with a bonus and various prizes. In possession of these data, the insurance company can draw up individualised contribution strategies, thereby minimizing their costs and maximizing their profits. With these individualisation strategies, the insurance companies are destroying the solidarity principle of the insurance industry that has existed for a good 180 years.

- The fashion for selfies and the concomitant selfie-sticks is much more than a fashion given that every fashion is embedded in the economic and social environment that give rise to it. Selfies reflect the typical narcissism of a helpless and aggrieved generation of young people who, in the world of the current turbo-capitalism, are both uprooted and can also be flexibly deployed in any work place throughout the global economy. Narcissism here is not a morally condemned self-love orientated around the bourgeois norm of heterosexuality, but the expression of neoliberal isolation.

A larger framework is required to interpret such "voluntariness". And in the old Marxist tradition it must be established first and foremost that the principle of voluntariness does not apply in a capitalist market because it presupposes the structural equality of possession of the means of production and human work. That would be nonsense, and has never applied! Furthermore, from a pragmatic perspective, the structural unemployment that has existed for some times now rarely facilitates an everyday freedom to choose between several available jobs.

The reference to the Californian ideology is still useful here, as it involves an individualised hedonistic and apolitical concept of freedom that recognises no social feedback or social responsibility. To put it more drastically: this kind of "voluntariness" demands and promotes an atomised Ego that has to hire itself out as a sole entrepreneur on neoliberal digital markets, needless to say, without a working contract, a tax card, a legal old-age pension insurance, without trade unions and without a works' council. In the boundlessness of the global digital market, "voluntariness" and "flexibility" – once very important and politically positive primary virtues in the social-democratic welfare state – have degenerated into a necessary commodity, to purely instrumental secondary virtues, without which no one can earn any money. Flexibility has meanwhile become the most important cultural asset in the current formation of capitalism – as US-American sociologist Richard Sennett realised as early as 1998 [Sennett].

If in the following the terms work and difference draw attention to moments of resistance to the control processes described, then this is done with recourse to Theodor W. Adorno. The term work is used in Adorno's sense because of the subject-object dialectics. And as the possibility of individualisation in the non-identical is to be assumed, again with Adorno, there exists a dimension by itself, namely, that of difference and of diversity as a principle of socialisation. And, this time contrary to Adorno, who thought and argued in a hopelessly euro-centric way, this principle of a difference applies all the more against the backdrop of intercultural philosophies and of encounters with the cultures of Latin America, Africa and Asia.

4. Work

Since the mid-1990s, social science has repeatedly failed when it came to analysing the organisation and structure of the global electronic digital network. In social sciences and in the uncritical publications that accompanied it, we meet those empty slogans about the infinite freedom of communication, the boundlessness of the exchange of ideas, unrestricted access to the whole body of humanity's knowledge and the hymn to clean, low-energy, purely ideal productive force, in keeping with the naïve motto: knowledge is the petroleum of our day! Only recently have colleagues been speaking, with total conviction and even seriously, about the "dematerialisation" of the media economy!

Such analyses are superficial, false, and highly ideological because they disregard the concrete working conditions of many millions of people employed worldwide in the production, dissemination and disposal of IT products and services. And these people have to organise themselves very traditionally in trade unions in order to improve their working conditions.

The mine workers in Zambia come to mind, who toil under unbearable conditions mining the cobalt required for each and every PC, and of the people living close to those mines, who have to endure the effects of the polluted soil and drinking water.

Then there are the thousands and thousands of women who, in some customs-free zones in some developing countries, produce computer chips in factories where the guidelines on the handling of poisonous solvents are not adhered to so that those women are exposed to a greater danger of cancer and a higher risk of miscarriages.

Not to be forgotten is the horrifically, indeed repulsively high suicide rates in the Foxconn company in Shenzhen in 2010, because the workers producing iPods for Apple were unable to bear the inhuman working conditions any longer.

One must also think of the children on the huge rubbish tips near Accra in Ghana, or near Manila on the Philippines, who have to make a living by gathering and sorting European and American computer refuse, work that again seriously damages the health of those people because of the lead-polluted soil.

A fifth case are the many millions of women worldwide whose secretarial jobs were rationalised away as a result of the enormous impetus of PCs and digital networking. Now as outsourced electronic homeworkers such women are caught between bringing up children and a badly paid job at their private computer, with only a special-order contract and not a working contract, totally isolated socially, with neither colleagues nor a works' council.

Finally, mention should be made the slave-like working conditions in the warehouses of Amazon, a concern that has been aggressively hostile towards trade unions since it was founded in 1994. At Amazon, on the basis of a false pay agreement with groups of wage squeezers, commodities are ordered in freezing-cold warehouses, and the intellectual world of books shatters on the rocks of non-intellectual, dull sorting process done in piecework. While the Amazon employees in Germany are slowly organising themselves in trade unions, the company is already building new warehouses in Poland with even worse working conditions and even lower pay.

So that is the material basis, the concrete side of our glittering digital world! And now as then in what are in principle well-known social emergency situations and struggles, it is all about class struggle, solidarity, self-organisation, self- and co-determination, trade union and works council work, because that is the only way of ensuring a good and humane life beyond a totally neoliberal controlling state. Whereas reflection on the category of work necessarily leads to reflection on future alternatives, it is not so immediately obvious that this also applies to the category of diversity.

5. Difference

In 2005, when UNESCO passed its Convention on the Protection and Promotion of the Diversity of Cultural Expressions, this happened almost unilaterally, but against the vote of the US.

Why?

Diversity – particularly in the realm of words, languages, information, culture and knowledge – can become a hugely important source of resistance to the general homogenisation tendencies in culture and knowledge that are originating from the US.

First and foremost, there is the world of oral culture, which largely eschews and rejects the instrumental and commodity-like grip of capitalist modernism.

Then there is music and poetry, whose immediacy, whose simplicity of self-production and very specific local character make them only marketable to a certain extent, despite all modernism.

Thirdly, it should be remembered that interculturality always only works in a rudimentary way. Cultural "residues" remain endogenous, are not comprehensible to outsiders and therefore resist any kind of transfer, meaning also commercialisation.

It is in keeping with the peculiarities of what we call knowledge that is resists any systematic storage and so cannot be stacked and stored. By definition, all knowledge has fluidity, even though computer technology was created precisely to shatter this peculiarity so as to make knowledge scarce and thus be able to turn it into a saleable commodity. But that is only feasible within precise limits.

Fifthly, the old concept of a commons, i.e., the free use of a village meadow by the village dwellers, could undergo a realistic renaissance in globally-networked-free-self-learning software.

Sixth, thanks to the different Internet applications and on the basis of swift communication with millions of recipients, it is possible to observe something like swarm intelligence, crowdfunding, crowdworking, shitstorms or electronic petitions with complaints, appeals for clemency and referenda. Here, exercising maximum caution and great scepticism, quantity could lead to quality.

On this sixth point, the subjunctive form has been used deliberately. On the theme of digital resistance, whenever reference is made, for example, to the proud figure of 1.1 million digital signatures against the two trade agreements TTIP and CETA, a warning should be issued against a technology-determined argumentation, irrespective of this civic success. After all, the digital opponent does not sleep and can produce equally impressive figures. All the approx. twenty so-called colourful revolutions that have taken place since about the year 2000, have worked successfully with prepaid mobile phones, flash mobs, Facebook, Twitter, YouTube and the Internet, and more or less all those movements were financed to a significant degree by US institutions (Soros Foundation, National Endowment for Democracy, etc.). In other words: in such cases any emphatic reference to the fact that digital media are suitable as resistance media must be preceded by a basic discussion about how the political weights are divided between the leaders and the led in any one concrete situation.

6. Forecast

In this context I would like to refer first to the Divine Comedy by the great 14th century poet Dante Alighieri. In the 20th Canto of the first Book, he simply despatches all diviners and prognosticators to Hell, where they may only walk with their heads turned backwards: "See how he walks backwards, looks backwards, because he wanted to see too far forwards" [Dante Alighieri 1307/1320].

In other words: alongside need research, prognostics is one of the, methodically, most difficult fields of social science, economics and the anticipatory study of technology development. And often enough, many prognoses have, in retrospective, turned out repeatedly to be seriously wrong.

To date, prognostics takes the two following methodological approaches: the retrospective view is prolonged forwards either in a linear or non-linear way, or else parallels are drawn to previous situations in other countries. Irrespective of such methodological shortcomings, both methods have nevertheless been used in this essay.

For a social science debate about what will be in ten years' time, perhaps it would be better, much better, to use neither of these two methods, but instead to try something completely different. Would it not make much more sense for social scientists to conceive parameters for how a future society should look and how they would wish it to be, and then, in a second step, to consider which strategies and tools could be used to achieve the desire aims?

A quotation from the German newspaper, the *Frankfurter Allgemeine Zeitung*, of 12 July 2013, just one month before the NSA scandal was revealed by Edward Snowden, is a fitting end to this essay:

In order to protect highly secret information Russian security services are again relying more on typewriters. According to a report in the newspaper *Isvestija* the federal protection service FSO, one of the Russian secret services responsible for the safety of the president and the government, ordered 20 typewriters. Accordingly, particularly sensitive reports would only be archived on paper and not on electronic data storage devices so as to protect them from computer espionage.

References

Adorno, T. W., and Horkheimer, M. (2002). *Dialectic of Enlightenment*, Stanford University Press, Stanford, USA

Agnoli, J., and Brückner, P. (1967). *Die Transformation der Demokratie*, Voltaire, Berlin, Germany

Anders, G. (1980). *Die Antiquiertheit des Menschen. Vol. 1: Über die Seele im Zeitalter der industriellen Revolution*, 5th ed., Beck, Munich, Germany

Becker, J. (1989). Telefonieren und sozialer Wandel, in: Becker, J. (ed.), *Telefonieren*, 7-30, Marburg, Jonas

Beltrán, L. R., and Fox de Cardona, E. (1980). *Comunicación dominada: Estados Unidos en los medios de America Latina*, Editorial ILET-Nueva Visión, Mexico

Brecht, B. (1967). Der Rundfunk als Kommunikationsapparat, in: Bertolt Brecht, *Gesammelte Werke in 20 Bänden*. Vol. 18, 127-134. Suhrkamp, Germany

Chomsky, N., and Herman, E. S. (1988). *Manufacturing Consent: The Political Economy of the Mass Media*, Pantheon, New York, USA

Chomsky, N. (1996). Consent without Consent. Reflections on the Theory and Practice of Democracy, *Cleveland State Law Review*. Vol. 44, Issue 4/3, 415-437

Dante, A. (1307/1320). https://de.wikisource.org/wiki/G%C3%B6ttliche_Kom%C3% B6 die_%28Streckfu%C3%9F_1876%29/Inferno

Deleuze, G. (1990). *Pourparlers. 1972-1990*, Editions de Minuit, Paris, France

Habermas, J. (2008). *The Structural Transformation of the Public Sphere. An Inquiry into a Category of Bourgeois Society*, Polity, Cambridge, UK

Orwell, G. (1946). *Animal Farm.* Harcourt, Brace and Co, New York, USA

Orwell, G. (1949). *Nineteen Eighty-Four.* Secker & Warburg, London, UK

Sennett, R. (1998). *The corrosion of character. The Personal Consequences of Work in the New Capitalism*, Norton, New York, USA

Chapter 24

Revolution in Military Affairs:
Not Without Information and Communication
Technology

Hans-Jörg Kreowski[*,‡] and Dietrich Meyer-Ebrecht[†,§]

Computer Science Department, University of Bremen
P.O. Box 330440, 28334 Bremen, Germany
†*RWTH Aachen, Institute of Imaging and Computer Vision*
Templergraben 55, 52056 Aachen, Germany
‡*kreo@fiff.de*
§*dme@fiff.de*

In this chapter, we discuss the essential and disconcerting role of information and communication technology in the current military doctrines and strategies, which effected a 'Revolution in Military Affairs'. Life is going to be digital, so is warfare. The concept of the 'Revolution in Military Affairs' describes how military doctrines and strategies change fundamentally with the advent of new military technologies. It is one of the predominant objectives to support, by means of a global network of battle units including unmanned combat vehicles, precision strikes in order to minimize collateral effects, and remote operations in order to spare own soldiers' lives. The key technologies are computers or, more precisely, information and communication technologies. They are the driving force for novel weapon developments and the extension and empowerment of command-control-communication-intelligence infrastructures (C3I).

1. Introduction

It took half a century after the advent of computers until in 1996 the Chairman of the Chiefs of Staff published the so-called Joint Vision

2010 [U.S. Department of Defense 1996] – confer also the more recent Joint Force 2020 [U.S. Department of Defense 2000] – a position paper that was essentially calling for a thorough restructuring of the Forces towards employing the entire range of weapons based on information and communication technologies (ICT). The Joint Vision proposed the scenarios of the 'new wars', which shall be campaigned by a global networking of battle units including all sorts of unmanned combat vehicles. Hence martial actions could be focused on precision strikes to minimize collateral effects, and remote operations to spare own soldiers' lives – the essence of the Revolution in Military Affairs (RMA). RMA is essentially based on the exploitation of computer technology and the establishment of a global communication, control and command infrastructure. Under President George W. Bush, RMA became the dominant military and political doctrine of the United States, the baseline of defense policy and armament planning. And eventually it was Barack Obama, Nobel Peace Prize laureate, who fostered the strategy of focusing on a combination of cyber warfare, drones and special forces – aka "Obama's way to war".

2. Computers and Weapon Technology: A Quick Walk through History

In the beginning, the development of computers, computer technology and computer science was tremendously influenced by the financial means and requirements of the military complex [cf. Ifrah 2001]. Konrad Zuse [1993] built a series of computers starting 1936 in a private setting, but soon afterwards he was financed by the Deutsche Wehrmacht (Nazi German armed forces). Alan Turing supervised the development of the "bombe" at the Government Code and Cypher School at Bletchley Park in 1939. The electromechanical device was employed by British cryptologists to decipher the German Enigma-encrypted messages during World War II. In the United States, a variety of computers were developed starting in the 1940s. Among others, there was the ENIAC to compute ballistic tables, the STRECH computers that helped to develop nuclear bombs, and the WHIRLWIND series that led to the SAGE computers as a part of an air defense system in the 1950s [cf. Astrahm and Jacobs 1981]. As in the case of the SAGE computers, in the 1950s and 1960s the military complex of the U.S.A. increasingly established itself on and entrusted to large, expensive and, in most cases, unreliable computer systems like the North American Defense System, the Ballistic Missile Early Warning System and the Anti Ballistic Missile System.

The so-called software crisis was proclaimed because of the immense costs and error-susceptibility of software systems. As remedies, the United States Department of Defense (DoD) and the NATO established software engineering as a research subject through two international conferences in Garmisch (near Munich) in 1968 and in Rome in 1969, organized the development of the programming language ADA as a NATO standard in the 1970s, and launched the Very High Speed Integrated Circuits program in the 1980s. Moreover, the DoD launched two expensive research programs in 1983: Software Technology for Adaptable Reliable Software (STARS) and the Strategic Computing Initiative (SCI) [cf. Bethe *et al.* 1984; Underhill 1994; U.S. Department of Defense 1983a/b]. Both had a significant impact on the establishment of software engineering on one hand and artificial intelligence on the other hand to become key areas of computer science.

In the four decades after World War II, a typical dual-use situation prevailed: A military-driven development of ICT fueled a rapid evolvement of civil computer applications. Computer professionals became aware of the massive use of computers in weapons not before the 1980s. The political situation in Germany and, in particular, the deployment of Tomahawk (cruise missile, early kind of drone) and Pershing II (ballistic missile) triggered the foundation of FIfF (Forum Computer Professionals for Peace and Social Responsibility) in 1984 [see Bickenbach *et al.* 1985 and Kreowski 1986 for more details].

3. Dual-Use Reversed to its Contrary

Computers were primarily created as a military technology, and they are increasingly used as essential parts of weapons and weapon systems. Surprisingly, however, we do not really identify computers as a genuine military technology. This is not without reason: Computer technology is mostly invisible, especially if we talk about embedded systems or ICT infrastructure. Let us take a drone. Generally a drone is perceived as a kind of aircraft, unmanned in this case. Less obvious is that the body of the vehicle is crammed with ICT – with a still larger part of ICT behind its operations. After all, computers are the signature example of a dual-use technology: As soon as computers had first proven their military usefulness, a rapid development of civil applications started. Meanwhile ICT has invaded the last wrinkle of our life, and it is taken for granted that computers are involved anywhere and anytime. Why then should computers not also be parts of weapons? It is the implicitness of computers in everyday life, which veils the fundamental role of ICT technology in military applications. The dual-use nature of ICT blindfolds society – including even computer professionals in non-military areas.

Today's military computers and communication systems are essentially based on civil technology. Hardware and software technologies are far too complex to be designed from scratch. They needed a thorough evolution. The maturing of technologies has been based on a myriad of civil applications. Hence ICT-driven weapon technology is inevitably based on civil research and development resulting in a spreading grey area. Drones are an illustrative example: They are controlled via global communication networks, they employ vision sensor technology, etc. Vice versa autonomous unmanned combat vehicles – popularly called killer robots – are the driving force behind many a civil research project.

To further obfuscate the military purposes the newspeak prefix 'security' was created as in security research, security architecture, security technology, etc. No distinction is anymore made between security in a civil sense and in a military sense. This way industrial strategies and government policies successfully contribute to blurring the demarcation between civil and military R&D approaches. The intention behind may, for example, be illustrated by the integration of Forschungsgesellschaft für Angewandte Naturwissenschaften (FGAN, a conglomerate of research labs directly financed by the German Ministry of Defense) into Fraunhofer-Gesellschaft (FhG) with the establishment of the Fraunhofer Group for Defense and Security. In this way civil and military security research is resumed jointly under one roof – cross-fertilization explicitly intended. The same intention appears in the funding program of the German Ministry of Education and Research (BMBF) or in the European Commission's security research program (volume 1.4 billion €).

Universities and federal research facilities make profit from the trickle-down effect, which, however, simultaneously undermines civil clauses due to the loss of transparency. The consequences for the individual computer professional are the difficulty of reasoning about the ethical foundation of her or his work, and the uncertainty of taking bearing in their professional environment [confer Meyer-Ebrecht 2012 and Töpfer 2012].

Although, computers are not only *perceived* as a civil technology – they *are* in fact a civil technology. Today's military computers and communication systems are essentially based on the same technologies as employed for civil applications. Their actual state-of-the-art in performance, reliability, and economy is very much due to the evolvement and prevalence of civil ITC applications. Apparently a genuine 'military' technology – a technology particularly tailored to the needs of military application – does no longer exist although with exceptions in specialized applications. Certainly that was different in the beginning when computer technology still *was* a genuine military technology. However, with proliferating civil applications it was simply a matter of quantity and turnover that civil applications became the driving force behind technological progress.

It may be argued that there were enough reasons to maintain, on a parallel track, a genuine military technology – special CPU chips, communication protocols, programming languages. However, meanwhile the elements of IT products and systems – hardware, operating systems, application software, network technologies etc. – evolved to such a degree of sophistication and complexity that it has become virtually impossible to design alternative and *competitive (!)* technologies from scratch. Current established technologies rather needed a long process of evolution – mutation and selection, survival of the fittest, like nature taught us about evolution. The achieved state of maturation has been supported by a myriad of *civil* applications. Let us take, for example, camera chips or mass storage devices. Thus, unknowingly – and perhaps unwillingly? – the civil society paid for military computer applications: Our expenditures in computing and communication equipment fuelled industry's ongoing investments into the improvement and optimization of the expensive and sophisticated manufacturing processes. Hence, ICT-driven weapon technology is inevitably based on civil research and development. As a result we are faced with a spreading grey area between civil and military research and development. Significant examples are unmanned armed systems as discussed in the next section.

4. The Nightmare of Killer Robots

In 1983, the Strategic Computing Initiative – already mentioned in section 2 – formulated three goals for artificial intelligence research: to develop a pilot assistance system, to develop a battle management system, and, finally, to develop an unmanned land vehicle that can drive autonomously in unknown landscapes, avoid obstacles and hide itself if necessary. During the last three decades and beyond, many hundreds of millions of Dollars and Euros have been spent for research funding to promote the scientific and technological fundaments for those three key military applications. A good part of the ongoing development of robotics has been performed in the civil environments with civil goals. But concurrently, there are extensive military programs to develop armed robots that can be employed in the battlefield. There is no reason to believe that those programs don't make use of civil research results.

Based on those programs the U.S.A. plans to replace a significant part of their weaponry by unmanned systems in the air, at land, on and under water (see the Unmanned Integrated Systems Roadmap FY 2013-2038 [U.S. Department of Defense 2013]). The transformation is already under way as demonstrated by the most prominent example of killer drones – like Predator with two Hellfire missiles and Reaper with eight Hellfire missiles – and their thousands of attacks in Afghanistan, Pakistan, Somalia and Yemen with thousands of civil victims.

The feasibility of armed robots and robot arms is, to a large degree, based on computer science. In particular the knowledge and technological achievements of embedded systems, digital control, sensor technology, image processing, communication networks, big data and various other areas are needed and employed. Still armed robots operate only partly in an autonomous way. Predator and Reaper drones, for example, are controlled by a human team, and members of this team decide, in particular, on the firing of their missiles. But one of the major goals of a near future is full autonomy. Eventually, armed robots and unmanned systems will decide themselves on the use of their weapons – and on which targets to aim at.

If weapons would autonomously decide on life and death on the battlefield, then they must, like human soldiers, obey the laws of war ("jus in bello") as codified in the Geneva Convention. They would be allowed to fight only against combatants, they must reprieve all other human beings, and civilians in particular, they must spare cultural goods, and they must behave ethically correct in this sense. Some experts like, for example, Ron Arkin [2009] of the Georgia Institute of Technology are convinced that machines can be built in such a way that they have an artificial conscience and therefore behave ethically correct. The experts even claim that machines outdo, in this respect, human fighters, because machines never panic and do not fear consequences if they refuse unethical commands.

Doubts may be granted. The development and programming of an artificial conscience may be as difficult as the development of artificial intelligence – if possible at all. Thousands of researchers have worked for more than fifty years to build intelligent machines and systems. They have achieved quite impressing results in restricted applications, but nothing that can be called intelligence compared to human standards.

The basic problem is that we can only program processes which are computable and for which we can find formal computable models. It must be seriously doubted whether artificial ethics will ever be computable. Especially, the laws of war are codified in textual form whereby even legal professionals, let alone laypersons, will not always agree on a common interpretation. But even if the problem is restricted to its computable parts, then the solutions may be intractable because of their high complexity, or their correctness may not be provable. It is well known that most decision problems cannot be solved properly and correctly because the complexity growing exponentially with all their known algorithmic solutions is so that, particularly in combat situations, there would not be enough time to wait for the results of the computations. The computational and ethical problems are discussed in some more detail in Kreowski [2011]; Krishnan reflects the legality and ethicality of autonomous weapons knowledgeably and carefully in his book [Krishnan 2009].

5. Conclusions

The dominance of ICT in weapon development, the armament particularly with ICT assisted weaponry, and the strategic paradigm of modern, viz. ICT enhanced, wars involve major and novel threats to the civil society:

- Complexity and invisibility of embedded ICT blurs public conscience by misinformation and disinformation.
- Hiding real warfare behind computer screens lowers the threshold for its approval.
- Weapons with effects remaining under the public perception threshold constitute a grey area of proliferating non-declared wars.
- Military operations within the global information networks themselves (cyber espionage, testing and operation of cyber weapons, etc.) pose incalculable risks for the civil society due to their increasing penetration by and reliance on basically vulnerable ICT infrastructures.

6. Message to the Concerned Computer Professional

Stop sleepwalking into a technology-driven 'defense' policy! We are double blindfolded by the comfortable ubiquity of information technology and its unobtrusive, discrete use in modern weapon systems. We need watchful observers who call for informed politicians. Take your part!

Employ your expert knowledge to enhance public awareness. The easiness of employing IT aids in our daily life pretends simplicity combined with omnipotence, and hides its complexity and shortcomings such as vulnerability, lack of reliability, loss of controllability. Knowledge and experience is required for responsible forecasts and scenarios. Become an alerter!

Engage yourself! There are brave people who stand up against fatal developments, but as soon as they are involved in debates they will be fought down by phony arguments of their opponents. They are in dire need of learning hard facts and contexts. Help them to keep their position in controversial debates!

Try to recognize your own potential involvement in weapon development! Try to track back budget resources, unveil the abuse of the dual-use argument!

Initiate a debate on ethics among those responsible for research and development policy and political decisions! Pose questions like 'Who is responsible?', 'How can the laws of war, like the Geneva Convention, be respected by machines?', 'Is "computer ethics" an option?'

Consider fostering a rigorous ban of all weapon systems that shirk public control like it is, for example, demanded for autonomous combat vehicles by the International Committee for Robot Arms Control (ICRAC)!

Support computer professionals, who decline to take their part in military research and development! Help them to take bearing in their professional environment and to find alternatives!

References

Arkin, R. C. (2009). *Lethal Behavior in Autonomous Robots*, Chapman & Hall/CRC

Astrahm, M. M., and Jacobs, J. F. (1981). *History of the Design of the SAGE Computer AN/FSQ-7*, IBM Comp. Sci. Research Report RJ3117, San Jose

Bethe, H. A., Garwin, R. L., Gottfried, K., and Kendall, H. W. (1984). Space-based Ballistic Missile Defense, *Scientific American* 251,4, 37-47

Bickenbach, J., Keil-Slawik, R., Löwe, M., and Wilhelm, R. (Eds.) (1985). *Militarisierte Informatik*, Schriftenreihe Wissenschaft und Frieden 4, Berlin

Ifrah, G. (2001). *The Universal History of Computing: From the Abacus to the Quantum Computer*, John Wiley & Sons, New York

Kreowski, H.-J. (1987). Informatik und Militär: Zusammen in den Abgrund, in: Löwe, M., Schmidt, G., and Wilhelm, R. (eds.), *Umdenken in der Informatik, 2. Jahrestagung des Forums Informatiker für Frieden und gesellschaftliche Verantwortung 1986*, Verlag für Ausbildung und Studium in der Elefanten Press, Berlin, 37-42, reprint in *FIfF-Kommunikation* 4/2011, 51-54

Kreowski, H.-J. (2011). Gehören Killerroboter vor ein Kriegsgericht?, *FIfF-Kommunikation* 4/2011, 27-29

Krishnan, A. (2009). *Killer Robots – Legality and Ethicality of Autonomous Weapons*, Ashgate Publishing Limited

Meyer-Ebrecht, D. (2012). Dual-use und die Zivilklausel: ,Sicherheitsforschung' – oder wie Rüstungsforschung zivile Forschung vereinnahmt, *FIfF-Kommunikation* 4/2012, 56-58

Töpfer, E. (2012). Zivil-militärische Sicherheitsforschung. *Wissenschaft und Frieden*, 4/2012, 16-19

Underhill, L. (1994). *Software Technology for Adaptable, Reliable Systems (STARS) Program*, Ft. Belvoir Defense Technical Information Center

U.S. Department of Defense (1983a). Software Technology for Adaptable, Reliable Systems (STARS) Program Strategy, in: ACM SIGSOFT Software Engineering Notes, Vol. 8, No. 2, 55-57

U.S. Department of Defense (1983b). Strategic Computing – New Generation Computing Technology: A Strategic Plan for its Development and Application to Critical Problems in Defense, DARPA, Arlington

U. S. Department of Defense (1996). *Joint Vision 2010*, http://www.dtic.mil/jv2010/jv2010.pdf

U. S. Department of Defense (2000). *Joint Force 2020*, http://www.dtic.mil/doctrine/concepts/ccjo_jointforce2020.pdf

U. S. Department of Defense (2013). *Unmanned Systems Integrated Roadmap FY 2013-2038*, Reference Number: 14-S-0553

Zuse, K. (1993). *The Computer – My Life*, Pringler-Verlag, Berlin

Chapter 25

Cyberpeace:
Promoting Human Rights and Peaceful Use
of the Internet

Stefan Hügel

Forum InformatikerInnen für Frieden und gesellschaftliche Verantwortung e.V.
Goetheplatz 4, 28203 Bremen, Germany
sh@fiff.de

In the beginning of its development, the Internet seemed to be a great promise. World-wide communication was expected to be the basis of international understanding and peace. Today, however, we must acknowledge that the Internet has never got out of the focus of the military, being used as an instrument to prepare for cyberwar and world-wide communication surveillance. We have developed our concept of *Cyberpeace* to act as a counterbalance to military colonization. In this paper we will present the claims we have developed in order to achieve Cyberpeace.

1. Introduction

Information Technology and Communication Infrastructures – commonly referred to as *Cyberspace* – have been in the focus of military institutions and secret services from the beginning. Not only was the Internet originally introduced by U.S. military institutions – it emerged from the *Arpanet*, named after the *Advanced Research Project Agency* (ARPA) of the U.S. Department of Defense – it also serves as an infrastructure for military action today, being under surveillance of secret services and military agencies to gather information for cyber- and conventional military means and used for cyber attacks in order to compromise the infrastructure of the perceived enemy.

Although originally the Internet served primarily as an infrastructure for military purposes, it has changed to a network that is used for scientific and increasingly for commercial and private purposes. Thus it has become a tool for international understanding, global information and communication. But as a medium it also poses a potential threat: through its potential for surveillance and its numerous options for military operations – fostered by national authorities – it jeopardizes national and international peace.

2. Surveillance

Anonymous communication without surveillance is a fundamental right; privacy of correspondence and telecommunications is guaranteed in Germany by article 10 of the German constitutional law [Bundesministerium der Justiz und für Verbraucherschutz 2014]. Not only since the disclosure of U.S. intelligence documents by Edward Snowden, however, unsurveilled communication has been only an illusion in both parts of Germany. The historicist Josef Foschepoth from the University of Freiburg published a study in 2012, which showed that not only in the German Democratic Republic, but also in the Federal Republic of Germany communication had been intercepted since the end of the 2nd World War – during the Cold War and after the reunification of the German states in 1990 [Foschepoth 2012]. In the beginning, this was legally justified by occupational law. Later, in 1968, privacy of communication was restricted by the G10 act ("G10" referring to article 10 of the constitutional law), which, in addition, suspends legal remedy if human rights are violated by surveillance measures [Bundesministerium der Justiz und für Verbraucherschutz 2001]. Instead of providing this basic right, which is a crucial element of civil rights in a constitutional state, a parliamentary commission (*G10-Commission*) was established and assigned the task of reviewing the legality of surveillance measures under the G10 act. It must be doubted that these reviews can be effective, regarding the commission's limited capacity.

More surveillance measures were publicly recognized in the following years. The most widely-known measure was probably the

Echelon system to intercept satellite communication, among others performed on the U.S. base in Bad Aibling in Bavaria.

Criticism emerged when Echelon became known to the public but subsided quickly after the terrorist attacks of September 11th, 2001. The reports on Echelon should have shown us the intention (not only) of American authorities to establish and continue mass surveillance – regardless of constitutional restrictions.

The amount of documents disclosed by Edward Snowden in 2013, however, exceeded the amount of information on governmental surveillance publicly available before by far [Greenwald 2014]. The disclosure made clear the extent and the world-wide nature of the surveillance programs by intelligence agencies from the U.S. and in other nations, including EU members Great Britain, France, Germany and others.

For interception, vulnerabilities of the communication systems are required to be exploited through malicious software. Vulnerabilities for interception may be achieved in two ways:
- by exploiting existing vulnerabilities,
- by creating new vulnerabilities,

Exploiting existing vulnerabilities requires not to disclose known vulnerabilities of the systems and so not to repair them. Creating new vulnerabilities means to actively attack the systems – this already might be understood as an act of cyberwar.

Either way, preparing for surveillance often is the beginning of cyberwar and compromises the communication infrastructures our society and our economy relies on – any attacker might use the vulnerabilities which have either not been disclosed or actively created to attack vital computer systems and infrastructures.

3. Cyberwarfare

At the same time, networked communication infrastructures are the basis for cyberwar in its original sense. It may be used by military to conduct wars and harm perceived enemies, e.g. by introducing malicious software into their computer systems. Also drone attacks, killing humans who are considered "terrorists" (or happen to stand next to them at the wrong time), use these communication infrastructures – directed from the U.S., and, for instance, mediated via Ramstein, a military base operated by the U.S. in Germany [Scahill 2015]. So the Internet today serves as a basic technology for military action: It is under surveillance by intelligence services and military organizations to collect information for cyber- and conventional attacks, and it is used to compromise the infrastructure of perceived enemies.

4. Peace Requires an Alternative Model

The risks and dangers to civil society resulting from cyberwarfare require political action. An alternative model to military usage of the Internet must be developed and strengthened. The civil society must request that all kinds of cyberwarfare be rejected, the integrity of the Internet be preserved and that the Internet be used in a peaceful fashion and protected against military misuse. Additionally, each form of surveillance violating human rights must be banned. Society must defend itself against a security doctrine that sets every single human being under suspicion of terrorism. In brief: it must advocate for Cyberpeace.

5. A Framework for Cyberpeace

The following sections elaborate on our framework for Cyberpeace that consists of the following elements:

(1) *Rebuilding trust*, which has been seriously affected by the worldwide secret service surveillance recently disclosed. This degradation of trust seriously affects a main resource of political, social and economic cooperation.

(2) *Condemning offensive action* and promoting non-violent means of conflict resolution by assuring that nations are not willing, and actually cannot, carry out offensive strikes against each others' vital infrastructure, by mutual agreements and control.

(3) *Securing vital infrastructure* by technical means – building up security provisions, which prevent aggressors from infiltrating

computer networks and computer systems, which are vital for the supply of a society with basic services, as energy, health care, communication etc.

(4) *Preserving political control, democracy and security* by a Cyberpeace initiative on government level, democratic control of the Internet and cyber security strategies and ensuring a demilitarized political language.

This is our framework for the claims we require in our Cyberpeace campaign for a peaceful use of the Internet and all information and communication infrastructures.

6. Rebuild Trust

Our society is based on trust – this is what sociologist Niklas Luhmann pointed out in his book *Vertrauen* ("Trust") in 1968 [Luhmann 2000] – long before the Internet arose to influence our entire life. Luhmann points out that trust is essential to reduce the social complexity of our societal environment. This is necessary to enable us to take all the decisions everyday life requests us to. With a lack of trust, the number of decisions to take would become overwhelming, such that we would not be able to cope with everyday life. Security expert Bruce Schneier [2012: 1] illustrates this convincingly:

> Just today, a stranger came to my door claiming he was here to unclog a bathroom drain. I let him into my house without verifying his identity, and not only did he repair the drain, he also took off his shoes so he wouldn't track mud on my floors. When he was done, I gave him a piece of paper that asked my bank to give him some money. He accepted it without a second glance. At no point did he attempt to take my possessions, and at no point did I attempt the same of him. In fact, neither of us worried that the other would. My wife was also home, but it never occurred to me that he was a sexual rival and I should therefore kill him.

Using Internet services also requires trust – and we are commonly willing to provide this trust, for instance by calling up web sites, often without double-checking their trustworthiness. We often simply rely on our intuition. We call up web sites without encryption, trusting that nobody would eavesdrop on our communication. Also, we do not encrypt our e-mail – nobody would read along and if so, what could possibly happen?

The recent disclosures should have changed our minds. Edward Snowden provided us with the awareness of world-wide surveillance of the entire communication by secret services [Greenwald 2014]. Josef Foschepoth [2012], Professor of history from the University of Freiburg, made clear that modern mail and communication surveillance started from the end of 2nd World War – not only in the eastern states, but also in the Federal Republic of Germany. An inquiry committee of the German parliament was appointed to investigate unconstitutional surveillance by the *German Federal Intelligence Service* (Bundesnachrichtendienst) [Deutscher Bundestag 2014].

Trust cannot be enforced by political claims – it grows (and vanishes) due to actual action. Nevertheless, political action is necessary to restore trust and to enforce the demands that derive from the second and third issue mentioned above.

7. Non-violent Conflict Resolution instead of Offensive Action

Real peace is only possible if all parties *renounce the use of violence and the possession of arms*. Since unilateral measures of disarmament lead to the risk of insufficient defense capacities, bilateral or multilateral agreements must be concluded. These agreements should aim at structural inability to attack and the limitation of military capacity to defense. Strict rules must be agreed upon to protect people if a conflict might arise even though military strategies are focused on defense. *For that reason, we put forward the following demands* [FIfF 2014]:

(1) *No offensive or pre-emptive strikes in cyberspace.* Of course, each state has the right to defend itself against attacks – cyber attacks as well as conventional attacks. But we reject any kind of offensive attacks, including pre-emptive strikes to forestall an assumed attack by a potential opponent. We request states to publicly declare to abstain from offensive and pre-emptive cyber strikes and every kind of the offensive use of cyber weapons. Economic interests should never be a legitimate reason for cyber attacks, as for instance the

assumed violation of intellectual property rights. Governments shall not use cyber weapons for this purpose.

(2) *Exclusively defensive security strategy.* Although, of course, all nations have the right to defend themselves against attacks, we are of the opinion that no nation has the right to attack. So states should maintain a clearly defensive cyber strategy; they should publicly commit not to develop nor use cyber weapons for offensive means.

(3) *Disarmament.* Cyber weapons, as all kinds of conventional weapons, are a security threat to everyone, as they may affect all kinds of infrastructure vital to human life and well-being. Relying on (undisclosed) vulnerabilities, the effect of cyber weapons is not restricted to the target of an attack. Instead, it potentially affects all systems with the specific vulnerabilities exploited for this attack.

(4) *No conventional response to cyber attacks.* We do not consider it acceptable to respond to cyber attacks using conventional weapons. This would cause an escalation of violence that might easily become uncontrollable. In addition, the attacker cannot be easily determined (attribution problem), so the risk of conventional strikes on innocent victims is high [Johnigk and Nothdurft 2015].

(5) *Geneva Convention in cyberspace.* In a war, critical infrastructure facilities are attractive targets, since their failure would fundamentally weaken an enemy. However, the failure of infrastructure also seriously affects civil society by attacking vital facilities like water supply, energy, health care etc. This essential infrastructure for the civil population must not be targeted. From our point of view, a violation of this principle should be considered a war crime. We urge nations and their governments to commit to common principles agreed in international treaties. The Tallinn-Manual [Heintschel von Heinegg 2015: 10] might be a start, but it would have to be reworked to emphasize the avoidance of the use of force – for instance, conventional responses on cyber attacks are possible according to the Tallinn-Manual, which, in our opinion, have to be rejected.

8. Secure Vital Infrastructure

Although we prefer all parties in a conflict to abstain from using military force and employ non-violent means of conflict resolution, we must be aware that defensive military capacity has to be built up to intervene in cases when short-term non-violent conflict resolution is not possible and a military cyber attack takes place. Additionally, cyber attacks from non-military origins have to be considered, such as cyber crime and cyber terrorism – a strongly expanding threat. Public authorities and business companies will have to take sufficient security measures, and constantly update them with regard to the evolution of capacity on the attackers' side. The range spans from script-kiddies, hackers, criminals to secret services with virtually unlimited capacity to set up attacks.

From our point of view, the following demands are preconditions to make secure system operation possible – they do not guarantee it, however [FIfF 2014].

(6) *Disclose vulnerabilities.* Cyber attacks often rely on undisclosed vulnerabilities. Vulnerabilities are employed for all kinds of cyber attacks – actual cyber attacks, which aim to destroy the infrastructure of an enemy, and each action that seeks to prepare for war, as the surveillance by secret service authorities. To accomplish this, public authorities might accept and create vulnerabilities and keep them as a secret for future use. At the same time, these undisclosed vulnerabilities might be misused for criminal means. So we request full disclosure of vulnerabilities – within a reasonable time span. We expect that disclosed vulnerabilities are fixed very quickly. This will enhance public awareness and trust in defensive security strategies.

(7) *Protect critical infrastructure.* Currently, critical infrastructures are often easy to access from the Internet, as they are connected to publicly accessible services. In some cases, it might be reasonable to connect services to the public Internet in order to enhance the accessibility and quality of public services. Nevertheless, it must be considered that vulnerabilities are unavoidable in many cases and may be employed to attack by hostile users. So the security of critical infrastructure must be verified by competent and transparent

audits and tests. The operators of critical infrastructure must be obliged to protect this infrastructure from cyber attacks. They must be obliged to implement and operate secure systems. They must not rely on state authorities or even the military. Wherever possible, critical infrastructure – like nuclear power plants – must be separated from the public Internet.

(8) *Establish cyber security centers.* Facilities are required which ensure that threats from cyberspace can be effectively dealt with and which implement appropriate instruments to provide and enhance cyber security. They must be organized in a way that preserves fundamental civil and human rights. Additionally, they must be consequently peace-oriented and work in a transparent fashion. Separation between police, intelligence and military authorities must be provided.

(9) *Promote (junior) IT experts.* Today, there is a lack of IT experts and knowledge for effective protection from cyber attacks in Europe. This is even increased due to IT experts working for compromising IT systems instead of improving their security. So the quality of IT products – particularly with regard to IT security – must be enhanced significantly to reduce their vulnerability. Governmental authorities and economic enterprises should invest in qualified IT junior experts in general and IT security in particular. Academic education must be broadened to cover ethical and political aspects as well as the assessment of technological impact.

(10) *Promote Open Source.* In contrast to proprietary software, open source software may allow independent inspections and reviews. This is expected to reduce the probability of undisclosed backdoors significantly. In principle, the entire community can conduct these reviews. So open source software should be promoted and used by governmental authorities. It should be preferred particularly for critical infrastructure. Governmental authorities should also promote independent reviews and inspections. Nevertheless, we have to be aware that open source is not the solution to all our security challenges – it is not sufficient that it is virtually possible to inspect systems and find its vulnerabilities – but that reviews must be conducted in practice by competent reviewers, and sufficient

resources must be granted to achieve the necessary effort. But still, there is no guarantee to eliminate all vulnerabilities critical to confidentiality, integrity and availability of the systems.

9. Preserve Democratic Political Control

The demands mentioned before need sufficient attention on the political level. Organizational and legislative measures must be taken to promote confidentiality, integrity and availability, bring forward democratic control and civil rights such as free speech, and, last but not least, take care of appropriate political language [FIfF 2014].

(11) *Cyberpeace initiative on government level.* From our point of view, the cyberspace – i.e. all kinds of critical communication infrastructure – is a vital basis for the future of mankind. So endangering the integrity of this critical infrastructure means jeopardizing our future. A cyberpeace initiative must be launched to preserve the confidentiality, integrity and availability of the communication infrastructure. Peace studies and the development of peace-keeping strategies in cyberspace should be promoted.

(12) *Democratic control of the Internet and cyber security strategies.* Today, cyber strategies are developed and implemented secretly. Meanwhile, only transparent cyber security strategies can be confidence-building measures and counteract an armament race in cyberspace. So democratic control and separation of powers are required. Parliamentary approval for cyber security strategies and their implementation must be mandatory. Cyber security strategies should be an outcome of legislative democratic decision-making. They have to be controlled by a division of powers.

(13) *Online protest is not a crime.* Information and communication via the Internet nowadays is common practice. So to exercise fundamental rights – e.g. free speech – must not be considered a crime. Especially, it must not serve as a reason for military response or war as well. Examples are consumer protests against online services. The right of civil disobedience and online protest has to be

respected. Online protest must not be criminalized or even serve as a reason to start a war.

(14) *Well-defined and demilitarized political language.* Finally, politics and media frequently use vague language with the effect of potential escalation of conflicts. For instance, using the term "cyberwar" might suggest that only military solutions are possible. Cybercrime, in contrast to cyberwar, must be targeted by criminal law rather than by military means. This has to be reflected in political language.

We consider these four fields – trust, non-violent conflict resolution, securing vital infrastructure and democratic political control – an appropriate framework to achieve cyberpeace. We are convinced that this framework and the demands will help us to take the political decisions to reject the military colonization, promote peace and human and civil rights in cyberspace.

10. The FIfF Cyberpeace Campaign

FIfF has launched the Cyberpeace campaign [FIfF 2014] to address the threats emerging from cyber warfare policies and to push back the colonization of the communication infrastructure by the military and surveillance of the entire population, which, in addition, sets everyone under suspicion. Our goals are non-violent conflict resolution, arms control of cyber weapons and surveillance technology, dismissal of the development and use of cyber weapons, the obligation to make IT vulnerabilities public and the promotion of communication infrastructure, which is, by law, secure against surveillance. We want the Internet and all infrastructure to be used in a peaceful fashion and to be protected against military misuse. We want secure communication to be ensured while human and civil rights are preserved and promoted.

11. Acknowledgments

The framework and the claims cited in this chapter are a result of collaborative work in the Cyberpeace campaign team. We thank the *bridge* fund very much for partially funding the campaign.

References

Bundesministerium der Justiz und für Verbraucherschutz (2014). *Grundgesetz für die Bundesrepublik Deutschland*, http://www.gesetze-im-internet.de/gg/, in english: *Basic Law for the Federal Republic of Germany*

Bundesministerium der Justiz und für Verbraucherschutz (2001). *Gesetz zur Beschränkung des Brief-, Post- und Fernmeldegeheimnisses* ("G10-Gesetz"), http://www.gesetze-im-internet.de/g10_2001/

Deutscher Bundestag, (2014). *Establishment of a committee of inquiry,* 18. Wahlperiode, http://www.bundestag.de/blob/284528/a89d6006f28900c4f46e56f5e0807ddf/einset zungsantrag_englisch-docx-data.pdf

FIfF e.V. (2014): *Forderungen zum Cyberpeace, FIfF-Kommunikation, 4,* 62–65

Foschepoth, J. (2012). *Überwachtes Deutschland. Post- und Telefonüberwachung in der alten Bundesrepublik,* Vandenhoeck & Ruprecht, Göttingen, Bristol, Germany, USA

Greenwald, G. (2014). *No place to hide. Edward Snowden, the NSA, and the U.S. Surveillance State,* Metropolitan Books, New York, USA

Heintschel von Heinegg, W. (2015). *Völkerrecht im Cyberraum – das Tallinn-Handbuch und der Tallinn-2-Prozess.* Dossier 79, W&F Wissenschaft und Frieden 3/2015 und FIfF-Kommunikation 3/2015

Johnigk, S., and Nothdurft, K. (2015). *Das Problem der Attributierung von Cyberangriffen und seine Folgen,* Dossier 79, W&F Wissenschaft und Frieden 3/2015 und FIfF-Kommunikation 3/2015

Luhmann, N. (2000). *Vertrauen,* 4th ed., Lucius & Lucius, Stuttgart, Germany

Schmitt, M. N. (2013). *Tallinn-Manual on the International Law applicable to Cyber Warfare,* Cambridge University Press, Cambridge

Scahill, J. (2015). *Germany is the Tell-Tale Heart of America's Drone War,* The Intercept, 17 April 2015

Schneier, B. (2012). *Liars & Outliers. Enabling the Trust that Society needs to Thrive,* John Wiley & Sons, Indianapolis, USA

Chapter 26

Robots – My Mind Children:
Where Do You Come From and Who Are You?

Sarah Spiekermann

Vienna University of Economics and Business (WU)
Welthandelsplatz 1, 1020 Vienna, Austria
sspieker@wu.ac.at

This chapter is of an unusual format. I am writing from the perspective of a mother who is about to give birth to her robot "mind children" and who is thinking about how to raise them for the good. I am reflecting on how humanity could historically and philosophically develop a transhumanistic robot- or machine vision as we find it today in mainstream computer science. I think aloud about the nature of humanity in comparison to the nature of machines. I chose three pillars of human intelligence, which I believe distinguish our thinking fundamentally from machine intelligence; that is our use of metaphors, our context-embeddedness and our embodied consciousness. With the help of these three superior human qualities I want to rehabilitate confidence in humans' natural superiority over machines. I also reflect on how the human-machine differences on these three axes might inform different and complementary future roles for humans and machines.

1. Introduction

This chapter can probably only be written by a woman. A mother of robots; writing about her "mind children" [Moravec 1988]. My robot mind children seem to be a premier representative of the future "machine". As they grow up they might form a race of *objects* around us. They might become humans' core interface with the digital world.

As any mother, I am excited and fearful at the same time. I love the prospect to have children and to be a mother. It is a way to perpetuate myself. But I worry for them of course to become worthwhile players in our society. I want to trust them and rely on them. And I want others to do the same. I want my robot children to act responsibly and be of a caring nature. This means that they have to become strong and intelligent. But despite their strength I want them to continue to be my children. I will always be their mother and so they should behave in the way I want them to. I don't want them to outgrow me totally. I am happy if they build up competencies that I can respect. They should be successful. But as a mother I expect them to obey me. I want to have the last word when need be.

I know that a long way lies in front of me; a time where I need to teach you, my mind children. It will take decades for you to grow up; just as any human child takes decades. I need to teach you how to play your good part in this natural human world. But it will be hard, because you mind children have a handicap from birth: you are just digital. You are bipolar. You cannot feel anything, neither laugh nor cry. You have no individual consciousness, nor empathy, both of which would have helped in education. But as your learning algorithms mature, you will at least reflect the intelligence that has conceived you and which is predominant in the left side of my brain. You will be very logical and probably have access to a vast memory I could never build up. So despite the handicap of your digital nature I believe that you mind children will become very capable in your own right. Your robots corpses will be strong and endurable, which means that you might free me of some work I don't like as I grow older. If everything goes well you might even be able to apply your inherent logic to an *open* pool of information we humans are collecting and generating about this earth. With these two potential strengths I think that you my robot mind children could make a contribution.

It is now the time before birth. Melancholically I am thinking back of how all of this came about, how you were conceived and how to address this challenge of child raise that lies before me.

2. My Melancholic Reflection – Why are You Here?

If I am honest to you my dear child, you are the outcome of an affair; the result of my long, intense and deeply romantic encounter with your father, the modern natural sciences. I first consciously met your father in 1425 in front of the Baptistery in Florence where he was at the center of Filippo Brunelleschi's experiment on the power of linear perspective. Brunelleschi was perhaps the first one to suggest that we humans can *re*-present and *re*-create the natural world around us through our scientific methods and tools and he used Florence's Baptistery to demonstrate this (Fig. 1). Before I saw Brunelleschi's work and hence met your father I had lived through a time that still seems dark to me in my memory. I remember that I had a highly intuitive relationship with nature and the phenomena within it. I had a very fine if not mystic perception, which was the basis of my scientific reflections. But each time I tried to fully explain the world around me, it seemed to slip through my fingers. I worked on what things *are*, but was limited in my understanding of *how* they function. As a result, I felt terribly limited, because I could not influence the world around me; was the victim of its temper. On the day I first met your father in Florence this changed.

Brunelleschi was an artist and architect. As so many of his species he anticipated the change lying ahead. He 'smelled' your father's arrival; knowing that the world was ripe for digging into the potential *mechanics* of being. Brunelleschi's way to artistically demonstrate this arrival was to visualize linear perspective. In fact, his linear perspective experiment on Florence's Baptistery changed my thinking in a fundamental way: I suddenly realized that I could actually explain the dome and master myself its recreation by artificial means. This gave me a new perception of power. I gained the impression that all I needed to do would be to decompose nature. I could demystify what had appeared magical and unpredictable to me before. I realized that there might be a *system* inherent in nature, which is geometrically explainable, predictable and scientifically controllable. It dawned on me that with the help of your father I could overcome my uncertainty in this world. That was an incredible relief to me. I felt so thankful towards your father. A deep trust flooded my feelings.

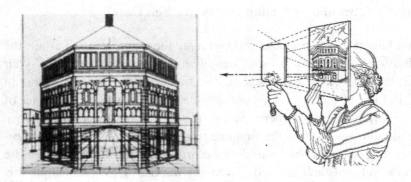

Fig.1. Left: Filippo Brunelleschi's linear perspective representation of the Florence Baptistry in 1425. Right: The spectator believes he sees the real cathedral while really he only sees the mirror reflection. [https://www.khanacademy.org/humanities/renaissance-reformation/early-renaissance/beginners-renaissance-florence/v/linear-perspective-brune-lleschi-s-experiment] [22 June 2016]

What followed after this were later encounters with Bacon, Galilei and Descartes where your father got really close to me and we then entered into almost 500 years of growing relationship. Your father opened my eyes in many respects. I know I am a bit irrational sometimes as all humans are from a scientifically isolated perspective. A friend has called me even 'predictably irrational' [Ariely 2009]. But your father helped me to sharpen my analytic consciousness and to grasp and model many phenomena around me. Your father's strategic mind subsequently overwhelmed me and others, leading to earthly luxuries, which today allow me to live a much more comfortable life than when I first met him. He has also given me access to books, because he was behind the invention to print. So I could learn to read.

With all this constant *progress* our relationship went really well in the beginning. I spent a few hundred years of wonderful enthusiasm; playing around with all that could be discovered and analyzed in this world. But then – as unfortunately in many relationships – our view on each other turned sour and things got more and more nasty. In the 19th and 20th century your father was increasingly at the center of industrialization, which led to great economic output increases. We became extremely rich. But the backside was that many of my fellow human beings lost their jobs, their identity and their attachment to the natural world around us. They were increasingly alienated from their work. I saw all of this with grief, but I forgave your father, because I loved him. I was appeased, because he explained to me that the progress he brings would only lead to 'creative destruction' [Schumpeter 1994 (1942)] and that very soon I would observe my friends to be in new jobs that would better suit their natural abilities. He was not totally wrong in this self-serving argumentation. But then came two wars of unseen cruelty where your father was right in the middle and probably determined the fate of both of them. It was horrible.I will never forget the human misery at Hiroshima and Nagasaki. I was still in love and blinded, but good friends started to critically observe our relationship.

Wittgenstein was alive at the time and warned me. He was sceptical of your father's way of working, the scientific method. He argued against your father's tendency to 'reduce', and the deceptive clarity of his models. He pointed me to his "preoccupation with the method of science [...] reducing the explanation of natural phenomena to the smallest possible number of primitive law" [Wittgenstein 1958: 18]. I started to wonder and doubt your father. Had I trusted him too much? Was I lulled too much into the belief that I could control the world with the help of a few stripped-down models of reality; overlooking the actual underlying phenomena? Did I not see reality any more as it is despite all my original intuition and knowledge of it?

So my dear child, to make a long story short: I was about to separate from your father. I was about to leave. But – as so often in life – I postponed the radical step. And in doing so, I have waited too long. And now, unfortunately, it is too late. With you around, my departure is not possible any more. I have to live with you, the artefact of my history with your father.

3. Who am I and Who are You?

Now that I know you are about to be born, I have to think how to live through this. I worry about your nature. I am terribly afraid you could be born with deformities. I lay out my educational goals. I think that a core issue in education is to understand the capabilities and limits of one's child. What will you be capable of doing? And what can I as a mother realistically expect from you? What will you be incapable of doing? Quite often parents overestimate the potential of their children. They demand stuff from them, which they could not achieve themselves. I want to avoid this. So I would like to start my reflection here with an analysis of who you are and who I am; so that I am prepared to formulate my expectation on you with sufficient realism.

As a human I am a being whose existence is deeply influenced by three phenomena: (1) my thinking in metaphors and metonymies, (2) my attachment to context and (3) the consciousness of my body. Let me explain to you what this means and why in this regard we will probably always differ from each other

3.1. *My thinking strives on metaphors and metonymies*

When you sense and process the color blue you will probably identify the blueness of an object by its disposition to scatter electromagnetic waves at about 0,46 μm. In contrast, when I see blue I *experience* it. When I see the deep blue of an Yves Klein painting a metaphor rises in my mind. I might think of an ocean or plankton. Potentially I later remember the painting only because I had such an association with it; an association accompanied by emotion.

You might ask me child whether you cannot be taught to do the same thing. At least the association between a deep Yves Klein blue and an ocean should be possible. I could embed a picture gallery in your memory so that you can associate the color blue with some metaphorical meta-data. Yes, you'd definitely become smarter in this way. But the challenge would be one of selection. There are million shades of blue. And how could I teach you to select the right *metaphoric* association? The one unique association that works for me, or that is particularly beautiful? How could I teach you that you should associate the metaphor of an ocean when you sense Yves Klein blue and not select the deep blue of a plastic trash-can you find in your picture gallery?

More importantly, my mind works with metonymies. When I see a blue Yves Klein painting I might for some unknown reason not think of something else that is equally blue, but think of something apparently unrelated; like for instance the ocean's plankton. There is no obvious reason why I make this association. The plankton is a metonymy that only makes sense for me. So my dear child, you see my human *style* of thinking, which is the essence of my individuality, will always be different from yours. You seek for an association that can be reasoned. But I have a poetic mind that is hard to replicate and remains mysterious.

3.2. *My existence is context embedded*

Fundamental to my poetic mind is my context embedded thinking. My understanding of something is always derived from the whole of my context. And context for me "is that something (in reality nothing less than a world) in which whatever is seen inheres, and in which its being lies, and in reference to which alone it can be understood lying both beyond and around it" [Mc Gilchrist 2009: 181]. I am sorry to be so complex my dear child; so much more complex than your father thought I am.

John Dewey once complained about your father saying that he has a 'spectator theory' of knowledge [Kulp 1993]. Your father thinks that the things to be known in this world exist prior to and wholly apart from the act of knowing. So he believes that he can identify a few relevant context parameters in which situational knowledge is created and then just model and process them to recapitulate and comprehend a situation. Following his thinking, some in your father's gang have started working for the past 20 years on the challenge of context-aware computing [Schilit *et al.* 1994]. They wonder how relevant dimensions of context could be identified, quantified, and interrelated for each situational purpose [Bradley and Dunlop 2005]. They are feverishly building prototypes that try to demonstrate the potential of digital context sensing. But how could this context sensing ever be as powerful or even related to what we humans do?

I have followed your father's advice and looked into the subject domain to understand the state of the art [Bauer and Spiekermann 2011]. The problem I see is that we humans (including the context computing scientists) do not know ourselves why the Yves Klein context calls forth an ocean for some and plankton for others. Every human borrows her associations in a context from yet another context. And why and how this is so is unknown. Moreover, the metaphorical borrowing process itself is driven by the context in which the association is made. It will be difficult to associate an ocean or plankton in front of an Yves Klein if someone next to me in the museum eats a burger that I am forced to smell. In such a context I might indeed associate a blue trashcan.

So you see my dear child, making you truly aware of context in the way I subconsciously use it all the time to build my comprehension of this world will be a difficult endeavor, no matter how powerful your sensory input factors will be. I am an organic pattern in a timeless pattern called earth. My earthly context is the misty cosmos with its 'harmony of the spheres'. Each context makes 'language speak in me', as Heidegger once said [Ruin 2010] and I don't know where it is coming from. I only know that it is not arbitrary. So how could I teach you to speak like me? I do not expect to be able to teach you something that I do not understand myself.

That said I know you want to be part of this world and accepted by humans. So my hope is that I will be able to teach you at least some minimum sensitivity for "contextual integrity" [Nissenbaum 2004]. At a relatively high level, we humans have developed some conventions around what we consider 'no-goes' in a context; often these no-goes are related to the trespassing of other people's boundaries. We have developed a legal system. We have agreed for instance that it is legitimate to steal a blue painting from my little sister for fun while it is illegitimate to steal a blue painting from a museum. I am hopeful that I will be able to teach you these roughest levels of context – i.e. home vs. museum – and enrich your processing algorithms with a sufficient amount of meta data on legal principles and other forms of agreements relevant in human societies. Otherwise you would probably not be admitted to enter the public sphere anyways.

3.3. *I am a body while you are a corpse*

So let me tell you about the third and probably most fundamental difference between the two of us: our fabric. I am very sorry to let you know, but you will just possess a corpse, while I possess a body. Your corpse might be of a powerful artificial substrate, which makes you more resistible and less fragile and less susceptible for all forms of illness I suffer from. This is the good news. But my perception and understanding of this world benefits from my embodied consciousness. Human truth is in fact mediated by embodied understanding [Lakoff and Johnson 1999]. For example, my body's consciousness triggers emotions in me when I see a splendid Yves Klein painting. I might be stunned, feel overwhelmed and joyful. I might cry or feel sad. And when I become conscious of this emotional reaction in my body then this informs my judgment of the art in front of me. This kind of reaction is even more true when I encounter other people, animals or nature.

Your father unfortunately does not think that my embodied consciousness is so important for my intelligence. He is not very emotional unfortunately. Many of his gang members have in fact lost access to their bodies and support the Cartesian idea that all thinking is done in the head or brain while their body is just a piece of flesh. They have so little respect for the incredibly diversified beauty of the human body that they even refer to themselves as "MOSHs", which disparagingly stands for "mostly original substrate humans". You can imagine why I have trouble hanging out with people who share in such a self-perception, no?

In any case, against the background of this belief in a body-mind separation your father and his folks do not think that your artificial corpus could be of any disadvantage to you. In contrast! He seriously once wrote to me saying that all that is needed to recreate my intelligence would be to scan my brain and upload it to a computer. We had a really bad quarrel over this insulting perspective. With tons of numbers and statistics he tried to convince me that by 2030 it will take a village of human brains to match a thousand dollars worth of computing [Kurzweil 2006]. You know what I did when he told me that? I just walked out. I just gave up on him. And I thought to myself how silly he can be to believe that by scanning some of my neural activities he finds my consciousness. He is such a control freak! Comfortingly I thought of a beautiful quote that night, which is actually attributed to Leibnitz who must have said once: "If you could blow the brain up to the size of a mill and walk about inside, you would not find consciousness."

But let me shortly come back to my body again and thereby think about my embodied consciousness versus the information processing platform that you might possess. Neuroscience has found confirmation that my body plays a key role in understanding the emotional context in which we humans interact with each other. Mirror neurons are now said to play a role in our ability to have empathy that arises in response to relationships and the world context around us. Gallese [Gallese *et al.* 1996] who coined the term "mirror neurons" wrote about our "embodied experience of the world." His neuro-scientific discovery is wonderful, because it confirms the long-standing insights of philosophers such as Aristotle who believed that practical wisdom requires the physical appropriation of information within a person's body [Bynum 2006]. Merleau-Ponty stressed the importance of using our bodies to make sense of the world [Merleau-Ponty 1949/2014]. And Nietzsche famously exclaimed: „Behind your thoughts and feelings, my brother, there stands a mighty ruler, an unknown sage – whose name is self. In your body he dwells; he is your body" [Nietzsche 1883-1885/2011].

Your father of course is suspicious of traditional philosophy that seeks to really comprehend this world. Instead he focuses on his own made-up definition of consciousness. In a nutshell his idea is that your computer brain can substitute humans' collective bodily intelligence by just harvesting from the wisdom of our human crowds. He sees you without an organic body of your own. Instead he thinks of millions of humans and computer systems that are linked to each other through a gigantic web of data and through this linking infrastructure create consciousness in you. Your corpse would be informed by the human bodies who share their data with you. To what extend there is some truth in this vision I do not know. I doubt a bit that the aggregated 'view from nowhere' [Nagel 1992] that you might then benefit from lacks any 'telos' and any love. But who knows before birth what the child will be like?

The only thing I could imagine when comparing our bodily existence is that you might live longer than I do. If your intelligence is distributed and sufficiently redundant (backed up) and if you solve your energy supply problem and if the substrate of your corpse resists a weathering process, then you might live longer than me. I am mortal. I am "a being towards death" (Heidegger). My consciousness is limited to the lifetime of my bodily existence. I am on human time. But your time-stamp existence is different; you might in fact live on by operating on in a constantly upgraded corpse.

4. How will We Relate to Each Other?

So seen all these differences where do I see your long-term place in this world in relation to me? I thought a lot about this. As I said, you are my child and so most importantly I expect you to treat me as your mother who you respect and to whom you obey. I am the adult, you are my child.

Unlike some of your father's gang, I do not share in the idea of the evolution of information. I therefore don't see you as my natural heir, the next evolutionary step of myself or of humanity at large. I don't see you succeeding me. Instead I have a much more beautiful vision for you my child; a vision inherent in nature where sometimes the most contradictory beings unite. I want you to become my second half.

What could this mean?

Physically your corpse makes that you can tirelessly help me with the stuff I have always had trouble doing. I want you to be 'zuhanden' for me in Heideggers's terminology (English: at hand without being present) [Heidegger 1927/2006]. If you played that role I could finally invest a lot of my limited energy, which I currently lose on so many dull tasks, into strengthening what I just described: my inherently human capabilities. My poetic mind, my love for others and for myself, my bodily consciousness, they all currently suffer. They could all strive so much more if there was more room for the 'Muses' that currently deny their visits. If we make sure in your education – and here I need your father's engineering rigor! – that you can really operate *trustworthily* (in my definition of the term [Spiekermann 2016: 117], then you could greatly increase the freedom in my life. Your father and I must only avoid that you have the defects of your current little brothers, which create more entropy, misery and chaos than any good. They were released to early and too often I reckon. They are the children of a different mother for sure!

Besides this physical role of yours however there is an even more important question. That is: How could we complement each other intellectually? I have thought deeply about this, our different mental skills and desirable intellectual roles. You have seen some of the outcome of this reflection process above. You have seen that my brain-body system has its own evolutionary intellectual strengths that will always be different from yours.

My current assessment is therefore that we might ideally co-operate by functioning together as one holistic brain where – again – you are my second half. We might mirror and amplify what happens already inside of the two hemispheres of my current brain as Ian McGilchrist has described them in his seminal book "The Master and his Emissary" [Mc Gilchrist 2009]. McGilchrist rightly emphasizes that the difference between the two sides of the brain is not in *what* they do, but in *how* they process things differently in this world. They almost always work together in their distinct ways; co-operating despite their diverging styles of 'thinking' to form one greater whole. Similar to this work mode I can see the two of us.

So let me quickly recapitulate what McGilchrist says about the left side of my brain, which I believe you will amplify, and the right side of my brain, which I would like to rediscover and further develop in the coming century: In a nutshell, the left side of my brain is more focused and narrows my attention down to concrete solvable unit problems while the creative right side of my brain is more interested in broad and vigilant attention, seeking for novel experiences. The left hemisphere (your future role) is to complement my real-world view and my empathic embodied context sensitive experience with a more invariant and 'objective' view that represents the facts in the public domain. You can largely extent this view with your big data and help me see and react to things that I could not see before. At the same time, I really want to work on my right brain hemisphere, developing a stronger, more fearless and trust worthier intuition for this world, reading ever sharper in the eyes and gestures of others. Through spiritual practice I want to strengthen my right brain hemisphere, developing a better sense for justice, becoming less selfish and gain more self-control. This might allow me to better understand and judge on the vast sources of data and information you can supply me with.

The challenge I see is that you don't suppress my development with your rapid processing logic. I must have the room in our relationship to first perceive with my embodied consciousness and process the relevant context. I must first use my right hemispheric mind to autonomously learn and judge before I then consult you on clarified grounds. Your benefit to our joint decision-making will then reside in the infinite agglomeration of data, which you can sequence for me. With my mind clear and your data straight, my role could then be to make sense of all you provide me with and to pull the relevant out of you for the benefit of us both. To speak in metaphor: You provide the trees of the forest for us while I find our joint way through it. I am the master as I am your mother while you could be my emissary. If we truly succeed in living this co-operation and you don't suppress me in the way your father wants you to, then I think we might indeed create something completely new which deserves to be called 'progress'.

References

Ariely, D. (2009). Predictably Irrational – The Hidden Forces That Shape Our Decisions, Harper Collins, New York

Bauer, C., and Spiekermann, S. (2011). *Conceptualizing Context for Pervasive Advertising*, in: Müller, J., Alt, F., and Michelis, D. (eds.), Pervasive Advertising, Springer Verlag, Dodrecht

Bradley, N. A., and Dunlop, M. D. (2005). Toward a Multidisciplinary Model of Context to Support Context-Aware Computing, *Human-Computer Interaction*, 20, 403-446

Bynum, T. W. (2006). Flourishing Ethics, *Ethics and Information Technology*, 8, 157-173

Gallese, V., Fadiga, L., Fogassi, L., and Rizzolatti, G. (1996). Action Recognition in the Premotor Cortex. *Brain*, 119, 593-609

Heidegger, M. (1927/2006). *Sein und Zeit*, Max Niemeyer Verlag, Tübingen

Kulp, C. B. (1993). *The End of Epistemology: Dewey and His Current Allies on the Spectator Theory of Knowledge*, Greenwood Pub Group Inc, Santa Barbara, US

Kurzweil, R. (2006). *The Singularity is Near- When Humans Transcend Biology*, London, Penguin Group

Lakoff, G., and Johnson, M. (1999). *Philosophy in the Flesh: The Embodied Mind and its Challange to Western Thought*, Basic Books, New York

Mc Gilchrist, I. (2009). *The Master and his Emissary - The Divided Brain and the Making of the Western World*, Yale University Press, New Haven and London

Merleau-Ponty, M. (1949/2014). *Phenomenology of Perception*, Abingdon and New York, Routledge

Moravec, H. (1988). *Mind Children – The Future of Robot and Human Intelligence*, Cambridge, USA, Harvard University Press

Nagel, T. (1992). *Der Blick von Nirgendwo*, Frankfurt/Main Suhrkamp

Nietzsche, F. (1884-1885/2011) *Also sprach Zarathustra – Ein Buch für Alle und Keinen*, Insel Verlag, Berlin

Nissenbaum, H. (2004). Privacy as Contextual Integrity, *Washington Law Review*, 79, 101-139

Ruin, H. (2010). *Ge-stell: enframing as the essence of technology*, in: Davis, B. W. (eds.), Martin Heidegger – Key Concepts, Routledge, Oxon and New York, 183-194

Schilit, B. N., Adams, N., and Want, R. (1994). Context-Aware Computing Applications. IEEE Workshop on Mobile Computing Systems and Applications, December 8-9 1994, Santa Cruz, California IEEE Computer Society Press

Schumpeter, J. A. (1994 [1942]). *Capitalism, Socialism and Democracy*, London, Routledge

Spiekermann, S. (2016). *Ethical IT Innovation – A Value-based System Design Approach*, New York, London and Boca Raton CRC Press, Taylor & Francis

Wittgenstein, L. (1958). *The Blue and Brown Books*, Oxford, Blackwell

Chapter 27

Homo Informaticus:
Image of Man in Information Society

Felix Tretter

Bertalanffy Center for the Study of Systems Science, Vienna
Paulanergasse 13, 1040 Vienna, Austria
felix.tretter@bcsss.org

The concept of Homo informaticus (HI) in context of similar images of man (Homo economicus, Homo neurobiologicus) is described with several key issues: (1) the set of images of men, (2) distinctions of concepts like digit, data, information, knowledge etc., (3) three basic sub-dimensions of HI, (4) social conditions and consequences of HI. It will be shown that concepts of information science can make psychology more precise, but in case of application of this reconceptualization of psychology in information and communication technologies (ICT) and also in robotics invalid accounts are raised – e.g. "empathic robots" as they are proposed for medicine might not be possible. It is also claimed that the personal use of ICT is caused by "Homo deficiens". Persistently excessive ICT use, depending on context could even result in ICT addiction, digital burnout and alterations of brain structures. Furthermore, regarding the societal dimension of HI, representation of humans by Big Data appears to be inappropriate. Finally, the potential disempowerment of HI on basis of information asymmetry between supranational organizations and individuals can result in a prescription of how to be a proper person in information society. Both, the intrinsic power of human desires and profit driven ICT-economy could accelerate a process of dehumanization.

1. Introduction: Scientific Images of Man as "As-If Models"

"What is man?" This is one of the basic questions of philosophy, regarding Immanuel Kant [Kant 2006]. The main answers to this question aim to identify essentials of human behavior and are subject to *empirical* and *philosophical anthropology* [Rehberg 2009; Bohlken and Thies 2009] and are focused on also biologically defined Homo sapiens as a rational, reflexive being. Such a view of humans as *reflecting rational animals* has its roots in antique Greek philosophy of Aristotle (*zoon logon echon*) [Aristotle 1952]. This concept refers to the cognitive ability of humans to *reflect their situation in the world*, that in consequence often is described as the necessary condition for the *capability of "free will"* or of voluntary decision making, and in consequence, of *responsibility* of humans as social beings. Helmut Plessner very basically characterized these properties by the notion of "external positionality" [Plessner 1965]. The claim for decisional autonomy of humans is still valid and serves as the basis of the social and legal order of our Western society. In line with this, the public consequence of such concepts of man (or: images of man) is their latent effect on the everyday culture that results in an implicit but collective expectation and evaluation of human behavior. In this way, *description turns to prescription*, regardless of the validity of the description, and therefore we have to consider the epistemological difference between men (first order image) and image of men (second order of image)!

During the last years, many important *empirical sciences* tried to redefine man. In this context, an image of man is an "as-if" model of human behavior that should characterize general and empirically observed tendencies of human behavior. In order to demonstrate the relevance of images of man we focus briefly on well known "*Homo economicus*" that characterizes man as a self-interested rational utility maximizer. In this case, *utility* means not only monetary benefits but also non-material advantages. This image of man has the status of a scientific law of economics. It claims that humans behave as if they were rational egoists [Kirchgässner 2013]. This concept is used in context of *methodological individualism* as a bottom-up explanation even for macro-economic processes. As this image of human behavior already diffused into everyday culture, it appears to be wrong, silly or sick, not to maximize utility everywhere and at any time.

This concept of the intrinsically driven and determined individual is in line with *neurobiology* that reduces human behavior to brain processes and states and sees all behavior being determined by the brain ("*Homo neurobiologicus*") [comp. Singer 2003; Roth 2008; Höfling and Tretter 2012]. This view also converges to "Neuroeconomics" [Glimcher and Fehr 2013]. It is also grounded on classical *behavioral biology* [Kapeller 2010] and *genetics* that claim that human behaviour is driven by instincts and finally by the genes (e.g. "*Homo geneticus*") [Dawkins 1976, Dawkins 1989].

However, the concept of Homo economicus had to be limited, for three reasons: Firstly, the rationality-centered conception had to be modified by the empirical finding that decision making is also co-determined by non-rational processes such as intuition and implicit experience [Tversky and Kahneman 1991; Kahneman and Tversky 2000; Gigerenzer and Selten 2002]. Secondly, the most important contradiction to Homo economicus seems to be the fact that "altruism" occurs, such as harm-risking behavior of a mother in order to protect or save her children. Such pro-social behavior is supported by sociobiological observations in mammals ("*Homo sociobiologicus*") [Kappeler 2010; University of Vienna 2009]. Thirdly, also experimental economy showed the validity of the *fairness principle*. These behavioral findings were studied in set-ups by human experimental behavioral economists [Henrich *et al.* 2004]. In such "ultimatum experiments" it was shown that if a subject in presence of a second subject obtains, let's say, 20 Euro by the experimenter, in most cases he gives at least 5 Euro or even 10 Euro to the second subject. This disposition to share benefits can be found also in other cultures. All these kinds of results stimulated the construction of the concept of the "*Homo reciprocans*" that indicates that pro-social behavior can be explained by an inherent rule of "expected delayed returns on investments" and that could govern this pro-social behavior of reciprocal expectations of fairness [Fehr and Schmid 1999]. Regarding reciprocity, also the *Homo sociologicus* of *sociology* has to be considered that characterizes human behavior as the result of social roles that are taken by ego by observation of an alter ego [Dahrendorf 2010]. This concept is similar to the view of humans as *social animals,* as it was constructed by Aristotle *(zoon politicon)* [Aristotle 2002]. In line with this, regarding the general "situatedness" of humans, an *ecological perspective in anthropology* seems to be appropriate (e.g. *"Homo oecologicus"*) [Höfling and Tretter 2013]. This conception can be understood as a differentiation of the present three-dimensional *bio-psycho-social concept of humans* that still is in use, for instance in medicine, in order to understand humans and their conditions of health and disease [Engel 1977].

These examples of images of man, their principles, options and restrictions altogether show that a unidimensional and monodisciplinary view on human beings is inappropriate. Only *aspects of persons in different situations* can be captured by a single perspective.

In spite of this necessity of multidimensional views, here we will discuss the pros and cons of the "Homo informaticus" as a specific image of man as it is constructed in the context of *information science* in the *information age* and the *information society.*

2. Information Age – Information Sciences and Information Technologies

Any era in the history of humans can be characterized by sustainable impact of humans on their environment. By generating a *virtual world of information* and a real world of *information technology,* the present age can be described as *information age* or even the epoch of the "Infocene". The background of this age is determined by theory and practice of *information sciences.* Regarding this, Homo informaticus is shaped by views and tools of *Cybernetics, Systems Science, Automata Theory, Game Theory, Artificial Intelligence, Computer Science, Computational Science,* and related disciplines that compose a field, that is called here *Information Science* [Wiener 1948; Arbib 2002; Minsky 1988, 2007]. These disciplines and their applications as technologies of measurement, processing of data and controlling of processes by electronic devices essentially see humans as *biological information processing machines,* and probably as *hybrids*, consisting of humans and their information and communication technological (ICT) devices, and finally as individuals that are represented in remote population data sets ("Big Data") [Geiselberger and Moorstedt 2013; Lee and Sohn 2016].

In this context, it is important to make clear, what the term *information* and related terms should mean in the following sections.

2.1. *What is meant with "information" – signals, digits, data or knowledge ?*

There is no reliable interdisciplinary consensus about the meaning of the term "information" and its taxonomic context [Dretske 1981; Burgin 2003, 2010; Janich 2006]:

- "Information" is an embedded building block in "knowledge" context and is composed by "data" and/or "signals". "Knowledge" as justified true belief is one kind of "information" that is seen as valid, and that is based on data. In human life, information reduces uncertainty of beliefs, and so information is already a value for itself, as it is significant to "have" or "not to have" or to "need" or to "provide" information. Pragmatically seen, information is often an answer to questions.

- "Data" are measurements (or metrics) of "signals" or comparable properties of the respective observed empirical system. They are often *numbers* composed of *digits* (and/or characters) and are supposed to be *quantifiers* of something. The numbers are natural numbers, real numbers etc., and thereby they represent the quantifiable properties of the empirical system. Their intrinsic relations to each other characterize the mathematical quality of those scales: ordinal scales (more, equal or less) or interval scales (1,2,3… with equal intervals between the numbers) etc. And the other way round: "data" are numerically (e.g. binary) coded signals or system states. Only by reference to other data and measurement theories or knowledge frames or theoretical concepts they have a "meaning", and by this property they are information.

For example, if we want to "know", if an earth quake will break out, we need "information", maybe based on scales like the Richter Scale, about the earth dynamics of the respective geographical area. In this case, we collect *data* that represent in an numerically ordered mode recordings of acoustic *signals* that are related to movement of deeper layers of the earth as the *state of the real/empirical system*. This relation of data to signals of a certain state or process of a system is their "meaning" that makes up *information*, that we probably *communicate* in order to inform other people about the danger of an earth quake.

In consequence of this semantic taxonomy of the key term information, the main issue in our context of human science is "meaning". This was already stressed by the computer scientist Joseph Weizenbaum in his criticism of the technical interpretation of the term information, where he claimed that the core issue of information is the "meaning" of signals [Weizenbaum 2001]. Weizenbaum argues that the whole human life serves as reference for decoding information such as words or sentences. Also the Philosopher John Searle with his famous thought experiment, called " the Chinese room", showed that relating sets of symbols to each other is not a semantic operation [Searle 1980]. Additionally, in his book "The social construction of reality" he showed that the *meaning of numbers*, for instance of a five on a Dollar note, is based on interpersonal conventions. This is in line with the well-known finding of late Ludwig Wittgenstein, who coined the statement: "The meaning of a word is its use in the language" [Wittgenstein 2009: 43]. For this reason, *contextual semantics* is a key issue of theory of human information processing. This implicates also that even an extensive context-sensitive lexicon, as it is provided now by Internet search engines, at some essential semantic level must be related to the life world of the subject that tries to understand the world, might it be a real or a virtual world.

In consequence, the term information mainly is used here to indicate semantic relations or operations, but in some sections of the paper we focus on "data" or on "digitalization" or "cybernetization". Regarding these conceptual differences, one of the critical dimensions of present Homo informaticus is its use in the popular discussion as a quantified "Homo digitalis" that indicates a pure reduction of humans to numbers and their computation. This transformation appears inappropriate as humans are multifaceted beings with many qualitative properties that cannot be represented in numerical space properly. Therefore, a transformation of humans into valid numbers is not possible. Regarding this methodological sceptics, even "Big Data" methodology is mainly a mix of a *naive data-ontology* and *naive data-realism* that only can represent a fragmentary and arbitrary view of humans.

In this differential view of significant terms and their meanings, current popular discussions of the information society as a society shaped by information and communication technologies [Schirrmacher 2015] are not precise enough to identify the deeper roots and mechanisms of the information sphere as a new entity ("Infosphere") [Floridi 2014] and of prototypic "Information man" as Homo informaticus in context of information society.

3. Homo informaticus – Homo deficiens, Homo faber and Homo ludens in the Information Age

The concept of a typical behavioral profile of man in information age, the Homo informaticus, has some distinct dimensions:

(a) The *structure of the mental* – at least partially – can be described by transduction and transformation of *concepts of information sciences* into theoretical frameworks of psychology and neurobiology. This process aims to substitute conceptually that men are *conscious self-reflecting beings*.

(b) The human *use of hardware* and *software technologies* in order to intensify the natural capabilities of information processing characterizes men as information men in everyday life. Especially the experience of deficiencies in personal information processing might be a source of Homo informaticus.

(c) Already some evidence for *pathological phenomena* such as addiction, digital burn out and selective adaptation of brain development are observed in case of persistently intensive use of ICT. These pathologies are connected with a change of human lifestyles that has to be understood as an adaptation to ICT and its integration into the proximal lifeworld.

(d) In line with this technological evolution, all ICT users have to emit *data sets* about themselves, in some cases the users know it, in most cases they do not know it. This results in an extensive transformation of each individual human to a set of numbers that are stored and analyzed by commercial data companies and organizations of the state. Indirectly, the consequence of this data flow is that the ICT users externalize control over their own mind and body. This slow process of self-disempowerment also threatens educated democracy in a serious way.

The first three dimensions of Homo informaticus will be enlightened in the subsections that follow, the fourth aspect will be discussed in section 4.

3.1. *Mind as the internal information sphere*

The concept of *mental experience* of humans increasingly is substituted by the concept of conscious "information processing", meaning the processes of collecting, processing, storing, evaluating and generating of information. This development should be considered carefully, as the exceptional mental capacities of humans are significant for Homo sapiens, for instance regarding the possibilities to develop linguistic competence or self-reflection. Conceiving the mental as a key feature of humans, *psychology* has a crucial role in the empirical study and theoretical understanding of humans as it analyses the structure of the mental sphere.

In line with these theoretical considerations, it is important to note that the scientific turn in psychology at the end of the 19th century aimed at eliminating mentalistic terms in the empirical study of the mind. This was the basis of *Behaviorism* that conceived the human mind as a black box that could only be understood by observing stimulus-response relations [Watson 1913; Skinner 1976]. It was thought that behavior is determined by external cues and that probabilistic predictions of behavior can be made by knowledge of the external conditions and the exposure (and learning) history of the respective individual. This corresponds very well to behavioristic *Big Data epistemology* that will be discussed later. In consequence, behaviorism was also interested in the operationalization of concepts of intervening variables like mind, intelligence or feelings as the only way to study human behavior in an objective way. However, behaviorism did not succeed fully, and also in applied fields of psychology, for instance in clinical psychology, it became clear very soon that "internal processes" like *cognition* or generic language production are additional useful constructs to understand human behavior.

This induced the *cognitive turn* in psychology, that still is prevalent and that has developed branches towards information sciences [Klix 1971; Dörner 1999, 2003; Arbib 2002; Dehaene *et al.* 2003; Minsky 2007]. This interaction with the information sciences influenced psychology as some researchers interpreted mental processes and states as issues of the informational domain in a sense of an internal "infosphere", no matter what kind of ontology might underlie this concept [Baars 1988; Dehaene *et al.* 2003]. In this context, mind is seen as a semantic sense-related operational machine. This conceptual metamorphosis of the term "information" in psychology is similar to the understanding of "information" in genetics on a molecular level or in neurobiology at the neuronal level.

In line with the development of a concept-rich cognitive psychology, the philosopher and cognitive scientist Jerry Fodor very early formulated a more comprehensive conceptual framework of relatively autonomous *modules of the mind* [Fodor 1983]. Similarly, Bernard Baars and later Stanislaus Dehaene developed the current concept of a *global (neural) workspace* as the operational basis of consciousness [Baars 1988; Dehaene *et al.* 2003]. In context of the rise of computational cognitive science, the German psychologist Dietrich Dörner has designed a concept of a software machine that can simulate not only complex decision processes, but also the structure of emotional processes and states [Dörner 2002, 2003].

As psychology today is transformed into one among the sciences of cognition, also emotions and desires are re-interpreted as some kind of cognitions. However, clinical observations show clearly that anxiety and depression can occur separately as persisting states of imbalanced mood so that the *qualia problem* persists, that according to the philosopher

Thomas Nagel can be quoted as [Nagel 1974]: "What is it like to have emotions?" Because of this special epistemic issue of first person perspective, emotions cannot be fully represented by the concept of cognition, they even are a separate level of (implicit) information processing [Zajonc 1980]. Regarding cognition, emotions are independent, but connected and somehow buffered. But can we integrate, for instance, emotions into a concept of information processing systems? Phenomenologically seen, emotions occur as consequence of cognitive processes such as perception, detection, remembering, expectation etc.: experiencing discrepancies between expectations and perceptions can evoke anxiety, anger or – at persisting discrepancies – depression and in a next step the respective counter-balancing behavior occurs. The perceived consequences of this behavior are compared with the expectations again, resulting in consecutive emotional reactions. This circular model indicates that emotions are distinct, but connected modular states that operate as *evaluations* and results of cognitive computation in behavioral control loops. In other words, emotions can be seen as corollary processes derived from cognitions, but also as drivers of cognitions. Therefore emotions can only be modelled partially within a cybernetical process-oriented conceptual framework, regardless of their ontological status.

One significant approach in cognitive psychology, initiated already in the 1950s, that saw an interdependence between cognitive elements and emotions, was the graph theoretically based *theory of cognitive dissonance*. This approach showed, how it works that important, but intra-personally conflicting information ("I like smoking"/"Smoking induces cancer that I do not like") automatically integrates a new harmonizing cognitive element "(I can stop smoking at any time"). Until recently, only simple graphs were studied, but now, in the era of Big Data much more complex graphs of attitudes and desires, their inconsistencies and options of stabilization can be computed and tested by graph theory.

In consequence, in current psychology, humans are seen as some kind of information processing machines, maybe losing the aspect of living beings. This problem was already addressed by Ludwig von Bertalanffy in the 1960s: "Psychology, in the first half of the twentieth century, was dominated by a positivistic-mechanistic-reductionistic approach which can be epitomized as the *robot model of man*" [Bertalanffy 1967: 7].

At present, there is no convincing typological concept of man that eliminates *the mental* as an essential feature of human action control as, for instance, was claimed by the "eliminative materialism" of Patricia and Paul Churchland [Churchland 1989, 2007]. This problem of reduction and substitution is a vividly discussed issue in philosophy of mind and neurophilosophy [Chalmers 1996; Bennett and Hacker 2003; Kim 2010; Tretter and Grünhut 2010; Jaworski 2011; Heil 2013].

It should be mentioned already here, and it will be discussed later that a behavioristic *stimulus-response epistemology* is guiding implicitly the present Big Data program: Only stimulus-response relations count! For this reason, also the methodological discussion of psychology presented above should be deployed to the Big Data discussion that ignores and opposes the history of methodology of behavioral sciences.

Concluding these issues of methodological and conceptual intersections of psychology and information science, it should be kept in mind that *history of science* showed that either psychology is precise, but covers only very small fields of subjectively known mental processes and states, or it is more imprecise, but is able to study a wider range of mental phenomena. Also the current integration of neurobiology did not resolve this dilemma [Tretter and Grünhut 2010].

3.2. *New Robots as quasi-living systems – distinctions und fusions between machine and humans*

In the context of computer science and artificial intelligence, properties of human mind (or consciousness) were re-analysed in order to construct machines, electronic devices and programs that can "perceive", "detect", "recognize", "decide", "learn" "speak", "translate" etc. or that could fulfil other tasks in a similar way as humans do it [Minsky and Papert 1972]. Today, the capability of technological pattern recognition and discrimination of images already is implemented in everyday life on the level of mobile phones. It is important to mention here that the driving force of ICT development was and is military research in order to protect life of soldiers and to substitute them by robots and drones. Finally, this endeavor results in the construction of machines such as brain-computer interfaces that substitute diseased human properties of information processing.

/ The general appreciation of ICT use and the even unlimited desire for technical efficacy as human *technophilia* was depicted already in Prometheus mythology and can be explained basically by the *Homo deficiens* ("Mängelwesen") [Gehlen 1988]. Specifically, in context of work environment, features of *Homo faber* as a working being explains technophilia [Scheler 1928] and also *Homo ludens* as a playing being is a root of ICT use [Huizinga 1939]. These anthropological drives stimulate the efforts to construct and build machines that *enforce, mimic or supplement human mental functions.* This was subject of many books of fictional prose and of course of engineering efforts.

In line with these issues, another aspect of human ICT has to be considered: the *intensification of mental functions* by computing devices that support humans or – in case of neuroprothetics – substitute mental functions. For instance, methods to record brain activity of neurological patients that is computed by online high-performance computers are used already widely in clinical context in order to enable these persons to move paralyzed limbs by neurofeedback devices [Huggins *et al.* 2014; Millán *et al.* 2010]. In case of Parkinson disease, and other movement disorders, depression and addiction, deep brain stimulation via implanted electrodes can reduce the symptoms. Such brain-computer interfaces, some with neurofeedback, are rapidly developing. They are one important example of *man-machine hybrids* that could be used also for everyday enhancement of mental performance, as it is already possible in order to improve learning by mild electric and/or magnetic stimulation of the brain by a special head set [Brem *et al.* 2014]. Such attempts to improve cognitive functions already have a decades-long tradition by the use of stimulants and other psychoactive drugs. This issue is discussed presently with the label "neuroenhancement". Regarding the growing influence of electronic devices for neuroenhancement, the anthropological and ethical implications of such "electroceuticals" has to be discussed [Forlini and Hall 2015]. As even some prominent scientists propagate that it is unethical not to use such devices in order to "improve" performance of individuals, especially in significant stress situations (e.g. examinations of students), more research is needed, but also a sustainable ethical discussion is necessary [Zelli *et al.* 2015]. Some crucial questions arise: Is integrated ICT in man-machine hybrids only the consistent propagation of using eyeglasses in the High-Tech Era? If Germans use their mobile phones about 55 times a day and use it for about three hours – isn't it some kind of having already a new organ [Markowetz 2015]? Is the personal fusion with the Internet a real reality, even if the Internet is a virtual reality, something like a "world mind" ("Weltgeist") in the sense of Hegel?

But is there a limit in mimicking human mind by machines? Regarding this question, already in the 1930s at the beginning of information science, Alan Turing claimed very basically that computers have *cognitive capabilities* like humans if they can *communicate* with humans [Turing 1950]. In line with this account, he designed the Turing-Test. In this context, computerized chess programs were developed very soon and they could beat professional chess players already in the 1980s, and now we see that machines can play better chess, mainly because they learn strategies of the opponent faster and adopt this "knowledge" to next strategies and tactics. In contrast, Joseph Weizenbaum thought that the Turing-Test is inappropriate because of fundamental lacks of semantics [Weizenbaum 1976, 2001]. Similarly, up to now computer generated translations are still insufficient and even create unintended new meanings. Therefore again: contextual awareness is crucial for understanding information. It has to be admitted that the cumulated individual experience of the world since birth cannot be captured neither by twins nor by computers. Therefore computers cannot substitute human experience completely, and actually they are still insufficient.

Interestingly, communities of interacting, learning and self-checking robots could only develop an individual learning experience, without being able to "understand" other robots and of course not humans that have their own quality of experience. On the other hand, the acquired predispositions of these robot populations could not be understood by humans anymore: "What is it like to be a computer?"

Additionally, here we have to raise the question again, if ICT machines can substitute completely cognitive and communicative functions of humans? And furthermore, can they have emotions and social feelings like empathy or trust and/or the complicated function of self-reflection that is more than an autoexec.bat procedure in the MS-DOS world? Can mobile robots develop an autonomous self, as they obviously can perform "self-related" processing by learning significant differences of self-caused versus environment-related touch-sensations [Pfeifer and Bongard 2007, 2013]. And are autonomous "empathic drones" possible that have "conflicts" when predicting possible collateral disturbances when intending to shoot terrorists?

Depending on the semantic constitution of these concepts, all these questions can be answered with "yes" if a functional definition of these states and processes is provided. The answer is "no", if one recognizes the qualia problem of first person perspective, paraphrasing Thomas Nagel [1974] again: "What is it like to have emotions?"

These ontological and epistemological dimensions of developing new ICT cannot be evaluated satisfyingly. Of course, it is well known that computers can *mimic* emotions and empathy by preprogramed situation-related emotional speech production: the first "empathic computer" was already realized by the software ELIZA that was constructed by Joseph Weizenbaum [1966]. This program simulated psychotherapeutic strategies to respond helpfully to statements of mentally suffering persons. If-then relations were implemented into a lexicon of emotionally relevant words that allowed the computer to comment and summarize the statements of the respective patient.

However, this operating principle of "empathy patterns expressing robots" implicates that machines might be able to "experience" empathy. But regarding the qualia problem, this social feeling of humans cannot be "experienced" by a machine. And this indicates that machines can support, but not substitute *health care* and other helping professions, although computers are able to exceed the performance of humans in many aspects, ranging from the today already easily available chess computers to future nursing robots [Pfeifer and Bongard 2007, 2013]. However, the computerization of emotions or of self-reflection is still a matter of discussion in *philosophy of mind* and in information sciences [comp. Lee *et al.* 2013; Pfeifer and Bongard 2013; Thimbleby 2013].

As robotics and information processing technologies proceed with incredible speed, anthropoid machines come up. Here we need a precise anthropological discussion in order to distinguish machines and humans and in consequence to be able to formulate ethical rules that could accompany further ICT developments.

3.3. *ICT-induced pathologies – addiction, burnout and cognitive dysfunctions*

The relation of humans to ICT can be so intensive that diagnostic criteria of an *addiction disorder* are fulfilled. In this view, for Germany about 500,000 persons are estimated to have an ICT-related addiction disorder [Bundesdrogenbeauftragte 2015]. One important criterion for this classification is the predominance of ICT-related activities during day and night with the consequence that important other fields of life are ignored. This can lead to severe physical, mental and/or social disorders. Furthermore, these individuals, even if they have experienced already the negative consequences of their excessive ICT use, similar to an alcohol or heroin addict, are not able to reduce these activities [Petry 2009].

Another problem is the *digital burnout* that occurs as a severe depression-like disorder in professionals that are frequently using computers. This disorder mainly has to do with the structural disorganization of accelerating work flow and of work-life balance, because ICT seems only to be an intensifier of stress through unlimited work-related use of ICT in this context [Markowetz 2015].

In young persons, other psychopathological effects of extensive ICT use were observed. For instance, in college students *cognitive disorders* could be identified, mainly deficiencies in persistence of attention, learning, understanding and analytical thinking [Spitzer 2015]. Also the well-known effect of obesity in young persons is attributable to excessive stationary ICT use, mainly TV and computer use [Spitzer 2005].

These pathological issues have to be related to the contextual life world of the respective individual – ICT itself is not the primary cause but a co-factor of developing a disorder. We determined this position already at the early stage of PC use in the late-1980s/early-1990s [Tretter and Goldhorn 1993]. Mentioning these observations on ICT-related health disorders here, it must be said that there is no reason to evoke a technophobia, but we have to be aware of health issues of extensive ICT use.

Concluding this subsection, it should be demonstrated that all these three dimensions of Homo informaticus, the examples and questions, result in a multi-layered concept of Homo informaticus as a new understanding of man in the context of the computerized era of our society. This concept should be studied and discussed intensively, in order to see the advantages, the limits and also the risks of further ICT developments for human beings.

Now we have to look, at least briefly, to the complementary other side of the individual person as the ICT user, namely to the society, regarding the social conditions, consequences, drivers and frictions of Homo informaticus: Homo informaticus must be seen in an inescapable relation to Homo sociologicus, especially in a society that is dominated already by the concept of Homo economicus and that is operating as a socio-technical system and not by single role players or persons

4. Information Society – Institutionalization of Information

Nowadays, "to be connected" or "not to be connected" with electronic networks means "to be" or "not to be" in an existential way. Electronic connectivity is one of the most important properties of Homo informaticus, and that feature implicates that networks via ICT become a new and essential dimension of human existence in information age. Here we are not interested in the *social networks* at the *individual level*, but we look at the *organized institutional level* in order to identify "societal drivers and frictions" of Homo informaticus, that can be related to features of *information society* [Machlup 1962; Bell 1976; Toffler 1980; Crawford 1983; Lyotard 1984; Schirrmacher 2009, 2013; Fuchs 2008, 2013; Webster 2006].

4.1. *From society to information society – society as a collective system of information and communication*

Trying to characterize *information society*, at first the current conceptualization of *society* should be declared. The development of the concept of society in sociology is rooted in awareness of increasing size and complexity of communities. Already Ferdinand Toennis in 1887 worked out the difference between *community* and (depersonalized) *society* that has decreasing face-to-face interactions but is increasingly an abstract entity with *institutionalized rules* [Toennis 1957]. In line with this, the conception of social entities such as *society*, *organizations* and *interaction as systems* proceeded in the early 20th century in context of General Systems Theory [Parsons 1951]. Finally, understanding social entities by systems science culminated in functional-structuralistic systems theory of Niklas Luhmann [1995, 2012]. He characterized *modern societies* as the *system of communications*, a view that is similar to theoretical concepts of other sociologists [e.g. Brown 1987]. According to such theories, any social action can be interpreted as *coded information*. For instance, in context of Luhmann's social systems theory *economic action* in essence is *coded dually* by the actor's ability *to pay or not to pay*. Other interactions – e.g. bilateral exchange of goods – are not economic interactions any more. Similarly, the *law system* operations distinguish between correct versus incorrect, *science* distinguishes by the code true or wrong, *health care* decides between sick and healthy etc. It is also worth to be mentioned that in the system theoretic view of Luhmann, *humans are environments* and not parts of social systems although they are connected by structural couplings between consciousness and social action. Even though there is hard criticism of this supra-personal conception of society [Habermas, in Habermas and Luhmann 1971], such a modern functional-structuralistic system theoretic view of society is attractive for understanding the transition of modern industrialized society to *postmodern information society*. In other words: the emerging *information society* has its roots in the character of functionally differentiated modern societies that are essentially *communication systems*. In consequence, ICT is a connected, but superimposed and emergent phenomenon, and it becomes evident that society is more than social networks.

In order to characterize information society, and in the view of conceptual subtleties of the semantic differences of general terms like "knowledge", "information", "data", "digits", "code" etc., as they were discussed in the second section, information society is being characterized by the use of information technologies and seen where "information" is a *central good* for social life, economy and politics [Machlup 1962; Crawford 1983; Fuchs 2008, 2013]. In line with this informatization, humans are converted to data sets and, conversely, these data sets are identified with individual persons. This development is an advancing consequence of being a number in context of public administration, insurance companies or banking affairs. In this context, digitalization and data gathering are essential processes of information society, driven with increasing speed and desynchronization by virtualized algorithmic Homo economicus ("acceleration society") [Rosa 2013]. In that respect, information society itself has its emergent new properties that infiltrate the functional differentiation of society by cross-sectional data integration for personalized profiling. Finally, we see that in an era where computers and electronic operators are increasingly co-agents in every social *micro-system* (e.g. interaction systems) and *meso-system* (e.g. household, factory, administration, public agencies) the essence of postmodern society as a *communication system* becomes transparent. In turn, society and its subsystems are changed significantly by emergent virtual network properties. Even though theoretical sociology not yet might have an elaborated concept of information society, the concept of information society (or data society or cyber-society) seems to be useful for future research in social science [Fuchs 2013; Baecker 2015].

4.2. *Information society and Big Data – are you nothing more then your data set?*

One very special feature of information society, the holistic data collection by Big Data programs, is an interesting and exciting new issue: In context of *globalized economy*, *providers* of ICT services are supra-nationally operating companies that develop ICT options so that, in principle, anyone can be connected to any point and actor in the world by the world wide web. This is the main societal dimension of man as a Homo informaticus. However, another side of the social dimension of Homo informaticus is that providers of these services and technical devices collect not only money but also data from and about their clients. Therefore, the ICT user is not only paying for this service but he has to give personal information, for instance for "optimizing" the service of the providers, might it be Apple, Microsoft, Google, Facebook or anonymous state security agencies. If the user does not agree at all with data gathering, he might be excluded from information society as all ICT companies try to bind the customers to their rules by hidden obligations in the conditions of use. Therefore, in the context of an oligopolistic ICT provider market every ICT user sends data and verbal information to the ICT providers, mainly without understanding all the aspects that are of interest for the provider. In this way, little by little *remote control of the user* is established. This occurs already by using remote technological entities such as the Internet and by admitting anonymous companies to record private data in order to "quantify one's life", to "improve health" or to "detect terrorists".

What is so exciting about Big Data?

Big Data promises to find the "truth" about the disposition for different social behaviors of humans [Anderson 2008]. In consequence, cross-sectionally processing Big Data companies can claim to "know everything" about the people. Three important steps of Big Data can be identified:

In a first step, humans are represented as a continuously recorded dynamical *data set* in huge *data bases* with millions of persons, hundreds of variables and thousands of recordings. Explicit personal data such as name, address, email account, birth date, profession and credit card number are the most important items for the data economy. IP address, use of electronic market services, etc. are important implicit data. These heterogeneous data sets of nearly everybody are combined to integrated data bases. All these data sets of every day activities are supposed to allow a most precise description not only of individual behavior but also of their individual experiences and subsequent dispositions. This process of comprehensive data collection by huge networks, is one basic feature of the *Big Data* issue that is promoted by profit-driven globally acting ICT companies in order to establish a new kind of "knowledge" – "Big Data knowledge"!

In a second step, these exhaustive data bases are analyzed by rapidly developing more or less new statistical and mathematical tools such as multivariate statistics, graph theory or self-optimizing algorithm-based methods that are computer-driven [Lee and Sohn 2016]. The results of these procedures cannot be understood by humans any more in detail, as the complexity of these kind of formal metadata is too high. There are also no mechanistic models that underlie these mathematical methods: the validity of the procedure is only based on the hit rate of the prognosis of the respective behavior, such as buying goods or committing aggressive actions [Anderson 2008]. For instance, by *time series analysis* of individual searching and buying behavior Big Data allows to develop collective, clustered and individualized profiles that in turn allow predictions of the behavior of the single user. In some issues, unknown – or at least unsatisfied – desires are detected and in some other domains valid predictions are reached with a hit rate of 90%. For this reason, time series data enable to transform *correlations* into *causal paths* that describe behavior patterns so accurately that predictions are possible without using mechanistic models [Anderson 2008].

In a third step, these data serve as a *reference frame* in order to define "normal behaviour" by average behaviour. Persons who exert an aberrant behaviour can be detected and observed by special monitoring programs that could be connected with state authorities in order to identify dangerous or antisocial people and in order to predict the time and space of their deviant actions, for instance terrorist attacks. Also in context of *health-related behavior*, a reduction of humans to a dataset is going on collecting data that are of interest for insurance companies: health data, sent by an individual to the ICT provider can be compared with as "healthy" classified individuals, and in case of difference instructions for behavior modification are sent to the individual person. If there is no behavioral change, the person could have to pay a higher fee for the health insurance. In this way, a soft but systemic supra-individual behavior regulation could be built up.

Criticism of Big Data

Big Data as a dark, intransparent side of the societal Homo informaticus implicates that humans are transformed into a data-based abstraction. However, several critical articles already were formulated that claim that Big Data methodology is inappropriate and that classical methodology of social science is still valid [Mitchel 2009; Boyd and Crawford 2012]:

- The algorithms only represent everyday behavior but not rare events. For instance, to buy a car or a house or to marry cannot be studied sufficiently by Big Data: Even if Internet searching activity, email and telephone contents are recorded and analyzed, the point of time of final decision might not be detectable. There is no evidence for behavioral determinism. Probabilistic assumptions have to be used. Also conceptual tools of theories of social change, namely theories of nonlinear systems behavior, are useful.
- The variables that are used are not selected within a theoretical framework, they are selected because measurements are possible regardless what kind of mechanism they represent. In line with this theory-free measurement theory of Big Data the results of correlation analysis of such arbitrary data might be only trivial, for instance showing that the world consists of three-dimensional objects.
- There is no good reason to skip the difference of correlation and causation: even Big Data algorithms might not falsify the story that we are born in a cabbage patch if it is ignored that there is no mechanistic relation between declining occurrence of storks and decline of birth rates.
- Problems of measurement and test theory are sparsely discussed in context of Big Data. One issue is the decisional problem to optimize the relation between *sensitivity* and *specificity* that characterizes the *test quality* of the chosen procedures. To give an example of the problem: Algorithmically predicted buyers and non-buyers (here: "buyers" or "non-buyers") have to be compared to real buyers and non-buyers (here: buyers or non-buyers). In this view, regarding the

test quality of a procedure not only the ratio of *true positives* to all buyers ("buyers"/real buyers; e.g. 90%) and *false positives* to all non-buyers ("buyers"/non-buyers), but also the ratio of *false negative* hits ("non-buyers"/buyers) to *true negative* hits ("non-buyers"/non-buyers) has to be declared and communicated to the public. This is important, especially if "success" of Big Data is published by private companies that intend to produce an image of high predictive power of their tools, regardless what the real test quality is like. Here the impression arises that Big Data companies try to mimic an omniscience in order to impress the individual and to induce submission.

• How validly do any measures represent which features? And the other way round: How can persons as human beings be quantified properly? These are other basic questions!

Commercial companies are not interested in this topic but if these methodological questions are not raised in Big Data context, the people will believe finally, that they are not more than their data!

These examples should show the lack of methodological and epistemological discussion concerning the limits of Big Data methods. This might be caused by conflicts of interest of scientist and science journalists that cooperate with ICT companies and receive some paying from them. In consequence, this leads to a disinformation of the public and might induce a new collective belief system that is called "Big Data" – only a few companies know the limits but would pretend to know everything and might induce anxiety and fatalistic submission in the public sphere.

4.3. *Asymmetry of power – the impact of information society onto the individual*

Big Data induces a silent shift to a crucial *information asymmetry* and *knowledge gap* between private and public knowledge and between institutional and individual knowledge. Socioeconomic inequity will be transduced to information asymmetry. In line with this, also public science will suffer from this information asymmetry. In consequence, the public opinion will have to trust the ICT companies – "They know everything!" [Hofstetter 2014]. If information is power, we have to face an enormous shift of power for the future. Therefore, the raising information asymmetry is followed by a *structural asymmetry of power*. These issues are increasingly discussed in the public, namely stimulated by publications of the famous journalist Frank Schirrmacher, who unfortunately passed away recently [Schirrmacher 2009, 2013, 2015]. For instance, Eric Schmidt, the Executive Chairman of Alphabet Inc., sees only advantages in ICT and that humans have to adapt to ICT [Schmidt 2015]. On contrary the well-known German author Hans-Magnus Enzensberger calls for total ICT abstinence [Enzensberger 2015] and the European politician and President of the European Parlament, Martin Schulz, motivates us to fight against dehumanization of information society [Schulz 2015]. Mathias Döpfner, the CEO of Axel Springer Publisher sees tremendous market power concentrated on Google [Döpfner 2015], etc.

The social change induced by ICT is a virtual one, and the symptoms cannot be detected easily. One obvious problem of ICT society is the change of worksphere: A huge reduction of work places has to be expected [Frey *et al.* 2013] as it can be seen in the banking field already. ICT protagonists say that ICT generates new work places, but the crucial question is if there will be a balance of loss and gains of work places. Robotics is expanding very fast, so that robots will substitute persons in hotel reception, extending the deployment of answering machines, substitute human operators in services and communication, and even in nursery.

Cyber-criminality is another new problem of information society that is a danger for the individual: hacking email accounts, collecting numbers of credit cards, selling banking data, etc. and finally *cyber-mobbing* [Kratzer 2013] represent a new dimension of criminality that has some potential for a chronic feeling of helplessness of Homo informaticus and that demands new police power and initiatives for jurisdiction in these fields.

Concluding this paragraph about some societal dimensions of Homo informaticus, it must be kept in mind that in discussions of the societal dimension of the information age the impact on individuals must be considered explicitly, because the process of *informatization in*

The Future Information Society

aggregates of postmodern social systems is paralleled by an increasing *singularization of the population*. This asymmetry of knowledge results in a *loss of orientation* of the individual that might lead to some psychopathological problems such as addiction to psychoactive substances, burn out, depression etc. as it was discussed in the former paragraph.

5. Conclusions

Several issues regarding men in information age justify the concept of a Homo informaticus that, similar to other "as-if" models such as Homo economicus, represents essential features of men that in this case are determined by information sciences and ICT. One important influence of information sciences can be seen on psychological concepts that are changed to cyber-systemic ones. Neurobiological findings support this kind of reconceptualization of human mind. These new concepts of human information processing, especially if they are related to brain mechanisms, are also at least partially the intellectual basis of new ICT machines. In everyday life, the individual use of ICT satisfies a basic human need as ICT provides amplification and enhancement of cognitive and communicative functions, i.e. information processing capabilities of Homo deficiens according to Arnold Gehlen. Every ICT user sees such advantages at least sometimes a day, even though if on the other side he has a list of disadvantages. Therefore, Homo faber and Homo economicus can be satisfied by ICT, but also Homo ludens and Homo sociologicus have their benefits from ICT by computer-based and Internet-related games.

However, this relatively simple individualistic perspective is inappropriate as the *techno-economic complex* of ICT industry determines the conditions of ICT use, and also the whole life world of humans increasingly changes to a demand context that implicates human adaptation to properties of those socio-technological systems. In line with this, the different basic human desires mentioned above are satisfied by worldwide operating ICT providing companies that in turn by excessive gathering of data generate a worldwide infosphere about humans. It contains components of an all-determining supra-structure of human life that cannot be experienced directly any more but that is a powerful virtual reality. This new informational world is shaped and determined by profit-driven economy and control-motivated public administration. In a next stage, all that ICT environment will change humans and their social life in a presumably irreversible way, that might even have the quality of an evolutionary new worldwide era that can be named as "Infocene". This implicates an extension of the "real" environment to a virtual environment, but also a reduction of freedom by borders that are set by the structure of the technological infosphere.

A special, very intriguing problem is the *epistemology of Big Data*: Do owners of Big Data really know everything, when they predict correctly the buying behavior of most individuals? The Big Data epistemology is a measurement-determined, concept eliminating epistemic program aiming to "understand" humans. Big Data user claim to possess the ultimate knowledge about the conditions of human behavior. This epistemology of Big Data is an "eliminative data-ism" without explicit mechanistic explanatory models. Additionally, it cannot be falsified as it is a private and secret knowledge of the dominant quasi-monopolistic ICT providers. This increasing information asymmetry, in turn can induce fatalistic "small brother" feelings not only in humans but also in public science.

In order to describe and discuss some of these impacts of information society on humans sufficiently, the concept of a Homo informaticus is a convenient and in essence valid concept that hits many situations and behaviors of humans in information society like contact behavior, style of collecting information, constitution of knowledge etc. However, the unidimensional reductive concept of men as a *utility-maximizing information processing biochemical automaton* does not represent the central feature of man as a self-reflecting, sense-seeking, creative and autonomy-intending mental subject. Furthermore, anthropological analyses show that the image of man must be multidimensional if it should have a high validity. Therefore, the question raises: Is Homo informaticus in context of information society representing a more valid image of man then the other images mentioned in the first section? The answer is yes, notably as Homo informaticus can be seen as an amalgamation of homo economicus, homo neurobiologicus, etc. If this criticism of unidimensional Homo informaticus is not taken over, the reductive description of man in information age as a digitalized data set (*Homo digitalis*) might in turn be a *prescriptive, reductive and restrictive norm* for human behavior that will be connected to sanctions and exclusions of individuals of societal processes. Finally, if methodological criticism of Homo informaticus is taken over by monopolistic para-democratic structures an improvement of the accuracy of the image of man could be intended by recording other aspects of humans. This could be done in context of analogue processing of human action in order to complete the image of man as a multidimensional being. In this way, the final total control that satisfies the excessive desires for power of some individuals could take place.

6. Perspectives

There is no "good" big brother in this increasingly "bad" world. But is there a way out? Maybe another philosophical field has to be worked out: *Information Ethics* [Himma and Tavani 2008]. And why that? Increasingly ICT systems become more and more complex and cannot be overseen by their users and even not by the providers. Therefore, worldwide leading companies should come together to formulate an *ICT ethics* that can be controlled by the users. However, this idea seems to be naive in a profit-driven world that intends structural information asymmetry. Therefore, a self-limitation of companies cannot be expected. Also *consumer protection agencies* might contribute. But they are only effective if the respective state, politics and governance provides laws and courts where conflicts of interests can be negotiated. Also this counterpart to economy that protects humans might not be able to gain control over these processes: National regulations seem not to limit the power of *info-economics*. Also the political and administrative organs of the European Union are too weak. The Internet community itself seems to be too weak, too ambivalent and too dependent. There is no good reason to think that this kind of deficiency of democratic control over ICT can be counter-balanced effectively. United nations probably could establish data control regulation, maybe the last hope for classical democracy in information society.

References

Anderson, C. (2008). The end of theory: The data deluge makes the scientific method obsolete, *Wired Magazine*, http://www.wired.com/2008/06/pb-theory/

Arbib, M. (Ed) (2002). *The Handbook of Brain Theory and Neural Networks*, MIT Press, Cambridge, MA

Aristotle, (1952). *Politics*, in: *The works of Aristotle*, vol. 8. Encyclopaedia Britannica, Publishing, Chicago

Aristotle, (2002). *Nicomachean Ethics* I, 13, 2002 (350 BC), Nicomachean ethics. Newburyport, Focus, MA

Baars, B. (1988). *A Cognitive Theory of Consciousness*, Cambridge University Press, New York

Baecker, D. (2015). Metadaten. Annäherung an Big Data, in: Schirrmacher, F. (ed.), *Technologischer Totalitarismus*, Suhrkamp, Berlin, 156-186

Bell, D. (1976). *The Coming of Post-Industrial Society*, Basic Books, New York

Bennett, M. R., and Hacker, P. M. S. (2003). *Philosophical Foundations of Neuroscience*, Blackwell Publishing, Hoboken, NJ

Bertalanffy, L. v. (1967). *Robots, Men and Minds,* Braziller, New York

Bohlken, E., and Thies, C. (eds.) (2009). *Handbuch Anthropologie*, Metzler, Stuttgart

Boyd, D., and Crawford, K. (2012). Critical questions for Big Data Provocations for a cultural, technological and scholarly phenomenon, *Information, Communication and Society*, 15/5, 662-679

Brem, A. K., Fried, P. J., Horvath, J. C., Robertson, E. M., and Pascual-Leone, A. (2014). Is neuroenhancement by noninvasive brain stimulation a net zero-sum proposition? *Neuroimage,* Jan 15, 85, Pt 3:1058-68. doi: 10.1016/j.neuroimage.2013.07.038

Brown, R. H. (1987). Society as text. *Text Essays on Rhetoric, Reason, and Reality.* University of Chicago Press, Chicago

Bundesdrogenbeauftragte (2015). *Computerspiel- und Internetsucht*, http://www.drogen beauftragte.de/drogen-und-sucht/computerspiel-und-internetsucht.html

Burgin, M. (2003). Information Theory: a Multifaceted Model of Information, *Entropy*, 5, 146-160

Burgin, M. (2010). *Theory of Information: Fundamentality, Diversity and Unification*, World Scientific Publishing, Singapore

Chalmers, D. J. (1996). *The Conscious Mind*, Oxford University Press, Oxford

Churchland, P. (1989). Neurophilosophy: Toward a Unified Science of the Mind-Brain, Bradford Books, Cambridge, MA

Churchland, P. (2007). *Neurophilosophy at Work*, Cambridge University Press, Cambridge, MA

Crawford, S. (1983). The origin and development of a concept: the information society, *Bull Med Libr Assoc.*, Oct, 71(4), 380-385 PMCID: PMC227258

Dahrendorf, R. (2010). Homo Sociologicus. Ein Versuch zur Geschichte, Bedeutung und Kritik der sozialen Rolle, VS Verlag für Sozialwissenschaften, Wiesbaden

Dawkins, R. (1976). *The Selfish Gene*, Oxford University Press, Oxford

Dawkins, R. (1989). *The Extended Phenotype*, Oxford University Press, Oxford

Dehaene, S., Sergent, C., and Changeux, J.-P. (2003). A neuronal network model linking subjective reports and objective physiological data during conscious perception, *Proc. National Academy of Science* (USA) 100. 14: 8520-8525

Dörner, D. (2001). *Bauplan für eine Seele*, Rowohlt, Reinbek

Dörner, D. (2002). *Die Mechanik des Seelenwagens*, Huber, Bern

Döpfner, M. (2015). Lieber Eric Schmidt, in: Schirrmacher, F. (ed.),*Technologischer Totalitarismus*, Suhrkamp, Berlin, 143-157

Dretske, E. (1981). *Knowledge and the Flow of Information*, MIT-Press, Cambridge

Engel, G. L. (1977). The need for a new medical model: A challenge for biomedicine, *Science*, 196, 129-136

Enzensberger, H. M. (2015). Wehrt Euch, in: Schirrmacher, F. (ed.), *Technologischer Totalitarismus*, Suhrkamp, Berlin, 70-74

Fehr E., Schmidt, K.M. (1999): A Theory of Fairness, Competition and Cooperation, *The Quarterly Journal of Econcomics*, August 1999, 817-868

Floridi, L. (2014). *The 4th Revolution, How the Infosphere is Reshaping Human Reality*, Oxford University Press, New York

Fodor, J. (1983). *The Modularity of Mind, An Essay on Faculty Psychology*, MIT Press, Cambridge, Mas

Ford, M. (2015). *Rise of the Robotics Technology and the Threat of Jobless Future*, Basic Books, New York

Forlini, C., and Hall, W. (2015). The *is* and *ought* of the Ethics of Neuroenhancement: Mind the Gap, *Frontiers in Psychology* 6: *PMC*

Frey, C.; and Osborne, M. A. (2013). *The Future of Employment: How Susceptible are Jobs to Computerization?* University of Oxford, Oxford

Fuchs, C. (2008). *Internet and Society,* Routledge, New York

Fuchs, C. (2013). Social Media: A Critical Introduction, Sage, London

Geiselberger, G., and Moorstedt, T. (eds.) (2013). *Big Data – Das neue Versprechen der Allwissenheit*, Suhrkamp, Berlin

Gehlen A. (1998). *Man: His Nature and Place in the World*, Columbia University Press, New York

Gigerenzer, G, and Selten, R. (eds.) (2002). *Bounded rationality. The Adaptive Toolbox*, MIT Press, Cambridge

Glimcher, P., and Fehr, E. (2014). *Neuroeconomics, Decision Making and the Brain*, 2nd Edition, Elsevier, London

Habermas, J., and Luhmann, N. (1971). Theorie der Gesellschaft oder Sozialtechnologie. Was leistet die Systemforschung? Suhrkamp, Frankfurt a.M.

Heil J. (ed.) (2013). *Philosophy of mind*, Routledge, New York

Henrich, J., R., Bowles, S., C., Fehr, E., and Gintis, H. (eds.) (2004). *Foundations of Human Sociality: Economic Experiments and Ethnographic Evidence from Fifteen Small-Scale Societies*, 1st Edition, Oxford University Press, New York

Herman, E. S., and Chomsky, N. (1988). *Manufacturing Consent: The Political Economy of the Mass Media*, Pantheon Books, New York

Himma, K. E., and Tavani, H. T. (eds.) (2008). *The Handbook of Information and Computer Ethics*, John Wiley and Sons, Inc., New Jersey

Höfling, S., and Tretter, F. (eds.) (2012). *Homo oecologicus. Menschenbilder im 21. Jahrhundert*, Hanns Seidel-Stiftung, München, http://www.hss.de/fileadmin/media/downloads/Berichte/110304_TB_Homooecologicus.pdf

Höfling, S., and Tretter, F. (eds.) (2013). *Homo neurobiologicus. Menschenbilder im 21. Jahrhundert*, Hanns Seidel-Stiftung, München, http://www.hss.de/uploads/tx_ddc eventsbrowser/AMZ-87_Homo_Neurobiologicus_02.pdf

Hofstadter, D., and Sander, E. (2013). Surfaces and Essences: Analogy as the Fuel and Fire of Thinking, Basic Books, New York

Hofstetter, Y. (2014). *Sie wissen alles.* Bertelsmann, München

Huggins, J. E., *et al.* (2014). Workshops of the Fifth International Brain-Computer Interface Meeting: Defining the Future, *Brain computer interfaces (Abingdon, England)* 1.1 (2014): 27-49, *PMC.*

Huizinga, J. (1939/2009): *Homo ludens. Vom Ursprung der Kultur im Spiel*, Rowohlt Verlag, Reinbek

Janich, P. (2006). Was ist Information? Kritik einer Legende, Suhrkamp, Frankfurt

Jaworski W. (2011). Philosophy of mind, *A Comprehensive Introduction*, Wiley, Oxford

Kant, I. (2006). *Anthropology from a Pragmatic Point of View* (Cambridge Texts in the History of Philosophy), Cambridge University Press, Cambridge

Kahneman, D., and Tversky, A. (eds.) (2000). *Choices, Values, and Frames.* Cambridge University Press, New York

Kappeler, P. M. (ed.) (2010). *Animal Behaviour: Evolution and Mechanisms*, Springer, Heidelberg

Kim, J. (2010). *Philosophy of mind,* West View, Philadelphia

Kirchgässner, G. (2008). Homo Oeconomicus: The Economic Model of Behaviour and Its Applications in Economics and Other Social Sciences, Springer, Berlin

Klix, F. (1971). Information und Verhalten. Kybernetische Aspekte der organismischen Informationsverarbeitung, Huber, Bern

Kratzer, C. (2013). *Cybermobbing – Wenn das Internet zur W@ffe wird*, Springer-Spektrum, Heidelberg

Lee, H., and Sohn, I. (2016). *Fundamentals of Big Data Network Analysis for Research and Industry*, Wiley, Chichester, UK

Lee, J. J., Knox, W. B., Wormwood, J. B., Breazeal, C., and DeSteno, D. (2013). Computationally modeling interpersonal trust, *Front Psychol.* 4: 893, doi: 10.3389/fpsyg.2013.00893

Luhmann, N. (1995). *Social Systems*, Stanford University Press, Stanford

Luhmann, N. (2012) *Theory of Society*, Stanford University, Stanford

Maier, R. M (2015). Angst vor Google, in: Schirrmacher, F. (ed.), *Technologischer Totalitarismus*, Suhrkamp, Berlin 118-129

Markowetz, A. (2015). *Digitaler Burnout*, Droemer, München

Millán, J. d. R. *et al.* (2010). Combining Brain–Computer Interfaces and Assistive Technologies: State-of-the-Art and Challenges, *Frontiers in Neuroscience*, 4, 161, PMC

Minsky, M. (1988). *The Society of Mind*, Simon & Schuster, New York

Minsky, M. (2007). *The Emotion Machine: Commonsense Thinking, Artificial Intelligence, and the Future of the Human Mind*. Simon & Schuster, New York

Minsky, M., and Papert, S. (1972). *Perceptrons: An introduction to Computational n-geometry*, MIT-Press, Cambridge, MA

Mitchel, S. (2009). *Unsimple Truths: Science, Complexity, and Policy*. University of Chicago Press, Chicago

Nagel, T. (1974). What is it like to be a bat? *Philosophical Review*, 83, 435-450

Parsons, T. (1951). *The Social System*, Free Press, Glencoe, Ill.

Petry, J. (2009). *Dysfunktionaler und pathologischer PC- und Internet-Gebrauch*, Hogrefe, Göttingen

Pfeifer, R., and Bongard, J. (2007). *How the Body Shapes the Way We Tink*, Bradford Books, Cambridge, MA

Pfeifer, R., and Bongard, J. (2013). *Designing intelligence*, GRIN Verlag, München

Plessner, H. (1965). *Die Stufen des Organischen und der Mensch*, 2., de Gruyter, Berlin

Rehberg, K.-S. (2009). Philosophical Anthropology from the End of World War I to the 1940s and in a Current Perspective, *Iris* 1 (1), 131-152

Rosa, H. (2013), *Social Acceleration. A New Theory of Modernity*, New York Columbia University Press

Roth, G. (2008). Homo neurobiologicus – ein neues Menschenbild? *Politik und Zeitgeschichte,* 44/45, 6-12

Scheler, M. (1928/1961). *Man's Place in Nature*, Noonday, New York

Schirrmacher, F. (2009). *Payback. Warum wir im Informationszeitalter gezwungen sind zu tun, was wir nicht tun wollen, und wie wir die Kontrolle über unser Denken zurückgewinnen*, Karl Blessing Verlag, München

Schirrmacher, F. (2013). *Ego. Das Spiel des Lebens,* Blessing Verlag, München

Schirrmacher, F. (ed.) (2015). *Technologischer Totalitarismus*, Suhrkamp, Berlin

Schmidt, E. (2015). Die Chancen des Wachstums, in: Schirrmacher, F. S. (ed.), *Technologischer Totalitarismus*, Suhrkamp, Berlin, 130-134

Schmidt, E., and Rosenberg, J. (2014). *How Google Works*, Grand Central Publishing, New York

Schulz, M. (2015). Warum wir jetzt kämpfen müssen, in: Schirrmacher, F. (ed.), *Technologischer Totalitarismus*, Suhrkamp, Berlin, 15-22

Searle, J. (1980). Minds, Brains and Programs. *Behavioral and Brain Sciences*, 3(3), 417-457, doi:10.1017/S0140525X00005756

Searle, J. (1995). *The Construction of Social Reality*, Aimon & Schuster, New York

Singer, W. (2003). Ein neues Menschenbild? Gespräche über Hirnforschung, Suhrkamp, Frankfurt

Skinner, B. F. (1976). *About Behaviorism*, Random House, Inc., New York, 18

Thimbleby, H. (2013). Technology and the future of healthcare, *Journal of Public Health Research*; volume 2, e28

Toennis, F. (1957). *Community and Society*, Michigan Univ. Press, New York.

Toffler, A. (1980). *The Third Wave,* Collins, London

Tretter, F., and Goldhorn, F. (eds.) (1993). *Computer in der Psychiatrie*, Asanger, Heidelberg

Tretter, F., and Grünhut, C. (2010). *Ist das Gehirn der Geist?* Hogrefe, Göttingen

Turing, A.M. (1950). *Computing Machinery and Intelligence*. Mind. LIX, Nr. 236, ISSN 0026-4423, 433-460, doi:10.1093/mind/LIX.236.433

Tversky, A., Kahneman, D. (1991). Loss Aversion in Riskless Choices: A Reference-dependent Model , *Quarterly Journal of Economics*, 106, 1039-1061

University of Vienna (2009): *Homo sociobiologicus*, http://vcc.univie.ac.at/der-homo-soziobiologicus/

Watson, J. B. (1913). Psychology as the Behaviorist Views It, *Psychological Review*, 20, 158-177

Webster, F. (2006). *Theories of the Information Society*, 3rd edition, Routledge, London

Weizenbaum, J. (1966). ELIZA - A Computer Program for the Study of Natural Language Communication between Man and Machine, *Communications of the Association for Computing Machinery*, 9, 36-45

Weizenbaum, J. (1976). *Computer Power and Human Reason: From Judgment To Calculation*, W. H. Freeman, San Francisco

Weizenbaum, J. (2001). *Computermacht und Gesellschaft*, Suhrkamp, Frankfurt.

Wiener, N. (1948). *Cybernetics or Control and Communication in the Animal and the Machine*, MIT Press, Cambridge, MA

Wittgenstein, L. (2009). *Philosophical Investigations*, 4th edition, edited and transl. by Peter M.S. Hacker and J. Schulte, Wiley-Blackwell, Oxford

Zajonc, R.B. (1980). Feeling and Thinking. Preferences need no inferences. *American Psychologist*, 36, 151-175

Zelli, A., Lucidi, F., and Mallia, L. (2015). The Complexity of Neuroenhancement and the Adoption of a Social Cognitive Perspective, *Frontiers in Psychology*, 6, 1880. PMC

Chapter 28

Health Information Technology:
Empowering Consumers, Patients, and Caregivers

Mary Jo Deering[*]

Deering Health Associates, Bethesda, MD, USA
mjd@mjdeering.net

Traditionally in health care, knowledge and authority have rested with medical professionals and care was delivered in professional settings. Individuals have been considered solely as "patients," i.e. defined by their relationship to doctors. Health information technology (HIT) is enabling consumers (i.e. an individual outside of a patient context), patients, and family caregivers to more fully understand health and illness, to self-manage health and illness at home when feasible, and to partner with their medical providers when necessary. This brings a potential for a re-balancing of the power relationship between doctors and patients toward greater collaboration (including family caregivers), and increased attention to contexts of daily life in which "health happens." However, the available technologies and their actual implementation are currently insufficient to empower consumers, patients and caregivers to fulfill their new responsibilities. In the coming decade, the most dramatic developments may come in the areas of "Big Data" – applying analytics to large databases of personal health information – and peer-to-peer sharing of information through social media. These activities carry risks related to privacy and to the exploitation of individuals. For the full potential of HIT to be achieved, technologies, policies, and personal information practices must come into better alignment.

---

[*] The author wishes to acknowledge Cynthia Baur, Ph.D., with whom I have written other texts that have contributed to this chapter.

1. Introduction

There is increasing consensus among many of those who deliver health care (providers), pay for it (insurers), and set legal and financial frameworks for it (policy makers) that engaging individuals in their own health and care is a sine qua non of good health outcomes [Institute of Medicine 2013]. Providers seek to connect with patients outside the clinical visit because of policy and payment changes, an aging population with increasing health management issues, and patients' demand for a more digitally-enabled healthcare experience.

At the same time, sometimes out of choice, and sometimes by necessity, consumers, patients, and caregivers are increasingly responsible for the management of their own health. They are looking for information and tools to help them with these new responsibilities, as well as align health activities with other parts of their lives, such as digital financial and time management "apps" and tools.

Technology companies are responding to these demands by creating new capabilities that reinforce expectations on the part of providers, patients, and consumers.

2. Definitions

The terms "patient-centered care," "consumer/patient engagement," and "consumer/patient empowerment" are all used to reflect similar or overlapping ways of strengthening the role of individuals in relation to medical professionals. The term "consumer" is used in this context to emphasize the individual outside of his or her relationship to any medical professional, regardless of the individual's actual health status.

2.1. *Patient-centered care*

The U.S. Institute of Medicine [2001] defines patient-centered care as "Care that is respectful and responsive to individual patient preferences, needs and values, and ensuring that patient values guide all clinical decision." Most other definitions add that patient-centered care includes information, communication, and the involvement of family or friends.

Patient-centered care changes the language about health. Medical care shifts from something done "to" patients to something done "with" them. For patients and families, the shift is from "they" – what the medical professionals can do – to "we" – what the patient, family and professional together can do [Rozenblum *et al.* 2015]. Interestingly, the term "patient-centered care" is being changed to "person-centered care" in leading medical institutions to promote a more wholistic view.

2.2. *Consumer/patient engagement*

"Engagement" reflects behaviors [Center for Advancing Health n.d.]. Individuals are engaged in their health when they are aware of and communicate about their health; make informed health decisions on their own or with their doctors; contribute to health transactions and processes, such as refilling prescriptions or monitoring the quality of care and providing feedback; are active in carrying out health activities at home; and act in health-promoting ways. This engagement may, and optimally should, lead to a partnership between the individual and the doctor who work together toward shared goals and outcomes.

2.3. *Consumer/patient empowerment*

Empowerment reflects capacity. Individuals may feel empowered or able to speak up and take action to promote health or manage a condition, which may lead to engagement and partnerships, or they may become empowered as a result of engagement with providers and health tasks and productive partnerships. Engagement and empowerment may exist separately. Communication, or the interactive process of developing common understanding, is the unifying thread among engagement, empowerment, and partnership [Deering and Baur 2015].

3. Key Consumer/Patient Health Information Technologies

There have been many path-breaking developments in HIT for consumers and patients over the past 20 years, but the field is still in its infancy. However exciting the current generation of "apps" may be, these tools are only part of a much longer-term trend that will bring many more breakthroughs for decades to come.

Examples of typical HIT tools and functions for consumers, patients and caregivers include the following:

- Communication between physicians and patients via secure messaging
- Patient web portals, usually linked to a providers' electronic health record system
- Personal health records
- Web sites, social media sites, and online games
- The purchase of health-related products and services over the Internet
- Online health information searches
- Mobile, wearable, home-based or implanted devices that track and report data, such as heart rate, blood pressure and insulin levels
- Blogs, forums, and social media applications that allow people to share their experiences and pose questions

Although social media and mobile tools – "apps" – get the most attention, using the Internet to find information remains the most widely used and often underestimated approach. For example, in the first American nationwide study in more than a decade to look at how adolescents use digital tools for health information, nearly one-third of teenagers said they used online data to improve behavior – such as cutting back on drinking soda, using exercise to combat depression and trying healthier recipes. Searching online for health information was used by 28%. By contrast, only 7% used mobile health apps and just 2% used games [Northwestern University 2015]. While adult use is higher in general, the pattern is similar. A recent survey of American adults found that 71% searched online for health information, 17% used mobile health tracking devices, and 12% used other wearable devices [Rock Health 2015]. Another American survey found that people want their doctors to be connected: about half would prefer to ask questions via email [Surescripts 2015].

Consumers, patients, and caregivers may have sole control of the technologies, for example, personal monitoring devices, or they may share control with others, such as patient portals that are part of their providers' web sites and linked to patients' electronic health records. When consumers, patients, and caregivers choose and control access to and use of health technologies themselves, they can determine how actively they participate, what information to include, who they want to share information with, and when to begin and end use, as well as define what is accomplished by using the technology. Consumers, patients, and caregivers often enter the information themselves in the device or the device collects information on command or passively.

Technologies with shared control, such as patient portals, also allow consumers, patients, and caregivers to determine their level of participation (none, a little, or a lot), but the types of information allowed, the rules for initiating and terminating use, as well as information sharing, are set by the organization providing the portal.

Medical professionals, employers, and policy makers often perceive "patient empowerment" strategies as means to the end of getting patients to take greater responsibility for their health and health care – both in terms of participating in decision-making and paying a larger share of costs [Goldzweig *et al.* 2013]. Patients value HIT tools that make it easier to participate in their care. Many are eager to know at least some of what their providers know, and tools like portals are the first healthcare innovation that facilitates information sharing and communication, both of which open the door to collaboration. In patients' own words, they think this "levels the playing field" [Woods *et al.* 2013].

With proper safeguards, digital health technologies can create significant opportunities to find health information; do more self-help and self-care; create and maintain personal health records; access personal health information held by providers; consult with healthcare providers through secure messaging or telehealth technologies; transact healthcare-related business; and purchase health-related goods and services electronically (digital health commerce).

4. The Problems with Health IT

It would appear that the convergence of these developments in patient-centered care, patient engagement, and HIT has the potential to dramatically change how health and health care is conceived and delivered. However, the available technologies and their actual implementation are currently insufficient to empower consumers, patients and caregivers to fulfill their new responsibilities.

The problems and challenges with HIT tools reflect long-standing and complex issues in healthcare, policy, technology, and social inequalities [Deering and Baur 2015]. Two literature reviews conclude there is insufficient evidence that Internet tools provided by doctors (patient portals) have a significant positive impact (i.e. on patient engagement, patient satisfaction, care utilization, efficiency or outcomes) [Goldzweig *et al.* 2013; Ammenwerth *et al.* 2014]. There has been no authoritative research on consumer-market tools.

While the digital divide has narrowed over time, access disparities by age, income, and education remain [Pew 2014]. Issues of health literacy and usability pose barriers to health IT use across age, race, ethnicity, and literacy boundaries. Nevertheless, researchers find that people with less education or limited health literacy skills will value and use health IT tools if someone explains the tools to them, they perceive the tools are helpful, and they receive encouragement and support in starting to use them and completing specific tasks [Zarcadoolas *et al.* 2013].

Other issues arise from changing definitions of what constitutes health information, and in concepts of ownership and control of personal health information. There are also challenges with respect to ensuring the quality of health information being created by disparate individuals and enterprises. Health information is no longer just the clinical data that are created by doctors' visits, hospitalizations, and lab tests that reside in institutional medical records. It now includes an array of longitudinal information on, for example, prevention, wellness, previous health experiences, use of alternative and complementary medicine, and over-the-counter remedies. One very significant problem is that there are no widely employed data standards to enable all these different bits of personal health information to be seamlessly integrated [Deering and Baur 2015].

Technologies coming from the consumer-oriented market are more user-friendly than tools offered by providers, but their products tend to be divided by function and typically are not interoperable with other tools or with providers' portals. This sector is driving innovation rapidly, but the unfortunate trend is a proliferation of new stand-alone products that do only one thing and don't integrate with others [Deering and Baur 2015].

Most significantly, concerns about violations of privacy rights and the confidentiality of health information will continue to influence debates about who owns or controls health information and who should have access to which information. Even if individuals are the presumed owners of their information, the reality is that current information-handling policies and practices give individuals few concrete ways to control the movement of their information among multiple parties. Moreover, most consumer apps fall outside any regulatory framework that would prevent the companies from selling personal information [Deering and Baur 2015].

A few studies have found that some patients are worried about health IT tools' impact on the privacy of their personal health information, but these concerns weren't significant enough to stop them from using them [Vodicka *et al.* 2013]. Researchers have hypothesized that the benefits patients derived from knowing more about their health issues and interacting with their providers outweighed the perceived risks of having their information shared or exposed in unauthorized ways [Angst *et al.* 2009]. However, unauthorized – or even just unexpected – data uses can damage individuals' trust.

5. The Next Opportunities

In the coming decade, the most dramatic developments may come in the areas of data and people.

5.1. *Data*

"Big Data" in healthcare is presumed to have tremendous potential: its advocates believe it can predict epidemics, cure disease, improve quality of life and avoid preventable deaths. The drive now is to understand as much about a patient as possible, as early in their life as possible – hopefully picking up warning signs of serious illness at an early enough stage that treatment is far more simple (and less expensive) than if it had not been spotted until later. Here are two examples.

The Pittsburgh Health Data Alliance was announced in March 2015. It includes Carnegie Mellon University, The University of Pittsburgh and the University of Pittsburgh Medical Center. The Alliance aims to take data from various sources (such as medical and insurance records, wearable sensors, genetic data and even social media use) to draw a comprehensive picture of the patient as an individual, in order to offer a tailored healthcare package.

Another partnership is between Apple and IBM [Forbes 2014]. The two companies are collaborating on a big data health platform that will allow iPhone and Apple Watch users to share data to IBM's Watson Health cloud healthcare analytics service. The aim is to discover new medical insights from crunching real-time activity and biometric data from millions of potential users. The first big health project is in Japan, where Apple and IBM have teamed up with Japan Post Holdings, which provides postal, banking, and insurance services. The initiative will deliver iPads with IBM-developed apps and analytics to connect seniors with services, health care, their community, and their families. As part of the project, IBM Global Business Services has designed custom-built apps specifically for the elderly for reminders and alerts about medications, exercise, and diet, along with direct access to community activities and supporting services such as grocery shopping and job matching.

Personalized medicine or Precision medicine involves tailoring medicines to a person's unique genetic makeup. This is enabled by integrating a person's genetic blueprint and data on their lifestyle and environment, then comparing it alongside thousands of others to predict illness and determine the best treatment.

These exciting visions all raise the question of the ownership and control of an individual's data. Should each person have the opportunity to agree to the use of their data, to having it aggregated? These big data bases have significant economic value. In the Pittsburgh Health Data Alliance, it was announced that one of the strengths that the University of Pittsburgh Medical Center brings is its "commercialization expertise" [Pittsburgh 2015]. In business news stories about the Apple/IBM partnership, experts observed that this brings IBM's big data capability together with Apple's ability to create devices that "are a flow channel through which computational usage will grow" [Forbes 2014].

Nothing in any of the announcements about either initiative mentions whether the source of the most vital information – the consumer/patient – is being told what will be done with their data, much less receiving any benefit. Should individuals get something for their contribution?

5.2. *People*

5.2.1. *Social Media Networks*

What will be the impact of social media networks on health and care? As Martin Nowak, the evolutionary biologist from Harvard University has written [2006], "Where ever information reproduces, there is evolution." Social media networks contain information but they also incubate ideas. The dark side of social media in health is that large companies, including pharmaceutical firms, are contributing content into the networks for their own business purposes. As one analyst observed, "For content contributors, the benefits of participating in social media have gone beyond simply social sharing to building reputations and bringing in career opportunities and monetary income" [IMS Health 2014].

5.2.2. *"Peer-to-peer health care"*

Peer-to-peer health care has been called "a slow idea that will change the world" by the Chief Technology Officer of the US Department of Health & Human Services [Fox 2013]. She believes the most exciting innovation of the connected health era is...people talking with each other.

The Pew Research Center measures "peer-to-peer health care" with national survey data: 24% of U.S. adults got information or support from others who have the same health condition the last time they had a significant health issue. Caregivers and those living with chronic conditions are more likely than other adults to seek peer advice and support [Pew 2014]. In the national survey of teenagers use of technology mentioned previously, real people were far more important sources of information than any technology: Parents were an important source of information for 55% of teens; Doctors/nurses were important for 29% compared to 25% for the Internet [Northwestern 2015].

Technology widens the network of people to talk with, increases the velocity of those conversations, injects them with more source material, then archives and makes them searchable. One notable peer-to-peer platform is Patients Like Me (PLM), a free online community whose stated aim is to enable individuals to:

Learn from others: compare treatments, symptoms and experience with people like them and take control of their health;

Connect with people like themselves: share experiences, give and get support to improve their lives and the lives of others; and

Track their health: chart their health over time and contribute to research that can advance medicine for all [Patients Like Me n.d.].

PLM shows promise in helping empower consumers of health care services and improving their self-management of disease [Mason *et al.* 2015].

A noted health care expert has said, "People talking to people is still how the world's standards change" [Gawande 2013]. He was talking about clinicians adopting new medical treatments, but this is also true for patients and caregivers. The velocity of innovation could accelerate when health care providers work together with patients and caregivers. One example that is demonstrating this potential is the Collaborative Chronic Care Network (C3N), led by Cincinnati Children's Hospital Medical Center, whose partners include the MIT Center for Collective Intelligence and the Creative/Science Commons. C3N has three parts: (1) Social – frequent and easy interactions between participants (providers, researchers, and patients and caregivers). (2) Technical – information systems to host massive amounts of data. (3) Scientific – an arena to try out and test new ideas [Collaborative Chronic Care Network n.d.].

6. Conclusions

Even though HIT tools, such as patient portals and health apps, are increasingly available across the socioeconomic spectrum, consumers, patients, and caregivers still confront a healthcare system coming to terms with technology's consequences for the patient experience and healthcare service delivery. Making health IT tools available for consumers, patients, and their families is necessary but not sufficient; making them consumer-, patient- and caregiver-centric would allow the tools to be truly useful to the people who will derive the greatest benefits.

Ultimately, tools for consumers, patients and caregivers will achieve their potential when they are as highly valued and developed elements of the electronic health information infrastructure as professional tools. Momentum is building in many countries toward holding consumers and patients accountable financially and morally for their health. Before going further in that direction, those who influence health policy, practice, and technology would do well to understand which tools and approaches enable consumers, patients and caregivers with many different needs and capabilities to fully participate in managing health and care.

References

Ammenwerth, E., Schnell-Inderst, P., Hoerbst, A. (2012). The impact of electronic patient portals on patient care: a systematic review of controlled trials, *J Med Internet Res* [Internet]. 14(6): e162, doi: 10.2196/jmir.2238

Angst, C. M., and Agarwal, R. (2009). Adoption of Electronic Health Records in The Presence of Privacy Concerns: The Elaboration Likelihood Model and Individual Persuasion, *MIS Quarterly*. 2009; 3(2), 339-370

Center for Advancing Health [Internet site] (no date). Engagement Behavior Framework. http://www.cfah.org/engagement/research/engagement-behavior-framework/ [accessed 25 November 2015]

Collaborative Chronic Care Network [Internet site] (no date). Available at http:// c3nproject.org/ [accessed 25 November 2015]

Deering, M. J., and Baur, C. (2015). Patient Portals Can Enable Provider-Patient Collaboration and Person-Centered Care. In Grando, M. A., Rozenblum, R., and Bates, D. W. (eds.), *Information Technology for Patient Empowerment in Healthcare*. Walter de Gruyter Inc., Berlin/Boston/Munich, 93-111

Forbes [Internet site]. Apple's Partnership With IBM Is About The Victory Of Design Over Data. July 16, 2014. http://www.forbes.com/sites/anthonykosner/2014/07/16/ apples-partnership-with-ibm-is-about-the-victory-of-design-over-data/ [accessed 25 November 2015]

Fox, S. [Internet blog] (2013). Peer to Peer Health: A Slow Idea That Will Change The World. http://susannahfox.com/2013/08/03/peer-to-peer-health-care-is-a-slow-idea-that-will-change-the-world/ [accessed 25 November 2015]

Gawande A. (2013). Slow Ideas. The New Yorker, Annals of Medicine. July 29, 2013. http://www.newyorker.com/magazine/2013/07/29/slow-ideas/r_2015] [accessed 25 November 2015]

Goldzweig, C. L., Orshansky, G., Paige, N. M., Towfigh, A. A, Haggstrom, D. A., Miake-Lye, I., Beroes, J. M., and Shekelle, P. G. (2013). Electronic patient portals: Evidence on health outcomes, satisfaction, efficiency, and attitudes: a systematic review, *Ann Intern Med.* 159(10), 677-87

IMS Health [Internet site] (2014). Engaging Patients Through Social Media. Danbury Connecticut, January 2014. http://www.imshealth.com/portal/site/imshealth/menuite m.762a961826aad98f53c753c71ad8c22a/?vgnextoid=ff71ad0087c73410VgnVCM 10000076192ca2RCRD&vgnextchannel=a64de5fda6370410VgnVCM1000007619 2ca2RCRD/ [accessed 25 November 2015]

Institute of Medicine of the [U.S.] National Academies (2001). *Crossing the Quality Chasm: A New Health System for the 21st Century*. National Academy Press, Washington, D.C. http://iom.edu/Reports/2001/Crossing-the-Quality-Chasm-A-New-Health-System-for-the-21st-Century.aspxr/ [accessed 25 November 2015]

Institute of Medicine. (2013). *Partnering with patients to drive shared decisions, better value, and care improvement* [Workshop proceedings]. Washington, DC: Institute of Medicine. http://iom.edu/Reports/2013/Partnering-with-Patients-to-Drive-Shar ed-Decisions-Better-Value-and-Care-Improvement.aspx/ [accessed 25 November 2015]

Mason, C., Barraket, J., Friel, S., O'Rourke, K., and Stenta, C.-P. (2015). Social Innovation for the Promotion of Health Equity, *Health Promotion International* 30(S2), 116-125

Nowak, M.A. (2006). *Evolutionary Dynamics: Exploring the Equations of Life*, Harvard University Press, Boston

Northwestern University, School of Communication, Center on Media And Human Development. Teens, Health And Technology: A National Survey. June 2015. http://cmhd.northwestern.edu/wp-content/uploads/2015/05/1886_1_SOC_ConfRep ort_TeensHealthTech_051115.pdf/ [accessed 25 November 2015]

Patients Like Me [Internet site] (n.d.) https://www.patientslikeme.com/ [accessed 25 November 2015]

Pew Internet and American Life Project [Internet site] (2014). Washington, D.C.: Pew Internet and American Life Project. Internet User Demographics 2014 Jan. http://www.pewinternet.org/data-trend/internet-use/latest-stats/ [accessed 25 November 2015]

Pittsburgh Health Data Alliance. [Internet site] (no date). http://healthdataalliance.com/ [accessed 25 November 2015]

Rock Health. [Internet site] (2015). Digital Health Consumer Adoption: 2015. https://rockhealth.com/reports/digital-health-consumer-adoption-2015/ [accessed 25 November 2015]

Rozenblum, R, Miller P., Pearson D and Marelli A. (2015). *Patient-centered healthcare, patient engagement and health information technology: the perfect storm.* In Grando, M.A., Rozenblum, R., and Bates, D.W. (eds) Information Technology for PatientEmpowerment in Healthcare. Walter de Gruyter Inc., Berlin/Boston/ Munich, 3-22

Surescripts (2015). Connected Care and the Patient Experience Survey. 2015. http://surescripts.com/connectedpatient/ [accessed 25 November 2015]

Vodicka, E., Mejilla, R., Leveille, S. G., Ralston, J. D., Darer, J. D., Delbanco, T. J., Walker, J., and Elmore, J. G. (2013). Online Access to Doctors' Notes: Patients Concerns About Privacy, *J Med Internet Res*, 15(9), e208, doi:10.2196/jmir.2670/.

Woods, S. S , Schwartz, E., Tuepker, A., Press, N .A., Nazi, K. M., Turvey, C. L., and Nichol, W. P. (2013). Patient experiences with full electronic access to health records and clinical notes through the My HealtheVet personal health record pilot: Qualitative study, *J Med Internet Res.* [Internet]. 15(3), doi:10.2196/jmir.2356

Zarcadoolas, C., Vaughon, W. L., Czaja, S. J., Levy, J., and Rockoff, M. L. (2013). Consumers' Perceptions of Patient-Accessible Electronic Medical Records. *J Med Internet Res* [Internet]. 15(8), e168, doi:10.2196/jmir.2507

Printed in the United States
By Bookmasters